REVIEW 4

REVIEW

Volume 4 1982

Edited by

James O. Hoge and
James L. W. West III

University Press of Virginia
Charlottesville

THE UNIVERSITY PRESS OF VIRGINIA
Copyright © 1982 by the Rector and Visitors
of the University of Virginia

First published 1982

ISSN 0190-3233
ISBN 0-8139-0974-0

Printed in the United States of America

Contents

Byron Refreshed   1
   by Ian Jack
     Review of *Byron's Letters and Journals*, ed. Leslie A. Marchand, 12 Vols.; *Lord Byron: The Complete Poetical Works*, ed. Jerome J. McGann, Vols. I–III.

The Garrick Years   19
   by Harold Love
     Review of Richard W. Bevis, *The Laughing Tradition: Stage Comedy in Garrick's Day;* Allardyce Nicoll, *The Garrick Stage: Theatres and Audience in the Eighteenth Century; The Plays of David Garrick,* ed. Harry W. Pedicord and Fredrick L. Bergmann

A Critic's Burden: R. P. Blackmur's Reading of Henry Adams   31
   by William E. Cain
     Review of R. P. Blackmur, *Henry Adams,* ed. and with an Introduction by Veronica A. Makowsky

Swinburne's Life and Works   51
   by T. A. J. Burnett
     Review of Donald Thomas, *Swinburne: The Poet in His World*

The Comic Grotesque in Elizabethan Prose and Drama   59
   by Robert S. Kinsman
     Review of Leland H. Carlson, *"Martin Marprelate, Gentleman": Master Job Throkmorton Laid Open in His Colors;* Neil Rhodes, *Elizabethan Grotesque*

The Modern Short Story 89
  by Samuel Pickering, Jr.
    Review of Walter Allen, *The Short Story in English*

The Clarendon *David Copperfield* 97
  by Richard J. Dunn
    Review of *David Copperfield*, ed. Nina Burgis

Dunbar, Henryson, and Other Makars 113
  by J. A. Burrow
    Review of *The Poems of William Dunbar,* ed. James Kinsley; *The Poems of Robert Henryson,* ed. Denton Fox; Edmund Reiss, *William Dunbar;* Douglas Gray, *Robert Henryson;* Gregory Kratzmann, *Anglo-Scottish Literary Relations 1430–1550*

Impressionistic Literature and Narrative Theory: Stephen Crane 129
  by M. E. Kronegger
    Review of James Nagel, *Stephen Crane and Literary Impressionism*

Romanticism as Movement 135
  by Stuart Curran
    Review of Leopold Damrosch, Jr., *Symbol and Truth in Blake's Myth;* Diana Hume George, *Blake and Freud;* V. A. De Luca, *Thomas De Quincey: The Prose of Vision;* Tilottama Rajan, *Dark Interpreter: The Discourse of Romanticism;* Thomas McFarland, *Romanticism and the Forms of Ruin: Wordsworth, Coleridge, and Modalities of Fragmentation*

Lawrence Enters the Pantheon 159
  by Richard Kuczkowski
    Review of *Apocalypse and the Writings on Revelation,* Vol. I of the Cambridge Edition of the Works of D. H. Lawrence, ed. Mara Kalnins

Contents

Medieval Literature in Historical Context — 171
  by Derek Pearsall
    Review of Janet Coleman, *English Literature in History 1350–1400: Medieval Readers and Writers*

Responsible and Irresponsible Authorship: Recent Henry James Criticism — 179
  by Ross Posnock
    Review of Alwyn Berland, *Culture and Conduct in the Novels of Henry James;* Nicola Bradbury, *Henry James: The Later Novels;* Laurence Bedwell Holland, *The Expense of Vision: Essays on the Craft of Henry James;* Susanne Kappeler, *Writing and Reading in Henry James;* Philip Sicker, *Love and the Quest for Identity in the Fiction of Henry James;* H. Peter Stowell, *Literary Impressionism: James and Chekhov*

Hoy's Bowers's Dekker — 207
  by T. H. Howard-Hill
    Review of Cyrus Hoy, *Introductions, Notes, and Commentaries to Texts in* The Dramatic Works of Thomas Dekker, ed. Fredson Bowers

Tennyson and the Histories of Criticism — 219
  by Jerome J. McGann
    Review of *The Letters of Alfred Lord Tennyson*, ed. Cecil Y. Lang and Edgar F. Shannon, Jr.; *The Letters of Edward FitzGerald*, ed. Alfred McKinley Terhune and Annabelle Burdick Terhune; *The Letters of Arthur Henry Hallam*, ed. Jack Kolb; Robert Bernard Martin, *Tennyson: The Unquiet Heart;* Peter Allen, *The Cambridge Apostles: The Early Years;* June Steffensen Hagen, *Tennyson and His Publishers;* Henry Kozicki, *Tennyson and Clio: History in the Major Poems;* Robert Pattison, *Tennyson and Tradition*

The Reader as Hero and Bully: Stanley Fish and F. R.
Leavis   255
   by Alan C. Purves
      Review of Stanley Fish, *Is There a Text in This Class?
      The Authority of Interpretive Communities;* William Walsh,
      F. R. Leavis

Annihilating the Poet in Donne   265
   by John T. Shawcross
      Review of John Carey, *John Donne: Life, Mind, and Art*

The (De)Construction of Sister George: Eliot's Second Hundred Years   275
   by Victoria S. Middleton
      Review of Jeannette King, *Tragedy in the Victorian Novel:
      Theory and Practice in the Novels of George Eliot, Thomas
      Hardy, and Henry James;* Hugh Witemeyer, *George Eliot
      and the Visual Arts;* U. C. Knoepflmacher and George
      Levine, eds., *Nineteenth-Century Fiction, Special Issue:
      George Eliot, 1880–1980;* Judith Wilt, *Ghosts of the Gothic:
      Austen, Eliot, and Lawrence*

Merton's Affirmation and Affirmation of Merton: Writing
about Silence   295
   by Victor A. Kramer
      Review of Thomas Merton, *The Collected Poems of Thomas
      Merton;* Thomas Merton, *Merton on St. Bernard;* Thomas
      Merton, *Love and Living;* Thomas Merton and Robert
      Lax, *A Catch of Anti-Letters;* Deba Patnaik, ed., *Geography
      of Holiness: The Photography of Thomas Merton;*
      William H. Shannon, *Thomas Merton's Dark Path: The
      Inner Experience of a Contemplative;* Monica Furlong,
      Merton: A Biography; James Forest, *Thomas Merton: A
      Pictorial Biography;* George Woodcock, *Thomas Merton,*

Monk and Poet: A Critical Study; Ross Labrie, *The Art of Thomas Merton;* Sister Thérèse Lentfoehr, *Words and Silence: On the Poetry of Thomas Merton;* James Finley, *Merton's Palace of Nowhere: A Search for God through Awareness of the True Self;* Daniel J. Adams, *Thomas Merton's Shared Contemplation: A Protestant Perspective;* Elena Malits, *The Solitary Explorer: Thomas Merton's Transforming Journey;* Gerald Twomey, ed., *Thomas Merton: Prophet in the Belly of a Paradox;* Brother Patrick Hart, ed., *The Message of Thomas Merton*

An Eleventh-Century *Beowulf?* 335
  by Ashley Crandell Amos
    Review of Kevin S. Kiernan, Beowulf, *and the* Beowulf *Manuscript*

Contributors 349

Editorial Board

Felicia Bonaparte
City College, CUNY

Jerome H. Buckley
Harvard University

Paul Connolly
Yeshiva University

A. S. G. Edwards
University of Victoria

Ian Jack
*Pembroke College,
Oxford University*

Robert Kellogg
University of Virginia

James R. Kincaid
University of Colorado

Cecil Y. Lang
University of Virginia

James B. Meriwether
University of South Carolina

Hershel Parker
University of Delaware

Martin Roth
University of Minnesota

George Stade
Columbia University

John L. Sharpe III
Duke University

G. Thomas Tanselle
*John Simon Guggenheim
Memorial Foundation*

Stanley Weintraub
Pennsylvania State University

Byron Refreshed

Ian Jack

Byron's Letters and Journals, ed. Leslie A. Marchand, 12 vols., London: John Murray, 1973–1982; Cambridge: Harvard University Press, Belknap Press.

Lord Byron: The Complete Poetical Works, ed. Jerome J. McGann, Vols. I–III, New York: Oxford University Press, 1980–1981.

Byron was a role player before he was a poet. He grew up in the knowledge that he would be one of his country's hereditary legislators, and when he assured his mother that he would "cut . . . a path through the world or perish in the attempt" (I, 49), it was not of poetry that he was thinking. When his mother (for her part) assured John Hanson that she had "*no* doubt of his being a great Man," she was anticipating for him a career embracing politics and public life.[1] While he "subside[d] into poetry" (IX, 43), he never became a dedicated poet. He believed, and unwisely informed the readers of *Hours of Idleness,* that it was "highly improbable, from my situation, and pursuits hereafter," that he should ever obtrude himself "a second time on the Public." Ill-judged as was the tone of that preface, he already expected his readers to be interested in the poet as well as his poetry, and the manner in which he cultivated and encouraged that interest did a great deal to determine the shape of his career. When he put his name to the second edition of *Childe Harold* I and II, he realized that he was making it inevitable that the Childe (originally "Childe Burun" in the title of the Murray MS.) should be identified with himself, and in the notes he encouraged the tendency by identifying the friend lamented in I, xci as "The Honourable J.* W.** of the Guards," whom he had known for "ten years, the better half of his life, and the happiest part of mine," continuing: "In the short space of one month I have lost *her* who gave me being, and most of those who had made that being tolerable." His reference to "The parent, friend, and now the more than friend" at II, xcvi and the mourning of the "lov'd and lovely one" in the previous stanza, a reference (as we now know) to John Edleston, offered readers the same irresistible temptation. In his later work he was to carry the same process further, deviating (in *The Corsair*) "into the gloomy vanity of 'drawing from self' " and obviously relishing the "odd report,—that *I* am the actual Conrad, the veritable Corsair, and that part of my travels are supposed to have passed in privacy [piracy?]"[2] and taking pains that the poem to his wife on the separation and his poems to his half sister, Augusta, should be privately printed and passed round some of Murray's circle, so ensuring that public interest in his own life and personality should be as intense as interest in his poetry.

This makes it fortunate that the new edition of his *Letters and Journals* should have reached completion as the new edition of his *Poetical Works* is coming out. Eighty years after the publication of Rowland E. Prothero's edition of the *Letters and Journals* and Ernest Hartley Coleridge's complementary edition of the *Poetry*, we are now presented with more accurate texts illuminated by a great deal of fresh supporting material. While interest in Byron has never flagged, the publication of the successive volumes of Professor Marchand's edition of the *Letters and Journals* over the last eight years has once again kept him constantly in the public eye. It is to be hoped that Professor McGann's fine edition of *The Complete Poetical Works* will enjoy something of the same success.

If the idea of republishing the letters and journals in slim volumes, at a rate of better than one a year, was John Murray's, it is clear that he has inherited the shrewd business sense of the distinguished founder of the firm. The pleasant format of these books, each of them containing some 250 pages accompanied by a well-chosen frontispiece and a note on the life of Byron during the period in question, at the top of the contents page, is much more inviting than that of the large volumes in which we are accustomed to find authoritative texts of the letters of literary men, while the moderate price of the first volume or two (I can no longer remember what it was, but it would still no doubt buy several cups of coffee) lured admirers of Byron into becoming purchasers. Only the twelfth volume strikes me as overpriced. The index is of course indispensable, and it has been reasonably well done. While some of the entries—those on Alfieri, Ariosto, and Dryden, for example—are somewhat laconic, the most important—notably *"Don Juan"* and "John Murray"—are full and helpful. The idea of prefixing 36 pages of "Memorable Passages" to plump the book out was not a happy one, however: they are indifferently chosen, and it is disagreeable to find three of Byron's objectionable observations on Keats here presented as "bons mots."

Byron would have liked the edition, since many of his letters —and in particular a great many of those to John Murray— were not private communications at all but rather fragments of autobiography intended for the inner circle of his friends during his lifetime and for a much wider readership after his death. When Thomas Moore's *Letters and Journals of Lord Byron: With Notices of His Life* appeared in 1830, it had the intended effect of keeping Byron in the forefront of public attention, and the work of the Brontës may serve to remind us of the importance of the idea of Byron in the early Victorian period. To the 561 letters published by Moore, Prothero added another 637 at the end of the century, and subsequently important additions have been made by John Murray IV, Peter Quennell, Iris Origo, and others. Marchand estimates that some 2,500 were in print when he began his edition, and to these he has been able to add more than 400. It is astonishing how letters keep turning up: as recently as 1976 a trunk was discovered in the vaults of Barclays Bank which contained, along with a wealth of other material, fifteen new Byron letters. These are included in Marchand's eleventh volume, by amicable arrangement with T. A. J. Burnett, whose study of Scrope Davies—*The Rise and Fall of a Regency Dandy*—was published last year. Finality is not to be expected, or indeed hoped for; but we have to thank Marchand for providing what now probably comes near to a complete collection of the letters of one of the finest letter writers in the language. When we lament the fate of the Memoirs, we should remember that one of the men who assented to their destruction, John Cam Hobhouse, was responsible for the survival of most of these letters and journals.

Marchand provides us with a text which is in general much preferable to that of earlier editors. As we should expect, Moore and Prothero both omitted and bowdlerized on many occasions—though Moore, as Marchand points out, was more honest in that he usually indicated by asterisks that a passage had been omitted. Marchand has no need to resort to asterisks, and so we find Byron telling Hobhouse that he has "fucked" one beautiful girl "twice a day for the last six—today is the seventh—but no Sabbath day—for we meet at Midnight at her Milliners—She is the prettiest Bacchante in the world—& a piece to perish *in*" (VI, 40). On occasion the manuscript itself omits a letter or two, sometimes more in the spirit of Sterne than of Bowdler. On 6 April 1819, for example, Byron tells Hobhouse that if he had been in England he would "have f——d Caroline Lamb out of her 'two hundred votes' " on his behalf, "although at the expense of a testicle," adding: "I think I could have neutralized her zeal with a little management—but alas! who could have thought of that Cuckold's family ⟨sitting⟩ *standing* for a *member*—I suppose it is the first time that George Lamb ever *stood* for any thing—& William with his 'Corni Cazzo da Seno!' (as we Venetians say—it means—Penis *in earnest*)." In another letter little remarkable for its reticence Byron tells Hobhouse and Douglas Kinnaird: "what I get by my brains—I will spend on my b——ks—as long as I have a tester or a testicle remaining" (VI, 92).

The most obvious exception to the normally very high accuracy of the text of the letters is Marchand's handling of quotations from Latin. At I, 244, we can be certain that Byron wrote "giving him a 'mittimus' to his own Country," not "mittamus," and that at IV, 249, he did not write "Vede note on Number 2" but "Vide." At VII, 144, it is highly probable that "negatio" for "negotio" is Marchand's error, not Byron's. Marchand's shaky Latin is exemplified in the note to II, 14, where we are given "Caesare" for "Caesar" in a quotation from the

Pharsalia. As for Greek, we may safely guess that ἅγιον ορος at II, 33, is a misreading of ἅγιον ὄρος, that at II, 10, Byron wrote εὐμόρφῳ not εὔμορφω, and that at IV, 51, αρισον is a misreading of αριστον (as the footnote implicitly acknowledges). It is also most unlikely that Byron used σ at the ends of words instead of the terminal form of the letter, ς, which we sometimes find here. The annotation of classical references is occasionally inadequate, too, as at II, 89n[2], where Prothero's note is preferable. At II, 133, Marchand translates the first words of Pindar's first Olympian Ode, but fails to recognize the source. At VIII, 35n[2], he tells us that Socrates' remark, "which is best, life or death, the gods only know," comes from the *Phaedo*, although it is evident that its source is the *Apology*. At IX, 76n[2], we have the strange reference "1,7,84" for Persius III, 84. Little attempt is made to identify quotations from Italian.

Marchand tells us that he has "tried to make the footnotes as brief and informative as possible," but while we must acknowledge that what he terms "the leisurely expansiveness of R. E. Prothero" is no longer possible, we are bound occasionally to wish that he had annotated more fully. He is at his best in annotations relating to Byron's life and friends, and the brief biographical sketches given at the ends of many of the volumes are admirably done. While the additions and corrections included in Volume XI deal with some of the more surprising omissions in the earlier volumes (such as the failure to identify "Mr. R. P. K" at III, 33), disappointing omissions remain. Whether or not it would be easy to identify "Mr. or Mrs. Ellis" to whom Byron refers in a letter to his wife at V, 30, "Mr. Bainbridge's legacy" in the same letter could surely be run down. Marchand's dealings with Joe Manton the gunsmith illustrate the editor's limitations. At V, 71, Byron is angry with Manton because "he has put a very bad brush into the pistol case ... for cleaning the *locks* of my pistols." Whereas that reference is indexed and requires no note, there is an unindexed reference at VI, 211, when Byron tells Kinnaird that Hobhouse "should have wafered [Major Cartwright] with Mantons." It is true that *OED* gives "Manton" as a noun meaning "a fowling piece" (citing *The Antiquary*), but "wafered" is a verb unknown to the *Dictionary;*

it should surely have been annotated (as it could have been from "Wafer 5. *Gunnery.* A kind of primer"). At VIII, 31, Byron writes of "*wafering* or shooting." At VI, 212, "Mantoned" has become a verb. At VII, 78, we have an unannotated reference to "*Manton's best powder,*" where an explanation of the type of powder intended should surely be provided.[3] At III, 66, "Murray, the αναξ of publishers, the Anac of stationers" would not have required a note fifty years ago, or perhaps thirty, but now I believe it does. At IX, 61, some explanation should have been provided of Byron's acknowledgment that "assuredly Murray will be displaced if he publishes it" (*The Vision of Judgment*), and no one could be better equipped to provide the explanation than Marchand. At IV, 151, he errs in describing "Gut" as "an epithet that Byron used for the Strait of Gibraltar," as the word is neither an epithet nor peculiar to Byron.

The notes referring to writers other than Byron himself are occasionally at fault. At III, 229n, the reference to *A Sentimental Journey* could be more precise, while the quotation immediately following is not from Sterne but from an unsympathetic critic. On the same page no source is provided for a quotation from Italian verse. At IV, 103, the play by Rochester is presumably *Sodom.* There is no "tragedy called *Ian*" by Mrs. Wilmot (IV, 290n). *The Baviad* was published in 1791, not 1794 (VII, 175n). At VII, 191n, the date of publication of Boswell's *Life of Johnson* seems to be given as 1780, until we realize that it is the particular episode referred to which occurred in that year. At VII, 200n, the reference to Lucretius should be given: IV.1133–34. At VIII, 112n, a simple reference to *The Lay of the Last Minstrel* is inadequate: the reference is to Canto I, stanza xxii, last line (which Marchand slightly misquotes). The lack of precision of the reference to Johnson's *Life of Edmund Smith* at IX, 69, is not serious (in fact II, 14, in Birkbeck Hill's edition), but at VIII, 115, "Dryden's Life" is quite inadequate (I, 475–76 in the same edition). The editor of Dryden in an unnecessarily elaborate reference at VII, 153n, should not be "Kingsley" but Kinsley.

While the additions and corrections at the end of Volume XI go far to improve the level of the literary annotations, it is surprising how many remain unidentified. At III, 121, a poet called J. Thomson who published a volume c. 1813 which included a Drury Lane Address should surely be identifiable (" 'Dejected Addresses' " at II, 249n, is a witless misprint). At III, 51, " 'a guide philosopher & friend' " should be identified as a quotation from *An Essay on Man*, IV.390. (Jerome J. McGann notices a quotation of the same line in Byron's "Farewell Petition to J[ohn]C[am] H[obhouse], Esq.," line 35). At III, 96n, two lines of Moore's verse are quoted, without a reference; at XI, 223 we are told to "add source: *LJ*, II, 250n.," but when we do so we find that while Prothero quotes the lines he does not tell us where to find them. In fact they come from *The Twopenny Post-Bag*, VI.32–33. At IV, 337, it seems extraordinary to find "this 'best of all possible worlds' " without a reference to *Candide*, Ch. I. With the help of Prothero, Marchand catches many of the echoes from the Waverley Novels, which Byron claimed to know by heart; but he misses others. The words " 'my vocation' " at IV, 183, for example, are a quotation from Edie Ochiltree in *The Antiquary*. At VII, 83, Marchand does not realize that "remeid" is a Scots form of "remedy," and is therefore in no need of an editorial *sic*. Byron may have had it from Scott or (as the passage here suggests) from Dunbar's great "Lament for the Makaris." Marchand also misses several obvious quotations and misquotations from Shakespeare: at II, 144, "eye hath not seen, ear hath not heard, nor can the heart of man conceive" spoils *A Midsummer Night's Dream* IV.ix.211–12; at IV, 187, " 'both your houses' " is an obvious quotation from *Romeo and Juliet* III.i.106; at IV, 226 " 'mine inn' " is from *The Comedy of Errors* I.ii.14; while "The exquisite reason" at VII, 206, alludes to *Twelfth Night* III.iii.143. At I, 57, " 'A talkative woman is like an Adder's tongue' " is surely a reminiscence of *3 Henry VI*, I.iv.112, in spite of Byron's ascription of it to "one of the prophets." At V, 25, " 'a drop of that immortal man' " refers to Shakespeare, as the context makes clear: Byron is quoting from the last line of Garrick's prologue to *Florizel and Perdita*. His tendency to misquote is illustrated at II, 127, where " 'To those who trifle with more grace & care / Whose trifling pleases, & whom trifles please' " turns out to be the last two lines of Pope's *Second*

Epistle of the Second Book of Horace, deprived of rhyme and masquerading as blank verse.

To such minute and niggling criticisms Marchand has of course the perfect answer. He has completed his task, and he has every reason to feel proud that his retirement has enabled him so splendidly to crown a career in which he has thrown more light on Byron than any other scholar of his generation.

An edition as elaborate as McGann's *Complete Poetical Works,* edited by the man who is Professor Marchand's predestined successor as the leading authority on Byron, can only be properly assessed after repeated use; but even a preliminary survey makes it clear that if the remaining volumes are comparable to the first three, this will be one of the finest editions we have of any of the Romantic poets. McGann has built splendidly on the foundation provided by Prothero and others, and by incorporating a great deal of new material (often of his own discovery) he has produced an edition greatly superior to his predecessor's which anyone seeking the fullest possible information about Byron's poetry must now regard as canonical.

The jacket flap informs us that McGann's aim is "to correct the texts of the known works, and to print for the first time as complete an edition of the poetical works as possible," and we are told that "more than eighty new poems or poetic fragments" are now first collected. While McGann has indeed corrected the text of many of the poems (most notably, perhaps, that of *Hints from Horace*), and while some of the new poems and scraps are of real interest (notably the Latin lines to John Edleston previously printed only in an exhibition catalogue), it seems to me that the principal importance of McGann's work consists in the wealth of information which he presents in the commentary at the end of each volume. Before I consider the commentaries, however, I wish to say something about the arrangement of the poems.

With a few exceptions the arrangement of the poems follows "the chronological order of their composition," an ordering which has become increasingly popular since the success of the Longmans "Annotated English Poets." The first surviving poem of Byron's, Poem no. 1, is an epigram on an old woman:

> In Nottingham county there lives at Swine Green,
> As curst an old lady as ever was seen;
> And when she does die, which I hope will be soon,
> She firmly believes she will go to the moon.

We are told that "Moore had the lines orally from B's nurse May Gray, and though he raised a question about their originality, he allowed them to be collected." Do they form a felicitous opening to the works of a great poet? If we apply the strictly chronological method to Browning, we are obliged to begin with the couplet: "Good people all who want to see / A boy take physic look at me," and to follow it with the two lines he once quoted from a poem he had written to ingratiate himself with his schoolmaster, and justly described as "great bosh": "We boys are privates in our Regiment's ranks— / 'Tis to our Captain that we all owe thanks."[4] One is reminded of Charlotte Brontë's comment that "usually, it seems a sort of injustice to expose in print the crude thoughts of the unripe mind, the rude efforts of the unpractised hand."[5] Of course we are inured to such injustice: academic competition now makes it inevitable that every scrap of verse by a major poet will be published somewhere, by someone. But the proper place for juvenilia or trivia is a biography or an appendix to the poet's works reserved for such curiosities. While we accept the Autolycus-like role of the scholar in this matter, surely we can still expect him to show some discretion in the display of his "unconsider'd trifles." It is not fair to a poet that they should be given the same prominence as the poetry which he wrote for publication.

While it must be accepted as one of the solutions to the problem of arranging a poet's work, a strict following of chronology has a great deal to be said against it, and the most obvious thing is that it pays no regard at all to the poet's own wishes when those are known or may plausibly be guessed at. I do not wish to consider here the case of poets who rearranged their work for collected editions, as did so many of the poets of the nineteenth century; but leaving that question aside, there is the obvious distinction to which I have just referred, that between poems published by the poet himself (or intended for publication), and poems not published and probably not so intended. Very often (I would maintain) the proper course is to give as the principal part of the poetical works the contents of the volumes which the poet published in his lifetime, with subsequent sections devoted to any poems which he would probably have published if he had lived longer, other poems (published, perhaps, but not collected), and perhaps juvenilia and fugitive pieces. That is substantially the method followed by H. W. Garrod in his Oxford English Texts edition of Keats, which ends with a section of "Trivia" which includes the lines which Keats wrote during a lecture, "Give me women, wine and snuff." In the Longmans edition, in which all poems are equal, Miriam Allott gives these immediately after one of the poems printed in the *Poems* of 1817, the epistle "To George Felton Mathew." It is fortunate that the lines were not written between the "Ode to a Nightingale" and the "Ode on a Grecian Urn." To print poems automatically in the order of their composition is surely to reduce them to documents illustrating the poet's life and development. Would anyone have the gall to treat the poems in *The Temple* in this manner, if by some mischance we knew the order in which they were written? In fact one scholar, G. H. Palmer, would have liked to do so, and although he had to acknowledge that there was insufficient evidence he did go so far as to divide the poems into "three broad Divisions." His notes remain of value, but hardly anyone now approves of his rearrangement. The problem is an interesting one, and I shall be considering it in "A Choice of Orders," a contribution to a volume of essays to be published by the Huntington Library next year.

While I am glad to have the thirty poems which precede the first of the *Hours of Idleness* poems, and give McGann due credit for the fact that seventeen of them are unpublished or uncollected, I should rather have seen them in an appendix entitled "Juvenilia." But I am glad that McGann departs from chronological order when it would lead him into some obvious absurdity: Cantos III and IV of *Childe Harold* are printed after Cantos I and II in his second volume, while *Don Juan* will similarly be printed as a unit. For a less obvious reason—because he prints the early published poems in a sequence following that in *Poems Original and Translated* (1808)—he gives "On the Death of a Young Lady," first printed in the earlier volume *Hours of Idleness* and there accompanied by a note stating that it had been written "at an earlier period than the rest" of the poems there published, after many poems written later.

McGann's deference to the principle of chronology may be associated with the singularly unhelpful running heads of these volumes. The legend that one finds at the top of every page of the text, left hand or right hand, is simply "POETICAL WORKS 1804" (at the outset) and so on to "1816" by the end of Volume 3. I cannot understand why we are not given the title of the longer poems (at least) on the right hand pages, or why no indication of the canto or part of the poem is given, in the case of the longer poems. In Volume 1 we cannot quickly find *English Bards and Scotch Reviewers* or *Hints from Horace,* except by consulting the contents, in Volume 2 we do not know at which canto of *Childe Harold* we have opened the page, while in Volume 3 we are similarly at a loss with the Eastern Tales. By an unhappy oversight every page of the text of Volume 2 is headed by the date "1812," although Canto III was published in 1816 and Canto IV in 1818.

The same lack of helpfulness at the top of the page is to be found in the commentary which is printed at the end of each volume. The proper place for explanatory notes is of course the bottom of the text: if they are printed, for the sake of economy, at the end of the book, the reader should at least be able to see by a glance at the top of the page which poems are there commented on. In fact not even the number of the poem is given there, and in Volume 3 confusion is confounded because Byron's own (published) notes are quite properly given before the commentary (again without any guidance at the top of the page). It follows that anyone who wishes to discover whether Byron has a note on any line or passage, and what light McGann has to throw on it, has his work cut out. This is the more regrettable because the quality of the commentary is of the highest. With the longer poems we have sections on "MS.

and Proofs," "Publishing History," and "Literary and Historical Background," followed by full detailed annotation.

It is ironical that one or two errors crept into the commentary on *Hours of Idleness* and attracted the eye of the *TLS* reviewer, who gave them a prominence which was unfair in the course of a relatively brief review. As Byron's first published volume was preceded by two privately printed collections, *Fugitive Pieces* and *Poems on Various Occasions,* and succeeded by a second edition entitled *Poems Original and Translated,* and since many poems appear in two or more of these collections (often revised), the editor is presented with a perplexing task, and the table given on page 363 to enable the reader to see at a glance the poems printed in *Fugitive Pieces* errs because of McGann's discovery of one further poem at a relatively late date. As a consequence "30,68,69" should read "31,69,70." To use the phrase "complete nonsense" is unfair and suggests that the reviewer is without experience in the trying task of seeing a long and very complicated piece of printing through the press. In fact the general commentary on *Hours of Idleness* is of great value, while the opening of the commentary on one of the individual poems, "Oscar of Alva," may serve to exemplify McGann's command of his complex material: "The MS. scraps of the poem which survive are from B's draft MS., which he gave to E. Pigot to copy for the *HI* printing. Miss Pigot evidently cut the draft MS. into smaller pieces, and these subsequently given away or sold. The surviving fragments include: 93–6, . . . 125–36 (*MS. Hn,* location: Huntington); 137–68 (*MS. B,* location: Bodmer); 179–84, 193–6 (*MS. P,* location: Pforzheimer); 257–60, 267–72 (*MS. Ne,* location: Trevelyan Papers, Newcastle Univ. Library); . . . 293–6 (*MS. S,* location: presently unknown; sold at Sotheby's 14 Dec. 1976, lot 179.) Published in *HI, POT.*" The commentary on "Childish Recollections" is similary impressive. It begins with this paragraph: "The original MS . . . written late in 1806 for printing in *POVO,* does not survive. Early in 1807 B revised and augmented the poem for printing in *HI*. All later collected editions ultimately depend on *HI,* which is copy text here. At the beginning of 1808 B began making further revisions for the *POT* printing, where it was in fact set up in type . . . with a second epigraph from Virgil (see *BLJ* I.152 and *Wise*, I.II). But B was reconciled to Dr. Butler, the Pomposus of the poem, in Feb. 1808, and he therefore decided to remove the work from *POT*, a decision made during the course of printing which forced a delay in publication." McGann has searched a great deal, traveled a great deal, and tirelessly analyzed his evidence. He excels at locating manuscripts, proofs, private printings, and collateral material and utilizing it all to throw light on the poem in question. The account of *Hints from Horace* is outstanding, and while "it has not been feasible" to print the parallel passages from Horace, as Byron desired—why not?—a list of the principal Horatian passages is at least given for reference. The authority with which McGann has earned the right to speak may be illustrated by one of his comments on *The Curse of Minerva:* "Every critic and editor . . . has accepted the dating of the poem which B indicated in the note he placed before the text in *Curse 1812:* 'Athens. Capuchin Convent, 17 Mar., 1811.' But this date is quite misleading. In fact, most of *Curse* was written in Nov. 1811, after B had returned from the Levant. The dating on *MS. B* itself suggests two phases of composition."

The commentaries in the other two volumes are equally valuable. That on *Childe Harold*, for example, provides a great deal which is of direct use to the critic, who is unlikely to know Rodwell Wright's *Horae Ionicae* and Richard Polewhele's "Grecian Prospects" as well as does McGann. Here and elsewhere (as in the case of *English Bards and Scotch Reviewers*) Byron's own manuscript annotations are of particular interest. The commentaries on the Eastern Tales are full of meat. The composition of *The Giaour*, the revisions and accretions of which are rightly described by McGann as "among the most extensive and complex" in the whole body of Byron's work, is clarified by four tables. The first two of these "list and briefly describe the different MSS., Proofs, and Revises," the third "describes the content of the poem from its first MS. state to its ultimate form in the seventh edition," while the last "outlines the order of composition of the various parts of the poem." Only after seven pages devoted to these difficult yet important matters do we reach the editor's comments on the "Literary and Historical Background" of the poem, and his annotations to particular passages. As to *The Siege of Corinth,* it is true that "B's remarks on the composition . . . , and later commentators' speculations about the MSS., have created some confusion," and while McGann does not claim to have solved every difficulty, he demonstrates the limitations of Robert Gleckner's account of the matter and clarifies the problems most helpfully. It is characteristic of McGann's scholarship that he knows no fewer than five drafts and eight corrected proofs of one of the most important minor poems in the volume, the "Address, Spoken at the Opening of Drury-lane Theatre."

The annotations to particular lines and passages which make up the greater part of the commentary are extremely well done. Whereas Marchand occasionally seems to have grown weary of the labor of tracing Byron's reading, McGann revels in it and proves remarkably successful. He notes the innumerable references to *Macbeth* and to Shakespeare's other plays (mentioning that the Commonplace Book now in the Folger principally contains "extracts from Shakespeare," and incidentally correcting the library's dating of it), to the Bible, Virgil, Horace, Pope (above all *An Essay on Criticism*), and other standard authors and works; but he also identifies quotations from less obvious writers: Sir William Jones, Maturin, Kirke White, Ossian, Waller, Richard Savage, Thomas Tickell, Edward Young (*The Revenge* as well as *Night Thoughts*), Otway, Mathias, Bowles, Richard Mant (*The Simpliciad*), Lady Anne Hamilton (*Epics of the Ton*), and Henry Bunbury, whose "The Little Grey Man" so few of us have read. At II, 279, he points out that two lines of Latin verse which Byron ascribes to Aulus Gellius are actually from Varro's "Papiapapae," IV.

Confining myself to Volume 1, I have one or two criticisms to make of the notes. Commenting on the line "The chance, which has lost, may in future redeem you," McGann remarks that "B probably wishes 'has lost' to be read 'has been lost,'" but surely he means (rather) that "just as it has happened that we are now lost to one another, so in the future it may happen that we come together again." Here and elsewhere we notice that Byron lacked the deep respect for the English language characteristic of our very greatest poets: paradoxically, he shows a greater respect for the English idiom once he has discovered his later informal style. On page 385 McGann twice describes "lay" (as in "Where now my head must lay") as an "irregular usage," but it is not so in Scots. On page 386 he is uncharacteristically careless in describing Lavater as "inventor of the science of Phrenology (which he called Physiognomy)," which sounds like something from *1066 and All That*. On page 408 he understandably fails to see the pun in the proposed motto for the *Edinburgh Review:* "tenui . . . avena" means "a few oats" (a little porridge) as well as "a slender pipe." On page 413 Byron's comment on "sundry novels in the style of the first edition of the Monk" refers to the salacious passages which were omitted from later editions of the book. On page 431 the couplet from Pope is from the *Epistle to Burlington* (*Moral Essays III*), lines 339–40. On page 432 I assume that the "English newspaper, which finds its way abroad wherever there are Englishmen" is *Galignani's Messenger*. On page 438 Byron's reminiscence of his fifth-form translation of a chorus from the *Prometheus Vinctus* "wherein was a pestilent expression about 'staining a voice'" should have a cross-reference to Poem 55, a fragment deriving from this exercise in which the pestilent expression has given way to "My voice shall raise no impious strain."

McGann is much more careful with Greek and Latin than Marchand, and indeed the errata slip in Volume 2 shows that at times he is overanxious. The form ὅπου, which he wishes to substitute for the correct ὄπου, can only result from misreading a carelessly written breathing above the initial letter—it was common enough to indicate a breathing, rough or smooth, by a mark which is indistinguishable from an accent, but there is no point in converting the slipshod into the erroneous. None of the apparent or actual errors in Hobhouse's Greek on pages 328–34 seems worth perpetuating: it is unlikely that he wrote ἀντος rather than αὐτὸς, for example, and if he did it can have been no more than a slip of the pen. No one who knows Greek would write ἀντοῦ for αὐτοῦ. If Hobhouse wrote 'sed' for 'sub' in the quotation from the *Ars Amatoria* on page 330, the correct reading appears in my copy of the first edition. In Volume 1 McGann has misread the word νεικει in the quotation from the *Iliad* given as the first epigraph to *Hours of Idleness,* and on page 431 he has "Genius Irritabile" for "Genus Irritabile," so raising the question whether he gives a misreading on page 428, line 18: if Byron is responsible for this error, it would have been as well to point it out. On page 201 of the same volume Ἐαυτòν should be Ἑαυτòν, and probably originates in another carelessly written breathing.

A writer in the *Edinburgh Review* commented, on the publication of *Childe Harold IV:* "It is not enough to say that the veil is torn off. It is a nobler creature that is before us." If the devoted labors of Marchand and McGann do not present us with "a nobler creature," that is emphatically not what we would have desired. What they have done is rather to sharpen the focus, so that we can see Byron more precisely than before.

Notes

1. Leslie A. Marchand, *Byron: A Biography,* 3 vols. (New York: Knopf, 1957), I, 145.

2. *Letters and Journals,* II, 399. The only authority for the text of this Journal is Moore. It seems clear that "privacy" should read "piracy," and I silently emended the word in my *English Literature 1815–1832* (Oxford: Clarendon, 1963), p. 58. Marchand gives it as a possible alternative reading. Others no doubt thought of the emendation before myself, as it is an obvious one.

3. In his *Biography* (I, 145n) Marchand quotes an amusing anecdote about Byron and Manton from Gronow's *Reminiscences:* "When in London, Byron used to go to Manton's shooting-gallery, in Davies Street, to try his hand, as he said, at a wafer. Wedderburn Webster was present when the poet, intensely delighted with his own skill, boasted to Joe Manton that he considered himself the best shot in London. 'No, my lord,' replied Manton, 'not the best; but

your shooting today was respectable.' Whereupon Byron waxed wroth, and left the shop in a violent passion."

4. The lines are to be found in *The Life of Robert Browning*, by W. Hall Griffin and H. C. Minchin (London: Methuen, 1910), pp. 29–30.

5. Prefatory note to "Selections from Poems by Ellis Bell," *Wuthering Heights*, 2d ed. (London: Smith, Elder, 1850).

The Garrick Years

Harold Love

Richard W. Bevis. *The Laughing Tradition: Stage Comedy in Garrick's Day.* Athens: University of Georgia Press, 1980. x, 282 pp.

Allardyce Nicoll. *The Garrick Stage: Theatres and Audience in the Eighteenth Century.* Athens: University of Georgia Press, 1980. viii, 184 pp.

The Plays of David Garrick. Vols. I–II *Garrick's Own Plays, 1740–1775;* Vols. III–IV *Garrick's Adaptations of Shakespeare 1744–1773,* ed. Harry W. Pedicord and Fredrick L. Bergmann. Carbondale and Edwardsville: Southern Illinois University Press, 1980–1981. xxx, 437 pp.; xviii, 385 pp.; xxvi, 469 pp.; xviii, 472 pp.

Few areas of cultural history have been so comprehensively enriched over the last two decades as the study of the eighteenth-century English stage. Readers of 1960 seeking up-to-date scholarly information would have found themselves largely restricted to the two relevant volumes of Allardyce Nicoll's *History of English Drama 1660–1900* and a handful of more specialized studies, of which Harry W. Pedicord's *The Theatrical Public in the Time of Garrick* has proved the most enduring. Then came the eleven data-packed volumes of *The London Stage* followed more recently by the huge *Biographical Dictionary of Actors, Actresses, Musicians, Dancers, Managers and Other Stage Personnel in London, 1660–1800,* which have between them made available a vast fund of information that previously had to be searched out from early stage memoirs and original copies of contemporary newspapers. Just as importantly, almost the entire body of printed play-texts of the period, along with the invaluable Larpent collection of acting scripts submitted to the Lord Chamberlain's Examiner of Plays, had become available on microcard in the early sixties as part of the Readex collection, *Three Centuries of English Drama*. With many of the magazines and reviews of the century reprinted in University Microfilms' *English Literary Periodicals* series, and a number of the basic memoirs and controversial sources available in reprint collections such as Garland's fifty-volume *The English Stage: Attack and Defense 1577–1730*, resources for examining eighteenth-century English drama have now been effectively globalized. In response, the last decade has brought a succession of new studies, including Robert D. Hume's *The Development of English Drama in the Late Seventeenth Century* and Judith Milhous's *Thomas Betterton and the Management of Lincoln's Inn Fields, 1695–1708* for the earlier part of the period, and Cecil Price's *Theatre in the Age of Garrick*, John Loftis's *Sheridan and the Drama of Georgian England,* Leo Hughes's *The Drama's Patrons,* and George Winchester Stone, Jr., and George M. Kahrl's *David Garrick: A Critical Biography* for the latter, along with Curtis A. Price's and Roger Fiske's studies of theater music, Dene Barnett's series of papers on eighteenth-century acting published in *Theatre Research International,*[1] and the fifth and sixth volumes of the *Revels History of Drama in English.* Richard Bevis's new study of eighteenth-century comedy and Allardyce Nicoll's posthumously published account of the theater of Garrick's time are worthy additions to this list.

It may seem disappointing in the light of such enormous advances in our understanding of repertoire and performing conditions that the original drama of the period still remains something of a poor relation. Literary readers, with their standard of excellence set by Shakespeare and the Jacobeans, have usually found more to interest them in the comedy and heroic drama of the Restoration than in its eighteenth-century successors and, with some justice, have diagnosed a progressive retreat from the notion that a good stage play should attempt to grapple with the tensions and complexities of real life. Those, on the other hand, whose concern was with the populist theater of spectacle, burlesque, and emotionalism have always been more drawn to its Victorian high tide than its Georgian beginnings. Consequently, accounts of the century in general histories have tended to lay main stress on its Garrick-inspired tradition of Shakespearean performance, and have looked little beyond Farquhar, Gay, Goldsmith, Sheridan and two or three token tragedies for its original creations.

Bevis's exhaustive study does little to challenge this evaluation. Although he is alert to performance values, he nowhere suggests that among the many long-neglected scripts he has conscientiously traversed there is any unacknowledged masterpiece that might emulate the success of the Royal Shakespeare Company's 1977 revival of O'Keefe's *Wild Oats*. With only a handful of exceptions, these plays were conceived as vehicles for particular performers and died either with those performers themselves or when the salient features of their performances ceased to be transmitted from one actor to the next by direct imitation. Both Bevis's title and his opening chapters seem to betray a certain impatience with this situation—as if he felt that by now some major new discovery or interpretation should have been forthcoming. Bevis devotes considerable polemic vigor to assailing the view that most original comic writing in the eighteenth century was of a "sentimental" cast in the special sense given to the word by theater historians. That this was evidently not the case and that the bulk of new comedies and afterpieces performed on the eighteenth-century stage were firmly orientated toward the hearty chuckle and sometimes the belly laugh was a point well worth making. But this valid observation hardly justifies the emphasis Bevis gives it, especially as his position has been foreshadowed by other writers and a good deal of his argument depends on a definition of *sentimental* that may not have been accepted by those he is contradicting. Rather more disconcertingly, the reader often has the sense that he is being invited to join in a crusade, not just against those who have overstated the prevalence of sentimental drama, but against the thing itself, as if the appearance of sentimental drama marked some kind of pathological departure from an ideal of theatrical sanity represented by uncomplicated laughter. Bevis's epilogue confirms that this is in fact his position; yet the task of a historian of theatrical tastes is not, at least initially, one of passing judgment but rather one of helping us understand what the appeal of a vanished mode may have been and why that appeal came to be felt when and where it did. His conclusion that the "humanitarian" period in drama was "an age better for society than for comedy" (p. 231) ignores the fact that, for many theatergoers, humanitarianism served up à-la-mode was marvelously entertaining. And nothing, after all, is surer than that the tides of theatrical taste will someday sweep in a new age of tearful benevolence.

The primary importance of Bevis's book, then, does not lie in its ostensible thesis so much as in that it presents us with a welcome mapping of a little visited dramatic territory. As Bevis is a careful and intelligent writer with an excellent understanding both of the period and of the morphology of comic forms, it is a good map, comparable in its informativeness, though of more limited scope, with Hume's of Restoration drama, and it must be regarded as superseding Nicoll's older and more impressionistic survey of the same territory in his *History*. There are useful special sections on the plays of Macklin, Murphy, Foote, Colman the elder, and Garrick and highly revealing analyses of the way Goldsmith and Sheridan draw on their immediate tradition. Its only serious limitation is that, in concentrating on the original comedies of the time, it ignores the enormous amount of creative energy that went into the pruning, refurbishing, and in some cases wholesale recomposition of older drama. But it is hard to see how both topics could be covered in one book.

A particular strength is the careful attention Bevis gives to the often disregarded afterpiece both in the form of farce and *petite comedie*. He sees these plays as constituting the major stronghold of his "laughing tradition" and, perhaps because he would have preferred them to offer a more respectable alternative in terms of originality and craftsmanship to the sentimental tradition, he is frequently critical of their stereotyped characterization and unadventurous recycling of Plautine plot formulae. Garrick's *Miss in Her Teens* provokes him to diagnose an "early lowering of tension frequently found in eighteenth-century comedy, especially in the afterpiece" (p. 142) and amply documented by his own analyses elsewhere in the book. Discussing Thomas Hull's *All in the Right,* he complains of a "warmed-over taste," adding that there "were many Georgian afterpieces in this vein, and only the playwright's skill at handling formulae and introducing twists kept an entertaining ritual from becoming tired, dry repetition" (p. 120). These criticisms are both as relevant and as irrelevant as they would be applied to television situation comedy. Viewed from Bevis's perspective, which here is basically that of an analyst of the history of comic forms, there is little to be found in method or resources that was not perfectly familiar to the audience of Menander in ancient Athens. And yet this ceases to be an objection when we see farce in the context of performance as an art which borrows the shells of preexisting forms in order to house a new vital tissue. Like situation comedy, farce is invariably a performers' art. Where the eighteenth-century afterpiece is concerned, both its enormous popularity and the fact that it was performed (and sometimes written) by the greatest actors and actresses of the day should warn us that here plot and dialogue are even less than usually reliable as guides to theatrical substance. That Bevis is aware of this fact is shown by his discussions of the satirical comedies of Samuel Foote where he is prepared to accept that the plot as such exists as no more than a conventional frame for the grotesqueries of the satiric butts. But to require a treatment of comic acting as well as of comedy is once again to demand a different book than the one Bevis set out to write.

Any deficiencies in the purely theatrical aspect of Bevis's treatment have, in any case, been rectified by the simultaneous appearance from the same press of Allardyce Nicoll's posthumously published *The Garrick Stage: Theatres and Audience in the Eighteenth Century.* This has been prepared for the press by Sybil Rosenfeld who describes her contribution as mainly concerned with the selection of the 116 illustrations (from a total of 700 assembled by the author) and the updating of the text to acknowledge recent research. A task of this kind is inevitably a difficult one and the editor can hardly be blamed for occasional awkwardnesses of style and for one or two passages that suggest Nicoll was drawing on material written some time previously which he would no doubt have subjected to further revision.

(A reference on p. 119 to the topic of stage illusion having "recently been widely explored" turns out to be to Richard Southern's 1952 *Changeable Scenery*.) Among a number of passing slips is the reference on p. 36 to the Restoration King's Company as the King's Men—a title which, however appropriate to its lineal predecessor of Jacobean times, would hardly have pleased its hard-working women. But on the whole this is a useful, well-produced book and no unworthy conclusion to a theatrical-historical oeuvre that is unlikely to be equaled in our century.

In case *The Garrick Stage* should be mistaken for something that it is not, it needs to be stated that the book is introductory rather than encyclopaedic in aim and scope, and that the serious student will need to supplement it on almost every topic from the more specialized studies cited at the beginning of this review. But in its careful treatment of theater design, audiences, lighting, scenery, and costume, it does provide exactly the kind of concise, sympathetic guide required by nonspecialist readers of the plays and intending performers. It also teaches two valuable lessons in scholarship. The first of these is skepticism. Nicoll never ceases to probe and sift his evidence and to explore alternative explanations for problematical stage phenomena. He presents a conclusion only when he is satisfied that there is nothing material that can be argued against that conclusion, and on other occasions he is content simply to offer us a group of rival hypotheses. In drawing on iconographical evidence, he shows through a series of detailed case studies that such evidence may feature a large degree of artistic license or straight-out deception, and, even when realistic in intent, may omit details that were so much taken for granted as to have become virtually invisible—such as the two onstage sentinels who were a fixture at each of the patent theaters for at least two-thirds of the century but appear in only one illustration. In considering costumes, he makes clear that the engravings in such collections as Bell's edition of *Shakespeare* and *The British Theatre* frequently show named performers in roles they seem never to have played, and that variant representations of a particular costume (his example is Garrick's Hungarian huzzar's get-up for the role of

The Garrick Years

Tancred) differ in ways which, while probably due to the artists, may still derive in some particulars from changes made by the performer. The second lesson, paradoxically, is that of the necessity of imaginativeness. Even Nicoll's skepticism has its imaginative side, as when he stresses at several points that if no item of data can be accepted wholly at its face value, it is also the case that no item of data should ever be wholly disregarded. Imaginativeness shows again in his insistence that theater historians should possess vivid images of the buildings with which they are concerned—that they should be able to enter them mentally and be aware not simply of their measurements but of sights, sounds and smells and the anarchic life of their auditoriums. His pursuit of this ideal leads him in the early chapters to employ a heavy-handed "time-machine" approach; but the intention is sound and the reader who is not put off by the archness of the proceeding can begin to discover how to experience the plays as compositions not simply for *the* theater, but *a* theater.

As a last instance of the virtues of Nicoll's approach, his treatment of the difficult matter of lighting levels might be compared with a recent discussion of the same subject in Donald Mullin's *Theatre Notebook*. Mullin pertinently points out that the entire candlepower available to illuminate the stage at Drury Lane before Garrick's reforms of 1765 probably did not exceed on aggregate that of a single modern hundred watt bulb, a level which he believes "must have given the steady theater-goer a permanent squint."[2] Nicoll likewise believes that the theaters were much dimmer than they are normally assumed to have been or than most illustrations represent them as being, but he points out that by eighteenth-century standards of nocturnal illumination they were still exceptionally bright:

We go to an hotel, entering a brilliantly lit reception hall, passing along equally bright corridors and eventually being ushered into a bedroom glittering with lamps overhead and on the tables. An eighteenth-century gentleman, if he were staying at an inn, would walk into a lobby provided with perhaps only a candle or two, a candle would be used to guide him along the corridors, and with the candle's tiny flame he would be left in his room. This means that, if we were suddenly enabled to be present at a performance in Garrick's Drury Lane, our eyes would certainly be continually conscious of and oppressed by its dim outlines. It may, on the other hand, be justifiable to suggest that the contemporary public, on entering the playhouse, must paradoxically have been impressed, and even afflicted, by its glare. [p. 116]

It seems to me that it is Nicoll here who has hold of the right end of the stick. It has not, as far as I know, been suggested that our twentieth-century exposure to the nocturnal brilliancies of electric illumination has had the same deleterious effect on our eyes as our ears are supposed to be suffering from traffic noise and rock music; but one has only to experience that other example of eighteenth-century minimalism—the sound of the clavichord—to realize that our senses are much more resilient than we give them credit for being. To eyes trained for a lifetime to see by candlelight, candlelight no doubt sufficed to see many things that would be invisible to us. But Nicoll does not stop here. He also wants us to realize that what was not clearly seen with the physical eye, and what might not even have been there to see, could still be experienced with great vividness in the eye of the imagination. Perhaps his most striking suggestion is that academic paintings of Shakespearean scenes set against nontheatrical backgrounds, which most scholars have rejected outright as evidence for stage practice, may yet show us what audiences *thought they saw* when they peered into the flickering recesses of Drury Lane's scenic area. Here Nicoll has remembered a vital point overlooked by Mullin—that the purpose of stagecraft is, after all, to deceive.

David Garrick, Nicoll claims, was "almost as important as a dramatist as he was a performer" (p. 3). Bevis is less complimentary, giving it as his considered view that "most of his comedies and farces are unexciting and highly derivative, though generally clever and 'stagey,' and even his most popular plays now seem rather pallid" (p. 139). Both views, as it happens, are perfectly correct. Garrick's original plays are inconsequential stage confections constructed out of well-tried plot formulae;

but he shows a marvelous touch with fops and grotesques—especially when he intended to play them himself—and his dialogue, even in cold print, is a continual delight to the ear. The first four volumes of the new Pedicord and Bergmann edition, two containing Garrick's own plays and two his Shakespeare adaptations, have as their main justification that they provide a charting at one remove of a transcendent actor's stage skills; but they will also give much pleasure to readers providing they are content to accept theatrical rather than literary criteria of excellence. The edition is handsomely printed, admirably complete, and, as we would expect, superbly documented with regard to theatrical genesis and stage history. It also establishes beyond reasonable doubt that it was Garrick and not the elder Colman who made the major contribution to *The Clandestine Marriage*.

Despite these virtues, textual scholars are going to shake their heads in sadness over this edition. At the most elementary level, no attempt seems to have been made to assess the nature of the printer's copy underlying the editions chosen as copy text or to identify press variation within these editions. More crucial still is the editors' generally dismissive attitude toward manuscript sources. Not only are these never chosen as copy text when a printed alternative is available, but the reader is not even favored with a list of their substantive variants, despite the fact that some contain autograph material. The editors give no explanation for these choices and provide no information concerning the place of the manuscripts in the textual stemma or the identities of their scribes and correctors. A sampling of the microcard reprints of the Huntington manuscripts reveals that they contain considerable substantive variation from the printed versions and much valuable evidence of the process of composition, including extensive deletions. In the case of *A Christmas Tale* (1773), or *The Christmas Tale* as the Larpent script calls it, the first edition follows the corrected, not the uncorrected, readings of the manuscript and may well have been descended from it. If this could be shown to be the case—but only then—the editors could plead that the status of the manuscript was closer to that of a draft than a publicly issued recension and that for this reason its variants did not belong to the history of the text proper (though this would still involve the dubious claim that performance did not constitute a mode of publication). But the moment the possibility is admitted that the printed and manuscript texts could be descended independently from a lost archetype, neither can be allowed to carry sole authority for the substantives of that archetype and each could theoretically function as copy text. An "old spelling" editor would at this point make his selection according to which best preserved the author's accidentals; however, even in a modernized edition, as here, the editor is still obliged to record the substantive variants of the other collaterally descended text and to emend his copy text when a reading of the other is more likely to represent the author's intention. *Florizel and Perdita,* according to the evidence of George Winchester Stone, Jr., quoted by Pedicord and Bergmann at III, 434–35, seems to require such treatment, with each of the two texts containing between forty and fifty lines unique to itself.

But even if we could assume (as the editors generally appear to do) that it was Garrick's habit to provide his publishers with an autograph fair copy representing his final intentions, a problem of editorial choice would still remain. Richard Bevis has accumulated a considerable body of evidence to suggest that published versions of plays of the Garrick period were revised to meet the tastes of a novel-reading rather than a theatergoing public, and cannot for that reason be relied upon as evidence for what was spoken from the stage (pp. 26–39). This may or may not have been Garrick's own practice—only the editors could tell us that—but it is common enough in Bevis's experience for him to insist that the study of eighteenth-century dramaturgy must be based primarily on the scripts and only secondarily on the editions. In the case of *Florizel and Perdita,* Stone was certainly of the view that the manuscript represented "'what the audience saw during the first season of performance'" (III, 434–35). The editors question this conclusion on the evidence of act division, and might well have added the rider that the Larpent scripts are by definition preproduction copies submitted for censorship and will not record the way a play evolves in performance. But the more important issue in this instance is whether the first edition may have contained readings designed to satisfy the expectations and prejudices of readers which were never spoken from the stage at all. (The existence of a text "regulated from the prompt book" will sometimes help resolve such questions; yet even here there may be doubt about the nature and extent of the "regulation.")

Clearly, the editors' low esteem for manuscript sources and failure to list manuscript variants are not only suspect on purely textual grounds but will create considerable difficulties for theater historians, who are, after all, likely to comprise the majority of serious users of the edition. In *Miss in Her Teens,* as Bevis points out, a whole opening scene between Sir Simon and Jasper has been omitted from the printed text (and therefore from the new edition). But it is certainly of Garrick's composition and we can have no assurance that it was not performed. If the editors' departures from the Bowers/CSE editorial model and their apparent vulnerability to Bevis's argument concerning the artistic primacy of the scripts are the result of mature choice rather than bibliographical naiveté, it is to be hoped that the considerations that led them to act as they have done will be fully explained in one of the remaining volumes. As things stand, however, an edition that in other respects would have been warmly welcomed both for itself and its distinguished dedicatees is left with a rather large question mark hanging over it.[3]

Notes

1. Dene Barnett, "The Performance Practice of Acting: The Eighteenth Century," *Theatre Research International,* 2 (1976–1977), 157–86; 3 (1977–1978), 1–19, 79–93; 5 (1979–1980), 1–36; 6 (1980–1981), 1–32.

2. Donald Mullin, "Lighting on the Eighteenth-century London Stage: A Reconsideration," *Theatre Notebook,* 34 (1980), 77.

3. There are also grounds for concern over the accuracy of the text. A collation of the two opening scenes of *The Jubilee* against a microcard of the copy text, the Huntington manuscript, revealed the following mistranscrip-

tions. The reading on the right is that of the manuscript. I.i.3 frightened] frighted; 10 "I durst not"] *Original blotted over: emendation seems too long to fit;* 18 aware] *corrected in MS to* 'ware; 30 his] *corrected in MS to* 's; 53 round house]*editors omit Garrick's explanatory note, apparently* "the amphi theatre"; 61 And] an'; 67 people] People to; 88 have] of; ii.0.2 *and*] w[i]th; 72 Pudding] Puddings; 94 country] County; 122 all] *all* [for emphasis]. In addition, three fragments of dialogue entered on the versos have been overlooked. The significance of the first two is not clear; however, the third—"Ive hear'd Vather zay how he holp'd Mob one Jew Bill out of Town. & now there's a plot for another. I wonder they dont sarve this so."—could well have been intended as a continuation of Ralph's speech at I.i.33–35. In lines 21–22 of the prologue, the edition gives the nonsensical "Each Magpie, your Honors, will peck at his brother, / And their nature's we've always to crib from each other." The manuscript reads "Natures" with the third letter of the following word blotted. While the original may well reveal more of what lies under the blot than the microcard, the context would seem to require "natures were."

A Critic's Burden: R. P. Blackmur's Reading of Henry Adams

William E. Cain

R. P. Blackmur. *Henry Adams.* Edited and with an Introduction by Veronica A. Makowsky. Foreword by Denis Donoghue. New York and London: Harcourt Brace Jovanovich, 1980. xxv, 354 pp.

One of the curiosities of modern criticism is that a number of its major works were never written or were not completed. One thinks, for example, of T. S. Eliot's study of seventeenth-century poetry, F. R. Leavis's systematic account of "the elements of practical criticism," Kenneth Burke's monograph on Coleridge, and John Crowe Ransom's book on aesthetic theory, "The Third Moment." Each was announced, and its publication declared to be imminent. But though parts and chapters did appear in journals, these were works that their writers were unable to finish or see through to publication. Other books took precedence as the critic's career moved forward, or else studies undertaken by other critics—this seems especially true in Eliot's case—made the planned job of work unnecessary.

R. P. Blackmur's book on Henry Adams is the most famous—and also the most infamous—example of this peculiar genre. Blackmur's first piece on Adams appeared in 1931, and other essays and reviews soon followed, all of which seemed to forecast that the publication of the book-length study was just a year or two away. But as each installment appeared, it became increasingly obvious that Blackmur had neither stopped working on Adams nor gotten any closer to wrapping up the book. So doubtful did the book's publication come to seem that, as Russell Fraser has noted, Blackmur's colleagues and acquaintances began to treat the project as a kind of farce, joking about the advances he had received from his publisher and the deadlines he kept failing to meet.[1]

There is admittedly something amusing as well as depressing about Blackmur's long struggle to complete the task he started in the 1930s. He often insisted that only a little more time and money would enable him, at last, to conclude his work. But it is apparent that this was no ordinary scholarly book and that Blackmur was involved in much more than a critical analysis. What began as criticism turned into autobiography; in examining and meditating upon Adams, Blackmur saw reflections of himself, and he used his subject as an opportunity to locate the terms of his own life and brood upon their meanings. He felt a deep kinship with Adams's sense of failure, loss, and inability to secure a satisfying life and career within society's institutions. And he was also drawn to Adams's keen and sometimes grotesque forms of irony and sense of distance between the intelligent observer and the events that swirl around him. Blackmur's favorite name for himself, Fraser reports, was "the outsider," the man without a place or vocation.[2]

Blackmur's identification with Adams is sometimes overbearing and suggestive of a certain intellectual arrogance. Though Blackmur is an extremely self-conscious writer, he does not often direct the bemused remark or ironic aside against himself or inquire into the nature of his obsession with Adams's ideas. He does not appear to recognize the degree to which he has accepted and absorbed Adams's myth of "failure," despair about human achievement, and pessimism about the course of history: it is as though these are doctrines to which one is obliged to pay homage. And Blackmur's kinship with Adams has its sadly self-punishing side. In 1941, for instance, this headnote preceded one of Blackmur's essays: "Scheduled for publication in 1941 are two critical studies, *The Spoils of Henry James* and *Henry Adams: A Critical Portrait.*"[3] It is eerie, comical, and disturbing all at once to witness Blackmur putting such pressure on himself; as if the Adams project were not demanding and difficult enough, he burdens himself with a second book, equally challenging and complex. This is the act of an ambitious critic, gifted beyond measure, who sets high goals for himself and voices

A Critic's Burden: Blackmur on Adams

them publically even as he knows that he will not be able to attain them. It is, one might say, the act of a man who needs to feel the pain and inescapability of failure. "Failure" perhaps was more meaningful for Blackmur than success, and he seems to have construed it as a sign of merit and authenticity. "Failure" carries the mystique that Adams assigned to it: it is the genuinely perceptive man who realizes that the "expense of greatness" is to fail and who understands that his most significant aspirations are those that he cannot fulfill.

Veronica A. Makowsky's edition of *Henry Adams* is not the book that Blackmur intended to write, and in its omission of important material it might even be judged unfaithful to his design. As Makowsky points out in her introduction, the revised outline for his study that Blackmur wrote in the late 1940s divides it into two sections. The first would begin with Adams's education at Harvard and would survey his life and career until the turn of the century, just before the major books, *Mont-Saint-Michel and Chartres* and *The Education of Henry Adams*, were composed. The second section would consist of a detailed analysis of both texts, with additional commentary on Adams's other later writings and theory of history, and it would conclude with a biographical review of Adams's final years.

Henry Adams, as Makowsky has organized it, is almost entirely focused on the second section of Blackmur's projected work. It opens with "The Expense of Greatness: Three Emphases on Henry Adams," a brief general account which first appeared in the *Virginia Quarterly Review* in 1936 and which Blackmur included in *The Expense of Greatness* (1940) and *The Lion and the Honeycomb* (1955). The next part of the book is titled "The Virgin and the Dynamo" and is more than 250 pages long. Most of this material appears here for the first time and provides us with Blackmur's interpretation of *Mont-Saint-Michel and Chartres* and the *Education*. Blackmur's manuscript for this section breaks off in midsentence, and at several points in the text he refers to chapters either he did not complete or Makowsky did not include. At times "The Virgin and the Dynamo" reads like work-in-progress in need of the revision and reshaping that Blackmur could not bring himself to perform. Part three, "King Richard's

Prison Song"—the title is taken from a medieval lyric that Adams loved—is also mostly new, though a section of it appeared in the *Kenyon Review* in 1940 and was reprinted in *A Primer of Ignorance* (1967). The book's fourth and final part, never published before, is titled "At Rock Creek: Adams: Images: Eidolon." Only a few pages long, it represents Blackmur's attempt to imagine Adams's meditations at his wife's graveside, next to the monument sculpted by Augustus St. Gaudens.

One must recognize how much has been omitted. Blackmur left among his unpublished papers essays dealing with Adams's *History of the United States of America during the Administrations of Jefferson and Madison,* the journalistic writings, and the biographies of Albert Gallatin and John Randolph. Makowsky decided not to include any of these four essays; in her introduction she contends that this kind of historical criticism does not display Blackmur at his best and adds that much of the analysis is based on sources which more recent scholarship has superseded. Also omitted are three essays on "Foreign Affairs 1895–1908," one of which appeared in the *Hudson Review* in 1952. Nor will the reader find reprinted in this volume Blackmur's essay on Adams's novels, *Democracy* and *Esther;* his review of Marian Adams's letters; his comparative study of Henry and Brooks Adams; and his treatment of Adams's letters to his niece, Louisa Hooper. For this material we will still have to consult Blackmur's other collections of essays (not all of which are in print) and the scholarly journals.

Even with these omissions *Henry Adams* is a 350-page book; and no doubt economic factors influenced Makowsky's and the publisher's decision not to give us, in a single volume, everything that Blackmur wrote about Adams. Still one's gratitude for the book is tempered by what has been left out. It may well be true, as Makowsky argues, that Blackmur rarely labored as a historian and that formalist criticism is where his real strength lies. Yet this might suggest a perfectly good reason for including samples of such historically grounded work. *Henry Adams* obviously appeals to readers interested in both Blackmur and Adams; we are eager to discover more about this critic's style and approach as well as to acquire new insights about his subject. To fail to

A Critic's Burden: Blackmur on Adams

include any of the material on foreign policy and politics is to narrow Blackmur's range, to portray him as more of a pure formalist than is actually the case. In addition, Makowsky too quickly assumes that Adams's writings of the 1900s constitute his best and most enduring work. Of course, there is a good deal of support for this judgment; B. L. Reid has recently stated that the *Education* is "the single book of highest distinction ever produced by an American."[4] But other critics have maintained that both *Mont-Saint-Michel and Chartres* and the *Education* are seriously flawed masterpieces, too often playful without purpose, marred by eccentricity, and excessively burdened by Adams's unremitting sense of irony. William Dusinberre, for example, in his stimulating *Henry Adams: The Myth of Failure*, has described the *History*, rather than the later books, as Adams's major achievement, one that rivals the work of Gibbon and Macaulay.[5] We can only regret that Blackmur's analysis of Adams's superbly crafted nine-volume *History* remains unpublished, still consigned to the Princeton University Library archives.

But until a second editor gathers the other writings on Adams, the book that Makowsky has constructed is the closest approximation we have to the book that Blackmur never finished. As it stands, *Henry Adams* is a very uneven, puzzling performance, and it calls for both the highest praise and the most severe judgments. Much of Blackmur's commentary is unquestionably thoughtful and penetrating. Blackmur is wonderfully skilled at treating the patterns, imagery, and formal systems of a text, and no critic has shown more vividly the dense, complex symbolic structures that Adams created in *Mont-Saint-Michel and Chartres* and the *Education*. Blackmur's argument cannot be summarized, in part because of the density of his writing, but even more because he is not, in this book, actually arguing his case and developing specific points. Denis Donoghue, in his foreword to the present volume, refers to Blackmur's criticism as a "supplication of texts" (p. viii), and this seems especially apt as a description of his writing on Adams. Blackmur carefully and patiently attends to Adams and serves the manifold organization of the texts. From one point of view, Blackmur might even be seen as engaged in his own act of re-creation, as he strives to reshape and illuminate the great symbols of the Virgin and the Dynamo in his own prose.

When Blackmur succeeds, the results are impressive. His analysis is shrewd and provocative, yet phrased in a manner that reveals a deep sympathy for and sensitivity to his subject. Sometimes Blackmur is merely repeating commonplaces, but even these are stated with just the right feeling for tone and nuance, as when he observes that Adams "had not the faith; only the apprehension of its need which made him struggle toward it all his life" (p. 17). Blackmur is also acute in noting Adams's "doubts" about his audience but ultimate faith in his symbols: "The waywardness of form and lightness of tone reflected doubt of his audience—doubt of the possibility of any bridge between the audience and himself—but of the validity of the symbols toward which he worked he had no doubt at all" (p. 28). Regrettably, Blackmur never managed to deal at length with Adams's response to his wife's suicide in 1885. But he does comment in some detail on the "gap" in the *Education* between the twentieth and twenty-first chapters—a gap that excludes from Adams's life story the years of his marriage, his wife's death, and his efforts to recover from the shock of losing her. "In leaving out twenty years," Blackmur explains, Adams

is not only making an enormous understatement; he is bringing to bear on all his later chapters the force of the unaccountable—the sum of all that had happened which is not recounted—by means of deliberately inexplicit or only partly explicit symbols. The feeling is thus thicker than the prose: the meaning continues after the words have stopped because it was active before the words began. We have thus a recapitulation, here and there in these chapters, of material that was never given in the book and yet refers both the reader and Adams to it with all the more strength because of its deliberate disguise as the shared unaccountable. [p. 96]

Blackmur has often been praised for his ability to demonstrate how words are used in literary texts. But as this passage suggests, he is also alert to the power generated in texts by what a writer leaves unspoken. In an early chapter of the *Education*,

Adams characterizes the writing he did as a young man at Harvard by saying, "At best it showed only a feeling for form; an instinct of exclusion."[6] For Adams, to "feel" the formal patterning of a work is to be aware of what must be excluded from it; the text, paradoxically, receives its greatest intensities from the facts and feelings that the writer does not express in words. Adams's critics, including Blackmur, have often examined the content of the *Education*—its ideas, themes, and historical generalizations. But Blackmur is exceptional in seeing that what is explicitly "said" is informed by Adams's exclusions. The form of the book is, in a word, *permeated* by Adams's sense of the formless, chaotic, and inexplicable. His deepest feelings are expressed not in words but through significant gaps, exclusions, and silences, which exist precisely at what might have been, in a different book, its most verbally active and fluent part.

When Blackmur addresses the later chapters of the *Education* and considers Adams's theory of history, his discussion is often incisive. He describes well, for example, the cruelty and curiosity evident in Adams's fascination with the sweep of history and the ruthless "tendency" of the forces of the universe. "Curiosity," Blackmur remarks, is "never livelier than about the cruelty of the mind to itself; nothing is of such vital interest as the means of death, nothing so terrifying as the means of rebirth" (p. 264). In Adams's last writings, we see "the cruelty of mind to mind pursued with the liveliest possible curiosity into a kind of desperate dogma." Particularly, Blackmur points out, in the two papers "A Letter to American Teachers of History" and "The Rule of Phase Applied to History," Adams

> plays with his dynamic theory as if it were fact, and in his play shows that combination of frivolity and seriousness which the man of the world and the stoic both think go best with surrender to the inevitable. In these papers physics is *all* physics, and everything else is physics, too; there is no metaphysics, no poetry, and no gesture—only the murderous sweep of law reaching, aspect by aspect, into the life of man. It is the other and lesser thing Adams might have done to finish his *Education;* it is the same thing he did do, but on a lower, more polemic, more practical, less meaningful level: at that level of play

which is the breakdown, rather than the completion, of the mature mind. [p. 265]

This is subtle, suggestive criticism, but it also marks one of the infrequent moments in *Henry Adams* when Blackmur makes a limiting judgment about his subject. For the most part, Blackmur's book is extremely uncritical, taking Adams at his own valuation and accepting the symbols, theories, and political attitudes without disagreement or even qualification. Blackmur's kinship with Adams often leads him to say provocative, intelligent things, but it also causes him to identify so closely with his subject that his writing loses its critical edge; he is not able, it seems, to detach himself from Adams and preserve a scrupulous critical distance from the texts that he is analyzing. Because *Henry Adams* is often stimulating, I hesitate to stress its shortcomings, but these do exist and are serious.

In some stretches *Henry Adams* is long-winded and wearying. There is a great deal of paraphrase and summary, not enough quotation and analysis, and too many occasions when Blackmur attempts to write prose poems, which transform his usually careful style into a series of bad lyrics. Blackmur also seems to me to be guilty of an excessive solemnity in this study; sometimes one feels that the critic's piety, his exaltation of Adams's symbols, and his respectful attention to the theories about man and the cosmos are more appropriate to a funeral oration than to a critical work. Blackmur is constantly raising questions that he does not answer, leading up to crucial arguments that he then dodges, and referring to passages that he either touches on briefly or does not examine at all. His book, to put the matter as directly as possible, suffers from a lack of proportion and judgment—a lack that is all the more striking when one recalls the early essays that Blackmur wrote on modern poetry. In those essays he is very alert to the need to prosecute an argument, to distinguish the good from the bad, to focus on and evaluate basic techniques, ideas, and structures of thought and feeling. In *Henry Adams,* however, Blackmur appears so absorbed in his subject that he can propose critical judgments only if he is certain that he can then diminish or explain away their impact. At one point, for example, Blackmur concedes that "there is a little plain nonsense" in Adams's symbols, "a little *hoc est corpus* turned hocus pocus" (p. 71). But instead of really tackling this issue, Blackmur in effect avoids it by saying in his next sentence, "Yet nonsense has a right in one's symbols; for there is nonsense at the center of the major as well as the minor contradictions in man's mind." How much "nonsense" is contained in *Mont-Saint-Michel and Chartres* and the *Education*? How much does it damage the books? And does its presence reveal something about the tragic self-imprisonment of Adams's mind in his later years? These are the questions that Blackmur's remark about "nonsense" implies, but he passes over them, settling for wordplay (sense and "non-sense") and generalizing the problem in such a way that he is not required to confront it. The nonsense that we may feel at times in the *Education,* he maintains, is not peculiar to Adams but defines the mind of man.

Even more disturbing is Blackmur's willingness to adopt Adams's terms as a means of interpreting the modern world. When he does this, his attitudes become coarse and his language toneless. "To preserve the absolute values in the new relation," Blackmur states, was Adams's "true problem,"

> and he was right to insist on it even if his view of the new relations was prejudiced and erroneous. It would have altered only his exaggerations and nothing of his judgments, had he seen how the population problem of India and Southeast Asia under the impetus of a mild injection of artificial energy in the absence of Western resources suggests the *need* of a mechanization of sex there. Even war, in itself, no longer cuts population much in areas dominated by new forces, and its effect on race in Russia is doubtful. Further, inertia of race among the decimated Jews seems to have intensified. Thus Adams was righter than he might have thought. [p. 251]

If George Orwell had known of this passage when he was writing "Politics and the English Language," he might have included it as an example of the relationship between deformed language and skewed thinking. Blackmur begins by noting the errors in Adams's diagnosis of social problems, but then concludes by affirming that whatever the errors, Adams was "righter" than he could have realized. Here and elsewhere in his book, Blackmur criticizes or corrects Adams only to progress to new reasons for admiration. And this produces a callousness in his voice that apparently he cannot hear. As Makowsky observes in her introduction, much of Blackmur's work on Adams was done in the 1940s and fifties. It was performed, that is, during the period when the war raged in Europe and the terrible truth of the Holocaust became public knowledge. And these facts of history make Blackmur's generalizations, layered in Adams-like language, all the more insensitive. To refer to the "decimated Jews" in such a shallow way and to leave gapingly unexamined the question of Adams's notorious anti-Semitism are glaring failures of critical responsibility.

Blackmur's uncritical relation to his subject manifests itself in other ways. While he comments acutely on the formal design of Adams's texts, he is sometimes inattentive to the resonances of particular passages. Blackmur's absorption in his material here exacts its cost, for it prevents him from being skeptical and suspicious about Adams's uses of language. A whole set of questions that Blackmur raises in his treatment of the modern poets is not introduced in this book. He does not, for instance, tell us in detail what Adams's language sounds like, how it moves from phrase to phrase, how sentences and paragraphs are put together and function. He appears to believe that Adams presents us with sacred texts that the critic cannot probe without violating their sanctity. And so the business of the critic never gets done.

Far too frequently in *Henry Adams* the reader is disappointed, let down by Blackmur's failure to provide the necessary analysis and make the essential discriminations. A notable case in point occurs when Blackmur quotes Adams's account of his feelings after hearing the news of his sister's death. "Impressions like these," Adams writes,

are not reasoned or catalogued in the mind; they are felt as part of violent emotion; and the mind that feels them is a different one from that which reasons; it is thought of a different power and a different person. The first serious consciousness of Nature's gesture—her attitude towards life—took form then as a phantasm, a nightmare, an insanity of force. For the first time, the stage-scenery of the senses collapsed; the human mind felt itself stripped naked, vibrating in a void of shapeless energies, with resistless mass, colliding, crushing, wasting, and destroying what these same energies had created and labored from eternity to perfect. Society became fantastic, a vision of pantomime with a mechanical motion; and its so-called thought merged in the mere sense of life, and pleasure in the sense. The usual anodynes of social medicine became evident artifice.[7]

Blackmur offers a few sentences about this passage, but they are more in the nature of fervent paraphrase than actual analysis. Adams's writing is impressive and grand here, and it is hard not to be awed by the effect. But it is the very sublimity of the passage that one cannot help wondering about. The rush of the participles ("colliding, crushing, wasting, and destroying"), the alliteration, and the other stylistic devices are very much on the surface. This is not, clearly, an instance of an art that seeks to conceal itself: the style, in all its brilliance, is more at the center of our attention than the feeling that Adams is evoking. And as one reflects upon the craftsmanship, the motives and aims of the passage become puzzling. It is not clear whether Adams's effort is primarily to stress the horror of his sister's death or instead to dramatize how intensely he responded to it—as though he alone could feel what the death meant, in its reverberating madness and cosmic significance. Adams's description is also informed by his specialized vocabulary of energy and force, which may, on the one hand, be faithful to his sense of his response, but which may, in addition, point up his attempt to incorporate this death, like the other incidents of his life story, into his theoretical patterns and schemes. The sister's death is compelling confirmation of the deathly tendencies of Nature, Adams believes, and he appears both horrified and captivated by his loss.

As one reads this passage and others in the *Education,* the foregrounding of Adams's own "evident artifice" is sometimes hard to fathom. Passages strike us as vivid, imposing, and brilliant, yet when they are looked at carefully, they appear evasive in intention and elusive in meaning. In part this is a shortcoming in Adams's book; as Tony Tanner has argued, in the *Education* "the feeling of verdict preceding evidence, of experience being subtly deformed by dogma, is sometimes very strong."[8] Yet it is also true that Adams revels in the complexities of his artifice, and takes great pleasure in the range and depth of his ironic performances. Adams sees his act of writing as an act of incessant irony, role playing, masking, and imposture; and it often happens that at just the moment when Adams appears finally to be revealing himself he is, once again, hiding his intentions from our view and practicing still other forms of evasion.

In his *Education,* Adams is always provoking his reader to ask questions, note disparities, contemplate what is irrational and inexplicable. And he is also anxious to make us pursue lines of force and sequences in his own narrative, to make us, in other words, see the relationships that group one incident or person with others. Adams's description of his sister's death, in all its stylistic power and extravagant feeling, is, I think, intensified by the fact of Marian Adams's suicide. The sister's death occurred in 1870, the wife's in 1885; one is vividly rendered, the other not at all. Yet it is the second, as Adams constructs his narrative, that the first might be seen to prefigure. It is the memory of the second death that informs the first one and heightens it. The language used to evoke the sister's death is extreme; it would be hard to imagine language that is more dramatized and elevated. And this makes the absence of language at the gap in the narrative, which leaves the wife's death in silence, all the more painful: here, imagination and language fail.

What we have, then, in *Henry Adams* is a book that is both brilliantly insightful and seriously flawed. Blackmur studies the formal structure of Adams's masterpieces more thoughtfully than any other critic has done. Yet at the same time, it must be said that he does not really consider Adams's ironic stances and profound play with language and is too enmeshed in Adams's theories and ideas. And it is because *Henry Adams* presents such extremes of distinction and failure that final assessments about it prove difficult to make. Depending upon one's point of view and approach, the book will seem primarily an achievement of the highest order or a disturbing example of the ways in which excessive sympathy interferes with the tasks of judgment and analysis. It is possible that Blackmur might have eliminated the failings in his book if he had been able to revise and restructure it. But I think that the problems in *Henry Adams* tell us something important about Blackmur's criticism as a whole. His critical writing combines a keen awareness of formal structures with an inability to perceive what they contain. As many passages in *Henry Adams* demonstrate and as his later work generally testifies, Blackmur is interested in ideology, politics, international affairs, and related topics; he is, in this respect, much more than a critical formalist. But his efforts to move beyond formalism are not often successful, both because they are filtered through Adams's terms and because they are themselves formalist in their basic orientation. Though Blackmur does treat issues and ideas, and not just technique and style, his analyses invariably take a "formal" direction. He nearly always is concerned to explain how values, beliefs, and attitudes function in texts—how, that is, they serve to undermine textual structures or make them more coherent. For the most part, it is formal questions and considerations to which he gives his sharpest scrutiny.

But no sooner does one say this than one feels obliged to qualify. In several essays in *The Lion and the Honeycomb* and *A Primer of Ignorance*, Blackmur deals perceptively with "the economy of the American writer," the "American literary expatriate," and other social and cultural matters. And he discusses them in a way that his formalist predilections neither mar nor distort. When you write about Blackmur, you always have to be prepared to take back what you say. He is difficult to pin down, for, like Adams, he appears anxious to avoid settling into a single role or position. It is not, however, merely the case that Blackmur wants to keep us off-balance and parry or sidestep our attempts to place him as one kind of critic or another. There is also a good deal of uncertainty and contradiction in Blackmur's work. He recognizes, on the one hand, that his talents are suited to formalist studies of a writer's craftsmanship. Yet he also feels constrained by a criticism that binds him to the words on the page, and so he seeks to devise a more elaborate, complex style and becomes a devotee of the religion of art.[9] When Blackmur acts as a high priest of criticism, his essays are obscure, silly, and seem a throwback to the aestheticism of Pater and Wilde. But—as if matters were not confusing enough—this is only part of the story, for Blackmur's solemn, sacramental essays sit in his collections alongside trenchant, sharply focused work on politics, economics, and the state of the modern world. In *this* work Blackmur is an incisive commentator on society, not at all a decadent escapist from it.

Like many contemporary critics, Blackmur wants to make major claims for the critic's activity but is ambivalent about how extraliterary these should be. Sometimes he seems to propose a direct, critical engagement with social problems, while on other occasions he implies that the best response is elevated disdain and absorption in the mysteries of art. In his 1961 essay "The Chain of Our Own Needles: Criticism and Our Culture," for example, Blackmur stresses that we need to "relate" the connections between literature and society, art and the modern world.[10] But except for some sketchy remarks about poetics, rhetoric, and the like, he is not able to explain the means by which these connections might be articulated. It is one thing to insist that literature and society ought to be brought into conjunction, and another to define the various ways through which this should be accomplished. And still another to commit oneself to acting on the basis of these definitions and the aims that they embody.

By stressing the difficulties in coming to terms with Blackmur's work and describing our problems in making judgments about it, I am going against the consensus. There is a standard account of Blackmur's career, one that few have questioned. He began, it is said, as a New Critic in the 1930s and during these years produced his best essays, including those on Stevens, Moore, Lawrence, and other poets. It is this period of Blackmur's career, when he was most purely a formalist, that the majority of his readers admire. Laurence B. Holland states that

Blackmur is "the most brilliant and durable of the New Critics"; A. Walton Litz contends that he "was in many ways the most satisfactory literary critic of his generation"; and Russell Fraser, most boldly of all, asserts that *The Double Agent* (1935) and *The Expense of Greatness* (1940) constitute "the best literary criticism produced in our time."[11] These citations could be supported by many others. Nearly everyone agrees that Blackmur is the best of the New Critics and that his formalist essays of the 1930s have achieved a classic status.

But this characterization of Blackmur as the exemplary New Critic is inaccurate, for he transcends this category as much as he belongs in it. John Crowe Ransom pointed to Blackmur as the typical "New Critic" in his preface to *The New Criticism,* a book that appeared in 1941 and assigned a name to the movement as a whole. Indeed, like many of the New Critics, Blackmur is a close, rigorous reader of texts. But, unlike the others, he rarely engages in full-fledged explications; his analyses often concentrate only on parts of texts, or are strategically placed to enforce a general argument about a poet's characteristic ways of working. Cleanth Brooks's readings of poems by Donne, Pope, Gray, Wordsworth, Keats, and others in *The Well Wrought Urn* (1947), which proceed through the text image by image, sometimes even word by word, are more representative of the usual New Critical procedure. This is not the kind of analysis that Blackmur prefers to engage in, however well equipped he is to carry it out when it does suit his purposes. In addition, Blackmur's verbal analysis generally involves other, more theoretical problems—"authority" in Hardy's poetry, the relation between literature and belief in Eliot's writing, the nature of artistic "consciousness" and dramatic "form" in Melville's novels. Nor is Blackmur's criticism geared towards pedagogy, which many of the New Critics emphasize and see as the resting ground for their interpretive tools.

Blackmur himself once wryly noted that "whenever any of my own work is attacked I am attacked as a New Critic. Usually when people wish to make more pleasant remarks about me they say how it is that I have departed from the New Criticism."[12] As "the outsider," Blackmur felt uneasy about being a member of a movement and did not wish to be portrayed as one of the leading executives in the business that Ransom described as "Criticism, Inc." In at least two essays, "The Lion and the Honeycomb" and "A Burden for Critics," Blackmur in fact treats the New Criticism quite harshly, condemning its narrow canon, its developments of methods that are "useless" when applied to Chaucer, Goethe, Racine, and Dante, and its bad effects on creative writing.[13] He is not a spokesman for the New Critical doctrines in his theoretical writings; his practice is not confined to textual explication as such; and when he does refer to the New Criticism and its advocates (Ransom, Brooks, and Robert Penn Warren, for example), he usually calls attention to defects and misplaced emphases.

Clearly many contemporary critics have a great stake in praising Blackmur as the exemplary New Critic, a fact that may reveal little about Blackmur but much about the state of contemporary criticism. Robert Boyers, for instance, honors Blackmur for his skills as a close reader; and like Holland, Litz, and Fraser, he singles out the early essays on the modern poets as Blackmur's best work.[14] In his concentration on poetic detail and "technical dynamics," Blackmur provides us, says Boyers, with a "model" for our own practice. "The early writings" demonstrate "right thinking" in action, the kind of probing, sensitive response to the text that is rarely seen in "critical discourse" today. As Boyers's frequent complaints about contemporary criticism suggest, he is opposed to the spread of literary theory and wishes to return criticism to the exchange between poet, text, and reader. For Boyers—and many others agree with him—criticism is, by definition, the type of formalist analysis that Blackmur undertakes in his early essays. Critics should not stray from the text itself, should not write "creatively" (as though they were artists themselves), and should not overwhelm the poem and the reader with an obsessive interest in terms and methodology. Boyers's assumptions—and again, many others share them—suggest the extent to which the New Criticism has become institutionalized—has gotten accepted, that is, as the very foundation of criticism itself. And these assumptions strongly determine, I think, the praise that Boyers bestows on the early Blackmur.

These assumptions also determine, in large measure, Boyers's hostile commentary on Blackmur's later work, as gathered in *The Lion and the Honeycomb, A Primer of Ignorance,* and *Eleven Essays in the European Novel* (1964). Like many before him, Boyers has nothing good to say about these essays. "Blackmur came to believe," he states,

> that he too had better things to do than to write the best essays on poets and poetry that anyone had ever written. He bought the notion that an ambitious critic was well advised to move away from texts, to discover Ideas, to talk about things instead of allowing his discourses to be penetrated by the voice and thought rhythms of poets and their verses. He pretends, in his position papers, to be as attached as ever to "technical judgment" and to be interested still in "recreating . . . a verbal sensibility capable of coping with the poetry." But he ceased effectively to write about poetry by the late forties, and much that he wrote in the period between 1950 and his death in 1965 is simply unreadable.[15]

In Boyers's view there is only one Blackmur. When Blackmur stopped seeing himself as a formalist and sought to enlarge his conception of the critic's job of work, he stopped being a good critic.

But it is precisely the later writings that have earned Blackmur the acclaim of a different group of contemporary critics—the critics that Boyers has in mind when he laments the state of the discipline and nominates Blackmur's early writings as an alternative. Geoffrey Hartman, for example, has described Blackmur as "perhaps the first of our witch critics," whose "involuted style betrays an extreme awareness of how the mind is textured by texts and how the critic's, if not the poet's, authority is always under the shadow of imposture."[16] Even more extravagantly, Edward Said has proclaimed that Blackmur is "the greatest genius American criticism has produced."[17] For Hartman, Said, and others on the critical and theoretical vanguard, Blackmur's greatness lies in his ability to range beyond the boundaries set by the New Criticism and in his willingness to enlarge the critic's commerce with other disciplines and society. From this perspective Blackmur's later criticism, where he strives to do more than simply treat the "technical dynamics" of poems, is the essential Blackmur. Here, his critical approach is also a creative one, and it aligns him with those who argue, as does Hartman in particular, for a critical style as dense, sophisticated, dextrous, and allusive as the primary text that it takes as a point of departure.

Blackmur is held in high esteem these days. Most readers still prefer the early essays, but now that a number of prominent critics and theorists have highlighted the later work, these essays too will win new admirers. But the more one reflects upon the nature of Blackmur's reputation, the more it seems that it involves not only a debate about his career but also one that concerns the definition and authority of the critic's role. If you propose ambitious tasks for the critic and if you believe that criticism must move beyond the words on the page, then your emphasis will fall on the later Blackmur. If, on the other hand, you equate criticism with close reading and formalist analysis conducted in a lucid style, then you will judge Blackmur's early work to be his best and view his later writings as a catastrophic decline, as misconceived and unreadable. As Adams observes in the *Education,* "One sees what one brings," and this applies not only to Blackmur's reading of Adams but to our reading of Blackmur as well.

Notes

1. Russell Fraser, "R. P. Blackmur and Henry Adams," *Southern Review,* 17 (January 1981), 69–96. Fraser's biography of Blackmur is forthcoming from Harcourt Brace Jovanovich. Harry Thomas is preparing an annotated bibliography, which will include both primary and secondary materials, for the Garland Press Bibliography Series on Modern Critics and Critical Schools. Until Thomas's work appears, the reader should consult Gerald Pannick's "R. P. Blackmur: A Bibliography," *Bulletin of Bibliography and Magazine Notes,* 31 (October–November 1974), 165–69, which is useful but incomplete and inaccurate in places.

Helpful discussions of Blackmur's criticism include: Stanley Edgar Hyman, *The Armed Vision: A Study in the Methods of Modern Literary Criticism* (1947; rev. ed. New York: Random House, 1955), pp. 197–236; Richard Foster, *The New Romantics: A Reappraisal of the New Criticism* (Bloomington: Indiana Univ. Press, 1962), pp. 83–106; Joseph Frank, "R. P. Blackmur: The Later Phase" in *The Widening Gyre: Crisis and Mastery in Modern Literature* (1963; rpt. Bloomington: Indiana Univ. Press, 1968), pp. 229–51; René Wellek, "R. P. Blackmur Re-Examined," *Southern Review*, 7 (July 1971), 825–45; and Grant Webster, *The Republic of Letters: A History of Postwar American Literary Opinion* (Baltimore: Johns Hopkins Univ. Press, 1979), pp. 149–61.

2. Russell Fraser, "R. P. Blackmur: The Politics of a New Critic," *Sewanee Review*, 87 (Fall 1979), p. 564.

3. See *American Issues*, II, ed. Willard Thorp, Merle Curti, and Carlos Baker (New York: J. B. Lippincott, 1941), p. 869.

4. B. L. Reid, "The View from the Side," *Sewanee Review*, 88 (Spring 1980), 229.

5. William Dusinberre, *Henry Adams: The Myth of Failure* (Charlottesville: Univ. Press of Virginia, 1980). This is one of the best recent books on Adams.

6. *The Education of Henry Adams*, ed. with an introduction and notes by Ernest Samuels (Boston: Houghton-Mifflin, 1973), p. 66. This edition includes nearly 200 pages of letters, documents, and notes and is by far the best one available.

7. *The Education of Henry Adams*, pp. 288–89.

8. Tony Tanner, "Henry James and Henry Adams," *TriQuarterly*, 11 (Winter 1968), 99.

9. See Quentin Anderson's complaint, in *The Imperial Self: An Essay in American Literary and Cultural History* (1971; rpt. New York: Vintage Books, 1972), that Blackmur is too often "where no critic ought to be, between the writer's pen and his page, or at least acting as a passionate acolyte at the altar, watching the consummation of the sacred mystery" (p. 195). See also Foster, *The New Romantics*, pp. 176–81.

10. R. P. Blackmur, "The Chain of Our Own Needles: Criticism and Our Culture," in *Modern Literary Criticism, 1900–1970*, ed. Lawrence L. Lipking and A. Walton Litz (New York: Atheneum, 1972), pp. 345–51.

11. Laurence B. Holland, "A Grammar of Assent," *Sewanee Review*, 88 (Spring 1980), 260; A. Walton Litz, introduction to *Modern Literary Criticism, 1900–1970*, p. 256; and Russell Fraser, "The Politics of a New Critic," 566.

12. R. P. Blackmur, *The New Criticism in the United States* (1959; rpt. Folcroft, Pa.: The Folcroft Press, 1970), p. 1.

13. Both essays are included in *The Lion and the Honeycomb: Essays in Solicitude and Critique* (New York: Harcourt, Brace, 1955), pp. 176–98, 199–212. See also *The New Criticism in the United States,* pp. 1–16.

14. Robert Boyers, *R. P. Blackmur: Poet-Critic, Toward a View of Poetic Objects* (Columbia: Univ. of Missouri Press, 1980).

15. Boyers, *R. P. Blackmur: Poet-Critic,* pp. 7–8.

16. Geoffrey Hartman, *Criticism in the Wilderness: The Study of Literature Today* (New Haven: Yale Univ. Press, 1980), p. 176.

17. Edward Said, "Interview," *Diacritics,* 6 (Fall 1976), 32.

Swinburne's Life and Works

T. A. J. Burnett

Donald Thomas. *Swinburne: The Poet in His World*. New York: Oxford University Press, 1979. vii, 256 pp.

Some individuals have their life and works encapsulated by a single book—a biography which understands and reveals their existence and their endeavors so well that it supersedes all previous works upon the subject and stands alone for several generations. Not forever, for there is no word so inappropriate when applied to works of scholarship than the much-abused adjective "definitive." In the case of others the truth does not fall to one well-concerted, powerful assault but must be reduced by the slow, meticulous construction of saps and trenches. The besieging army of scholars advances to final victory yard by painful yard.

Such is the case with Swinburne. Each successive biography has added a little to our knowledge of the poet's life—this is not quite true; a few have added nothing—but none has totally effaced its predecessors. What is worse, all have been affected by a fatal bias. The well-known peculiarities of Swinburne's manner, character, and sexual inclinations have made it difficult for biographers to approach him with true impartiality. The poet's masochism has led to sinister influences being detected where there were none, and his fantasies have been taken as sober truth. His addiction to alcohol and the contrast between his nervous energy and his frail physique have tempted biographers to make of him a figure of fun. Swinburne's superficially amusing and surprising activities have attracted interest, leaving the serious business of relating a life to a body of work still to be done.

Donald Thomas's new biography is an improvement on its predecessors. Thomas brings a healthy common sense to his discussion of the poet's sexual problems—helped no doubt by his previous work on the marquis de Sade and on the history of literary censorship in England—and many hoary myths, especially those concerning Swinburne's relationship with his father and with his housemaster at Eton, are dispelled. He has found some interesting new (to this reviewer at least) secondary sources. The book is readable and enjoyable, and on the whole it is a success. What it is not—and probably it did not set out to be such—is a synthesis of all that is so far known about Swinburne and his work. Thomas does not seem to me to have studied Swinburne's manuscripts. In the absence of a complete edition of Swinburne's poems (an absence that Professor Terry Meyers and I have been working for the last ten years to make good), a thorough examination of the manuscripts is essential if we are to have a balanced picture of Swinburne's output, and essential in order to establish a chronology for the composition of his poems. Furthermore, Thomas does not seem to have read the various articles in academic journals—*Victorian Poetry* for instance—which have, piece by piece, corrected errors and added small but important items to our knowledge of Swinburne. Nor has he ventured very far into the realm of literary criticism. If a life of Swinburne is to be more than the amusing tale of a droll eccentric, then he must be studied as a poet. The man is dead, but the poems, or many of them, will live forever. The value of a biography, therefore, especially when we are dealing with a life in which little happened in the way of action, lies in seeking to explain and understand the poems by relating them to the psychology and experience of the poet. It lies also in establishing as much objective fact as possible so that critics are not led up blind alleys through ignorance of the poet's attitudes, of seminal incidents in his life, of his social setting, and of the precise details surrounding the genesis of his poems. Clearly it is important that a biographer use such evidence as he finds in a critical and discriminating spirit. Distortion and bias in his sources should be seen for what they are and eliminated. This I think Thomas *has* done, except perhaps in the case of that distortion which began with the first and still the most influential of the many lives of Swinburne, that published by Edmund Gosse in 1917.[1]

That Gosse was prejudiced and fundamentally unable to sympathize with his subject has long been recognized, and I am by no means alone in pointing this out, nor indeed is this the first occasion on which I have done so. He has proved, however, a malignant spirit of a kind peculiarly hard to exorcise. This is perhaps because for many of the incidents which he recounts he is the sole authority, and he recounts them with style and malice. Whatever the source of his stories, and whether they are true or not, it is the tone which distorts the picture that he paints of Swinburne. It is consistently patronizing and belittling, holding the man and his antics up for our indulgent amusement, enjoying the failure of his plans and the occasions when the poet, all too often literally, fell flat upon his face. By a campaign of innuendo he robs Swinburne of any claim to dignity or consistency and distracts our attention from his achievement as a major poet. Unquestionably the motive behind Gosse's attitude was jealousy reinforced by injured pride. He recognized Swinburne's social, intellectual, and artistic superiority, and for him friendship with the poet was a powerful source of gratification. Swinburne for his part failed to perceive the relationship as one of friendship—at least in the intimate sense in which Gosse saw it. For Swinburne, Gosse was a journalist, a disciple, a little man who could be useful and who moreover commended himself by the possession of babies. He constantly forgot, or never realized, that Gosse thought of himself as something more.[2] The unconscious rebuffs that Swinburne gave to his would-be friend engendered in the latter an animus toward the poet that colors everything he has to say about him. It is noticeable that the quotations in Thomas's book from other contemporaries, while often critical and disapproving of Swinburne's uncontrolled or unconventional activities, do not have the same snide tone that is found in quotations from Gosse. Gosse's obvious rancor, together with the frequent inaccuracies in his book, suggest that his *Life* really should not be used as evidence without corroboration, and that quotations from it should be confined to footnotes.

In his first chapter, devoted to Swinburne's family and his time at Eton, Thomas makes two sound points—the first when he writes, "There is no evidence whatever to identify Captain Harewood, the sadistic father in *Love's Cross-Currents,* nor Denham, in *Lesbia Brandon,* with Captain Swinburne. As Swinburne admitted of Reginald Harewood in the earlier story, "Nothing can possibly be more different than *his parents* from mine." Thomas is awake to the danger of seeing too much biographical detail in Swinburne's novels, as he is to seeing it in another class of fiction, Swinburne's letters. Swinburne's extraordinary account in a letter to Lord Houghton of how his housemaster at Eton would burn incense in the room while beating him, or saturate his victim's face with eau de cologne, an account that has been seized upon by unwary biographers, Thomas quite rightly describes as "another of what Cecil Y. Lang aptly calls 'Algernonic hoaxes' " (p. 24). In some other passages, however, Thomas is not on such good ground. He follows all previous biographers from Georges Lafourcade to Philip Henderson in equating Swinburne's unfinished play *The Unhappy Revenge* with that described in his famous letter to John Churton Collins of 11 December 1876, where he says that he "first read *The Revenger's Tragedy* in [his] tutor's Dodsley at Eton . . . with infinite edification, and such profit that . . . [he] forthwith wrote a tragedy . . . into which . . . [he] had contrived to pack twice as many rapes and about three times as many murders as are contained in the model." As Edward P. Schuldt has pointed out in his 1976 doctoral dissertation, not only is it known that Swinburne completed at least three other Elizabethan tragedies at Eton, any one of which could equally well have been that referred to, but he also specifically says that he destroyed the one based on *The Revenger's Tragedy.*[3] What is more, *The Unhappy Revenge* resembles *The Revenger's Tragedy* in neither plot nor style, being much more closely related to Fletcher's *Valentinian* and Massinger's *The Virgin Martyr,* and to clinch the point it contains only one attempted but frustrated rape and three murders. *The Revenger's Tragedy* contains three rapes and over ten murders. At a more serious level there are also problems with the dating too complicated to be set forth here.

Thomas paints a lurid picture of Eton life in Swinburne's time. No doubt there was much that could have been improved in the organization of the school, but conditions were not as Thomas describes them. He quotes in several places from the Reverend C. A. Wilkinson's *Reminiscences of Eton* (1888). Wilkinson's book, however, is subtitled "Keate's Time," and Dr. Keate, the famous flogging headmaster, retired in 1834, fifteen years before Swinburne first went to Eton. In the intervening period there had been a reforming headmaster, Edward Hawtrey, and a reforming provost, Francis Hodgson. The days of rat hunting in Long Chamber, the dormitory formerly occupied by the Scholars, and tossing in a blanket were past. In any case, Swinburne was an Oppidan—that is to say, not a Scholar. Thomas also tells us of the career of Dr. Vaughan, headmaster of Harrow, an account which contrasts so comically with that given in the *Dictionary of National Biography* that it must serve once again to remind us how urgent it is that that indispensable reference work be rewritten. Both Wilkinson and Vaughan, however, are irrelevant to Swinburne. I suspect that Swinburne's career at Eton was attended by much less brutality than his fantasy letters and poems have led biographers to suppose. It is quite likely that he never suffered a flogging by the headmaster at all; and, leaving Eton prematurely, as he did, when he was quite recently sixteen, it is most unlikely that he was ever sufficiently senior to have witnessed one. But Thomas is quite right in suggesting that for Swinburne, as for other pre-Freudians, floggings were seen more as a test of courage than as any sort of a sexual trauma.

Chapter 2, devoted to Swinburne's time at Oxford, is sound as far as it goes; but it does not go far beyond what has already been said elsewhere, and it again points up the difficulty of writing a biography without studying the relevant manuscripts. During his Oxford years Swinburne filled a large number of notebooks with his poems, and many of them survive, though often in fragmentary condition. These apprentice years are obviously important for the study of the influences on Swinburne and the development of his style, as well as for the analysis of his subject matter. Many of the poems are devoted to Italian politics—these were, after all, the years of King Bomba's enormities in Naples—a fact that not only shows us that Swinburne's interest in political poetry long antedates his meeting with Mazzini but also serves as a counterweight to a statement such as that with which Thomas opens Chapter 3: "By the time of his departure from Oxford, it was at least doubtful whether anyone took Swinburne seriously, including himself. Hoax and burlesque played quite as prominent a part in his writing as lyric fervour" (p. 49). Thomas's treatment of Swinburne's Jacobean dramas, *The Laws of Corinth, The Loyal Servant,* and *Laugh and Lie Down,* is somewhat inadequate, and he again follows all earlier biographers—this time by paying too much attention to the supposed psychological insights which these dramas afford. In fact there was nothing unusual in the writing of pseudo-Elizabethan and pseudo-Jacobean plays. It was quite a fashion from the early nineteenth century on, and Swinburne had many distinguished predecessors, including Wordsworth, Coleridge, Landor, Beddoes, Tennyson, Browning, and Lamb. There was nothing eccentric in Swinburne's fascination with the originals. What is more, the originals outdo Swinburne in sadistic and sexually ambivalent passages. In *Laugh and Lie Down,* for instance, to quote Edward Schuldt, "three references to hermaphroditism, a harmless exchanging of clothing, and an uncomfortable excess of flagellatory description are enough to throw Lafourcade and with him all subsequent commentators right off the track. The main action of the comedy is totally ignored." These three plays, together with *The Unhappy Revenge* (written earlier at Eton), are important primarily for allowing us to follow Swinburne's development from close pastiche to original adaptation and to observe "his increasing awareness of the problems which face the serious dramatist."[4]

In his fourth, fifth, and sixth chapters Thomas treats the most important period of Swinburne's life, the years when he wrote *Atalanta in Calydon* (rather curiously described as "a Victorian Greek tragedy") and the poems published in *Poems and Ballads* (1866). Unfortunately, here again Thomas is mistaken about certain vital facts. As Jerome J. McGann indicates, just as to read Wordsworth's Lucy poems with no knowledge of the biographical facts behind their composition is to be condemned to an impoverished perspective, so it is to read Swinburne's

Poems and Ballads without understanding Swinburne's life when he wrote them. McGann believes that "when Swinburne spoke of 'The Triumph of Time' as the 'monument to the sole real love of [his] life,' *the person he had in mind* was Mary Gordon."[5] Whether or not McGann is correct, it is a pity that Thomas resurrects the old Gossean canard about Jane Faulkner and the poem "To Boo." One had thought that John S. Mayfield and Cecil Lang had buried that one once and for all. The problem that arises from any attempt to relate Swinburne's biography to his poems is that of establishing a date for the latter's composition. The day when Swinburne's "whole life's love" went down would seem to have fallen sometime late in 1863 or early in 1864, though it could possibly have been in the summer of 1864. Mary Gordon was married in June 1865 and presumably would have known of her forthcoming marriage a year or so previously. Does the evidence we possess as to the date of composition of the poems of loss fit those dates? This is a question to which Thomas does not address himself.

Despite various omissions and uncritical acceptances of earlier writers' errors, the first six chapters of *Swinburne: The Poet in His World* offer a much more balanced account of Swinburne's life than we have had before. After that point, however, I found the book disappointing. Certainly, *Tristram of Lyonesse* deserves more serious attention than Thomas gives it, and two of Swinburne's greatest poems, "The Lake of Gaube" and "A Nympholept," receive no mention at all. It is no wonder that Swinburne's later poetry seems thin when compared with his earlier work if one ignores the important pieces. And the influence of Gosse grows stronger toward the end of the book. (All the same, Thomas does try to do the right thing by Watts-Dunton and to combat the campaign of denigration and belittlement with which that "hero of friendship" has been assailed.) Thomas expresses surprise at "the speed with which the former disciple of Mazzini and apostle of revolution turned against those men and causes whom he might have been expected to support" (p. 206). But the question is not so simple as it seems. It can be argued that Swinburne's later unionist and imperialist views represent not an apostasy from his earlier revolutionary sympathies but a natural development—given the distinctive character of his early views and the general political climate. He was after all, like Byron, an aristocratic revolutionary and would no doubt have agreed with Byron when he, having expressed his admiration for Napoleon, went on to say, "But I don't want him here."[6] Swinburne's seemingly contradictory blend of liberalism and conservatism was far from being a special case; the views expressed in his poems accurately reflect the passions, ideals, and paradoxes that characterized Victorian opinion at large.

Notes

1. Edmund Gosse, *The Life of Algernon Charles Swinburne* (London: Macmillan, 1917).

2. The mortification felt by Gosse, the rejected suitor, who himself admitted that he had followed Swinburne around like a dog, emerges frequently in his letters to Theodore Watts (later Watts-Dunton). On 26 September 1879, he wrote, "He never writes to me, now, Swinburne. I am afraid he forgets his friends very easily." On 1 July 1886 the line was "I have written a letter to Swinburne, which I wish you to see,—if he will show it to you. I suppose it is the last that he will ever receive from me . . . he was born without a heart." On 4 March 1899, Gosse complained, "I have been, not to brag, a very faithful soldier of Swinburne's for nearly 30 years. . . . Of all this, of all my affection and loyalty for years, I don't think that Swinburne has the very least appreciation. I don't think he has ever observed it!" And on 26 May 1902: "I did not know how to approach the rather distasteful fact that on occasion of my having put myself out to reassert and define Swinburne's position at a moment when the fickleness of taste has for the time being retired from him, Swinburne himself should have no word of affection, or of sympathy, or of the very barest civility, to address to one of the oldest personal friends he possesses" (British Library, Ashley MSS. 822, ff. 21, 21b, 51, 51b, 63, 63b; B2014, f.144).

3. Edward P. Schuldt, ed., *Four Early Unpublished Plays of Algernon Charles Swinburne*, Diss., Reading Univ., 1976, pp. 98–101.

4. Ibid., pp. 261, 263.

5. Jerome J. McGann, *Swinburne: An Experiment in Criticism* (Chicago: Univ. of Chicago Press, 1972), pp. 210–12.

6. See Byron's Journal entry for 17 November 1813 in Leslie A. Marchand, ed., *Byron's Letters and Journals*, Vol. III (London: John Murray, 1974), p. 210.

The Comic Grotesque in Elizabethan Prose and Drama

Robert S. Kinsman

Leland H. Carlson. *"Martin Marprelate, Gentleman": Master Job Throkmorton Laid Open in His Colors.* San Marino, California: Huntington Library, 1981. xxi, 445 pp.

Neil Rhodes. *Elizabethan Grotesque.* London: Routledge and Kegan Paul, 1980. xiv, 207 pp.

At initial glance it may strike the reader that the two books presented here seem only casually related. The first, Leland Carlson's awesomely and arduously thorough study of that explosive outburst against the Church of England hierarchy in 1588–1589, set off by the "learned Epistle" of the "reverend and worthie Martin Marprelate, gentleman" (with five books and a broadside to follow), is primarily a study in authorship. It attempts convincingly to identify one man—not a composite author or a disguised cabal—Job Throkmorton (1555–1601), as the real Martin Marprelate, from a field of twenty-two candidates variously proposed over time, and to establish the canon of his works. The second book, Neil Rhodes's *Elizabethan Grotesque,* concerns itself in general with comic and satirical writing in the late Elizabethan and early Jacobean periods (roughly 1592–1614, the dates of Nashe's *Pierce Penilesse* and Jonson's *Bartholomew Fair*). In particular, it examines the nature of the grotesque in the new styles of comic prose that had developed during the 1590s and were to make a noticeable impact upon the drama of the period. And in doing so, Rhodes perforce considers the Marprelate controversy which brought into high prose relief inter alia the racy colloquialism, the "base comparison," unsavory references, and analogies to human and animal bodies, and unpleasantly punning variations on personal or vocational names (e.g., Thomas Cooper, Bishop of Winchester = cooper, "barrel or cask maker," with further allusion to the tubs, featured in the bath and whorehouses of the Bankside, "stews" owned by the bishop).

A second look thus will show that the two books are indeed joined in the searching out of styles by which to identify an author or characterize a cultural era: scurrilous "scoffs" and bitter invective, "fierie and vulcanicall satyrs," "gunpowder libels," and gallimaufries of kitchen rhetoric. Indeed, Carlson devotes two chapters wholly, and perhaps one-quarter of his text all told, to various indicators of Throkmorton's "stylistic characteristics and techniques" based on four letters, three parliamentary speeches, and one acknowledged book, as augmented by pseudonymous and anonymous works he convincingly claims for him. A bit of circularity here, one must confess, and unavoidable perhaps, however openly handled and persuasively argued.

There are other connections between the two books. One involves Thomas Nashe's almost certain entrance into the anti-Martin ranks with *An Almond for a Parrat, or Cuthbert Curry-Knaves Almes, Fit for the Knave Martin* (called in the book "Martin Makebate" [troublemaker] and "munckie face Machivell"—signs, as it were, of Nashe's known and later hand. The weight of recent scholarly opinion, at least, inclines the scales in favor of Nashe's being the most likely author of the piece, which thus forms a link between it, the last shot in the Marprelate battle, and Nashe's acknowledged success, *Pierce Penilesse* (1592). Whether or not Nashe wrote *An Almond for a Parrat* and thus participated directly in the Marprelate quarrel, we know from references in his preface to Greene's *Menaphon* and his own *Pierce Penilesse* that he was well aware of Martin and his pungent style.

Still a third connection exists between the two books. Both Carlson (pp. 72–74) and Rhodes (pp. 37–38) note the influence that "Martinism" had upon the popular stage of its immediate times. Carlson points out that "Mar-Martine," one of the earliest anti-Martinist writers, deplored the rampant colloquialism of

The Elizabethan Comic Grotesque

Richard Tarleton the antic comic actor and Martin Marprelate the Libeler:

> These tinkers terms, and barbers jestes,
>   first Tarleton on the stage
> Then Martin in his bookes of lies,
>   hath put in every page.

He also quotes lines from the author of "A Whip for an Ape, or Martin Displaced" in which a player, mimicking Martin's style ("Such rangings, ragings, revelings," "Such fleering, leering, jarring fooles bopeepe"), is made to leap in with a wild Morris dance and strike up "Dame Lawsens lustie lay" (Mistress Lawson had been accused of profligacy on accompanying a preacher and his wife "to Lambeth by water"). Rhodes cites a passage in *A Countercuffe given to Martin Junior* (1589) referring to a "May-game of Martinisme" in which Martin was lanced and wormed "at London upon the common stage," following which "hee had no other refuge but to run into a hole, and die as he lived, belching." Both Carlson and Rhodes are aware of Francis Bacon's admonition of 1589 that "an end and surseance [be] made of this immodest and deformed manner of writing [Martinism], whereby matters of religion are handled in the style of the stage."[1] And it is Carlson (pp. 73–74) who records that the Privy Council itself enjoined the archbishop of Canterbury, at this time, to appoint a person well versed in divinity to join with a representative appointed by the Lord Mayor of London and with the Master of the Revels to inspect plays for material "unfytt and indecent to be handled in playes, both for divinitie and State."[2]

Despite the fact that Carlson is massively equipped to approach problems of style (he tells us in his preface that he had originally contemplated carrying out a computer-aided study of the authorial problems in *Marprelate* but became convinced that "the computer" could not isolate salient stylistic characteristics), his book is essentially that of a deep-delving, dedicated historian, particularly adept at working with the archival records and documents of Elizabethan Nonconformity. His mastery of the compendious bibliography of the controversy seems complete; his survey of relevant materials, absolute; his arguments for Job Throkmorton's authorship of the Marprelate tracts, as opposed to Donald J. McGinn's championing of John Penry, severe but fair and fully founded (see especially pp. 297–300 and 303–7). His own book is almost literally packed with information from cover to cover: the front endpapers give us Job Throkmorton's line and kindred; the back, the Coughton Throkmorton line and the descent of Katherine Neville, Job's mother, back to Sir Edward Neville, first baron of Bergavenny, the sixth and youngest son of the first earl of Westmoreland. We are given a useful chronological outline of the main events in Throkmorton's life, particularly as it relates to the Marprelate controversy; a salient introduction to the causes provoking the Marprelate campaign; a synopsis of the Martin Marprelate books (six books and a broadside); a list of "dramatis personae" involved in the often fly-by-night production and distribution of the tracts (at least twenty-three persons working with the products of two presses); and "surmises" on the twenty-two candidates previously suggested for Martin's role.

With this background filled in, Carlson turns to his argument that Throkmorton was the author of the tracts and Penry the project manager and business agent. Thus Part II looks solidly at Job Throkmorton's life and writings, examining his early letters of protest (Carlson finds that Strype's printing of the manuscript of "An Answer" in his *Annals*, II.i.286–304 misreads twenty-seven words and omits 1,402 others), first printed works, and three speeches in the House of Commons. The life, proper, is succinctly presented. Throkmorton came from a numerous but proud and well-to-do family whose household included at least twenty servants and whose eldest son, Job, entered Queen's College, Oxford, in 1562, whence he graduated in February 1565/66. Although his polemical career had begun in 1572, with the death of his father, Throkmorton assumed the role of lord of the manor at Haseley and led the life of a squire for a decade or so. In 1586 he decided to stand for Parliament and was elected a burgess for Warwick, forcing his election by threatening to invoke the rights of the commonalty to vote. Carlson very nicely summarizes the three speeches (only recently discovered) that Throkmorton made in Parliament, 1586–87: "Againste the Scottish Queene," "On the Low Countries," and "The Bill and Book." All seemed clearly to convey a "rhetorical and Marprelatian power." In effect "Bill and Book" supported the revolutionary proposal of Sir Anthony Cope that the Calvinist and Reformed *Booke of the Forme of Common Prayers* supplant the Anglican *Book of Common Prayer,* that the existing ecclesiastical courts and laws be nullified, and in effect that Presbyterianism replace Anglicanism. Throkmorton, not without irony, pleaded as well for the freedom of utterance in the House of Commons and the elimination of "dumb" or nonpreaching clergy.

Since the complicated details of publication of the Marprelate tracts and of the government's gathering of evidence against and prosecution of those "Authors, Writers, Printers, or dispersers therof" (Throkmorton among them) constitutes Part I of Carlson's book (pp. 31–91), I shall not even try to analyze it here. Carlson, however, notices Throkmorton's intermittent presence in London, where in 1591 his advice and collaboration were sought by one Edmund Coppinger, "a naive Protestant visionary," long on fervent prayer and " 'phantasticall revelations,' " and thought to show some " 'crazing of the braine.' " We see Throkmorton at Westminster in Easter term, 1591, accused of intermeddling in the Martinist books; charged with slandering the bishops, the government, and the queen; and indicted for libeling the clergy in "a saucy and gibing manner" and for scoffing at matters of religion. Quite practically, and utterly unheroically, Job Throkmorton submitted, and the queen extended clemency.

In the summer of 1592, however, in a subdued style and modified manner, Throkmorton, Carlson believes, wrote *A Petition* defending the "uprightnesse of myne owne conscience." Here he strikes at his old adversaries in words that recall his earlier treatises but are now restrained sufficiently to accord with the fiction that he is petitioning Queen Elizabeth directly. Once again, nonetheless, Throkmorton becomes deeply enmeshed in controversy. Matthew Sutcliffe publishes an *Answer* to the *Petition,* accusing Throkmorton in effect of writing three Marprelate books and three works related to the controversy: "Libels and scoffes published under the name of Martin, as namely his theses, protestations, dialogues, arguments, laying men out in their colours."[3] Then in 1594, in a brief but fierce rejoinder of some thirty-nine pages, the only one of his polemics to bear his name, Job Throkmorton published his *Defence.* Accusing Sutcliffe of unfair treatment and venomous slander of himself and his Puritan friends in throwing out "the guantlet [sic] and chartell of defiance with one hande" and of shaking "the halter and [shewing] the hatchet with the other"—or rather, in plain terms, "to cut in sunder their windpipe first, and ... to aske them why they whoppe not or lewre [cry out] not afterward"—he proffers an ambiguous oath that he was not Martin (i.e., he is Job) and knew not Martin (a literary persona), and was as clear of the charges against him as a child unborn.[4]

From then on, save for an introductory epistle to the *Briefe Apologie* (1598) of his friend Thomas Cartwright, Job Throkmorton is silent. He does not reply to Sutcliffe's *Answere* of 180 pages (which included Throkmorton's *Defence in toto,* analyzed in the proportions of two or three pages of refutation to two or three paragraphs of the original). For our argument, he seemed even to ignore Sutcliffe's caustic comment on his style: "Forgetting the matter hee hath in hand, hee holoweth, shouteth, and whoopeth like a man of Bedlam, and crieth, so, ho, ho. Forgetting himselfe, he falleth in scorning, with termes unwoorthie to be spoken, or written."[5] There remain only a few glimpses of Job Throkmorton during the last four years of his life (1597–1601). Despite Sir Sidney Lee's religiously perfumed and mistaken account of Throkmorton's last-minute repentance and assurance of salvation, Job died an uneventful death, as Carlson calmly shows (pp. 128–29), having visited in London at the home of an old colleague in Parliament two months or so before he passed on.

Interesting and forcibly argued as is Carlson's account of this somewhat maculate pioneer in free speech, this fervent and jaundiced advocate-in-advance for the right not to testify against

The Elizabethan Comic Grotesque

oneself, this arguer before his time on the justice or injustice of *ex officio* and subscription oaths, my chief interest here, as earlier noted, lies in Carlson's arguments for Throkmorton's authorship of the Marprelate books, particularly as he seeks to identify Throkmorton's stylistic characteristics and techniques. We shall not itemize Carlson's careful approach book by book, although it is book by book that he constructs his argument for Throkmorton as the real Martin Marprelate. In essence, as he explains in Chapters 7 and 8, he endeavors to make a systematic comparative analysis of the writings of Penry, Throkmorton, and "Marprelate." For Penry he has nine books to go on, seven of which carried his name and two acknowledged; for Throkmorton twelve items on which he feels he can "certainly" bank (including five letters, three recently discovered parliamentary speeches, the preface to Cartwright's *Briefe Apologie, A Dialogue,* and *Master Some Laid Open*, these last two heavily relied on, while the pieces written in 1572–73, written fifteen or sixteen years before the Marprelate tracts, are resorted to sparingly). His main criteria are twelve: (1) parallels (of thought and expression) in Throkmorton's and "Marprelate's" writing; (2) strongly colloquial diction; (3) punningly coined words (such as "Divillitre," "paultripolitanship" (for "metropolitanship"), and "Percanterburikenolde," a three-step formal mock syllogism based on the name of three of his ecclesiastical opponents, the notorious turncoat, Andrew Perne; John Whitgift, Archbishop of Canterbury; and John Kennall, Archdeacon of Oxford and vice-chancellor of the University); (4) common phrases including references to betting, gambling, card playing, and drink; (5) "writing techniques" such as the prominent use of alliteration or, where appropriate, country turns of phrase or love of Latin tags; (6) use of conspicuous anecdotes; (7) noticeable reliance on proverbs; (8) inventiveness; (9) use of broad humor, irony, and raillery; (10) love of derisive epithets; (11) frequent and specific allusions to contemporary personalities; and (12) reliance on certain favorite topics and recurrent themes (such as prisons, praemunire and treason; printers, Puritans and writers). Used negatively, as it were, these criteria, singly and, better, in combination, rule out John Penry, Throkmorton's chief contender for the claim of Martin Marprelate. Penry, for example, seems not to use the proverb heavily, and, where one is found, it is likely to come from the formal sounding proverbs of the Old Testament. Where Throkmorton is given to invective and scoffing and dotes on derisive epithets, Penry "is above derision and invective, since he regards terms of opprobium as sinful, as expressions for which he must give ultimate account to his Maker in the Day of Judgement" (p. 214).

Satis quod sufficit; enough is as good as a feast. On every one of Carlson's commandments, John Penry, scriptural, earnest, somewhat heavy, gives way to Job Throkmorton, racy, mocking, and nimble. The prosaic Penry, brief in his arguments, clearly must yield to the jocular Throkmorton, lengthy in the presentation of his scurrilities. While there may in remote possibility exist some as yet undiscovered (or unrevealed) Elizabethan pamphleteer linked with Penry as "project manager" or Throkmorton as co-author, such an eventuality seems light years away from genuine belief. Carlson has stretched his net wide, has woven his cording tightly, and has set his reticulations nicely. His factual evidence is firmly set; his interpretations seem essentially unassailable.

The only criticism that one can advance stems, indeed, from the fullness of the evidence set before us. One could wish that the complicated matter of determining authorship on stylistic grounds could have lent itself more readily to elegance of statement and neatness of definition. At times the sheer bulk of Carlson's evidence, and the necessary repetitiousness of his book-by-book argument, defeat ease of statement and niceness of definition. One wonders, for example, why "Ka" is considered "colorful diction" (p. 224). It is a dialect form to be sure, a variant of *quo* (quoth) (see *OED*, ka v^2). Or on pp. 183–84, are we merely dealing with examples of "the use of *a* before words"? In the twenty-four examples there presented we have several separate functions at work. Some involve the use of the worn down proclitic form of the preposition "an" or "on." Accompanied by a gerund ("a praysing," "a studying"), the form presents process or action (*OED*, prep.,[1] senses 12 and 13). But in the phrase "a Gods name" it presents capacity: "in God's name."

In "to come a pace," on the other hand, the *a* perhaps reflects the fact that the English phrase derives from the medieval French *à pas* "on step," i.e., a good pace, swiftly (or may be a combination of *a, prep*,[1] "of manner" + *pace*). For one's hands to be "a colde," moreover, probably reflects a spelling of the adjective "acold," presumably a form of the past participle of the OE *acolian*, which regularly became "acooled" in the sixteenth century, but preserved the "o" sound before two consonants or by assimilation to the separate adjective *cold*. My point is this: while we are enormously grateful to Carlson for bringing in this vast catch, we need still to separate the elements of the haul for more useful purposes and more accurate analysis.

Similarly on page 205, under the heading "unusual parallels" we find that the phrase "is the winde in that dore" is used in one of Throkmorton's pieces and in one of the Marprelate tracts. In point of fact it is a proverb (Tilley, W419) and in that sense not "unusual" but seems rather to need classification under Throkmorton's pronounced penchant for proverbs. So, too, on page 206, we find under "Parallels with Three or Four Main Words" the phrase "not to say black was his eie (to your eies)," i.e., not to find fault with him (to lay anything to your charge). That is a proverb, also (Tilley, E52)—no wonder it is parallel. One last example, and I'm done. On pages 330 and 331, in examining ten parallels that indicate "similarities in language and ideas appearing in Throkmorton's and Martin's writings" we find variants on two proverbs "A Spade must be called a Spade" and "I must needs call a Spade a Spade," and "for never a barrel is better herring" and "never a barrel better hearring." Surely, by themselves, they do not make it "possible to perceive the author behind the distinctive style and diction." There is a lot more to be done to refine into their ultimate niceties the secrets of Martin's style and pose. But that would be another book and Carlson has already boiled two separate books down to make this one. For the clarity of his larger argument, despite its repetitiousness of method and resultant heaps of adequately but nonetheless coarsely sifted evidence, we should nonetheless be grateful. There is still a useful, full-scale book to arise from these precious piles, however.

Without wishing to belabor the point, we shall find ourselves well prepared for Neil Rhodes's *Elizabethan Grotesque* as a result of Carlson's careful laying open of Job Throkmorton. As Rhodes freely acknowledges, the most immediately available starting point for the gusty brand of comic and satiric prose available to Elizabethan writers of the 1590s was the Marprelate controversy. And whether the Marprelate battles directly and immediately involved Nashe or not, Rhodes points out that in the years which followed the fray, "the 'low' style of comic prose which it released was exploited chiefly by Nashe" (p. 4). What he learned from the controversy, together with what he may have learned from Aretino, was a "sense of the ebullient, physical power of words" (p. 156) and a sense of the personalized roles of mocking clown and threatening preacher, unstable or in conflict though they were, to be played by the comic and satirical writer, perhaps learned implicitly from the pen names "Martin Marprelate," "Martin Junior," and "Martin Senior." If, for example, Nashe really wrote *An Almond for a Parrat,* as is now generally conceded, surely he was consciously echoing Martin's signature in his Epistle ("by your learned and worthy brother, Martin Marprelate") when he signed his own preface "Thine in the way of brotherhood, Cuthbert Curry-knave," having dedicated the work to Will Kempe, the clown and player.

It would be inconceivable to think that a controversy as heated as the Marprelate, that had enlisted such a number of writers and had produced such a volume of titles over such a relatively short period of time, shouldn't have left its mark on the prose style of the nineties. As Rhodes notes, in his anti-Marprelate "Pappe with an Hatchet," Lyly abandoned his own artfully contrived and balanced style for "a style which was both more spontaneous and more brutal," while Nashe, adopting the Marprelate mask of antirhetorician, opened his first attack on Gabriel Harvey by declaring that he had taken "precise order ... not to be too eloquent" (p. 90). And where, incidentally, Rhodes proclaims that the "Elizabethan grotesque derives from the unstable coalescence of contrary images of the flesh: indulged, abused, purged and damned" (p. 4), we can recall that Carlson had called to our attention some sixty references to the body

The Elizabethan Comic Grotesque 69

in the writings of Throkmorton and "Martin" including frequent references to blisters and sores, to bowels, bones, cheeks and joints.

To a certain extent, Carlson's twelve categories of Throkmorton style provide reasonable parameters for a description of Nashe's peculiarities, although the matter of their degree of prominence must always be kept in mind. Both writers are anecdotal and off-handedly personal, both delight in outrageous coinages and unsavory epithets, in invective and gross exaggeration. Both rely on plain proverbs and proverb lore to a considerable extent, both have good ears for a racy, low diction. Each indulges in Latin and legal lardings, Nashe the more imaginative of the two with double and triple and sometimes "macaronic" puns on the Latin and English phrases so intertwined. Indeed, in them all, Nashe goes beyond Throkmorton, stimulated perhaps by his fierce predecessor to his own swashbuckling idiom.

Lest it seem that Rhodes's work is little more than his own rehash of *Martin Marprelate*, let me demonstrate how he moves out from his base to find extensions of Nashe in the writers of the period. In his chapter on the "Shakespearean grotesque" he looks at the Jack Cade scenes in *2 Henry VI*, at one time attributed to Nashe for the abundance of comic devices in his mode: parodies of rhetoric, abuses of logic, grotesquely physical language. "The most Nashian moment" in the play, Rhodes believes is found in IV.x, with Cade defying Iden in the latter's garden. As Cade brandishes his sword and threatens to "cut... out the burly-bon'd clown [Iden] in chines of beef," he resorts to an epithet (burly-bon'd) coined by the author of *An Almond for a Parrat* (Nashe?) and definitely used by Nashe in *Pierce Penilesse* and (later) in *The Unfortunate Traveller*. It is not found elsewhere in Shakespeare; it seems to indicate nonetheless that Shakespeare, now thought clearly responsible for the *Henry VI* plays in their entirety, was aware of the stylistic innovations of the Marprelate flytings and sought to capitalize on them.

While it is true, as Rhodes confesses in his preface, that *Elizabethan Grotesque* springs from a deep interest in Nashe and the resultant belief that his writing deserved a fuller critical discussion in a broad literary context, the book is not so much about Nashe as it is about "the origins and development of the comic grotesque in Elizabethan prose and drama, in which Nashe played a major role." Rhodes divides his book into two parts. The first takes up the nature of the grotesque and attempts to furnish a definition of the term in the context of late sixteenth-century culture. The second part turns our attention to the two great dramatists of the time in a detailed discussion of five plays, three by Shakespeare (*Henry IV,* 1 and 2, *The Merry Wives of Windsor* and discussion in passing of others) and two by Jonson (*Every Man Out of His Humour* and *Bartholomew Fair*). We should end where we began, with a realization that the grotesquerie of *Bartholomew Fair* emerges from a confluence of the forms of sermon, saturnalia, and satire "which from the beginning," Rhodes argues, "determines the modes of expression of Elizabethan grotesque" (p. 154).

Chapter 1 concerns itself with "Literary Grotesque: A Sixteenth Century Background." As it opens, it adumbrates comments on "the new satirical journalism" that will be developed in Chapters 2 and 4 relating to Nashe's boast of being a "second Aretino" and to the interrelationship between preaching, sermon literature, satire and comic polemicism of the Nasheian variety, further influenced by festive comedy and the spirit of saturnalia, a theme to be more fully advanced in Chapter 5. Basically the first chapter seeks to define literary grotesque in contradistinction to burlesque, both degrading modes. In the latter, "comedy derives from the demeaning of a lofty subject by an inappropriately low style" (p. 6); the grotesque, however, is "an exaggeration of the inappropriate to monstrous dimension," " 'an impossibly exaggerated caricature of something which should not exist in reality' " (p. 6, translating Heinrich Schneegans, *Geschicte der groteksen Satire* [1894]). Reflecting its origins, *grotto* paintings known for their fantastic quality, variety and strangeness, the grotesque provides a sense of "visual" shock often derived from grossly physical images of exaggeration and distortion. The sixteenth-century grotesque, deriving from the world of the body, reflects the sixteenth-century fascination with a mass of medical and physiological belief which lacked an esoteric medical terminology and thus contributes to satirical "anatomies," which profited from the blurring of distinction between technical and popular manuals. Thus the technical work *The Examination of Mens Wits,* translated from the Spanish of John Huarte in 1594, describes the inside of a fat man's head as having "abundance of matter . . . an evill token . . . as it befals in very big oranges, which opened, are found scarce of juice, and hard of rinde." The translation of Garzoni's *Hospitall of Incurable Fooles* (1600), a layman's work, tells of a man of "turbulent conceptions, wavering and inconstant motions, [and] broken sleep," whose "emptie soked head" is resembled to a "withered cucumber." In progressive deterioration of "medical" accuracy, Rhodes makes this series illuminatingly eventuate in Nashe's dream-fantastic image from *The Terrors of the Night,* devils with faces "far blacker than anie ball of Tobacco" and with "great glaring eyes that had whole shelves of Kentish oysters in them." Behind these sometimes monstrous images of physical deformity, Rhodes explains, lies the doctrine presented by Nashe in *Christs Tears:* sins are monsters of nature, "for as there is no monster ordinarily reputed, but is a swelling or excesse of forme, so there is no sinne but is a swelling or rebelling against God." Rhodes comments appositely that the sixteenth century was quite aware that "monstrous" derives from *monere,* with its Latin association of "portent" and "terrible warning."

At the same time one must be open to the contexts in which these monstrous things are made to appear. Gargantua's birth, at a Shrovetide tripe feast, is turned by the occasion into exuberance rather than unhappy grossness. In Nashe and his imitators, Rhodes argues, the old, rural festive forms have changed spirit as the active unsavoriness of the city underworld, or the intellectual apprehension of that unsavoriness, provides the material for the grotesque imagery of the new satirical journalism: "Saturnalia drifts toward satire, and the festive violence which is so typical of Rabelais is charged with the purgatorial spirit of contemporary didactic literature" (p. 16). He hastens to add, however, that the *enactments* of the drama sometimes resort to festive ritual so that the beating and baiting and vilification of certain plays depend upon "festive sanctification" which will govern the comic outcome of the plot.

The first half of Chapter 2 discusses the kinds of structure and style that accommodate the grotesque and seeks to explain how structure and style conduce to the proliferation of grotesque imagery. The second half of the chapter discusses Nashe's "indebtedness" to Aretino as a means of isolating the salient stylistic effects of Elizabethan grotesque in the new satirical journalism. The journalistic pamphlets of the 1590s are very loosely structured and are referred to by Rhodes as "rhapsodies" in the Greek sense: a stitching together of diverse material, an essentially oral method of composition which delights in aggregation and makes an almost indiscriminate blend of established literary topoi and themes. Relying on "residual oral techniques," the "low" style in which the pamphlets were written led to parody of the conventional or its replacement by "preposterously base allusions and images." Thus the literary *blason*, or itemization, of a person's physical characteristics from head-to-toe (or at least to shoulders or slightly lower) is supplanted by the *contre-blason*, as in Sidney's mock-itemization of the charms of Mopsa in Book I of the *Arcadia*.

The genuinely *grotesque* inversion of the *blason*, with its grossly absurd images and its patently vulgarized relation of them to the human body gives rise to the "anatomy," as in Middleton's description of the brains and lungs of a "tobacco-taker" in *The Blacke Booke*. This word in caps, as it were, when resorted to increasingly on title pages, indicates the extent to which, so Rhodes argues, "the Elizabethan grotesque springs from an oddly physical concept of literary composition itself" (p. 21). Parallel with the "anatomy" as the grotesque inversion of the *blason* is the "base comparison" as a "grotesque inversion of Euphuistic embellishments by similitude" (p. 22): pointed moustaches compared to shoemakers' awls, the face of a man seeking to enunciate elaborately compared to the stirring of a mustard pot. The last stylistic device conducing to the grotesque that Rhodes comments on is the coinage of either the "base" quasi-colloquial phrase or the "extravagant" neologism. The first stems from the writer's attempt to improvise fresh "boystrous" journalistic phrases derived from his lowlife surroundings in a super-idiomatic way. The second, in Nashe at least, arises from his somewhat pedantic attempt to coin "Italionate verbes which all end in Ize, as mummianize, tympanize, tirannize" or *palpabrize,* a verb which is used of priests handling the wafer. That word, Rhodes nicely argues, "perfectly articulates Nashe's transmutation of the verbal into the physical," rendering in solid reference what had been abstract concept (p. 26).

The remainder of Chapter 2, as indicated earlier, considers the possibility that Aretino and his satires, charged with almost physical, grotesque energies, had a major influence on Nashe's style. Such an influence, by implication, would be one that deepened and refurbished the impulses given Nashe's prose by the Marprelate Controversy. Although Rhodes accuses earlier scholars of being "curiously inconclusive" in their conjectures about the extent to which Aretino may have influenced Nashe, and, through him, Elizabethan satirical writing, his own arguments are no more decisive. They illuminate but do not, perhaps cannot, lead us to definitive proof. We shall have to remain content with Nashe's own remark: "Of all stiles I most affect & strive to imitate *Aretines*" (*Lenten Stuffe,* 1599). Nonetheless, the parallels between Aretino and Nashe that Rhodes advances highlight impressively the writers' spontaneity or seeming spontaneity, their rich fascination with the topical, the local (now vexatiously allusive), and the commonplace, their virtuosity in caricature. To paraphrase Rhodes, the "low style" with its peculiar system of conceits and amplification, typified in the "base comparison," is no longer a learned thing but seems to be part and parcel of their view on life. They are fascinated not merely by shocking images, but by images *of* shock. They have a strong feeling for the texture of things, expressed in a highly concrete and metaphysical way, impinging on physicality or verbal violence, yet brought down in incongruous ways to an everyday world, firmly brought within the grasp of the faculties of sensation.

Not surprisingly "Comedy and Violence in Elizabethan Pamphlet Literature" forms the basis of discussion in Chapter 3.

Here we return to the Marprelate Controversy and to the observations of Francis Bacon and others concerning the interrelationship by 1589 of Marprelate agitation and the popular theater, whereby matters of religion were handled in the style of the stage and religion turned into comedy or satire. One of those plays alluded to by the anti-Martinist author of *The Returne of Pasquill* was "The May-game of Martinism," probably not an actual reference but a pretext for working in an ironic preview of a "festive" game in which individuals might be mocked. Martin was presumably to be dressed as Maid Marian, his face muffled to cover his beard, with a great nosegay made of "flowers" assembled from his works. One cannot always fathom the thrust of Rhodes's argument in this chapter. One follows his distinction between the fictional account of Thomas Cartwright's death in an anti-Martinist pamphlet as too literally "correct" to be anything but disgusting and Rabelais's account of the death of Frère Jean, wherein the facts are "disgusting" but the pedantic chaos in which the account is embedded funny. But Rhodes does not quite make clear why the satirist Marston, inheritor of the ferocious weaponry of the Martinist quarrel, has a "verbal incontinence" of a different *kind* from Nashe's. It must lie in the difference in their powers of sustaining invention or in shifting scenes rapidly enough to sustain an imaginative sense of the grotesque. Rhodes's chief point throughout the chapter seems to be that in Nashe's violent images of the grotesque—in evisceration or of "guts as good for guts"—he keeps carnival associations in our minds, is prepared at the right time to release anguished tension by joking about his demons, an exorcising of fear through the demonic made trivial.

Mere sensationalism, Rhodes avows, is the nadir of the grotesque—as in Rowland's *Hells Broke Loose* (1605). The grotesque image seems to dictate to its skilled user the awareness of the warping of the natural order, and that awareness in turn should dictate an appropriate decorum of its own, however far beyond the bounds of normal it may seem. Thus Dekker in his pamphlet *The Wonderfull Yeare* (1603) believed that "mirth is both *Phisicall*, and wholesome against the Plague" and thus could resort to an "appropriate" grotesquerie for the individual horrors of the plague, of citizens seeking to avert the onset of the disease by "stuffing" rue and wormwood into their ears and nostrils, "looking like so many Bores heads stuck with branches of Rosemary, to be served in for Brawne at Christmas." As Rhodes remarks of this journalistic description, the "grim association of the plague with [Christmas] has the same force as the grotesque combination of execution and festivity in the Marprelate writings and in Nashe" (p. 48). Underlying the "aesthetic" use of the grotesque here, is the presentation of literary matter in such a way as primarily to suggest the disturbing and ultimate physical. At the same time it gave the reader an indirect but "distancing" reminder of more comforting spiritual ultimates.

The first division of Chapter 4, "Nashe and the Beginning of Satirical Journalism," associates preaching and satire. As the "new satirical journalism" took shape, it found itself intervening in topics formerly addressed exclusively from the pulpit: pride, envy, wrath, usury, lechery, conspicuous consumption, the moral implications of contemporary events. At the same time sermon literature offered a useful stance or persona to the fictionalizing journalist. At times, to be sure, the role of "preacher" seemed to conflict, in the excessiveness of Elizabethan prose satire, with the role of clown which the "low style" demanded. Perhaps, then, the violence or "hyper" state of Nashe's utterance may spring, Rhodes suggests, from his awareness of the dual personality of his cultural stance—clown mocking preacher, preacher frightening clown. A third point of contact between sermon and "moral" literature and the new satiric prose lies in the headlong resort to harangue, inveighing, and invective. This point, I dare say, has been made sufficiently clear as to obviate elucidation. As Rhodes shifts to the second division of his chapter, a discussion of the school of Nashe, nonetheless, he points out that Nashe differs from his contemporaries in maintaining a sense of personal connection with "admonitory literature." Lodge and Dekker may retain the format of admonitory literature, but they abandon the sense of personal crisis underlying such works and settle into "relatively coherent structures." "Hack journalism begins when the role of journalist is resolved" (p. 53). This means, with the dwindling of the personal authorial intrusion and the polemical or preaching voice, that direct social criticism begins to emerge, "uncluttered by the more histrionic kinds of moral fervour" (p. 54). With it the city comes to the center of the pamphleteering stage. This trend, Rhodes shows, becomes general in the school of Nashe. Lodge's *Wits Miserie* (1596), for example, shows the author ostensibly in earnest condemnation of dicing. Although Lodge uses the structure Nashe had used in *Pierce Penilesse*, that of the Seven Deadly Sins, Rhodes finds that the argument is manifestly a compilation and Lodge a ringmaster, not a performer directly involved as Nashe seems to be. Middleton in his *Blacke Booke*, to cite a second example presented in Chapter 4, uses specific material from Nashe's writings and shapes a direct sequel to *Pierce Penilesse*. In fact Middleton builds solidly upon Nashe's sketchy plans, so to speak, and in describing the ruins of Pierce's dwelling place (presumably that of Nashe himself), gives us a very early notion, perhaps the first in English journalism, of slum life in a big city. Grotesque imagery has become a more disciplined aspect of social criticism; as with Dekker's plague pamphlets, we have shifted to a social realism: "The secularisation of the prose pamphlet and ... its new perceptiveness about the economic bases of social life, introduce [a hitherto] unfamiliar note of compassion to popular literature" (p. 61).

Chapter 5 closes the first of the two major sections of *Elizabethan Grotesque*. It moves us in time into the late 1590s, some seven or eight years after *An Almond for a Parrat*, some five or six years after *Pierce Penilesse* and a year or two before the Bishop's Injunction of 1599, which as the result of the bitter, libelous wrangle between Nash and Gabriel Harvey, itself an ultimate outcropping of the Marprelate Controversy, decreed that no "Satyres or Epigrams be printed hereafter" and that all "Nashes bookes and Dr. Harveyes bookes be taken wheresoever they may be found and ... none ... bee ever printed hereafter." It presents us with a world of social disintegration evident in London toward the end of Elizabeth's reign. And it marks the beginning of a span of years between 1598 in which *Everyman In His Humour* appeared and 1605 in which *Eastward Ho* was produced, marked by the appearance of plays that tried to reflect and comment upon the viciously changing social scene through the medium of the newly forged satirical prose. Here Rhodes concentrates on the language and imagery of that prose "with its insistent physicality and constant attention to the uses and abuses of the human body" (p. 64), signs and symptoms of the diseased individual and of the diseased city or state.

As he examines the satirical drama of the period, citing *The Family of Love* (1602) and *Westward Ho* (1605), to name two of his titles, Rhodes notices that the chief factor in linking the vocabularies of violent abuse and of sex in such plays is the "syndromic" nature of the Elizabethan low comic imagery analyzed in his earlier chapters: oaths suggesting slaughter; slaughter, food; food, sex; sex, disease—in essence the grotesque world of the body, presented through the physicality of the new prose. In the second section of this chapter, Rhodes turns to the *Parnassus* plays and *Wily Beguiled*, possibly a Cambridge piece of the circle of Parnassus, together with Dekker's *Shoemaker's Holiday*, and the plays of Marston and Middleton, specifically to trace the language of the sexual grotesque, the symbolic debasing of the body into "flesh-food," as Rhodes a bit clumsily puts it, the "sex-food syndrome," corporality of oaths and "base comparisons."

An examination of the first and second parts of *The Return from Parnassus* (1599–1600, 1601–2) yields interesting results. They are modish attacks on fashionable literary trends; they attack the social and economic conditions that force would-be university wits into such base occupations as acting or writing for Shakespeare's company. One chain-linked image is that, literally, of nit-picking, an image that Nashe had used earlier, incidentally. In its multiple-faceted-imaged life, it finds a doctor sifting a patient's fecal specimen for diagnosis, sad vinegar wits souring at the bottom of a barrel, and hack writers appearing as bots and glanders of a printing house. In the views on love of Sir Fredrick, the salacious and crusty country gentleman of the second part of *The Return,* we encounter a kind of sexual grotesque that had become fashionable again in the translation of sex into terms of food to be consumed by the glutton: a piece of mutton (a wife of whom the husband is tired), gives way to "a messe of stewd broth" (several brothel "affairs"), which in turn yields to "an unlac'd Rabbit" (young woman) as best of all.

The same imagery of woman as food prepared for eating can be found in Marston's *Antonio and Mellida* (1600) with the difference that the grossness of the act is to be enshrined as an *impresa* boasting of Balurdo's gluttonous sexuality, "a good fat legge of ewe mutton, swimming in stewde broth of plummes," with the motto beneath it *"Holde my dish, whilst I spill my pottage."*

As Rhodes turns to Dekker's *Shoemaker's Holiday*, he points out that Simon Eyre's speech is characterized by the older tradition of comic vituperation, a mixture of festive abuse and excitement at the prospect of feasting, while Sybil, his daughter's maid, and Firke, one of his journeymen, are turned into caricaturists of the new caustic grotesque style. Rhodes finds that much of the boisterous zestfulness for which the play is acclaimed resides in a "grotesque reciprocation" in imagery among the characters, citing particularly Firke's abandonment of his satiric style at the sound of the Pancake bell, the reminder of the oncoming Shrovetide. At that point Firke's language shifts to that of Eyre's (V.ii). To sample Rhodes's analysis of the use of the grotesque in Dekker's *The Honest Whore* Parts I and II (1604, 1608), we shall look at the woman-as-cooked-flesh imagery. In Part I, for example, Bellafront comments that Sir Oliver Lollio, a tight-fisted client, "will eate Mutton till he be ready to burst, but the leane-jawde slave will not pay for the scraping of his trencher" (II.i.105–9). After Bellafront reforms in Part II, the very seamiest characters—Bots, a pandar, and Mistress Horseleach, a bawd, whose very names "sustain the theme of living off flesh"—pick up the baked meats motif: "stew'd meat for your Frechman, pretty light picking meat for your Italian, and that which is rotten roasted for Don Spaniardo" (III.iii.12–14). The reformed Bellafront finds herself "not worth a dish to hold [her] meate, for, poorer, [she wants] bread to eate" (IV.i.141–42). Matheo, now forcibly married to Bellafront for having initially seduced her, shows his nature through Nasheian oaths which debase the body into flesh-food, "the counterpart of the sexual grotesque which characterises the language of Bellafront's own fallen state" (p. 79). Rhodes

The Elizabethan Comic Grotesque 79

concludes his chapter and his first main division of the book with an examination of Middleton's use of another, if related, form of the grotesque, the conflict between the fat and the lean, between meat and fish, between Carnival and Lent, a conflict that will be of central importance to his discussion of the grotesque in Shakespeare and Jonson in Part II. His point is this: although the imagery involved had been inherited from earlier times, the "theme of the fat and the lean, while retaining its Carnival or Shrovetide associations, begins to acquire, through the sexual connotations of grease and fatty foods, an implicitly sexual meaning" (p. 83).

The main plot of Middleton's *Blurt, Master Constable* (1601–2) is devoted to love, that of the subplot to lust. Lazarillo, a lecherous, roving Spaniard, pines away with desire for the flesh (Imperia). Pilcher, his starveling page, pines for both flesh and fish—*food*. Curvetto, an aged contender for Imperia's favors, is considered a "gurnet's head" fit for "picking meat," but is dismissed by her as a dried stock fish that needs tawing (a process of softening). As the subplot progresses Imperia vengefully dampens Lazarillo's lust (expressed in terms of edible flesh, fat and lean) by welcoming him in his nocturnal sneaking with the scraps of many hearty meals, and then tricking him into a trapdoor into a cesspit, where he is further drenched with urine. The stream of imagery, Rhodes observes, spills over into the main ("romantic") plot in a very direct, almost parodic way (II.i.24–32), lending credence to a critical view that the play's purpose is to demonstrate that love is what D. M. Holmes has termed " 'a tawdry, glandular business' " (p. 84).[6]

Rhodes begins his sixth chapter, "Shakespearean Grotesque: The Falstaff Plays," with a reminder of the importance of Nasheian satirical journalism for the development of Shakespeare's prose style. The Nashe-Harvey dispute of the early and mid '90s, the Marprelate controversy redone on a directly ad hominem basis, as it were, seems clearly known to Shakespeare and to have been reflected by him in *Love's Labour's Lost*. Suffice it to say that Rhodes notes parallels between Shakespeare's presentation of Petruchio's skimble-skamble arrival at his wedding in *The Taming of the Shrew* (III.ii.41–59) and Nashe's descriptions of Dame Niggardize and John Leiden. He theorizes that the maturing Shakespeare is tentatively testing the preciousness of Arcadian prose against the energy of Nasheian prose as a means of presenting comic effect in dialogue, and that the "infusion of physicality into displays of wit, the increasing prominence of flyting as a dramatic element and a sense of the crowdedness of language are signals ... of a stylistic development [*pace* Nashe] which is to culminate in the Falstaff plays" (p. 98).

Rhodes interprets *1 Henry IV* essentially as "the drama of the body," chiefly Falstaff's monstrous boulting-hutch, but not excluding the lean pizzle Hal or by analogy and overt reference, the body politic. From the very beginning of the play Rhodes finds parallels between Nashe's "comparative tearmes" ("base comparisons") and Hal's "unsavory similes," by now a staple of the low style and the new grotesque. Shakespeare's reliance on the flyting between the "stuffed" Falstaff and the "starveling" Hal depends in part, Rhodes argues, on the stimulus of Nashe's masterfully vituperative *Have with You to Saffron Walden,* published a few months before the appearance of *1 Henry IV*. He comments, further, that at times it almost seems that Shakespeare is redeploying Nashe's imagery of the fat and lean so as to add a dimension beyond the politically moralistic in Hal's views of a man he must soon abandon. Noticing that Shakespeare has apparently drawn on Nashe's comparison in *Christs Tears* of a man's heavy wit to an ox with a pudding in its belly (*1 Henry IV* II.iv.434–38), Rhodes astutely notes how the Shakespearian images pursue a different course from one another, running the gamut of the grotesque from the physically repulsive to the physically exuberant, concluding with the image from Nashe with which Hal reluctantly but fascinatedly ends his sequence of invective, thus revealing a feeling for Falstaff beyond the logical or the moral.

Rhodes makes a valuable connection between the major and minor plots when he observes that in the flytings of the "serious" plot, particularly in the wrangling between Glendower and Hotspur, we find the "festive abuse" of the subplot clearly diffusing into the dissensions of the main plot "instilling it with the same

The Elizabethan Comic Grotesque

spirit of grotesque raillry" (p. 111). In Hotspur's retort to Glendower, in his jibe that the earth shook in "distemp'rature" at the earth's birth, Rhodes follows A. R. Humphreys in observing that Nashe had made a similar use of the noun in satirizing an absurd astrologer who seemed to have been at "the anatomizing of the Skies entrailes." He concludes his pursuit of the body grotesque in *1 Henry IV* with the remark that the analogies between the human body and the body politic seem submerged in this first part, but in *2 Henry IV* will appear as salient aspects of that part of the play. There we will find "The Body Purged." There age and disease subtly skirmish with Falstaff, undermining his "carnivalesque image with warnings of decrepitude" (p. 113).

As Rhodes reviews *2 Henry IV*, he takes a stand on Falstaff that runs counter to certain modern criticisms of Sir John. He believes that Falstaff's awareness of his own comic potential and "invention," combined with his willingness to exploit them, precludes a moral judgment of him. It is Hal who faces moral dilemmas, "and it is Hal's *dramatic* [my italics] subservience to Falstaff which forces those dilemmas into such stark isolation from the action of the play" (p. 114). Rather than talk of Falstaff's degeneration in Part 2, Rhodes prefers to consider the process one of evolution: "Falstaff evolves into an image of the play itself—an image which concentrates and embodies the themes of the play and unifies its separate plots" (p. 114). The comic subplot of *1 Henry IV,* he says, celebrates gluttony; Falstaff's obesity is a celebratory image. The comic subplot of *2 Henry IV* pivots on the medical admonition "Much meat, much malady." Within the context of the play and for the proverb, Rhodes traces the grotesque ramifications of consumption and decay. As the Chief Justice observes of Falstaff, "A candle, the better part burnt out"; and as Falstaff must acknowledge, wittily he seeks to restore the festive sense: "A wassail candle—all tallow." Instead of the Carnival of Part I, we have Lent in Part II; instead of the "sweet beef" of the first, we have the "apple-johns" (six dry, round, old, wither'd Knights) and "dry toasts" of the second. Hal is reduced to drinking small beer; Justice Shallow then takes over the prince's earlier role of Jack of Lent. Falstaff, too, dwindles away: "As a 'dead elm' and a 'withered elder' he has lost the power of natural lubrication which had fortified his earlier, festive self" (p. 116). As we learn, *2 Henry IV* moves close to the genre of satirical comedy in its subplot: its language makes unpleasant connections between gluttony, sex, and disease. In keeping with the purgative notions of such practicing satirists as Hal and Marston, we find throughout Part II a need to expel a growth or humor of the body. Food leads to sex; sex to disease: if the cook helps to make the gluttony, Doll helps to make disease. Falstaff has become a wen; he is surfeit-swelled; "and his body's final metamorphosis is into rank flesh in need of purgation" (p. 118).

At the same time, Rhodes nicely observes, references to gluttony, disease, and the need for purgative remedies are almost as prominent in the political scenes of the play. The two plots are thus interrelated. King Henry's nocturnal meditation (III.i.45 ff.), with its fears that the revolution of the times levels mountains and melts the continent into the sea, that the girdle of the coasts proves too wide for Neptune's hips, and that changes fill the "cup of alteration" with "divers liquors," reminds us of Falstaff, a "globe of sinful continents" (= "containers"), a "bulk" (= cargo ship), and one whose bulging girdle, expansive hips and brimming cup seem almost uncontrollably to emanate such images. The "political vocabulary" of *2 Henry IV* with its "surfeits," "beastly feeders," "glutton bosom," and "rank diseases" is barely to be distinguished from the comic vocabulary. And with this exposition Rhodes returns to his thesis: the patterns of imagery developed through Falstaff have grown into a cohesive statement about the state of England; Falstaff does not diminish in humanity but nonetheless remains "immune from simple moralistic judgments because the moral themes of the play are expressed in terms of purely physical processes" (p. 122), and Falstaff has been expanded, not diminished, in his symbolic functions as a force that unites significant elements, festive and political.

In the final section of this chapter on the Shakespearean grotesque, Rhodes deals with "The Death of Falstaff" (i.e., the reduction of Falstaff in *The Merry Wives of Windsor*). He argues that, quite in contrast to the expansiveness of his role in the *Henry IV* plays, Falstaff now must suffer diminution as a result of the narrowed, essentially bourgeois base of Windsor society and as the result of the formal restrictions of the Italianate plot of sexual intrigue (thwarting for Sir John). In a way this is the world of the container contained, the erstwhile "globe of sinful continents" contained in a clothes basket, crammed in with "stinking clothes that fretted in their own grease" (III.v.105–6). In this last phrase, as Rhodes indicates, we find another extension of grotesquerie centering in the image of "grease" that had earlier characterized Falstaff's vitality. In the basket he was as "subject to heat as butter; a man of continual dissolution and thaw." To be dumped into the Thames, "more than half-stew'd in grease," was to be transformed from a fine Spanish blade, hissing hot, into a mere horseshoe (III.v.106–13). Falstaff's power has indeed diminished.

One detects a sense of disappointment, on Rhodes's half, in Shakespeare's own diminished powers. By implication he fears that Shakespeare has reached the end of his experimentation in the low comic style and grotesque exuberance of the Nasheian manner. While the earlier Falstaffian plays had vigorously absorbed "the inchoate mixture of Nashe's literary material—sermon, satirical journalism and festive comedy"—the *Merry Wives* in its plotting turned tiredly away from the novel exploitation of the arguments from "body" in the *Henry IV* plays, arguments that there united plot. To be sure Falstaff is here ritual scapegoat rather than carnival celebrant, but "lacking a dramatic basis in sermon, satire or festive celebration, Falstaff's grotesque effusions have the air of being merely sporadic passages of *coloratura:* they are indeed his swan song" (pp. 127–28).

We are prepared to turn to Chapter 7 and its discussion of "Jonsonian grotesque" by Rhodes's comment, based on Sally Sewall's essay of four decades past, that *The Merry Wives* is Shakespeare's most Jonsonian play, to be epitomized as *Falstaff Knock'd Out of His Humour.*[7]

Since a discussion of Shakespeare's literary relationship with Nashe had formed the first step in Rhodes's discussion of Shakespearean grotesque, so in Chapter 7, "Jonsonian Grotesque," he first establishes Jonson's acquaintance with Nashe. Of course he is now on solid biographical grounds. We know that Nashe and Jonson collaborated on *The Isle of Dogs,* a play now long lost, but evidently mordantly satirical. We know, too, that Nashe, Shakespeare, and Jonson, each in his separate way, became embroiled with William Brooke, Lord Cobham, Lord Chamberlain from 1596 to 1597. As for Jonson's relationship to Shakespeare, it is likely that the manner of braggart Bobadella's awakening from drunken slumber is based on the discovery of Falstaff's drunken slumber behind the arras. Thorello, also of *Every Man In,* the play in which Shakespeare acted with the Chamberlain's Men, Rhodes notes, seems modelled on the Ford of *Merry Wives.* The first Jonsonian play discussed in Chapter 7, however, is *Every Man Out* (1599), a play that aggressively worked in the very sort of material that the bishops had banned in formal satire and polemical pamphleteering. The grotesque mode in comic prose is there with its "stabbing similes"—Puntevarlo looks like a "shield of brawn at Shrove-tide" or "a dry pole of ling upon Easter-eve, that has furnished the table all Lent." The subtheme of gluttony is there in reverse. Macilente cannot stand a dish as greasy as a loin of pork, protesting that it "varnishes" the face of those who serve it to look like "a gluepot." Sogliardo, to be sure, can defend it on a variety of fantastic grounds: man and swine are axiomatically related in natural philosophy—as churlish as a hog, as drunk as a sow. Had the Jews not been forbidden pork, they would never have murmured at their maker "out of garlick and onions"—they would have "gigantomachised." Buffone looks like "an image carved out of box, full of knots," with a face like a Dutch purse, "with the mouth downward, his beard the tassels." The Shrovetide contention is there, too, with its battle between Carnival and Lent, fat and lean. Linguistically, the grotesque, however, has had its own necessary layers of fat pared away: Jonson's idiom is lean, even if, in terms of total verbiage, the play is long. But the play lacks a dynamic center for its implications. Sogliardo, to a certain extent Falstaffian in language (he calls Macilente "a dry crust"), is treated more like a minor than a major vice. The central inn of the play, the Mitre, is not the Boar's Head;

and lean Macilente will need more than the audience's plaudits to become a Sir John Falstaff.

If *Every Man Out,* as Rhodes reads it, is Jonson's occasion for a rejection of the Nashean grotesque as verbally conveying significant themes (Buffone's remarks are "adulterate similes" in Jonson's terms), *Bartholomew Fair* is his apotheosis of the Elizabethan grotesque. In his interpretation Rhodes follows recent assessments of the play's staging, important because the central image of the fair is in itself the informing principle of the action: probably produced on a trestle-stage within a circular arena, with various mansions or *sedes* located in a symbolic fashion after the manner of the fifteenth century *Castle of Perseverance.* This theory lends a particular fruitfulness to Rhodes's vision of the play as centering in Ursula the pig woman's pork-roasting shanty, described by Knockem (but not without irony and ambiguity) as her "mansion" and her bower. There the fair-goer may have his "punk" and his "pig" in state, "both piping hot." Or as Rhodes summarizes it, "Acting as a tavern, a brothel, a public lavatory and a bank for stolen goods, the pig-booth is also the seedy metropolis in microcosm" (p. 142).

At this point in his exposition, Rhodes extends recent critical views and adds an extra critical dimension of his own. He seeks to demonstrate that in *Bartholomew Fair* Jonson makes a moral statement about human nature dissimilar from Shakespeare's "drama of the body" in the *Henry IV* plays, and from his own earlier versions of humanity. This departure is achieved by divesting Ursula of human personality and melting her away (only verbally) into the first rib, "mother o' the pigs." About her are made to accrete mythic qualities which symbolize the "disturbing obscurities of female sexuality" (pp. 147–48). Pig woman and termagant, great desire and womb, "all fire and fat," through her the Fair achieves a particular vision of the ineradicable human instincts with which we must all contend.

Although the themes of female appetite and male hypocrisy are common in Jacobean satirical comedy, the moral dimensions to which they have been extended in *Bartholomew Fair,* Rhodes contends, are not to be elsewhere found, since the play deliberately "removes the sins of the flesh from the realm of the demonic, and forces those who would condemn such a weakness first to acknowledge it in themselves" (p. 151). This statement leads him to examine Zeal-of-the-land Busy and his obviously fanatic apprehension of Ursula as bearing the marks of the three Enemies of Man upon her, even as he partakes of her roast pig. As a masterfully functional part of the play, the exposure of Busy's hypocrisy is more than a piece of anti-Puritan caricature, for it represents the dangers of the "reformed" view of human frailty, just as Overdo's attempt to ferret out enormities in his variety of disguises goes beyond an illustration of zealous law enforcement to the question of the human limitations of those who enforce the law. He who holds a truly "lawful calling" needs must correct, not destroy, build up, not tear down.

The contemplation of the actions of Busy and Overdo leads Rhodes to return to his opening pages. The grotesque emerges from the flowing together of forms of satire, sermon and saturnalia, each strand vital to the structure of the play, each held in check to give *Bartholomew Fair* its particular tone. Quarlous, Overdo and Busy rely on social, legal and religious "authority" for their harangues, but in each, Rhodes reasons, if to a varying degree, prevailing "authority" is undermined or revealed as limited or lacking. Real authority lies in the character of the madman "Trouble-all," who in questing for "warrant" (eventually teaching the disguised Overdo "compassion") does so with the departing wish "[God] quit you, and so multiply you." The "warrant" would seem to be the recognition that once the nature of reason and understanding can be established, one's own good will and "manners" can make life decently bearable, to paraphrase Grace Wellborn's statement in Act IV. In this way, so Rhodes reads the play, the character "Trouble-all," first appearing in Act IV, cryptically supersedes the Ursula of Acts I–III, his words invoking fertility replacing the image of the struggling and contradictory flesh, creation out of chaos. Female flesh and blood inevitably subvert the male-made, verbal authority of legal and religious prescription.

Elizabethan Grotesque is an intricately conceived book that covers an abundance of material, and suggests much more than it can selectively present. It teases and stimulates us into a rich if silent dialogue. At times its suggestibility seems indeed to have led Rhodes into the nearest teeming alley, preventing him from selecting what might have been the more rewarding path—a tendency that the author seems to acknowledge in his reluctance to establish a "universal" definition of the grotesque. Let me illustrate my point specifically by commenting only on Rhodes's presentation of the "grotesque" in *Bartholomew Fair*. I find it a bit odd that he doesn't examine more thoroughly the "roast pork" theme as a special indication of a pregnant woman's longings, with other sexually related overtones, such as a fear of "pig," the unclean beast, expressed by Dame Purecraft, for example. At the same time, he ignores a somewhat different sense of the grotesque in which the "Pig's Head," a sign, seems an "oracle" to Knockem and a reminder to Littlewit of a sort of Narragonia or Land of Cokaigne. And he passes over too lightly, perhaps, the "grotesque" implications of the puppet-play central to the "conversion" of Busy. One can understand Rhodes's desire to concentrate on the immediate "sources" of the satirical efflorescence of the 1590s. Nonetheless, it is a bit surprising to learn that the extent to which the older grotesqueries of Langland and Skelton were known in that decade is "unclear." True, perhaps, but evasive. *Piers Plowman* seems known to late Tudor writers and to the Elizabethan Puttenham, beyond doubt. Witness *Pyers Plowmans Exhortation unto the Lords, Knightes and Burgoysses* and *I, Playne Piers*—both of about 1550; witness, too, Robert Crowley's edition of *Piers Plowman* of 1550 and Rogers's reprint of Crowley's third issue in 1561, with its apocryphal addition of *The Crede of Pierce Plowman*. Why else the relevance of Nashe's title, *Pierce Penilesse*?

Ben Jonson clearly knew the grotesque *Tunning of Elynour Rummyng* as at least three of his masques patently show. Indeed, the "vices" of Skelton's *Magnyfycence*, a play probably very considerably used by Jonson in *Cynthia's Revels*, were as familiar with the sexual innuendoes of "mutton" as Marston or Dekker. And Skelton's ale-wines were as satirically insensitive to the evils of drink as any low-livers of early Jacobean social comedy.

Be that as it may, with Justice Overdo let me remark that my intentions are *ad correctionem, non ad destructionem.* Both books are nicely printed, nicely made. Of the two, Carlson's book is the more elegantly produced, designed as it was for the Huntington Library, although one wishes that the plate of Throkmorton's petition to Burghley, facing page 342, might have shown us a bit more of the right hand margin of the letter. Carlson's book otherwise seems remarkably near perfect in its production: I could find but one typographical error, a miracle to be commented on these days: in a section heading on page 202, surely "Parallels" reflects the author's own spelling. Rhodes's dashing book, from a commercial press, is not so sumptuously printed, although it has a handsome and appropriate image of gluttony on its dust jacket. It suffers, alas, from minor difficulties in typesetting or proofing: we should read, I take it, *voyage* for *voyate* (p. 104), *statement* for *tatement* (p. 144), *penknives* for *penk-nives* (p. 108). On page 112 a "distem-prature" seems not to be properly closed off in single quotes (the close-quote having been misplaced).

Notes

1. Francis Bacon, "Advertisement Touching the Controversies of the Church of England," *The Works of Francis Bacon,* ed. James Spedding, Robert Ellis, and Douglas Heath, 14 vols. (London: Longman, 1857–74) VIII, 76–77.

2. *Acts of the Privy Council, 1589–90,* ed. John Roche Dasent (Norwich: For Her Majesty's Stationery Office, 1899), VIII, 214–15.

3. Matthew Sutcliffe, *An Answere to a Certaine Libel Supplicatorie* (London: Christopher Barker, 1592), pp. 200–201.

4. Job Throkmorton, *The Defence of Job Throkmorton against the Slaunders of Maister Sutcliffe* (Middelburg: Richard Schilders, 1594/95), sig C4.

5. Sutcliffe, *An Answere,* p. 75.

6. D. M. Holmes, *The Art of Thomas Middleton: A Critical Study* (Oxford: Clarendon Press, 1970), p. 10.

7. Sally Sewall, "The Relationship between *The Merry Wives of Windsor* and Jonson's *Every Man in His Humour,*" *Shakespeare Association Bulletin,* 16 (1941), 175–89. Sewall establishes the relationship on the basis of resemblances of character and plot and on the choice of "identical foibles" then current for authorial ridicule.

The Modern Short Story

Samuel Pickering, Jr.

    Walter Allen. *The Short Story in English.* New York: Oxford University Press, 1981. x, 413 pp.

Nobody in Carthage, Tennessee, believed Cousin James Ligon would marry. One hot summer, though, when he was forty, James moved to Nashville. By September he had a wife. James did not introduce her around Carthage and naturally people wondered what she was like. Not long after the marriage my grandfather met old Mr. Ligon on the street. After discussing the weather, the crops, and local Republican doings, my grandfather brought up the marriage. "Knowing James as I do," he said, "I'm satisfied he married a fine person." "Yes, indeed, Sam," Mr. Ligon replied; "of course there are a couple of particulars. She's older than James. She's been married before. She's a nurse and she's a Catholic." Like James's bride, *The Short Story in English* is fine but there are a couple of particulars.
    Allen concentrates on what he calls "the modern short story." The modern short story and the novel, he argues, are similar; both present "more or less plausible representations of men and women as they behave in life." Before the appearance of the modern short story, the form, he believes, was an offshoot of romance. Unlike the novel and the modern short story, which depend upon realism and plausibility, romance depicts the extraordinary in order to surprise. Allen cites *The Thousand and One Nights* as an example of a romance which appeals almost singly to the "desire to be astonished." Allen's choice of the *Arabian Nights* is unfortunate. In *Hard Times* Sissy Jupe read her father stories from the *Arabian Nights*. Not simply diverting entertainment, the stories implicitly examine the theraputic effects of fiction. Fiction transforms one's view of life and thereby life itself. Not only did Scheherazade's stories deliver her from death and Sissy's father from despair, but they transformed

King Shahriyar's murderous, life-hating misogyny into enduring love. For the critical reader *The Thousand and One Nights* appeals less to the desire for sensational entertainment than it does to the creative imagination, Coleridge's "living Power and prime agent of all human Perception." Throughout the stories one sees the king, a despondent Everyman trapped by loss of belief in the possibility of decency, learning to see, in Coleridge's terms, the butterfly forming under the skin of the caterpillar.

Realism need not be limited to mimetic representation, as Allen implies, and many of the short stories in the *Arabian Nights* describe ordinary behavior. Some of the most astonishing events in the *Nights* occur in the Sinbad cycle. Sinbad, for example, crosses the sea on the back of a whale and flies through the heavens bound to the leg of a roc. Despite such occurrences, taken as a whole, the cycle presents a psychologically realistic depiction of the conflict between duty and dream as it occurs in most men. At the beginning of the cycle of stories, Sinbad the Porter staggers under a heavy load of goods. As he rests on a bench outside a fabulous palace, he reflects on his poverty and laments his laborious lot in life. Abruptly a page from the palace appears and invites the porter inside. There he meets the owner and his namesake Sinbad the Sailor. For seven days the sailor entertains the porter with accounts of his marvelous voyages. Emblematically the two Sinbads are different aspects of a single individual. One part of man, the Sinbad-the-Sailor part, makes him seek or at least dream of adventure in faraway places with strange sounding names. In contrast Sinbad the Porter represents the opposite part of man's nature—that part which dutifully shoulders responsibility and labors long through a conventional life. The cycle of tales implies that life mixes dreams and responsibilities. Frequently the result is harmonious; the two Sinbads meet in the morning and enjoy each other's company throughout the day. At night, however, they go separate ways, as in life dreams and responsibilities often diverge and pull a man in different directions.

For Allen the first modern short story is Scott's "The Two Drovers." Despite the attempt to fence the short story in with the barbed wire of external rather than psychological or poetic

The Modern Short Story

realism, the short story will roam. The date of the "Drovers," 1827, is too late for the beginning of "The Short Story in English." Tracing the ancestry of a person (much less a literary genre) very far is practically impossible. On his deathbed Toby Chuzzlewit was asked who was his grandfather. He answered, "The Lord No Zoo," whereupon his relatives concluded that the family was old and distinguished. The ancestry of the short story is as confused as Toby Chuzzlewit's, and critics, like members of the Chuzzlewit family who heard what they wanted to hear, are likely to discover what they set out to find. This aside, however, the family line of the modern short story is more complex than Allen implies. The historical critic can find a score of literary patriarchs in the eighteenth century alone. Although unbendingly instructive, the *Cheap Repository Tracts* (1795–1798), particularly those by Hannah More, are in Allen's terms realistic short stories. "Tawny Rachel" brilliantly describes the superstitious world of farm laborers and itinerant ragwomen; "Madge Blarney" depicts life in a tribe of gypsies; while "The Parish Nurse" paints the inhumanity of foundling homes. Many of the first children's books published in English were short stories or collections of short stories. Some of Dorothy Kilner's tales in *Anecdotes of a Boarding School* (c. 1783) and *The History of a Great Many Boys and Girls* (c. 1783) among others provide some of the best descriptions extant of childhood in the eighteenth century. Under the guise of biography, religious journals (particularly the *Evangelical Magazine* and the *Arminian—later Methodist— Magazine*) printed short stories. Short stories crowded the pages of magazines, as Robert Mayo has shown in his fine study *The English Novel in the Magazines 1740–1815*.

To what degree are fairy tales short stories? Any consideration of the short story's origin should address this question. Many of the psychological patterns found in the tales of Perrault and the Brothers Grimm are timeless and are consequently always modern. "Cinderella," for example, cannot simply be dismissed as an offshoot of romance or as a remnant of oral tradition. Modern short stories describe transformations, growth, and development more miraculous than that of Cinderella. As Cinderella lives amid the filth of the hearth yet dreams of attending a ball in a beautiful dress and being loved by the son of the king, so Rosabel in Katherine Mansfield's "The Tiredness of Rosabel" works as a salesgirl and lives in a fifth floor cold water flat yet dreams of champagne dinners and aristocratic lovers. Because they dream, both heroines are able to cope with their dreary lives. Peter Taylor's "A Spinster's Tale" and the Grimms' "The Frog Prince" are maturation stories that describe adolescent girls' fears of sexuality. As the Princess does not want to give up her golden ball, a childhood toy and an emblem of childhood itself, so Taylor's Betsy wants to remain prepubescent, in her case an innocent Alice in a land of naive wonder. Grimms' frog and Taylor's Mr. Speed represent those aspects of sexuality that appear grotesque to the girls. Unlike the Princess, who is forced to embrace the frog by her father and who discovers a prince (or that sexuality is something golden in its way), Betsy telephones the police against her father's wishes and has Mr. Speed, or her sexuality, dragged away and imprisoned.

Allen also neglects folktales, the literary kinsmen of fairy tales. He does not, for example, mention Joel Chandler Harris's stories of Uncle Remus, many of which can be traced to the Reynard the Fox cycle. Brer Rabbit is, of course, the trickster figure of a thousand faces from a thousand cultures and tales. "How Mr. Rabbit Succeeded in Raising a Dust" describes how the rabbit, the weakest of the animals and by extension a downtrodden everyman, wins a trial of strength and the hand of Miss Molly Cottontail. The "gals" tell their suitors that if they can raise dust by pounding a rock with a sledgehammer they will marry them. Brer Coon, Brer Possum, and Brer Fox roll back their sleeves but succeed only in wearing themselves out. Like any shrewd lover, or perhaps any successful man, Brer Rabbit relies on deception. He fills his slippers with dirt, and when he jumps up and down hitting the rock, the dust flies. The story is both humorous and serious. It teaches the weak person, and all people are ultimately weak, that if he uses his intelligence he can accomplish a great deal and triumph over adversity. The race in this world is not to the swift, the hard-working, or even the honest but to the clever.

The Modern Short Story

The Short Story in English lacks an informing critical principle. Only impressionistically does Allen discuss the mechanics of short stories: structure, tone, and narrative devices. Thus he writes that Bret Harte's stories "have a certain charm" but does not define the elements of this charm. The sentimentality of Harte's stories, he adds, "though gross, is in its way on the side of humanity." Vagueness is disastrous in sophisticated criticism, and "the side of humanity" is too broad to have any meaning.

Allen pays almost no attention to the cultural reasons behind the growth and popularity of "the modern short story." About the same time the short story came to be thought a distinct literary form, the lyric poem replaced the long poem in popularity. Are there cultural connections between the two occurrences? In the nineteenth century, literature lost its traditional social justification as a means of explaining existence. Only feeling remains when high social or moral seriousness disappears. The spasm in poetry or prose becomes more pervasive and persuasive than the creation of a rich and complex social texture embodying traditional world views. As the cultural center of society shatters, people drift to the margin and their vision becomes limited and thereby more suited to the short story than to the novel. Not only does the three-decker novel disappear by the end of the century but even during the time of its greatest success, shorter literary forms were becoming popular. The individual numbers of parts publication resembled short stories and appealed to a new group of readers who, because of expense or taste, would not read a three-decker novel.

The growth of the short story's popularity coincided with an expanded trade in magazines and newspapers. To what extent is the short story an appropriate form for an age of newspapers? The juxtaposition of tragedy and absurdity on the front page of a newspaper seems in itself an emblem of a fragmented social vision. For such an age the appropriate narrative form would seem to be the short story, which lends itself to an intense but narrow view of life. Examination of other genres would have revealed much about the short story and contemporary culture and would have provided a firm intellectual foundation for

Allen's book. How similar, for example, are the short story and the familiar essay? The best American essayists, writers like E. B. White and Joseph Epstein, often write, if not short stories, autobiographical fragments containing unfleshed tales. Epstein's "The Opinionated Librarian," an account of a man's pruning his library, is, if the books are taken as symbols of spiritual and intellectual states, a fine story of aging and loss and gain. If, as much postmodern criticism implies, fiction is only a comment on fiction, then perhaps the only true fiction left is autobiography as novel and the short story as familiar essay.

In the place of substantive consideration of the short story, Allen offers what is in effect a list of his favorite short stories in English. Although he skips African and Indian stories written in English, he ranges widely, from Britain to Ireland, the United States, Canada, South Africa, and Australia. He mentions important biographical events in the lives of most of the authors he discusses and often summarizes the stories which he believes to be the writer's best or most typical. Since the book examines the works of some eighty-five writers, Allen devotes little space to an individual. Thus Poe gets six pages, Hawthorne eight, and Kipling fifteen, while the writings of Fitzgerald, Hemingway, Maugham, Aumonier, Mansfield, Powys, Coppard, Faulkner, Katherine Anne Porter, and Erskine Caldwell are covered in only sixty pages. It is impossible to do either critical or celebratory justice to an author in so few pages. Examination of *In Our Time* is completed in two pages. It is impossible even to approach the complexity of *Winesburg, Ohio* in two and a half pages, and typically Allen here is reduced to the mundane and consequently the misleading. Winesburg's inhabitants are not "frozen into postures of estrangement and alienation." Like all men and women they have embraced truths and have become, to use Anderson's word, "grotesques." George Willard is not a vehicle which allows Anderson to discuss "the function of the writer in modern life." He is Anderson's portrait of the artist as a young man.

Subtlety disappears as Allen rushes from author to author and story to story. Stephen Crane's wonderful "The Bride Comes to Yellow Sky" is more than "a grimly sardonic rendering of how order came to the west" or "the final ironical comment on Bret Harte's stories of the gold rush." "A simple child of the earlier plains," Scratchy Wilson represents childhood and the youth of a civilization. His clothes resemble children's clothes; little boys in New England wear boots like his to go sledding in winter. Like Peck's Bad Boy throwing rocks at a cat, he teases a dog by shooting near it. He makes a great hullabaloo like a child playing when he chants "Apache scalp-music." Scratchy is the last "of the old gang." Age and marriage break up old gangs; there comes a time in the lives of individuals and nations when they put away childish things. A superbly emblematic gunfight concludes Crane's story. Scratchy draws his pistol on Jack Potter while Potter faces Scratchy with only a suitcase in his hand. A gun is no match for a suitcase and the maturing and civilizing forces it represents—marriage, responsibility, and property. Like an adolescent disappearing into the adult, Scratchy vanishes.

The faults of *The Short Story in English* are glaring. Yet the book does have, if not a saving grace, at least a redeeming feature. Allen summarizes neatly, and he interests one in reading the works of the authors he praises. Some of the authors, Stacy Aumonier and Leslie Halward for example, are forgotten, and Allen makes a case for searching out their writings. The bibliography is good and lists collected editions when they are available. In its account of the development of the modern short story and in its analysis of particular stories, *The Short Story in English* fails. But as a resource which lists collections of tales and suggests short stories to be read, the book is helpful.

The Clarendon *David Copperfield*

Richard J. Dunn

David Copperfield, ed. Nina Burgis. New York: The Clarendon Press, Oxford University Press, 1981. lxv, 781 pp.

The Clarendon Press's commitment to two long-term projects, an authoritative edition of Dickens's fiction and the massive Pilgrim Edition of his letters, continues in 1981 with the publication of the fifth volumes of each series. Although this article reviews *David Copperfield*, it is fitting that I acknowledge the new volume of letters, because the years covered, 1847–1849, include the time of the inception and appearance of *David Copperfield*'s first seven monthly numbers.[1] Novelists and editors seldom work similarly, and the difference between Dickens and his modern editors could hardly be greater. Although both Clarendon projects have published a volume on the average of every three years, Burgis and her predecessors have worked more than fifteen years with *Copperfield*. Dickens, on the other hand, constantly pressed by publication schedules and harassed by multiple distractions, worked at breakneck pace to compose and read proofs for each month's serial part. Seldom, if ever, would he refer to his manuscript when correcting proof. To edit such a reliable text as the Clarendon *Copperfield* demands a scholarly method antithetical to Dickens's own writing, and it is hardly surprising to find the editing taking more than five times as long as Dickens spent on his book.

The Clarendon Dickens editions, under the general editorship of Kathleen Tillotson, the late John Butt, and James Kinsley, intend "a text free from the numerous corruptions that disfigure modern reprints, with an apparatus of variants that will exhibit Dickens's progressive revision" (p. v). Should readers be unfamiliar with the controversy over the general editors' selection of first editions for copy-text, I refer them to Fredson Bowers's review of Tillotson's *Oliver Twist*.[2] Although I acknowledge a few problems with the general editors' policies, I do not think that the question of copy-text for these later volumes should be biased by Bowers's strictures. *Oliver Twist* was subjected to more extensive revision by Dickens himself than was usual, and modern editors did not have such complete manuscript and proof material for *Twist* as exists for a number of the later novels. In most instances a Greg-Bowers rationale of autograph manuscript for copy-text is apt "because it does not attempt to substitute an arbitrary rule for editorial judgment, but . . . enables [an editor] to maximize the chances of incorporating the author's wishes in instances where he otherwise has no basis for reaching a decision."[3] But for Dickens there often is another basis for editors' decisions—extant manuscript, proofs, and later editions that Dickens supervised. Because Dickens made the majority of his substantial revisions in proof and did not refer to the manuscript, it is reasonable that the modern editor should concentrate upon the textual changes from manuscript through proof to first edition, using the first edition as the copy-text. The principal choices the editor then faces are ones of how best to handle errors or omissions in proof. It is important to be as consistent as possible with Dickens's own practices, but when he neglected to catch an error in proof we cannot be certain whether he truly missed the change or tacitly admitted it.

Like Margaret Cardwell, Alan Horsman, and H. P. Sucksmith, who have edited the Clarendon editions of *The Mystery of Edwin Drood* (1972), *Dombey and Son* (1974), and *Little Dorrit* (1978), Nina Burgis adheres closely to the general editors' principles—a critical text with apparatus supplying substantive variants and providing the editor's selection of Dickens's "more interesting first thoughts" that may be determined from his manuscript cancelations. Although they provide an introduction and appendixes with details of the novel's composition and publication, the Clarendon editors eschew critical commentary and offer no explanatory annotation. Kathleen Tillotson appended a useful glossary of thieves' cant to *Oliver Twist,* and *David Copperfield* might profit from notes concerning East Anglian dialect, even though the dialect has been the subject of

The Clarendon *David Copperfield* 99

several studies and has attracted Burgis's attention in her introduction.[4]

The extensiveness of the materials available has both facilitated and complicated Burgis's work. Through the rich holdings of the Forster Collection she has had access to Dickens's number plans, sheets of trial titles, complete manuscript, and a full set of proofs (but with final proof for only the fifth monthly part). She finds important variants for part one in an unauthorized 1850 New York edition and in a few changes Dickens made for his 1858 Cheap Edition, 1858 two-volume Library Edition, and 1867 Charles Dickens Edition (the most frequently reprinted version). Although not having the author's final proof revises at hand for most of the novel, Burgis has been able to deduce their contents by collation of extant proof and first editions. The complications of her task are familiar to anyone who has confronted Dickens's closely written and heavily interlineated manuscript. The compositors set the book from this manuscript with surprisingly few errors, and the proofs indicate that Dickens's attention to those errors that did occur was seldom close and that he was inconsistent with many accidentals. As Burgis notes, the chief source of error in the 1850 copy-text "is the amount of interlineation, leading to the omission, in whole or in part, or misplacing, of interpolated matter, and the misreading of cramped words" (p. liii). She cites some two hundred instances of Dickens's failure to catch errors in proof, and she notes a number of other places where he made corrections which resulted in a substantive variant from manuscript. Generally, Burgis emends to reinstate the manuscript reading, "even in those few instances where the difference is so slight that the manuscript reading is not obviously superior" (p. liii).

In four of the five sample problems Philip Gaskell has discussed as important for definitive editing of *David Copperfield*, Burgis has shared Gaskell's preferences.[5] The one exception seems inconsistent with her practice of restoring manuscript readings, and it permits an inferior 1850 reading to stand when Dickens's intention is not certain. In an early speech of the sharp-tongued Miss Murdstone a compositor changed Dickens's "there is" to the less formal "there's." When he read the proof Dickens either missed or silently approved the change, and Burgis permits the contraction to stand, unfortunately without notation (p. 47). In her introduction she argues for admission of "a few readings originating in the proof; ... corrections of the manuscript such as Dickens would have wished made" (p.liii). However, not knowing what Dickens himself may have wished for this verb form, we are left to wonder whether the contraction makes Miss Murdstone sound less menacing. As Gaskell has observed, this would seem to be an instance where a modern editor should restore the manuscript version.

Dickens at times tuned his ear closely to the quality of his characters' speech, for even in a subsequently canceled passage he carefully revised the dialogue to have the suave Steerforth playfully echo the lamentations of Mrs. Gummidge (p. 270). But neither Dickens's care for variant spelling and pronunciation nor any great concern for the appearance of his text on the page are primary features of the *David Copperfield* proofs. Yet Burgis's choices of contracted verbs are puzzling, because just a few pages after she does not restore the manuscript "there is" she emends a contracted verb for a preferable proof version, and again her choice may affect our understanding of Dickens's characterization. David, reminiscing, mentions having heard a noise after having been locked in his room. In both proofs and published novel the passage declares that as a child "it had not occurred to" David that the noise came through a keyhole. By substituting the manuscript's "hadn't" for the more formal "had not" Burgis's emendation gives the same casualness to the adult David remembering as the text gives in direct quotations of the boy David in the succeeding paragraphs. Granted, Burgis is consistent in using the contracted forms in each example, and for the "hadn't" the textual notes show that this is an emendation made in the spirit of the kind of change Dickens might have made had he caught the compositor's slip.

The certainty of Dickens's intentions for the published text is not easy to determine from what he deleted, permitted to stand, or added to proof. When the proofs came back to him with overmatter for the monthly parts, he made cuts after having corrected the proof. He never restored the cuts even though he could have done so in 1858, 1859, and 1867 when preparing new editions. A number of these passages were published separately some years ago; many were appended to the 1958 Riverside Edition of *David Copperfield* and restored to the text in the 1962 Signet Edition. Clarendon copy-text policy does not admit these cuts to the text, but, including them in the apparatus, Burgis gives them their most accurate editing. Because the deletions represent a number of Dickens's most deliberate decisions about his first edition, it would be helpful if Burgis had been able to give them more prominence, discussing them further in the introduction or setting them more obviously apart from other details in the apparatus. On the other hand, for the few times where Dickens found himself short of the necessary length for the monthly numbers and added material in proof, the Clarendon text clearly identifies both the starting and concluding points of the passages which in proof became part of the 1850 copy-text.

Burgis's notes most often describe brief variants, trace the evolution of characters' names, and recover some false starts for chapter titles and chapter beginnings. I do not find the presence of apparatus intrusive on the pages of the text, and the footnote numbers are set in type small enough not to be annoying. The notes are easy to understand, but the two-column printing of them is sometimes cramped or strangely spaced. On page 415, for example, there are eight notes, a few more than for the average page. The first two notes are widely separated on a single line; the longer third note occupies the next line; there are three more on the third line; and a long note takes several lines before the short final note. Some poorly set text is more bothersome than awkwardly arranged notes. In early chapters a number of dipthongs, mainly "ou" combinations, are so badly set that word and line spacing is disrupted. Reviewers of earlier Clarendon volumes have asked for more editorial clarification of line-end hyphens,[6] but I think even without considering that as an issue in this *David Copperfield* we should hope for better word and letter spacing. In a few instances the spacing may affect our understanding of the character's manner of speaking. The extraordinary word separation in a line of one of Jane Murdstone's pronouncements led me to check the Clarendon (p. 117) against the first edition because I thought Dickens might have drawn out her words deliberately. He did not, but by giving her "it is of more importance than anything else—it is of paramount" an entire line of print, the Clarendon Edition gives her words a visible emphasis that they did not bear in the original. Although very few in number and certainly more the result of printer's than editor's imprecision, such cosmetic flaws are regrettable.

Despite these minor problems, Burgis's editing provides an accurate history of how Dickens developed his novel. We see the work growing before our eyes in the early numbers as we follow the author in his search for a narrative voice and in his selection of the final forms of characters' names. For Betsey Trotwood, later herself so sensitive to names, Dickens first used "Badger" as a surname, and for Little Em'ly he tried "Mary," which may not have been satisfactory because even more than a decade after Mary Hogarth's death he could not so directly designate his fond feelings for her. Our understanding of many of Dickens's motives remains speculative, but Burgis leads us to the exact point in the composition for Dickens's decisions about a number of details such as the change of "Crinkle" to "Creakle" for the schoolmaster's name at the beginning of Chapter 6.[7]

Thanks to Burgis we now have many fine points of textual history to consider in connection with a number of long-standing critical assumptions about *David Copperfield*. Our understanding of the book's autobiographical quality especially may benefit from both textual and extratextual study. Biographers have pointed to general and specific parallels between Dickens's life and the novel; critics have speculated about the emotional and psychological validity of *David Copperfield;* even casual readers remain impressed by the story's intimate narrative manner. The well-edited text helps us to understand the kind of control Dickens exercised in his most autobiographical fiction. The intimacy of the most remarkable passages is not simply that of a fictional adult remembering a fictional childhood; an embracing

The Clarendon *David Copperfield* 103

and omnipresent consciousness shares David's acts of remembrance, and *David Copperfield* thus often seems a tense construction of willed and involuntary memory.

Although Dickens was surprised when his friend John Forster mentioned that the hero's initials were the reverse of his own, the textual record suggests that Dickens very early had made efforts to conceal even as he revealed himself.[8] This is apparent in a well-known passage from the conclusion of the eleventh chapter when the narrator pauses to pity his earlier self as "an innocent romantic boy, making his imaginative world out of such strange experiences and sordid things." The Clarendon Edition shows that there was no substantial change from manuscript to text for this statement, but earlier in the same passage Dickens excised a revealing parenthetical remark from the proof. The first version had David speaking of "that slow agony of my youth (what it truly was no one can ever know but I)," but the published version protects the author's privacy by eliminating the parenthetical material and thereby makes the act of remembering less pointed.

Comparison of a section of the novel's fourteenth chapter with a passage Forster quotes from Dickens's lost autobiography shows Dickens's determination to conceal certain facts of his earlier life. As Burgis notes in her introduction, the fragment of autobiography published in Forster's *Life* concluded with the remark, "I have never, until I now impart it to this paper, in any burst of confidence with any one, my own wife not excepted, raised the curtain I then dropped, thank God" (p. xxix). With similar phrasing, David in the last paragraph of Chapter 14 points out that no one ever before raised the curtain on his previous experience as a working boy. He goes on to declare that he has "lifted it for a moment, even in this narrative, with a reluctant hand, and dropped it gladly. The remembrance of that life is fraught with so much pain to me, with so much mental suffering and want of hope, that I have never had the courage even to examine how long I was doomed to lead it." Here, as forthrightly as anywhere in *David Copperfield,* Dickens makes clear his ground rules for autobiographical fiction, and a minor change in the proof for this passage signals the care with which he controlled the tone of passages evoking painful memories. The manuscript simply reads, "That life is fraught with so much pain," but in proof Dickens added an initial phrase, "The remembrance of." Dickens thus stresses the act of remembering, and the change tempers pain which in the first version appears more direct and continuing. Choosing to remember or not remember is a more voluntary act than had been suggested in the manuscript's account of life fraught with pain. But when we turn later to the famous "Retrospect" chapters (18, 43, 53, 64), we see the novel translating fond memories vividly from past to present tense, carefully perpetuating more pleasant memories.

David as active recollector but often passive protagonist typifies a Dickensian imagination that may be both selective and spontaneous. In the autobiographical fragment Dickens had said that he was uncertain how long he had endured his childhood servitude, but he gives a different emphasis to the question of its duration in *David Copperfield*'s fourteenth chapter. In manuscript the chapter ended with the remark: "I only know how it began, went on and ended," but proof change produced: "I only know that it was, and ceased to be." Both versions add "and that I have written, and there I leave it." The change is small but pointed, for few autobiographical passages so forcefully enact a moment of literary closure. In contrast to the continuing vagueness of time Dickens had mentioned in his autobiography, the passage in the novel specifically declares that although he still has not solved the question of the original experience's duration, the writing superimposes its own definitive time scheme and frees the novelist to proceed with his story. Revision to the more concise "I only know that it was, and ceased to be" sharpens the sense of David's concluding both a chapter of his present story and of his past.

Extratextual sources confirm the ease with which Dickens worked once he began *David Copperfield*, and Nina Burgis's introduction is one of the most complete and lucid discussions of his progress with the book. There is much cross-reference between her introduction and the fifth volume of the Pilgrim Edition of Dickens's letters (although the Pilgrim editors misdate Burgis's book 1980). Newly published and newly ordered letters furnish more information than has been available hitherto concerning the novel's genesis. But for supporting her account of the autobiographical fragment, Burgis, like earlier commentators, depends upon the ambiguous information supplied by John Forster. In establishing a likely chronology for Dickens's work on the fragment and in recognizing its importance, Burgis well deserves Kathleen Tillotson's praise for presenting the best interpretation ever made of these problems (p. x). As Burgis realizes, Forster is often too allusive about the circumstances and date for the fragment, but she establishes that Dickens most likely started his autobiography as early as 1845 or 1846 and resumed it in the winter of 1848–1849. He began thinking of *David Copperfield* early in 1849, experimented with titles in February, and definitely was writing in March. The first serial part appeared in May.

Soon after Dickens's death in 1870, John Forster's biography made public many details about the hardship of Dickens's childhood and quoted the autobiographical fragment to state that Dickens had not shared its secrets with his wife and children. Twenty years after Forster's revelations, Charles Dickens the Younger, in an introduction to *David Copperfield,* declared that his mother had told him that Dickens had shared the autobiography with her in strict confidence and that, concerned about its presentation of Dickens's parents, she had advised against publication. The story is plausible, for Forster would not necessarily have known whether Dickens shared the autobiography with Catherine after telling Forster that he had never, his "own wife not excepted, raised the curtain" on his earlier life. If Dickens did indeed receive advice from his wife about the autobiography, it would seem that hers and Forster's suggestions could have had contrasting effects on the novel's mixture of fact and fiction. Forster had recommended a first-person narrative; he later praised Dickens's interweaving of his personal history with fiction. Catherine, on the other hand, evidently discouraged her husband from self-revelation, but we have no record of her reactions to the novel's parallels to Dickens's own life. But given Dickens's characteristic independence of mind (which biographers usually describe as a volatile mixture of pride and insecurity), it is difficult to regard him as more than temporarily hesitant because of suggestions from his closest associates. The scant information available from letters indicates that he acted with typical singleness of purpose, burning the manuscript autobiography when he found he could take it no farther than the part describing his thwarted courtship of Maria Beadnell, the prototype of the novel's Dora.

Soon after destroying the autobiography, Dickens began testing titles for the new novel. An appendix to Burgis's edition provides the first accurate chronological ordering of the seventeen title variants which are bound haphazardly with the manuscript. The story of the title development, from the cumbersome concept of "Mag's Diversions" to variations on the *Copperfield* idea (including "Charles" for the hero's first name), is fascinating because for a short time Dickens was uncertain about the shape he would give the book. Throughout late February he tested ideas on Forster, and as late as 21 April an advertisement cited an incorrect title for the serial that would begin the next month. However, as Burgis shows, Dickens had selected his final title sometime well before 21 April. Burgis has worked to set the garbled Forster chronology straight, but she, as well as the editors of the Pilgrim Letters, may have created some confusion about just when Dickens started writing *David Copperfield*. Relying on letters now accurately dated but with contents nonetheless open to differing interpretations, Burgis states that Dickens "began writing at the end of February" (p. xxvi). This may follow from Forster's account of Dickens beginning only after he had resolved his uncertainties about the title. The final choice eliminated "The Copperfield Survey of the World as it Rolled" from the title, but a letter of 28 February shows Dickens satisfied enough with the longer title to proceed: "The *Survey* has been my favourite from the first. . . . Therefore I have no doubt that it is indisputably the best title; and I will stick to it."[9] We should note, however, that this letter does not specify when Dickens did start the novel and cannot in itself substantiate Burgis's opinion that he began in February. She also notes a letter of 27 February to which Dickens added the postscript, "In the first agonies of a new book," and it is indeed possible that Dickens was speaking of the actual writing and not the agonies of finding a title for his book. If so, then another letter of 28 March stating that he had been "wallowing" in the novel for a month can be taken literally to designate a starting date in late February.

Without more precise dating than either the Pilgrim Letters or Nina Burgis is able to provide, we should consider the possibility that he started the novel in March because there is a textual suggestion of that date. *David Copperfield*'s opening account of the hero's birth stresses that he was Friday's child, but not many readers are so likely to remember that he was born in March, not, like Dickens himself, in February. Dickens may have given David a March birthday because he wanted to play down the autobiographical parallel, but if that were his principal motive he might also have given him another day of birth as well. I think it at least likely that he chose March as the month of birth simply because he had started writing the book in March. The first letter clearly stating that he was working on the novel itself is dated 5 March, when he told Forster, "Pen and ink before me! Am I not at work on *Copperfield!*"[10]

Despite my reservations over these minor details of Burgis's introduction, hers is an excellent account of the novel's genesis, composition, and publication which parallels but does not repeat John Butt's "*David Copperfield* Month by Month."[11] From John Forster's marginal notations in his copy of the 1867 edition of *David Copperfield*, Burgis obtains information about several autobiographical points and character prototypes, and she well describes Dickens's use of readers' recommendations concerning the Yarmouth characters' speech. Also Burgis mentions Dickens's incorporation of a number of allusions to current events that seem less tangential than the concern he expressed in Chapter 61 over issues of prison management. Although few directions from Dickens to his illustrator survive, Burgis publishes a series of preliminary sketches for one of the illustrations, and she notes a number of important relationships between text and illustrations. In addition to a superb ordering of the trial titles, the Clarendon appendixes present Dickens's number plans, his preface to the Charles Dickens Edition (where he at last confessed that he regarded this as his "favourite child"), and a list of the running headlines he prepared for this edition. Because Philip Collins has recently edited Dickens's public readings and because the reading adapted from *David Copperfield* in the 1860s had no bearing on the subsequent Charles Dickens Edition, Burgis does not need to include specific information about the reading version. Altogether, the Clarendon *David Copperfield* is nearly one hundred pages shorter than the Clarendon *Dombey and Son* although the original books were of similar length. It is too bad that cost of these books has increased so drastically—the *David Copperfield* lists for $110; the 1978 *Little Dorrit* was $62, and the 1974 *Dombey and Son* $37.50. Such increases are leading librarians to ask what many private purchasers have been asking in recent years: "Why buy this book?" The best answer is that for *David Copperfield*, and for all other Dickens novels except *Hard Times* and *Bleak House* (for which there are excellent Norton Critical Editions), there are no comparable editions. The Clarendon volumes provide an edited text with high quality reproduction of all the illustrations and useful supplementary accounts of Dickens's creative and editorial activities.

The general editors' policies, republished as prefaces to each Clarendon volume, define bounds which from novel to novel may seem arbitrary. In the case of *David Copperfield* it would be helpful to have had a few more pages. We could benefit from seeing the frontispieces and vignette title pages from editions published during Dickens's life; Burgis mentions these in her introduction, and the illustrations should be regarded as part of the record of what Dickens approved for his revised novel. Also the introduction might have discussed some of the novel's stage adaptations. Although Dickens did not himself write any stage version, he read the script and made some suggestions for a popular play, *Little Em'ly*, by his friend Andrew Halliday in 1869. But even before the novel's serial run had finished in November 1850 a loose adaptation, *Born With a Caul: or, the Personal Adventures of David Copperfield*, had appeared on the

London stage, and over the years *Copperfield* has been one of the most frequently dramatized of Dickens's novels.[12]

Modern editors of Dickens are the first to establish texts and select readings upon the authority of both composition and revision as they purify numerous careless reprintings and restore what we must regard as Dickens's own only partially fulfilled intentions. Necessarily reflective and analytical, the editor is a critic, who, as Philip Gaskell reminds us, must judge readings as works of art and must declare preferences.[13] As we have seen, most of Burgis's decisions are to restore manuscript when Dickens failed to spot errors in proof. Burgis's particular decisions may seldom seem major, for most often they involve only accidentals, single words, or short phrases. She favors the novelist's first impulses, and rightly, I think, because Dickens wrote with such rapidity and so little detailed revision. Burgis's straightforward introductory explanation of her practices and the great accuracy of her work should dispel any doubt over what the Clarendon Dickens intends by preserving the "most interesting" of his deletions from manuscript.[14] This edition of *David Copperfield*, then, lets us witness the confidence with which Dickens worked. The number plans indicate major directions and consider the story's timing—should he "move" a particular part of the tale in a given chapter or postpone it? Most tellingly, Dickens's general planning note for the tenth and eleventh chapters (two of the most intensely autobiographical) simply states, "what I know so well." So also was the inspiration clear for much else in *David Copperfield*. Proof and manuscript show some slight shifting of details such as the famous proof alteration of Mr. Dick's obsession from a bull in the china shop to King Charles's head. But much of the novel appears to have evolved with magical ease. There was astonishingly little revision necessary for achieving the impressive effects of Mr. Micawber's magniloquence or of Uriah Heep's oozings. In the few places where Dickens took great care with the verbal texture of his book, the Clarendon notes show him working hard to provide the most appropriate prose—cases in point are the retrospect chapters and his staging of the "explosion" in Canterbury when Mr. Micawber denounces Uriah (Chapter 52). But even in these instances of more revision than is common, it is obvious that Dickens wrote with a clear sense of what he expected to accomplish. A passage late in the book quietly but confidently declares the hero's determination that his fictions must speak for themselves: "In pursuance of my intention of referring to my own fictions only when their course should incidentally connect itself with the progress of my story, I do not enter on the aspirations, the delights, anxieties, and triumphs of my art. That I devoted myself to it with my strongest earnestness, and bestowed upon it every energy of my soul, I have already said" (p. 723). Although it is tantalizing to consider how David's self-descriptive statement applies also to Dickens, I point out simply that the Clarendon *David Copperfield* helps us to a better recognition of Dickens's aspirations, delights, anxieties, and triumphs.

Notes

1. *The Letters of Charles Dickens*, ed. Graham Storey and K. J. Fielding, Vol. V (Oxford: The Clarendon Press, 1981).

2. See *Nineteenth-Century Fiction*, 23 (1968), 226–39.

3. G. Thomas Tanselle, "Problems and Accomplishments in the Editing of the Novel," *Studies in the Novel*, 7 (1975), 333.

4. As Burgis indicates, the most reliable work on the novel's dialect is K. J. Fielding's "*David Copperfield* and Dialect," *TLS*, 30 April 1949, p. 288. As an example of the kind of misunderstanding some dialect terms have created, Mr. Peggotty's curious expression "Gormed!" has had several far-fetched explanations, but it probably is slang for "god-damned." See "Gormed!" *Dickensian*, 35 (1939), 72; also *N&Q*, 177 (1939), 118.

5. Philip Gaskell, "Dickens, *David Copperfield*, 1850," *From Writer to Reader: Studies in Editorial Method* (Oxford: The Clarendon Press, 1978), pp. 142–55.

6. The matter of line-end hyphens is one of a number of comparative issues Tanselle raises in comparing a number of recently edited novels (Tanselle, "Problems and Accomplishments in the Editing of the Novel," pp. 323–60).

7. Curiously, a highly inaccurate critical biography of Dickens in 1871

mistook Creakle's name, calling him, as did the manuscript, "Crinkle" (R. A. Hammond, *The Life and Writings of Charles Dickens, a Memorial Volume* [Toronto: A. H. Hovey, 1871], p. 265.)

8. There have been many commentaries on the relationship of David to Dickens. One of the first to recognize differences was an 1871 review of Forster's biography of Dickens which concluded that the novel left out the "shrewd, hard, acute side" of Dickens which became known through Forster's book ("David Copperfield and Charles Dickens," *Spectator*, 44 (1871), 1490–91); see also Robert L. Patten, "Autobiography into Autobiography: The Evolution of *David Copperfield*," in *Approaches to Victorian Autobiography*, ed. George P. Landow (Athens: Ohio Univ. Press, 1979), pp. 269–91; and also Stanley Tick, "On Not Being Charles Dickens," *Bucknell Review*, 16 (1968), 85–95.

9. *Letters*, V, 503.

10. Ibid., p. 505.

11. John Butt and Kathleen Tillotson, *Dickens at Work* (London: Methuen, 1957), pp. 114–76.

12. Two articles discuss the dramatic adaptations. See Richard Fulkerson, "*David Copperfield* in the Victorian Theatre," *Victorians Institute Journal*, 5 (1976), 29–36; Malcolm Morley, "Stage Appearances of *Copperfield*," *Dickensian*, 49 (1953), 77–85. For a reasonably full list of the plays, see Richard J. Dunn, *David Copperfield: An Annotated Bibliography* (New York: Garland, 1981), pp. 27–33.

13. Gaskell, *From Writer to Reader*, p. 2.

14. Apart from the difficulties I have mentioned concerning the typesetting, I find only one new error in the text, the spelling of "threshhold" on page 596.

Dunbar, Henryson, and Other Makars

J. A. Burrow

The Poems of William Dunbar, ed. James Kinsley. Oxford: Clarendon Press, 1979. xvii, 508 pp.

The Poems of Robert Henryson, ed. Denton Fox. Oxford: Clarendon Press, 1981. cxxiii, 596 pp.

Edmund Reiss. *William Dunbar.* Boston: Twayne Publishers, 1979. 183 pp.

Douglas Gray. *Robert Henryson.* Leiden: E. J. Brill, 1979. 283 pp.

Gregory Kratzmann. *Anglo-Scottish Literary Relations 1430–1550.* Cambridge: Cambridge University Press, 1980. xii, 282 pp.

In one of the ten poems given the title "To the King" by his most recent editor, William Dunbar complains to James IV that he does not receive the rewards granted to others who perform honorable crafts in the service of the king. Yet his work, he claims, will last just as long as that of lawyers, doctors, singers, coiners, printers, shipwrights, and the rest:

> Als lang in mynd my work sall hald,
> Als haill in everie circumstance,
> In forme, in mater and substance,
> But wering or consumptioun,
> Roust, canker or corruptioun,
> As ony of thair werkis all.
> [Kinsley, No. 44, lines 28–33]

This is the exact language of scholastic philosophy. Change and decay are caused by the imperfection and incompleteness of things ("Whatever dies was not mixed equally," Donne says in "The Good-Morrow"): and it is because they are complete ("haill") in every particular ("circumstance") that Dunbar expects his poems to hold out against the processes of decay. The "circumstances" are specified in Aristotelian terms. In his *De Anima*, Aristotle says that each substantial thing "includes on the one hand *matter*, which is not in itself any thing in particular; then, next, *form* or configuration, in respect of which a thing is called this particular thing; and, third, the *whole* constituted of these two." Dunbar's poems are substantial wholes, complete in matter and perfect in form, and so capable of lasting as long as any well-made coin, carving, or ship—or, we may infer, longer.

Both Dunbar and his predecessor Robert Henryson produced a good deal of poetry worthy of these high claims. Both poets are masters of form—the structure of a stanza, a story, or an argument—and both aspire to fullness in their treatment of a matter, whether it be abuse of a rival, celebration of Christ's resurrection, moralization of a fable, or description of the manufacture of flax. They do not always succeed in gratifying the appetite for both kinds of wholeness at once. Sometimes the poet's desire to display his subject "haill in everie circumstance" leads him to some sacrifice of that formal wholeness "in respect of which a thing is called this particular thing." The description of all seven planets in Henryson's *Testament of Cresseid*, for instance, goes beyond the proper requirements of this particular poem; and many readers consider that in the poem best known as "Lament for the Makaris," Dunbar's passion for the complete set leads to something too like a mere catalogue in his list of dead poets. But at their best—and they are often at their best—these two Scots poets combine fullness of matter with strong formal control. The result is well described in their own words. Dunbar speaks of his fellow-poet Mercer: "That did in luf so lifly write, / So schort, so quyk, of sentence hie" ("Lament," lines 74–75). Henryson says of the god Mercury: "Of rethorick the prettick he micht leir, / In breif sermone ane pregnant sentence wryte" ("*Testament*," lines 269–70). Such is their own work at its best: concise in form and expression, lively and pregnant with meaning. It is what Sir John Denham wished his own verse to be: "Strong without rage, without o'erflowing full." Thus Dunbar's "Surrexit Dominus de Sepulchro" encloses a whole thesaurus of traditional resurrection symbolism in five ringing stanzas; and the pleas of the mouse in Henryson's "Lion and the Mouse" (*The Fables,* lines 1431–1502) deploy in small compass and with great felicity every possible argument to excuse the impertinence of the mice. How effortlessly, for instance, does the following stanza advance three separate arguments for the defense:

> "We wer repleit, and had grit aboundance
> Off alkin thingis, sic as to us effeird;
> The sweit sesoun provokit us to dance
> And mak sic mirth as nature to us leird;
> Ye lay so still and law upon the eird
> That be my sawll we weind ye had bene deid;
> Elles wald we not have dancit over your heid."
> [lines 1440–46]

In this stanza the disciplines of rhetoric and the bar combine to yield a delectably lively economy of utterance, clinched by the typically decisive final rhyme.

Yet the poetry of Henryson and Dunbar did not in fact escape the "corruption" of which Dunbar spoke. On the contrary, the evidence for the text of their works is in general much less secure than for, say, Chaucer or Gower. The main witnesses are mostly late (the Bannatyne Manuscript was written in the 1560s, for instance, some fifty years after Dunbar's death); and they are corrupted not only by the normal errors of scribes and printers but also by a good deal of active rewriting, some of it inspired by Protestant zeal. The Scottish Text Society published major editions of both poets before the First World War; but since then there has been no major complete edition of either. W. Mackay Mackenzie's *Dunbar* and H. Harvey Wood's *Henryson* have long been cited as standard texts. In truth, however, both are somewhat sketchy pieces of work. Nor could the volumes of selections published in the Clarendon Medieval and Tudor Series (*Dunbar,* ed. Kinsley; *Henryson,* ed. Elliott) fill the gap.[1] It is therefore a matter of great satisfaction that we should now be given, within two years, full-scale new scholarly editions of both poets, in the majestic format of the Oxford English Texts. Both editions are long overdue. Their appearance marks a new era in the study of the riches of late medieval Scottish literature. They should be welcomed by those who already know how good these poets are and studied by those who do not. They offer a feast of good things, many of them little appreciated, to the reader of poetry in the English language.

Like Mackenzie before him, Kinsley divides Dunbar's poems up into types: Divine Poems, Poems of Love, Poems of Court Life, Visions and Nightmares, and Moralities. The classification is not entirely satisfactory (Why should "Tway Cummeris" count as a Morality?), but it serves to display the range of genres which is one of Dunbar's striking characteristics. The canon of his works (based mainly on early attributions) is not quite the same in Kinsley as in Mackenzie. Kinsley, rightly in my opinion, rejects two poems accepted by his predecessor ("Quhen the Gouvernour past in Fraunce" and "A Generall Satyre"), together with six of Mackenzie's *dubia* (Mackenzie, Nos. 85, 86, 87, 88, 92, 93). We are left with eighty poems ascribed to Dunbar by early authorities, together with three unascribed poems that Kinsley accepts. All three (Kinsley, Nos. 24, 31, 49) are addressed to Margaret, James's queen. They have a good deal in common and may all be Dunbar's; but the evidence produced for No. 49 is weaker than for the others.

The eighty-three poems present many textual problems. In a brief prefatory note the editor states his general impression of the main sources of the text: the superiority of the early Chepman and Myllar prints, where they are available; and the superiority of the Bannatyne to the Maitland Folio Manuscript. But, as he rightly says, each text has to be assessed separately, since "the route of one poem from the poet to the printer or the anthologists may have been different from that of another." His conclusion is that in each case the editor "must try to decide which text is the better . . . and stick to it. He takes over as little as possible from other witnesses, and then only *in extremis.*" The alternative, he says, is "magpie eclecticism." Opinions will differ about this policy. Two things are to be said in its favor. Most of the texts are too short for the relationships of the witnesses to be securely established; so it is not possible, in such cases, to use genealogical arguments to any effect. Also, Kinsley's policy is clearly stated and consistently followed, and the readings of other witnesses are clearly and fully recorded in the *apparatus criticus.* On the other hand, I do not see why the choice of one witness as giving the best text overall should mean that the readings of other witnesses are adopted only *"in extremis"* (unless, perhaps, those witnesses are notoriously unreliable). Is it "magpie eclecticism" to prefer a better reading when there is no reason for not doing so except that the witness in which it occurs is not judged to be in general the best? Judging a better reading is a tricky business, but then so is choosing the basis for one's text in the first place. Quite often Kinsley's fidelity to his chosen witness and fear of eclecticism lead him to reject a superior reading in some other witness. Thus the early Asloan Manuscript has a number of readings in Nos. 3, 52, and 54 which should, in my judgment, be adopted. In "The Passioun of Crist," Kinsley follows (misprinting *may* for *mair*) his chosen witness, Maitland:

> Agane thay rasit him on hie,
>   Reddie mair turmentis for to mak,
> O mankynd, for the luif of the.
>
> [lines 78–80]

But isn't Asloan's *tak* superior to Maitland's *mak*? Christ *takes* torments for the love of mankind. In "The Tabill of Confessioun," line 4, *hairt contreit* in Bannatyne seems preferable to the reading of Kinsley's chosen witness, which spoils the rhyme; in "The Goldyn Targe," line 187, the singular *anker* in Bannatyne and Maitland is preferable to the *ankers* of the early print; in the second line of "The Tretis of the Tua Mariit Wemen and the Wedo," Maitland's *meid* has a good claim to a place in the text, strengthening the alliteration and anticipating line 514;

in "All erdly Joy returnis in Pane," line 7, Maitland's Biblical *revert* is preferable to Bannatyne's *return,* which was presumably caught from the poem's refrain.

Besides such occasionally excessive fidelity to the chosen witness, Kinsley's texts can at times be faulted in their punctuation: e.g., No. 16, line 36, No. 44, line 63, No. 51, line 106, No. 69, line 17, and No. 71, line 21. But the texts are a great improvement on what was available previously; and they will surely be taken as standard in further work of Dunbar for years to come. Kinsley also provides an excellent glossary, the most essential of all aids for a reader of Dunbar, whose vocabulary is rich and often difficult. I noted only the omission of the adverb *but,* meaning "in the outer part of the house" ("Tua Mariit Wemen," lines 487 and 494), and *schewre* "tore off" ("The Fenȝeit Freir of Tungland," line 105). On the other hand, the commentary leaves something to be desired. The 153 pages of notes contain much useful and relevant information; but the treatment of the many difficulties is patchy and uneven. Too much space is occupied by cross-references to verbal parallels which are of no particular significance, while real difficulties sometimes go unremarked. The absence of any notes on the last three stanzas of "The Passioun of Crist" seems to be an accident; but there are a number of other places where the editor leaves the reader to his own devices. In "Tua Mariit Wemen" there are, for instance, no notes on lines 124 (where *traine* has been plausibly suggested for *trawe*), 129, or 143; and a line such as "Quhilk unrestorit helpis no confessioun" (No. 63, line 64) surely needs both its syntax and its theology explained. Where notes are provided, they are not always adequate for an edition such as this. On the passage quoted at the beginning of this review, the editor remarks only that "the claim . . . is familiar in Renaissance verse," without offering any explanation of the scholastic (and entirely medieval) terms of the argument. Some of the explanations are very doubtful. The line "Hutit be the halok lase a hundir yeir of eild" ("Tua Mariit Wemen," line 465) can hardly be rendered "derided may the guileless lass be till she is a hundred years old." It seems rather to be an adaptation of the tag from Isaiah, "puer centum annorum morietur, et peccator centum annorum maledictus erit" (65:20), commonly understood as a criticism of old people who show inappropriately immature characteristics—in this case, a lack of female guile. At their occasional worst, Kinsley's notes could be called amateurish, betraying an imperfect knowledge of current scholarship in medieval matters. It is extraordinary, in a book such as this, that a passage from the English version of Bartholomeus Anglicus should be cited from "Maurice Hussey, *Chaucer's World,* 1967, p. 114." Few readers will be able to trace a reference, mistranscribed from the bibliography in Whiting's proverb collection, to "*Die Burgsche Cato-Paraphrase.*"

Despite these faults, Professor Kinsley's edition is to be welcomed as a great advance on Mackenzie, the only complete edition previously available, in its text, its notes (imperfections apart), and above all its glossary. It is, however, not in the same class as Denton Fox's edition of Henryson, for the latter is an outstanding and rare achievement of scholarship—one of the best editions of a medieval poet to have appeared for many years. At times, by comparison with Kinsley, Fox may seem too much the medieval specialist; but his skeptical good sense saves him from all but the occasional overreading of the texts, and even his most abstruse discussions are freshened by curiosity and wit. Reading Henryson in this new edition is like standing (admittedly with a rather bulky catalogue in hand) before a wall of paintings by some old master which have been expertly cleaned and restored.

Of the thirteen short poems ascribed to Henryson, Fox includes twelve, excluding "The Want of Wyse Men" for good reasons and expressing grave doubts about the credentials of some of the others. They are a varied lot, including the somewhat overrated "Robene and Makyne," the patchily memorable "Bludy Serk," and "The Garmont of Gud Ladeis," with its odd anticipation of the winsome allegories of Emily Dickinson. Fox is at his best here with the obscure medical jokes of "Sum Practysis of Medecyne." But the heart of the Henryson corpus lies in his three longer poems: *Orpheus and Eurydice, The Testament of Cresseid,* and *The Fables. Orpheus* is the least successful of these, although Fox makes a good case for considering it, not as a narrative poem overloaded with digressions, but rather as an "encyclopaedic and cosmological poem" in the manner of Chaucer's *Hous of Fame* and Gavin Douglas's *Palice of Honour*. The editor provides a full transcript of Henryson's main source, Trivet's commentary on Boethius' *metrum* about Orpheus; and he explains the difficult musical allusions better than any of his predecessors. In the case of *The Testament of Cresseid*, Fox had already published a very full separate edition, in 1968. Here there is little to add, and he presents the same text (with only three changes), similarly introduced and annotated. He has discovered new blind Venuses (line 135n), runny noses (line 158n), and beaver hats (line 386n); but the main discovery since 1968 is a definite source for Henryson's stanza on the four horses of the sun (lines 211–17). Fox shows that the poet derived these from the *Graecismus* of Eberhard of Béthune, a schoolbook which he also used for his account of the Muses in *Orpheus*. This is a new and touching example of how the schoolmaster-poet's imagination struck roots in the textbooks of his trade: elsewhere he draws on the Distiches of Cato and the Fables of Gualterus Anglicus, both also texts over which he must have sweated with his Dunfermline charges.

The centerpiece of this edition, and its chief glory, is the presentation of *The Fables*—much the longest of Henryson's works, and also, it may now be clearly seen, his best. Like Wood and Elliott, Fox takes the Bassandyne print as his copy-text; but unlike them he treats it with a freedom won from exhaustive study of the whole textual tradition, which he discusses at length in the introduction. With such a long text it is possible—as it could not be for Kinsley—to establish the relationships between the surviving witnesses (which are fairly stable, as it turns out) and to use this knowledge in determining the text. Apart from two fragments in early manuscripts (Asloan and Makculloch), the text must rest on late and suspect witnesses. There are two branches to the tradition: one in the Bannatyne Manuscript, the other in the Bassandyne print and two related witnesses (Fox shows that one probably derives from Bassandyne itself, the other from the print from which Bassandyne derived). Where only these two traditions are represented, the editor simply has to choose between them. There are occasions where Fox's judgment may be thought to favor Bassandyne unduly (see lines 143, 252, 289, 300, 323–24, 356, 423, 438, 462, 723, 802, 822, 945, 1172, 1200, 1874, 1879); but in general his bolder treatment of the copy-text produces a text that does much better justice to Henryson's metrical art than do its predecessors (e.g., line 276) and also very frequently makes better sense (e.g., lines 697, 872). Most of the improved readings are drawn from Bannatyne. Fox is sparing with conjectural emendations, but makes some good ones: lines 741, 906 (*balterand* is excellent), 1190, 1438 (*prodissioun*). At line 527, he might have conjectured *we* for 3*e*.

The introduction and notes to *The Fables*, as to the other poems in the volume, are models of thoroughness and acumen. Fox's discussion of the sources is healthily skeptical (e.g., his remarks about the influence of Caxton); yet his account of the order of the fables presents a bold and radical justification for the structure of the whole work, seeing in it (following Roerecke) a symmetrical pattern and also a movement, at the halfway point, from comic to tragic. The notes are exceptionally full and helpful (typical instances are the three notes on pp. 417–28), never glossing over a difficulty, and displaying an encyclopaedic knowledge not only of medieval heraldry, law, and zoology, but also of *miniscula* such as the history of mousetraps. Fox's familiarity with Middle Scots idiom also commands admiration. Like Kinsley, he makes good use of the *Dictionary of the Older Scottish Tongue*. His glossary is excellent. It lacks the useful etymologies given in Kinsley but includes every word, as Kinsley does not.

There can now be no excuse for doubting that the poet displayed in Fox's edition is among the half dozen best poets writing in medieval English. Henryson ranks with Chaucer, Langland, the *Gawain* poet, Gower (perhaps), and his countryman Dunbar. Like Dunbar, he comes late in the period (though Fox is inclined to put him slightly earlier than some others have done); but both of them are completely medieval. Like Douglas Gray in his *Robert Henryson*, Fox firmly resists recent claims that Henryson's poetry shows the influence of Renaissance Italy: "Henryson was neither an ignorant countryman, writing naïvely about animals, nor a learned fifteenth-century humanist, abreast of all the latest developments" (p. xxiv). His poetry, in fact, grew out of the literature and learning of medieval Europe: Chaucer, but also schoolbooks such as "Aesop," and Boethius and his commentators.

Both these editions are handsomely produced, with no more than a sprinkling of printer's errors.[2] Although the surviving works of Henryson amount to less than those of Dunbar (roughly 5,000 lines to 6,000), Fox's book is considerably longer than Kinsley's, because of its long introduction (123 pages) and its much fuller notes (305 pages to 153 in Kinsley). Unfortunately, the reader must pay a price for Fox's old-fashioned spaciousness; his book is precisely twice the price of Kinsley's. Is there any possibility of a slimmed-down, less expensive version for students and general readers? Or a separate edition of *The Fables*?

If Henryson may be said to have fared better than Dunbar out of his recent editor, the advantage lies even more decisively with Henryson when one compares the two critical studies under review: Edmund Reiss's *Dunbar* and Gray's *Henryson*. Reiss's survey of Dunbar cannot profitably be considered at length in the present context. Like other volumes in the Twayne's English authors series, it is designed for student use, and it makes little claim to independent scholarship, as the dull and indecisive canvassing of others' opinions in the first chapter makes plain. In the ensuing critical discussions, Reiss is most at home with the Christian and moral poetry discussed in Chapter 4, of which he gives a workmanlike account. Elsewhere, he tends to reduce Dunbar to a conventional medieval moralist, critical of the court and ironical about love. He is right to find criticism and irony; but Dunbar surely cannot be understood in terms of vague Robertsonian pieties such as the following: "Though we might prefer literature which is humorous to that which is didactic, in Dunbar's time the humor would most properly be found on the surface of the poem and exist as a way of arriving at doctrinal truth" (p. 69). Reiss rightly stresses the range and virtuosity of Dunbar's skills as a makar; but, like other critics before him, he finds it "difficult to talk meaningfully about what Dunbar is like as a poet." Sentences such as these illustrate this difficulty: "The authorial voice should be viewed as that of the poet's persona, the narrator. Purposefully injected into the poems, even providing a context of sorts for what follows, this voice takes several forms and achieves various effects" (p. 127). If Dunbar is ever to be adequately described, it is not in language such as this.

Gray's book on Henryson is notable both for its wide range of reference (to the visual arts, music, and anthropology, as well as to the literatures of many countries) and for its exact and discriminating appreciation, lacking in Reiss, of the characteristics of the particular author, in the particular time and place. Chapter 1 gives a vivid and specific account of Henryson's world, drawing effectively on the burgh records of his own town of Dunfermline for details of local life. The remaining chapters present critical studies of all Henryson's writings. The chapters on the shorter poems and (especially) the *Orpheus* contain much that is fresh and interesting; but the main interest lies, inevitably, with the *Testament* and *The Fables*. Gray's reading of the former contains excellent things, such as these observations on Cresseid's act of blasphemy:

This sudden outburst of anger against the gods is certainly foolhardy, but there is something deliberate about it (emphasized by the details of closing the door, kneeling down) which gives it almost a touch of grandeur. For a fleeting moment this pathetic figure in the "orature" has something of the great *démesure* of a hero of a *chanson de geste* ("l'ardente révolte d'une âme déchirée"). At the same time it seems "out of character," as if in her extreme misery, this passive figure has been possessed by something like the ancient *ate* (or, as Henryson might more readily have thought of it, has become "fey," and has proceeded to act in the "doomed" way one would expect). The pattern of an ancient tragedy does not seem too far away. [p. 180]

The reference to "ancient tragedy" is not casual, for Gray reads the poem as "a medieval tragedy in the Senecan mode" (p. 166), invoking Seneca's tragedies in connection with Cresseid's complaints and the horror of her leprosy. He also sees something of the complexity of ancient tragedy in the poem's treatment of human suffering.

Gray's greatest contributions, however, come in the three chapters which he devotes to *The Fables*. Here, as in Fox's edition, we feel that justice is at last being done to this masterwork. The first chapter gives a wide-ranging account of the beast fable tradition, stressing among other things its affiliations with wisdom writings, the importance of pictorial illustrations (represented among the thirteen plates in the book), and its distinctive blend of simplicity and sophistication. This lively and cosmopolitan survey will be of particular value to readers of English literature, who tend to know little about a tradition that has, outside Henryson, few recognized representatives in insular writing. The following two chapters are devoted, respectively, to the narrative art and the moral bearings of the fables. The former, besides communicating something of the sheer delight of the stories, reveals much of their subtlety—in the discussion, for instance, of "The Wolf and the Wether" (pp. 103–7). This fable does indeed, in Henryson's version, "afford useful reflections to a grown man" (John Locke's comment on Aesop, quoted by Gray). The eager and dutiful sheep, who takes over the functions of a deceased sheepdog, wearing the dog's skin and so frightening predators away, is well described by Gray as a figure both "ludicrous" and "worrying." Carried away by his enthusiasm, the sheep follows a wolf in hot pursuit, crying "It is not the lamb, but *thee*, that I desire." It is bad luck that a briar should catch in his dogskin and rip it off, leaving him face to face with a very indignant wolf; but there is a deeper joke. What, after all, would have happened had the sheep achieved his aim and *caught* the wolf? It is here that the "worrying" reflection arises; for the sheep's behavior represents, in vivid fabular form, the way grown men often behave in roles and occupations which tempt them to act beyond their true capacities. The moral, here as often in *The Fables,* is "Know thyself."

Gray's discussion of the *moralitates* of the fables raises a number of interesting questions. Neither he nor Fox, I suppose, would claim to have made an exhaustive study of all the glossed and moralized "Aesops" surviving from the medieval schools.

No doubt new discoveries remain to be made about Henryson's use of these; but in the meantime Gray provides useful specimens of the tradition. The distinction which he draws between "clear" and "dark" moralizations, however, could have been more plainly stated, as a distinction between literal and allegorical. The difference is clearest in the case of "The Paddock and the Mouse," which has both sorts (marked off from each other, as Gray notes, by a change of stanza form). The reflection that one should choose one's associates with care arises as a simple generalization from the literal course of the story (the fact that the story is itself a beast allegory makes no difference here), whereas the ensuing "dark" interpretation of the mouse as the soul, the frog as the body, etc., takes the story allegorically as what Henryson calls a "similitude." The distinction is important because these two kinds of interpretation are governed by quite different rules. Literal moralizations have to be fair and true to the people and events in the story, but allegorical moralizations do not. It is not, properly understood, *unfair* to the cock in "The Cock and the Jasp" to say that he may be compared to a fool who neglects wisdom. Henryson does not say that he *is* a fool: he "*may* till ane fule be *peir*." So we need not look in the story itself for "a hidden pattern of irony at the expense of the cock" (Gray, p. 123), any more than we should look in the story for signs of grace in the rapist Aristaeus who is allegorized as "gude vertewe" in the *moralitas* to *Orpheus* (as Gray himself agrees on page 238). Such allegories are hard, perhaps impossible, for a modern reader to accept, because the moral responses set up by the story are, or may perfectly well be, negated in the *moralitas*. But that is how they are.

Henryson is fortunate to have found, within a couple of years, a critic such as Gray and an editor such as Fox. Like the edition, this critical study will add greatly to the appreciation of his work.

Gregory Kratzmann's *Anglo-Scottish Literary Relations 1430–1550* has two main topics. The first is the influence of English upon Scottish poetry in the period between 1430 and 1550. Kratzmann argues that the Scots poets learned little from any southern author other than Chaucer, because with Lydgate English poetry developed a tradition of "abstract, generalising and heavily explicit" allegory from which the northern poets had nothing to learn. Lydgate's poetry marks, in fact, "a literary watershed between Scotland and England." Kratzmann therefore devotes most of his attention to the relationships of James I, Henryson, Dunbar, Douglas, and others to the poetry of Chaucer. He suggests—in rather vague and general terms, it must be said—that these poets had in common with Chaucer, but not with Lydgate or his English successors, an intimate relation with a court audience, which encouraged them to follow Chaucer in boldly projecting their own authorial identities and cultivating a "talking" style. It is hard to see how this argument applies to Henryson, whose status as a court poet is entirely a matter of speculation. In any case, Kratzmann is most concerned to stress the independence of the Scots poets, even from their avowed master Chaucer. Although he at times overstates it, this is a valid point: the "Scottish Chaucerians" are very far from being mere imitators of the English master. Kratzmann suggests that they are, in general, more direct and affirmative in utterance than Chaucer. Indeed, he sees them (not always convincingly) as implying in their own work substantial criticism of Chaucer's detached and evasive ironies. Typical is the following comment, made in the course of an interesting comparison between Douglas's *Palice of Honour* and Chaucer's *Hous of Fame:* "Through his definition of Honour, Douglas offers an alternative to the ironic account of misdirected endeavour in *The Hous of Fame,* wherein Chaucer's indirectness and unwillingness to provide a religious perspective for his subject matter is replaced by a strong affirmation of the value which 'neuer mair sall end' " (p. 118). Kratzmann is less convincing on the affirmative nature of Henryson's *Testament of Cresseid.* He sees the poem as vindicating the justice of things. Cresseid's failure of integrity in love gets its deserts. Henryson portrays her sympathetically but does not, like Chaucer, evade judgment: she has sinned against nature. But it is hard to see the planets, following Kratzmann, as representing straightforwardly the natural order of things or "the laws that regulate human behaviour." Henryson's portrait of them seems to me, in fact, just as problematic as anything in Chaucer's *Troilus.*

Although Kratzmann's critical comparisons between the Scots poets and Chaucer are often acute, we might have hoped for a broader scholarly treatment of the whole subject of English sources in a book of this title. Is it true, for instance, that Gower's work evoked little interest north of the border, as Kratzmann indicates on page 17? And what about Hoccleve? The author's coupling of the latter with Lydgate as one who "eschews tonal variation in the interest of moral persuasion" (p. 258) makes one wonder what Hoccleve he has read. In treating his second main topic, the influence of Scottish poetry upon English in his period, Kratzmann presents a more thorough and detailed discussion of a less familiar subject. The influence of Gavin Douglas's *Eneados* upon Surrey's translation has been recognized before; but the author's discussion (original, so far as I know) of the possible Scottish influences upon Skelton deserves serious consideration by students of Dunbar's enigmatic English contemporary.

Notes

1. J. Small, A. J. G. Mackay, G. P. McNeill, W. Gregor, eds., *The Poems of William Dunbar*, Scottish Text Society, 2, 4, 16, 21, 29 (Edinburgh, 1884–93); G. G. Smith, ed., *The Poems of Robert Henryson*, Scottish Text Society, 55, 58, 64 (Edinburgh, 1906–14); W. M. Mackenzie, ed., *The Poems of William Dunbar* (London: Faber and Faber, 1932); H. H. Wood, ed., *The Poems and Fables of Robert Henryson* (Edinburgh: Oliver and Boyd, 1933); J. Kinsley, ed., *William Dunbar: Poems* (Oxford: Oxford Univ. Press, 1958); C. Elliott, ed., *Robert Henryson: Poems* (Oxford: Oxford Univ. Press, 1974).

2. *Dunbar:* "may," p. 9; omitted brackets, pp. 25, 263, 287, 357; omission of *Mercy*, p. 237; misplaced inverted comma, p. 257; "den," p. 261; "excercise," p. 279; shifted line, p. 286; "fragementary," p. 298; "elde" for "felde," p. 417; "gamaldis" for "gammaldis," p. 423. *Henryson:* "of" for "in," p. cv, n.2; misplaced numeral, p. 15; wrong line number, p. 49; "ind" for "in," p. 250; "rate" for "rare," p. 257; "*mensium*," p. 275.

Impressionistic Literature and Narrative Theory: Stephen Crane

M. E. Kronegger

James Nagel. *Stephen Crane and Literary Impressionism.* University Park: Pennsylvania State University Press, 1980.

Our awareness of "light" has become part of that general awareness, that heightening of sensibility so marvelously described in the novels of Flaubert, Gide, Proust, Claude Simon in France, Rilke and Musil in Germany, Stephen Crane and Henry James in America, Joseph Conrad and Virginia Woolf in England, Chekhov in Russia, which seemed, when we first read them, almost to give us new senses. They initiated a movement in fiction to adapt changes of consciousness, feelings, or sensations to the power of words, inventing a new language that by itself was capable of expressing the multiple nuances of the personality and feelings. Their discovery became the basis of modern literature and art; it is not what a sensation refers to in the outside world that matters, but what it evokes in the self. The writer treats it not as a fact but to produce a particular effect. He knows what color or word he must use to arouse a precise tone of joy or sorrow. The bouquet of sensations so composed will give off a fragrance of his own feelings capable of being communicated to others who have learned to "see."

An art of impression may vary from writer to writer, as whatever truth is described or suggested must relate to the artist himself as well as to nature. Impressionist literature and art were noted for the manner in which they attempted to render nature, more specifically, to render the impression, and the term *impression* was almost interchangeable with effect. This explains James Nagel's interest in modes of perception as reality filtered through a consciousness. In his *Stephen Crane and Literary Impressionism,* Nagel establishes the groundwork for impressionistic literature in America; he defines a poetics in terms of which the basic structure of all impressionistic literary works can be determined. He first views Crane's impressionistic literary work with the eyes of "Conrad's Complete Impressionist"[1] and from the vantage point of a large body of criticism dealing with three major questions: (1) What is the essence of perception? (2) What is the essence of consciousness? (3) How can language express the very specific effect of the elemental sensation, the impression? Nagel locates Crane's work, its structure and mode of existence, on the borderlines of realism, symbolism, and naturalism, and he links its impressionistic qualities to the impressionist painters' view of the nature of reality and to empirical data investigated by French positivists and chemists and British philosophers.

While Nagel's book makes an outstanding contribution to our knowledge and appreciation of Crane's major literary work, it also undertakes a remarkable investigation of the possible forms of impressionistic narrative methods, especially "the significance of perception as both a methodological and thematic component" (p. 53). Nagel is able to describe explicitly certain familiar aspects of Crane's discourse: the point of rendering life rather than narrating it, the truth-illusion theme, the aesthetic effect of the unified impression, the multiple visions at work in Crane's novels, the importance of anachronies, and the increasing discontinuity and ever more abrupt rhythm of the narrative. Nagel is the first critic to isolate other aspects that previously have been largely neglected by Crane scholars: the almost systematic elimination of meta-diegetic narrative; the relationships between the narrative text and the story it tells; the relationships between the narrative text and the narrating; and the relationships between the story and the narrating. More specifically, in *The Red Badge of Courage* Nagel studies the connections between the order in which narrated events have happened and the order in which they are introduced (p. 57). Nagel discusses the main modalities (distance and perspective) of narrative "representation," and the narrating act, its protagonist (narrator and narratee).

Thus, Stephen Crane, in effect, reveals a special relationship between man and nature, a particular manner of perceiving the world, an impressionistic manner considered to yield both objective and subjective truth. With Crane's perceptive experience, the reality of the novel changes; the traditional frozen forms of description set themselves into motion spatially.[2] The protagonists see reality from many angles of vision at once and the objects are released without losing sight of their earlier positions. Seen at a distance, no object has any clear and detailed outlines. Through unity of color, tint and tone, blurred outlines and vagueness of meaning, Crane achieves musical effects. As Nagel explains: "The narrative method of *Maggie* is an Impressionistic series of brief but sensorially vivid episodes, often discontinuous.... The sensory imagery evokes sight... sound... smell... and feeling" (p. 63). Thus, the subject itself is subordinated to the melodious effect of colors and sounds which then can be used to evoke a particular mood. There is a paradoxical coexistence of extreme mediation and utmost immediacy in the use of narrative parallax which "reveals his experimentation with points of view and his stress on the relativity of perspective" (pp. 76–77).

Nagel argues that "Impressionistic fiction is not often written in traditional first person because the standard first person narrator does not describe the immediacy of experience; he is recapitulating rather than experiencing, using memory rather than sensation. First person narratives enjoy spatial immediacy but temporal dislocation. There is customarily a double time: the time of the action presented from the time of the telling" (p. 24). Nagel explores the links between the duration of the events and the length of the narrative text: "Often a single episode will begin with a sensorially descriptive passage rendered before the narrator moves into the portrait to record dialogue and describe action from within the scene" (p. 84). He demonstrates that the one who speaks is not necessarily the one who sees. And he insists that "narrative restriction, limitations of sensory data, distorted interpretations of information, modulations among differing points of view, these are Crane's basic methods of presentation" (p. 77).

Crane's protagonists (narrator and narratee) come to know

objects in reality not through a single static position in space but rather through shifting and successive perceptions. Each act of perception seizes the perceived object only in a certain respect: "The result of Crane's narrative methodology, as suggested in *The Red Badge of Courage,* is to present an Impressionistic epistemology of a world in which the appearance of reality is constantly in flux, a kinetic world of light and shadow, of sensory multiplicity, of confusion and uncertainty" (p. 84). Thus, the perceived gives itself in the act of perception only by means of profiles. The impressionistic narrating act therefore represents a primordial and unadulterated vision of a reality which is not totally external. Nagel shows how the narrative language of Crane's impressionist works challenges the traditional notions of verisimilitude in society's mental codes and expected norms of realist, naturalist, and symbolist models which can be learned, repeated, and consumed. Both impressionism and phenomenology in literature experience a shifting of conventional forms which threatens to abolish the causalism of the realist novel by establishing a dialectic of synchronic and diachronic experiences. They reject the dichotomy between impression and language and see writing as bodily expression which is part of the ongoing primordial process of perception. The act of naming arranges a series of perceptual data, inaugurating rather than exhausting order.

Like most narratologists, Nagel devotes much of his attention to characterization, structure, and imagery. Crane's characters form a network of relationships, and the reader of *The Red Badge* must, in order to gain access to their world, become attuned to the numerous shifts of focus, or orientation, since their phenomenal world cannot be reduced to anything else than what appears in their field of perception. With Crane's dramatic revelation of characters, we have the impression of an emerging order, of individuals in the act of appearing, viewed not in linear, but in lived perspective. "The narrator of *The Red Badge* is perceptive and yet does not possess a preknowledge of the situation, the characters, or the meaning of events" (p. 119). To trace just a single outline of the individual character would sacrifice depth, the dimension of an inexhaustible human reality: "The humanizing function of this perspective extends beyond character description to the projection of war as seen from the point of view of a common soldier.... The novel presents little beyond what Henry can see and hear in battle, and his impressions are obscured by darkness and distance and distorted by fear and fantasy. Crane's use of epithets, far from being a weakness of his method, is thus a logical part of an epistemologically Impressionistic method of narration that made *The Red Badge of Courage* the finest American novel of the Civil War" (p. 119). The identity of Crane's characters keeps changing, as they seem to dissolve into a multiplicity and succession of selves in space and time.

In conclusion, the real appears to impressionistic protagonists in a field of perception constantly filled with a play of colors, noises, and fleeting tactile sensations, the background from which all acts stand out.[3] Crane's fiction derives from a narrator's projection in language of the thoughts and sensory experiences of a principal character. These are "impressions" in a fundamental sense, and they reveal the limitations of the center of intelligence and the psychological reality of his experience. The aim of Crane and other modern writers, painters, and musicians, then, contends Nagel, is the direct apprehension of reality. For them, perception is the basis of man's reflections, and the body, anchored in the world, is the basis of perception, perceiving and being perceived, a creative structure unfolding in time.

Nagel maintains that the relativistic realities of Crane's impressionism have had a major influence on the development of modernism, "especially in its sense of an indifferent and undefinable universe and a lack of individual significance.... The recognition of Crane's role as an Impressionist is thus a crucial determinant of his place in cultural history" (p. 125). With Crane and other impressionistic writers, the intellectual organization of the work of art is subsequent to impression. We cannot reduce the phenomenal to anything else than that which appears. The impressionistic novelist extends our field of vision dramatically, our possibility of seeing. With the act of seeing, Crane's text has a freedom of structure, inasmuch as the novel no longer represents a causal sequence that is coherent.

Nagel is exceedingly well informed. He makes several points which will continue to be very influential in impressionistic narrative theory, moving toward what Alexander Gelley has recently called a "phenomenological theory of description" in Crane's work and in the novel in general.[4] Nagel's book is quite useful to the person interested in the relevance of American literary impressionism to an international literary movement. And it will also interest the literary theorist who wishes to see the impressionist critical approach applied to the other arts. *Stephen Crane and Literary Impressionism* offers many intriguing judgments of the kind which evolve out of sound scholarship, with the methodologies of contemporary criticism, and with an impressive perceptiveness about the complex achievements of Crane's narrative art.

Notes

1. See Ian Watt's perceptive analysis of Conrad's literary impressionism in his *"Impressionism": Conrad and the Nineteenth Century* (London: Chatto and Windus, 1980), pp. 169–80.

2. Impressionist authors accentuate the internal power of the words themselves, a verbal experience in which the word carries a meaning that conveys a thought as a style, as an emotional value, as an existential mimicry rather than a conceptual statement. See in this connection M. E. Kronegger, "Stylistic Devices," *Literary Impressionism* (New Haven: College and University Press, 1973), pp. 69–85.

3. See Paul B. Armstrong, "Knowing in James: A Phenomenological View," *Novel*, 12, No. 1 (1978), 5–20.

4. Alexander Gelley, "The Represented World: Toward a Phenomenological Theory of Description in the Novel," *Journal of Aesthetics and Art Criticism*, 37 (Summer 1979), 415–22.

Romanticism as Movement

Stuart Curran

Leopold Damrosch, Jr. *Symbol and Truth in Blake's Myth.* Princeton: Princeton University Press, 1980. xiv, 395 pp.

Diana Hume George. *Blake and Freud.* Ithaca: Cornell University Press, 1980. 253 pp.

V. A. De Luca, *Thomas De Quincey: The Prose of Vision.* Toronto: University of Toronto Press, 1980. xv, 167 pp.

Tilottama Rajan, *Dark Interpreter: The Discourse of Romanticism.* Ithaca: Cornell University Press, 1980. 281 pp.

Thomas McFarland, *Romanticism and the Forms of Ruin: Wordsworth, Coleridge, and Modalities of Fragmentation.* Princeton: Princeton University Press, 1981. xxxiv, 432 pp.

The usual course for the author of an omnibus review is to bemoan the discontinuities of life, art, and criticism, recognizing that a specialized field or period is too tenuous a center to hold the anarchic impulses in check. It is thus with rare pleasure that one sets to review five books whose largest ends are congruent and mutually reflective and through which one can clearly discern an essential, significant wave of unified scholarly endeavor. An even rarer pleasure it is to acknowledge each a distinguished book, repaying close attention and contemplation with authentic intellectual growth. And yet, not to reduce these minds to a uniform sameness, I should acknowledge a paradox discernible even in the circumstances of the five books. Two are written by younger women scholars; three by more established male critics. Three are written by professors in Canadian universities; two by their counterparts in the United States. Two are distinguished by truly penetrating critical insight; three by their commitment to what in the large sense is an encompassing philosophical perspective. And three are richly based in a historical context, while two tend to read back from modern systems of thought to a discovery of their roots in an earlier time. The surface unity conceals an underlying duality, which is, one might argue, a mirror for the insistent intellectual pattern of all these studies and for what they epitomize as a wave of Romantics studies gathering force over the past decade. Whether the model is Freudian, Derridean, Hegelian, extrapolated from Blake, or revealed in De Quincey's obsessive recreation of his life out of the abysses of self-destruction, the pattern is insistently and complexly dialectical. As more and more of the literature and the conceptual preoccupations of English Romanticism become implicated in the mighty rhythms of linked contraries, traditional fixities must crumble. The great restructuring of Romantics studies in the last generation, which has witnessed the reclamation of Blake, the shifting of ground under Coleridge, and a wholesale revision of the simple verities once attributed to Shelley and Byron, has by no means run its course. As each of these volumes ably testifies—and in concert the voices are richly harmonious—the excitement of rediscovery and redefinition continues without diminishment.

If the current movement of scholarship in Romanticism might adopt Blake's maxim—"Without Contraries is no progression"—as its signpost, what equally distinguishes it is a collective recognition that such progress is by its nature tortuous, uncertain, even ambiguous. The actual rendition of that signpost is most fully conveyed by Leopold Damrosch, Jr., in *Symbol and Truth in Blake's Myth* when, having remarked that "no saying of Blake's is more famous," he himself withdraws dialectically into the admission that "none is more problematic" (p. 176). It is an apt key for the entire book, which attempts "to understand the shape of Blake's thought both as a structure of ideas and as a warfare of antitheses whose tremendous energy constantly threatens to break the structure apart" (p. 349). It is, one should say from the start, a splendid book, an exemplary combination of wide-ranging learning, incisive perception, and shrewd intelligence. Damrosch's critical perspective is based, very broadly speaking, on the philosophy of religion, in which he is more fully at home than any writer on Blake since Altizer. But he is not simply concerned with Blake's tradition, at least as it has customarily been construed. Indeed, his is the book one wishes that Raine's *Blake and Tradition* had been, just as learned and more pertinently so, free of the temptation to force Blake into systematic adherence to a received dogma. Damrosch rather sees Blake as grappling with age-old problems of theology and philosophy, here touching base with Plotinus, there with Gnostic thinkers, strongly influenced by the formulations of Boehme and Swedenborg, but hardly their disciple. Damrosch insists on "facing the implications of Blake's extraordinary isolation as poet and thinker," whose major result was that "it freed him to pursue his ideas with a special purity of commitment, and to launch a more penetrating critique of the whole structure of Western philosophy and psychology than anyone working comfortably within the tradition could have achieved" (p. 307).

The critic is as fervent an iconoclast as the figure whose thought he attempts to unravel. He is not only master of the history of philosophy and religion, but of the dizzying explosion of modern Blake criticism, which has erupted so precipitously that one tends to admire the fireworks and ignore the grounds from which they issue. Damrosch's philosophical perspective, his training in Enlightenment thought (he is the first eighteenth-century scholar since Hagstrum to take on Blake in a major way), and his simple hard-headedness lead him to question many of the assumptions of current Blake criticism as he questions Blake's own assumptions. Damrosch would say that, fundamentally, the large coherence of Blake's thought lies in its continual striving for coherence. In other words, Blake is absolutely a dialectical thinker, not a dogmatist. Others have said as much, if not at this length, but Damrosch goes much further. What often drives the dialectic in Blake's thought is, paradoxically, his very distaste for its terms, his desire for fixities, even those to be defined as Negations so that they can be thrust aside. To put this in the kind of traditional perspective Damrosch favors, "Blake is a dualist who wishes he were a monist" (p. 166).

This underlying division of impulse touches all aspects of Blake's art and thought. It is most clearly to be discerned in the complicated ambivalence of his view of sexuality, but it is no less central to his problematical attempts to retain Jesus while extirpating Jehovah, or to celebrate minute particulars yet collapse them all into univeral forms. The resonant nouns of Damrosch's title—symbol, truth, myth—are the loci for his testing of Blake's lifelong attempt to create a systematic vision that could at once convey truth and at the same time liberate the mind from dogma. Such a statement makes the process sound much easier than Damrosch shows it to be. The personal stresses revealed throughout the major prophecies, not to mention the evidence for a near breakdown at Felpham, suggest the gulf between the world of Generation and that of Eden as well as the intensity of Blake's compulsion to bridge it. A kind of personal craving, Damrosch demonstrates convincingly, enforces the monumental structure of Blake's myth as a means of saving him from the imprisoning, absolute order he partly desired.

Damrosch's is one of the subtlest, and at the same time most unsettling, accounts of Blake's thought. It is bound to excite controversy, bound also to be referred to for its insistent questioning, its analytical formulations, and its riches of learning. Occasionally Damrosch's desire to find ambiguity or second thoughts in Blake will seem excessive: I doubt that we are to worry about voyeurism in Oothoon's famous celebration of free love in *Visions of the Daughters of Albion*. Far more often than not, however, Damrosch's keenness of mind alerts us to significant problems that have been glossed over by others. Because of that, *Symbol and Truth in Blake's Myth* deserves a place as a milestone in the progress of Blake studies.

Curiously, given Damrosch's knowledge of the history of philosophy and psychology, there is only one section of the book that appears to miss its point directly, the ten pages suggesting the inapplicability of a comparison of Blake and Freud. Much of that exposition is taken up with showing that Urizen cannot be the superego nor Orc the id. It is one of the charms of Diana

Hume George's *Blake and Freud* that she tries out such correspondences and dismisses them all within a single parenthesis. If we adopt the right perspective on the two thinkers, she suggests, the comparison is not only pertinent, but capable of illuminating the psychic landscape of both. That perspective, however, necessitates a stance outside the "systems" of both writers, one that owns the universe to be more than the constellations of capitalized abstractions that once dominated Blake studies and more than the vortex of quasi-scientific jargon to which dogmatic Freudianism reverts as if by primal instinct. George is not just a Freudian critic; she is, more importantly, a critic of Freud, whose "science" she pointedly characterizes as "one of the most highly developed systems of symbolism ever devised, and one of the most radically metaphoric as well" (p. 66). From that perspective his affinity with Blake is a natural one, and their dialectical contention becomes in her hands a mutually revealing interpenetration of vast metaphorical structures.

The temperamental affinity, in George's view, also reaches toward a common intellectual and analytical viewpoint, which George represents with characteristic boldness: "My contention is that Blake knew everything that Freud knew; that the insights of psychoanalysis were anticipated in large part in Blake's poems and epics" (p. 71). And she goes even further, seeing in Blake's critique and revision of Milton the arguments for a similar confrontation with Freud, who was also a servant of memory, confused in his attitudes toward female sexuality, and inclined in the name of reason to undervalue the imagination. Moreover, Freud's scientific determinism gives ultimate authority to nature, denying the liberty that Blake designated as Jerusalem. George rightly remarks that the aims of Freudian revisionism, especially along the lines discriminated by Marcuse, are precisely those that Blake would have favored.

Having succinctly marked off these bones of contention, George turns to the comparative anatomy that is her true interest. There are numerous respects in which Freud and Blake have opposed visions, Freud seeing the progress of civilization as progressive, Blake as regressive, Freud regarding unconscious impulse as a tyranny, Blake as a means to liberate the mind from its circumscribing logic. But even where the conclusions appear diametrically at odds, the ground on which they are based is the same. For both identify sexuality, in its largest sense, as the fundamental fact of psychic life, and they are generally agreed on how it manifests itself in the process of human maturation. George's reading of the early poetry—the *Songs, The Book of Thel,* and *Visions of the Daughters of Albion*—insightfully concentrates on the nature of libidinal repression in the individual and society. She credits Blake with starting out where Freud came to rest in his theoretical formulation, with the recognition of dual drives—life-directed and death-oriented—compelling all human endeavor and often revealed in the dual perspectives we associate with Blake's early poetic technique. Her most interesting analysis, however, is of the enigmatic Oedipal triangle of *The Book of Urizen,* where her deep familiarity with Freud is of great advantage. But her recognition that in Blake the Oedipal situation first arises with the parents, who communicate it to the child (a recognition shared by Damrosch), also raises pertinent questions for psychoanalytic theory. Certainly it proves without question the extent to which Blake saw the "family romance" from a perspective similar to Freud's.

With the chapter on sexual dialectic in *Milton,* George drops her comparative method in order to follow Blake's ideas on their own. Many readers will think that decision a mistake. Though one grants George the importance of a direct confrontation of Blake and Freud on the nature of gender and of female psychology, the essential direction of the book has shifted; and the discussion is both protracted far beyond what is necessary and able to offer little more than the sympathetic recognition that culture and metaphor will limit even the best of minds. Perhaps it would be impossible systematically to compare Freud with the Blake of the prophecies, since the illustration of human development and the exploration of sexual response have given way in a sense to depth analysis and the uncertain paths of therapy (of self-therapy, Damrosch would argue). There is also another problem, one that George's highly successful linkage of early Blake and late Freud allows her to skirt in the shorter poems. One cannot penetrate to the core of the prophecies as psychological anatomies without coming to terms with Blake's cultural context. When Rintrah is identified with wrath and Palamabron with pity, or when the Sons and Daughters of Albion are identified as the "affections," we are in the realm of Enlightenment faculty psychology. What Blake derives from his culture, how he alters his inheritance, what he adds to it are, in the specific terms of psychology, questions that have yet to be addressed directly by scholars. The issues are exceedingly important, and they are simply sidestepped by George's decision to pursue feminist concerns. To be sure, a few glances are given to relevant psychological matters, but they lack the depth of penetration that characterizes the earlier discussion. The Spectre is much more than a "pure masculine principle, embodied aggression" (p. 158). Damrosch, who sees this figure as the embodiment of despair, treats Blake's increasing obsession with the Spectre at length and as evidence of something approaching paranoid schizophrenia during the Felpham years, thus reminding us of the personal stake Blake had in the intense psychological battles depicted in the prophecies.

In a footnote George calls her study introductory and looks forward to grappling with *The Four Zoas,* "probably the single richest and most resilient text for reading Blake as psychoanalytic theorist" (p. 241). One respects the author's honesty in not invading territory that cannot be adequately mapped as yet, especially when the author is as responsible and perceptive as the early chapters of *Blake and Freud* prove George to be. As encouragement to the further study she has promised, I would note areas that deserve attention that they do not receive or receive imperfectly here. The inheritance of faculty psychology is certainly one, for Blake's startling modernity creates a bridge, and we must know the other side if we are to traverse it confidently. But even from a modern perspective we need to fathom the various categories of states Blake devised, as well as the notion of states themselves: how would a contemporary analyst deal, for instance, with the collection of attributes Blake associates with Ulro? How adequately do Blake's Zoas and their emanations represent a psychic anatomy—or if not the Zoas, then the quaternity of Albion, his Spectre, Vala, and Jerusalem—from a post-Freudian perspective? Indeed, why are there these two quaternities in the first place? What does the very different mythic formulation of the Bard's Song in *Milton* mean as a representation of psychic breakdown? For that matter, what of the many such manifestations of breakdown that litter the prophecies? Finally and from the largest perspective, each of the three great prophecies traces a process of depth analysis. Blake appears to think humanity not just capable of understanding and accommodating neurosis but of being truly liberated from it. And yet, as the two versions of the turning point of *The Four Zoas,* Night VII, suggest, he was not of one mind about how this would occur. George has produced a study for which students of Blake and of Freud will have enduring gratitude. But if in the sequel she will explain just how Blake got Albion off the couch, the service will be that much more valuable. It will be aided, one respectfully submits, by a greater awareness of what previous writers—one thinks immediately of Jean Hagstrum—have been able to make out of Blake's deep concern with the psychosexual: the critical context of *Blake and Freud,* like its historical context, is more limited than the subject necessitates. It is a credit to its many virtues that this study is little inhibited by what it overlooks, but the comparative shortcomings of the treatment of *Milton* suggest that the next stage will require a more elaborate apparatus to support the quality of analysis of which George is capable.

One turns from the elegant nuances of Freudian theory and Blake's equally subtle premonitions of it to Thomas De Quincey's harrowing existence as to the thing itself, his life and mind as dark, impassioned, and inchoate as *The Four Zoas.* The effulgence of his prose notwithstanding, it is hard to like De Quincey's mind and impossible to be entirely comfortable in its presence. It is thus a high tribute to V. A. De Luca's *Thomas De Quincey: The Prose of Vision* to say that it carries one on with increasing fascination as it renders an art that seems never to have been as well understood, if truly understood at all, before. This is a bigger book than its apparent brevity might indicate, written with a chiseled, economic prose and commanding authority. It establishes a new plateau for our understanding of De Quincey as a creator of artistic structures, and one may assume that it will constitute the standard critical statement for some time.

De Luca's concerns, though they may appear primary, are not those that have motivated most writing on De Quincey. He is little interested in the life per se, though he is alert to De Quincey's penchant for rewriting fact to accord with imaginative pattern, and he recognizes in his life a unique characteristic: "There is little precedent in other major Romantic writers for the strangely late onset of De Quincey's chief phase as an imaginative artist, a phase that begins with the *Suspiria de Profundis* of his sixtieth year and continues for a dozen years more" (p. 57). De Luca is also little worried about the problems of identifying and accurately dating the canon that earlier scholars like Stuart Tave had to confront, though again he is incisive in recognizing changes of emphasis and structure in the various forms of and extracts from the *Confessions*. Nor is he much interested in De Quincey the literary critic of occasional force and depth of insight, nor, like Robert Maniquis, in the reactionary, almost bizarre, opinions on politics, economics, and racial superiority that De Quincey was wont to brazen forth. De Luca's eye is firmly on the deep structures that give De Quincey lasting claim to be taken seriously as an artist: "He is essentially one of those writers whose successive works refine a fundamental vision rather than alter it" (p. 34), and De Luca reads those works with a skill usually reserved for intricately wrought, complex poems.

The result is masterful, and it could not have been easy. For De Luca consistently represents De Quincey as an imaginative writer who, whatever the doctrinaire allegiances of his intellectual life, simply could not create his art—or his life—except in dialectical terms, terms which he compulsively forced to extremes. The early version of the *Confessions* exhibits "alternative visions of the self polarized in extremes of apotheosis and damnation" (p. 35), a pattern subsequently externalized in such works as "On the Knocking on the Gate in *Macbeth*." The older De Quincey grows, the greater the weight he attaches to each pole of this dialectic. In what De Luca calls "myths of the giant self," the famous prose poems at the end of the first part of the *Suspiria* "indicate the scope of De Quincey's aspirations as nothing less than the attainment of transcendence and spiritual resurrection in this life, an attainment based upon a knowing of all the modes of human experience" (p. 72). The imagination that can embody and give beauty to such an aspiration is conceived as a microcosm of God, invested with a Godlike inscrutability and, more to the point of the art it creates, containing not just multitudes but, as Keats put it, "sheer antipodes."

This becomes clear in De Luca's tour de force, the analysis of *The English Mail-Coach,* which he calls "the chief document in establishing De Quincey's claim to a place among the major English writers in the visionary tradition" (p. 83). The complex balancing act that De Quincey maintains as he attempts to fathom an abyss that is at once plenum and void is seen as informing all the works of this period. "In this vision the throne of God is conceived as a kind of dynamic vehicle moving ahead of and in the same linear direction as the expanding consciousness of the mortal perceiver gravitating towards it. Death is also conceived as a dynamic force, a 'wind' moving in the opposite direction from the throne and against the perceiver. The unstated but obvious corollary is that the wind of death must emanate from the region of the throne itself. Death and God are thus presented as powers in contrary motion but deriving their energy from the same mysterious point" (p. 84). The extremity of this dialectic is finally apocalyptic. The mail-coach becomes a symbol of enormous power, "the simultaneous embodiment in motion of two antithetical forces, triumphant joy and destructive power" (p. 111). And De Quincey as representative consciousness similarly "achieves a simultaneous identification with the destroyer and with the victims" (p. 106) in the famous scene where the coach bears down on the innocent couple in their carriage. The insistent conflation of opposite impulses goes to the heart of De Quincey's vision, which attempts to find a saving grace in self-destruction, with "consciousness divided against itself and attaining self-awareness in its sudden external awareness of an approaching destructive principle to which one is elusively but unarguably attached" (p. 106). For De Luca this explains on the deepest level why De Quincey represents so much of crucial experience through dreams, for dreams render it simultaneous, without explanation, a bodying forth of a vision that, for De Quincey at least, always subsumes opposites. The remarkable "Dream-Fugue" with which *The English Mail-Coach* ends is the epitome of De Quincey's obsession with the dialectical nature of dream, for, as De Luca incisively recognizes, the principle of counterpoint is as endemic to the fugue as it is to De Quincey's conception of the dream, and the large end of De Quincey's artistic aspirations is to render a charged, indissoluble, and virtually abstract *discordia concors*. De Luca's summary of this pattern is, as usual, succinct and eloquent: "*The English Mail-Coach* succeeds aesthetically by postulating a kind of gnostic universe where everything equates to its opposite, where every horror is a glory, every abyss a mighty house of the Lord, every experiential chaos a secret index of apocalyptic unification. All the opposites cancel each other and leave a void" (p. 147).

From such an art spun out of its own entropic impulses there is no means of continuing forward, and De Luca emphasizes the remarkable shift to be discerned in the final version of the *Confessions,* in which naturalistic detail and outward experience are added in abundance to balance the mythic self whose imaginings had earlier been so heroically projected. De Luca sees De Quincey as at last attempting to isolate points of equilibrium rather than violent confluence. But dialectical force is undiminished and no less universal as De Quincey patterns his early life, also no less perplexing: "The pathos of such a double vision," De Luca aptly remarks, "is that there is no way of bridging the gulf between the sensed worth of total knowledge and its sensed cost" (p. 143). That may seem a modern notion, but in fact it connects De Quincey to the contemporaries he outlived, to the Shelley of *The Triumph of Life* or the Byron of *Childe Harold's Pilgrimage*. But it is not with them that De Luca leaves his subject in a brief but valuable epilogue on De Quincey's place in the Romantic tradition, but rather with Wordsworth, whose imagination went on creating, then recreating, the self.

The final portrait is of "a figure balanced on a pivot between visionary transcendence and the absurd void, knowing that the precarious point is his true place, for all his searching, and the exemplification of his humanity" (p. 150). That is beautifully put, like so much of the writing of *Thomas De Quincey: The Prose of Vision*. V. A. De Luca cannot completely dispel one's sense of unease with De Quincey, but he presents him with a sympathy and complexity that make him more nearly attractive, and without question, indeed with distinctive force, he reveals the structure of a remarkable visionary art.

The dialectical rhythms that De Luca extrapolates from the De Quincey canon are, as the allusion to De Quincey in her title—*Dark Interpreter: The Discourse of Romanticism*—suggests, those that on a grand scale Tilottama Rajan sees interwoven throughout Romanticism. This, too, is a book of continually exhilarating subtlety. Notwithstanding occasional disagreements with strategies of exposition and particularities of reading, one wishes not so much to celebrate this book as to produce a fanfare for the arrival of a new, forceful voice in Romantic criticism, one from which we can eagerly anticipate further efforts. Without distracting in the least from her considerable independent achievement, a longtime admirer of her father's estimable writings on Milton cannot fail to note a striking family resemblance in the originality, the finely nuanced shading, and the simple eloquence of *Dark Interpreter*.

The signal achievement of this book is to take the theoretical formulations of deconstructionism and, without jargon, cant, or self-conscious gamesmanship, not simply to apply them to, but rather to derive them from, the Romantic movement itself: "The definitions of discourse developed by modern theorists such as Derrida, Heidegger, Sartre, and De Man can already be found in the work of certain Romantic theorists, and [thus] a deconstructive reading of Romantic poems is historically valid to the same degree as a logocentric reading." Moreover, "the current debate between organicist and deconstructionist critics over the nature of Romanticism was originally waged by the Romantics themselves and was not resolved in favor of either side" (p. 19). This is a conclusion which one would have thought the Yale School of Romantics studies would long ago have enunciated but which it has strangely passed by, perhaps in the fear that any actual historical context would taint the purity of its theoretical formulations. Still, the doubleness of purpose that Rajan remarks throughout English Romantic poetry is implicit, let us say, in the sense of the dialectical tensions of "Tintern Abbey" Bloom presents in *The Visionary Company*. However tendentious others may find the critical lines pursued by Bloom and De Man, the important point to emphasize is that Rajan almost wholly resists the tendency of deconstructionism to impose structures of thought on mute subjects. She uses what one might call the special sensitivity of an existentialist poetics to reveal the extent to which it existed within—even to which it is the hallmark of—the monuments of high Romanticism: "The Romantic period recognizes that the discourse of innocence is spoken from within experience. The simultaneously liberating and mimetic nature of art, arising from the fact that the unreal is created to free us from the world by a consciousness which stays in the world, makes of art a dialogue between illusion and its deconstruction" (p. 261). This statement could be used, with certain adjustments for local situations, to characterize the common theme of each of the five books considered in this review.

Like the school of criticism of which she is a revisionist exponent, Rajan believes it essential to have philosophical and aesthetic models to use for purposes of classification. These she draws from the progressive formulations of Schiller, Schopenhauer, and Nietzsche: the notion of a naive poetics with direct faith in an ideal is superseded by the sentimental, which recognizes the distance between one's consciousness and the ideal; this in turn gives way to a pessimistic dualism that creates fictions it recognizes to be empty, which is itself inverted in a stern optimism that forces the merger of Apollonian idealism and the Dionysiac anarchy threatening it. The distance between Schiller and Nietzsche is that figured between *Alastor* and *The Triumph of Life* or between *Hyperion* and *The Fall of Hyperion*. Aside from the evident anachronism of this progression, its very neatness requires a continual shifting of categories within a single poem, and at times the categories themselves require that the reader both delimit the connotations of a word like *sentimental* and suspend judgment on its absolute applicability. (Is the *Defence of Poetry* adequately summarized by that term?) One wonders too whether a truly encompassing knowledge of German Romantic philosophy, of the kind that Thomas McFarland so stunningly demonstrates, would not allow more historically accurate formulations. One observes, for instance, that Rajan quotes occasionally from A. W. Schlegel's *Course of Lectures on Dramatic Art and Literature* (1808), a work translated into English in 1815, which one can demonstrate was known to Byron, Coleridge, Haydon, Hazlitt, Hunt, Shelley, and probably Keats by 1818. The first chapter of the *Lectures* contains an impressive and influential definition of Romanticism as centering in a self-divided consciousness that embodies itself in a literature of continual irony. Thus, the recognition of an inherent doubling of impulse, if not necessarily of purpose, is endemic to the self-conceptions of at least the Younger Romantics, who receive the bulk of Rajan's attention. To be sure, her use of later writers reinforces her desire to keep the issues of the last two centuries of Western philosophy continually before our eyes. But that urge also drives McFarland's study, and he is perhaps more sophisticated in his ability to balance off cultural context against its still resonant legacy.

Whatever one's quibbles about the theoretical underpinnings of Rajan's analysis, she repeatedly demonstrates herself an interpretative critic of penetration and delicacy, and she is persuasive of the truth of her thesis far beyond what would be considered ample evidence. Her view "that Shelley's poetry can be read as a suppressed debate between his idealism and his skepticism" (p. 83) not only establishes an immediate link with the perspective Damrosch brings to Blake, but also sharply defines that within which the best Shelley criticism of recent years has been written (though the word "suppressed" might be a matter for contention). The analysis of *The Triumph of Life* reflects this balance perfectly. Discerning the extent to which images, episodes, and characters double and redouble themselves, yet are subtly played off against one another, Rajan concludes that Shelley "is deeply ambivalent about whether truth resides in the ideal or in the reality that desecrates it, and whether Rousseau's career is a victory of darkness over light or of knowledge over innocence and ignorance. . . . Truth is on both sides, in the terrible and chaotic and also in the beautiful and harmonious, in Apollo as well as Dionysus" (pp. 65, 68). This Nietzschean dialectic, one may agree, does not allow a reader successfully to resolve the poem toward either of its polarities without a reductionism that distorts its fluid terms. But the Nietzschean formula itself is forced into a dubious marriage with Eliot's version of the development of Shelley's canon, as Rajan goes back to *Alastor* and starts forward to show how distinctive is the leap that produces *The Triumph of Life*. Here the argument verges on the tendentious and is often enforced by mere assertion for which no real evidence can be adduced. Rather than see *Alastor* as an early, less sophisticated, less artistic attempt to create the same balance of antinomies, Rajan would have it continually attempt to evade its own skeptical impulses. Similarly, the *Defence of Poetry*, it is asserted, "engages in strategies of self-avoidance to escape being consumed by its own contradictions" (p. 75). In the same way, two Demogorgons are discovered in the one cave, supposedly a mark of Shelley's confusion of purpose. The problem with this approach—and it reappears at crucial junctures in the lengthy treatment of Keats—is that it depends so strongly on surmise, presuming an artist not in deliberate control of his own art and the critic's necessity a century and a half later to set him straight about his intentions. Whatever the problematic case of *Alastor*, which continues to spawn innumerable critical efforts at resolution, it is fair to say that Shelley carefully created Demogorgon as an emblem of a Power that is double-visaged, as it is in "Mont Blanc" and elsewhere in Shelley's work; and that this doubling is in exact accord with Rajan's thesis if she would only allow Shelley, and not Eliot, to live his own life.

Half of the critical exegeses of this book are devoted to Keats, and, given the richness and compression of Rajan's exposition, readers should be alerted that, whatever else it is, *Dark Interpreter* constitutes a major and provocative reading of Keats's mature poetry. As the repetitive and picayune nature of much Keats criticism testifies, this is a real achievement that should not be missed because of a book's title or its place on the library shelf. Again, one could raise questions about the extent to which the purity of a theoretical model forces interpretations that will not stand detached analysis. The distinctions that Rajan observes of *Hyperion* often are not in the poem, but rather come from what she thinks Keats's attitudes toward the Titans and Apollo should be. A truly earned knowledge of mythography would allow her to recognize how traditional is his conception of innocent Titans juxtaposed against the gods of experience (and would inform her as well that one of the few contemporary mythographers from whom she quotes, Edward Baldwin, is none other than the anarchist William Godwin attempting to inculcate juvenile minds under the guise of a pseudonym). The proof of the distortion that informs the early part of the argument on *Hyperion* is supplied by the critic herself: unless I too misread, the excellent understanding of the poem's dynamics offered on pages 182–83 fundamentally contradicts that expounded twenty pages earlier. One mentions this problem to isolate it as an occasional anomaly, to acknowledge that Rajan is not entirely free of the manipulative misprision that is the bane of deconstructive criticism, and perhaps also to suggest that an interpreter of dialectical thought cannot presume that anything goes under that rubric.

Elsewhere with Keats, Rajan reveals herself exceptionally alive to nuance of tone and image. The chapter focusing on *Isabella, The Eve of St. Agnes,* and *Lamia,* with perceptive side-glances at the odes, represents Keats as mediating between romance and antiromance in each of the poems, with a double consciousness that at once values and sees through imaginative illusion. Like Damrosch, Rajan is adept at reminding us that a critic's desire for simple formulations does not accord with our everyday sense of "the doubleness of existence," by which we explore "the possible conversion of contradiction into ambivalence" (p. 126). More than critical perception, there is true wisdom in the observation that "Keats seems to recognize that our contradictory need to sympathize with figures such as Lamia and to perceive their falsity derives from a sense that life itself respects the

Romanticism as Movement

radical innocence of beauty and yet sees through it" (p. 128). The highpoint of the treatment of Keats, however, is *The Fall of Hyperion,* which is viewed from a complex perspective akin to that informing Rajan's view of *The Triumph of Life.* Her comparison of the two poems, particularly in terms of the inherent tensions and layered textures of a dream vision, redeems, in a sustained and acute argument, what has for years been a classroom exercise.

The final, long chapter reverts to Wordsworth and Coleridge, especially the latter figure, where Rajan, as one might expect from her theoretical orientation, narrows her view to confront the problem of finding modes of discourse capable of truly effecting a marriage of the mind and nature. The gap between signifier and signified (my terms, for they are mercifully infrequent in Rajan's writing) is, she recognizes, of particular importance for Coleridge, and she traces the decline in quality of the later poems to his having exploded the supporting fictions of his conversation poems without having discovered anything with which to replace them: "The later poems are obsessively concerned with their own status as pseudo-poems, with the falsity of a poetry that finds itself without the sustaining interchange between image and reality furnished by a world in which the text of hope can converse with actuality through the medium of an auditor" (p. 238). The analysis of Coleridge thus leads Rajan back to the philosophical problems confronting Romanticism with which the book began, which really are the same that Damrosch derives from his reading of Blake. Call it sign, symbol, or myth, how, when you recognize yourself as its creator and manipulator, can you be certain that in any universal sense it accords with truth? And like George, Rajan recognizes that modern philosophical determinism, however austerely committed to the logic of its exposition, has something to learn from the bravery of the Romantic endeavor. What George sees as Blake's implicit critique of Freud is, in Rajan's terms, the challenge Romanticism poses for the line of Sartre, Derrida, and De Man: "It is the link between the imaginary and human freedom, explicitly made by Fichte in his distinction between imagination and cognition, that represents the continued challenge of Romantic idealism to recent existentialist aesthetics, which might seem to limit man to a recognition of his own nakedness" (p. 254). Rajan would locate the true modern response to this challenge in the thought of Nietzsche, at least if we may view the balance between the Apollonian and the Dionysiac as the creative tension persisting between transcendence and temporality. Insofar as this is precisely the culminating vision of Thomas McFarland's magisterial placement of Wordsworth and Coleridge against the flow of post-Kantian philosophy, we should turn our attention to this last—and, if one can be at all confident in one's sense of value, permanently lasting—book.

McFarland conceives of *Romanticism and the Forms of Ruin* as a multiprismed mirror of its subject matter, a fragmented book about fragmented personalities living in a fragmented culture; the basic model being that of Coleridge's meditative periodical *The Friend,* which moves by tortuous associations of its individual chapters to attain "landing-places" of the intellect and spirit. The structure of the study itself aspires to the condition of art, drawing us to see complex interactions among the spheres of its interest. And what is not among those interests? It is no diminution of Damrosch's achievement to say that McFarland's methodological range is at least as broad and his learning even more capacious. He is capable of analyzing in minute detail the dynamics of a biographical relationship in one chapter and in another treating us to a dazzling display of learning in intellectual history. Like Damrosch, McFarland is interested in problems of language and symbolic discourse as a humanistic mode of perception. Unique among this set of admirable critics, McFarland is also concerned with political philosophy, and his defense of Burke, and with him the mature Wordsworth, although it may not convince its readers to adopt so conscientious a conservative philosophy, is a deeply felt and wisely reasoned justification of its value amid the turbulence of post-Enlightenment history.

Although McFarland's carefully crafted approach to his subjects emphasizes their interrelatedness, his overarching recognition of abiding fragmentation will perhaps exonerate one's temptation to break apart the pieces in the interest of description. For the Romantic critic who insists on the importance of historical context, there are two symmetrically placed chapters that constitute major contributions to intellectual history. The first, "Fragmented Modalities and the Criteria of Romanticism," allows us to see how wholly the notion of the fragment suffused the Romantic imagination, whether German, English, or French. The actual term recurred to constantly throughout the book is diasparaction, the process of being rent asunder, and McFarland accepts as a given that what he defines as "the diasparactive triad"—incompleteness, fragmentation, and ruin—"are at the very center of life" (p. 5) and that awareness of this fact and of the limitations on our capacity for enclosing their fearful energies is of the essence of the Romantic sensibility. Even the familiar terms that promise a kind of enclosing wholeness—imagination, symbol, organicism—are themselves seen as responses, created virtually from despair, to this diasparactive awareness. The learning that supports this anatomy is simply massive, requiring of the reader something approaching the skill in languages, literatures, and philosophical systems of its author. And in an engagingly old-fashioned way McFarland aggressively underannotates the chapter, so that nonadepts will be unable to steal fruit from this orchard without acknowledging its source. The other such chapter (Chapter 5) is on notions of polarity in Romanticism, even more directly than the first an explanation of and justification for the prevalence of dialectical patterns of thought and artistic structure being emphasized in this review. In reaction against what he terms the "Anglocentric distortion of perspective" (p. 309), McFarland, with something of the satisfaction of a master magician, simply inundates us with the surprise of German Romantics discoursing on the dialectical structure of nature, the mind, society, and the course of universal history. And yet as his later recourse to Giordano Bruno and Boehme suggests, there are other means to this consciousness among the English Romantics. And there at last, in footnote 88, comes the most pronounced impetus of all, promulgated (as luck would have it) by an Englishman: Newton's third law, which McFarland immediately admits, albeit in a footnote, to be "undoubtedly the most important of all conceptions of polarity" (p. 323). The learning of this chapter is both awesome and accurate, but the concentration on German thinkers of the late-Enlightenment really distorts our perspective on what was a developing European mode of apprehension to which all the English Romantics had access. If McFarland had the temerity to bed down with the *Philosophical Transactions* with a zeal anything like that he brings to Kant's *Schriften*, he would, one predicts confidently, find a continual preoccupation with polarity—though not, to be sure, one conducted by the likes of Goethe, Kant, Schelling, and Hegel. Yet however one quibbles, this chapter, like the first, is a goldmine that scholars will tap for years.

On the other extreme are McFarland's penetrating analyses of the temperaments of Wordsworth and Coleridge, of how they nurtured one another and how, just as important and demonstrated with a sadly compelling authority, they eventually destroyed one another as well. Coleridge's demand that Wordsworth be a philosophical poet diverted him from his natural genius to a project that would forever remain unfinished. Wordsworth's demands on Coleridge to be a poet were equally frustrating, not only occasioning failure in that endeavor but contributing as well to his inability ever to assemble all the pieces of the legendary *Magnum Opus*. It and *The Recluse* are the monuments of their authors' ambitions and of their lived diasparaction. Of these excursuses into a broadly defined but truly inspired biography, that on "Coleridge's Anxiety" cannot help standing out. Published in an earlier collection by diverse hands, this weighty essay is reinforced by its present context. It is probably the greatest defense of the actual Coleridge ever mounted, not a product of special pleading, but rather a deeply moving, consistently humane recognition of flawed genius. Its distinctive character is epitomized by the simple power of this sentence: "Coleridge, I have always felt, is in a special way a hero of existence: though life bore him down, he fought from his knees" (p. 132). In attempting to comprehend the wholeness of Coleridge and Wordsworth, McFarland recognizes that the one could be duplicitous and faithless, the other mean and coldly

Romanticism as Movement

self-involved, and yet that both had their virtues, their naked vulnerabilities, not to say their considerable genius. To honor the latter without sentimentality or bardolatry gives McFarland's account of their ambiguous symbiotic relationship a depth of authenticity seldom encountered except in the finest biographies.

The two "landing places" of *Romanticism and the Forms of Ruin* are an attempt to define the poetic that governs a world of broken forms and the practice of poets who both measure and attempt to transcend it. The first of these is, in its large scheme, an effort to understand the relation of form and content, which McFarland transvalues into philosophical terms: *substantia* substituting for form, and content being divided between *ens,* an interpenetration of self and outer world, and *essentia,* the interpenetration of other temporal planes with the moment of the poem itself. The exploration of these terms is always enlightening, but as a definitive account of what makes poetry great they offer too limited a prescription. The bias is distinctly Wordsworthian, conservative, personalized, and thus far more appropriate to the lyric and dramatic than to a narrative mode. The special and hard-won achievement that Damrosch extrapolates from the stylistic and structural practices of Blake, for instance, cannot really be accommodated to this poetic. Nor in this view of him at least can Shelley, whom McFarland insists on seeing virtually as Leavis did, seemingly forgetting the work of his much praised mentor, Frederick Pottle, in demolishing the shaky scaffold from which the anathema blustered forth. Whatever one's taste in poets and critics, it is, I think, fair to say that any poetic that gives E. A. Robinson precedence over Shelley is open to serious question.

Of course, this may be part of McFarland's design, since there is much in the second landing place that implicitly questions the terms of the first. Perhaps this is an ultimate diasparactive awareness, a deliberate casting of a dialectical balance. For the poetry of the earth lauded in the earlier chapter is recognized as finally inadequate in the second, which concentrates on a meontic search for fictions of transcendence. Here the book turns grandly on its axis, reverting to the problems of fragmentation and Romantic strategies for enclosing its force and concentrating now on the urge toward wholeness by which humanity precariously balances its existence and restores its sense of purpose. McFarland fittingly ends by quoting the *Phaedrus*, reminding us that the Romantic sense of a falling away and the correlative thirst for the whole are as old as philosophy itself, as old and as universal.

There is perhaps a direct moral for the academic reviewer to be derived from McFarland's grand dialectical rhythm. Universities in general, and the humanities in particular, see themselves beset by a world of technology and of intellectual indifference. Standards of education appear in permanent decline; the connections between the specialized and the specious seem ever more sharply etched; the waste of talent casts a pall over the entire academic enterprise. Incompleteness, fragmentation, and ruin, the diasparative triad, can be discriminated everywhere one turns, if that is what one is looking for. And yet, I began by asserting that here, in these five books, was a center that could be seen to hold. It holds because, as McFarland's lived discourse reminds us, the urge to transcendental wholeness is the natural counterpart to the modalities of fragmentation in which we exist. It holds, too, because of the active assertion of the liberated imagination that both George and Rajan remind us is an essential component of the Romantic legacy. These books make it abundantly clear that driving intellectual energies have not waned in the academy. When two young women professors can hold their own with major scholars, should we be so quick to bemoan the failings of graduate education and the intolerable pressures of the tenure system and the patriarchal exclusions of the universities? When the Cornell University Press can foster two such aspiring minds in a single publishing season, or when the Princeton University Press can deliver us two tomes of such learning and stirring intellect, should we be quite certain that there are no bastions where standards do not alter when they alteration find? And when one is confronted by five books that, no matter how sharply delineated their subject matter, continually reach out for larger connections—aspire, indeed, to offer wisdom to their readers and to their culture—there is no need for question. An academy that sponsors and nourishes this level of collective intellection, whatever its problems, is in serious good health. The same must be said for Romantics studies.

Lawrence Enters the Pantheon
Richard Kuczkowski

Apocalypse and the Writings on Revelation, Vol. I of the Cambridge Edition of the Works of D. H. Lawrence, ed. Mara Kalnins. Cambridge: Cambridge University Press, 1980. xiii, 249 pp.

Apocalypse was the last book D. H. Lawrence wrote. It is a short work, less than a hundred pages, and, as Mara Kalnins points out, "although he rewrote some passages and deleted others, the published version is essentially a first writing" (p. 24). This first volume of the Cambridge Edition of Lawrence's works establishes texts for *Apocalypse,* three inconsequential deleted fragments published here for the first time, and short related pieces previously published as "A Review of *The Book of Revelation* by Dr. John Oman" and "Introduction to *The Dragon of the Apocalypse* by Frederick Carter." It also includes a chronology of Lawrence's life, extensive explanatory notes, textual apparatus, and an introduction which presents useful information on the genesis and context of these writings, the circumstances of their publication, and their critical reception. All this adds up to about 12 pages that Lawrence finished and published, fully 50 pages of material he discarded, about 110 pages of "first writing," and 84 pages of introductory material, textual apparatus, and notes.

These numbers presage hefty tomes indeed once scholars tackle the task of establishing texts for those of Lawrence's works which, like *The Rainbow, Women in Love,* and *Studies in Classic American Literature,* are longer and whose textual history is more complex. One hopes that the very magnitude of the undertaking will constrain scholars to moderate impulses toward nonfunctional notes. While it is useful and enlightening to anchor obscure passages to facts and history, the value to a scholarly text of footnoting (for example) Napoleon or Caesar with material indistinguishable from that in a general work of desk reference is questionable.

Minor excesses of this kind do not by any means vitiate Kalnins's work, however; the disproportion of introduction, notes, variants, and discarded material to text is a standard and necessary—if ironic—feature of textual study. The scholarly effort that goes into establishing the best possible texts for writings and clarifying their backgrounds has unquestioned value, especially for an author like Lawrence, who presents a host of special problems including censorship, personal style, and wholesale, often highly significant, revisions. But now that we have the best texts for Lawrence's writings on Revelation—most of them unfinished—what are we to make of them? This question receives minimal consideration in Kalnins's introduction, yet her remarks are worth notice:

> *Apocalypse* is an important document, not merely because it is Lawrence's last book, but because the ideas expressed in it—ranging over the entire system of his thought about Christianity, politics, man, God, religion, myth, art, and symbol—are the summing up of issues that preoccupied him throughout his life and that he also explored in the writings of the final years. Indeed, *Apocalypse* stands in the same relation to these writings—to *Lady Chatterley's Lover*, the *Last Poems*, *Etruscan Places* and *The Escaped Cock*—as "The Study of Thomas Hardy" and "The Crown" do to *The Rainbow* and *Women in Love*. The *Apocalypse* essays embody Lawrence's final vision of man and the cosmos and are a last testament of his belief in the symbolic value of art as the way to creative integration. [p. 24]

On the face of it, this seems like a good set of answers, but not all are quite convincing. First of all, Lawrence's strength lies in *not* being a single-barreled linear thinker, and these writings are by no means consistently and clearly focused on a single theme: Kalnins's last assertion seems to put undue emphasis on the role of art in them. The first statement implies that *Apocalypse* is closer to a *summa* than to a first draft and that Lawrence had developed a rigorous, systematic body of thought. Those dubious assertions overwhelm the more judicious and significant—but undeveloped—middle one.

Lawrence Enters the Pantheon

Kalnins resorts to rhetoric and exaggeration rather than analysis or explication to assert the importance of *Apocalypse:*

> It is a searching examination of our civilisation and a radical criticism of the Christianity and scientific technology that shaped it; but it is also the revelation of Lawrence's belief in man's power to create "a new heaven and a new earth" if he can destroy the "false, inorganic connections especially those related to money, and re-establish the living organic connections with the cosmos, the sun and earth, with mankind and nation and family." *Apocalypse* is a vigorously iconoclastic work, condemning nearly all our contemporary ways of life and searching for the causes of our malaise in the failure of Christian and democratic ideals as Lawrence saw them. Like Nietzsche before him, Lawrence criticized Christianity's emphasis on renunciation, love and equality, because he felt it denied individual potential and ignored the deep impulse to power in mankind. [pp. 22–23]

There follow pious attempts to dissociate Lawrence's thoughts on power from fascistic implications by likening them to portions of Blake, by omitting any reference to Lawrence's habitual sneering scorn for things Jewish, by quoting Lawrence's assertion that submission to a greater man puts an individual in touch with "far, far greater life than if he stood alone," and that "individualism is really an illusion. I am part of the great whole, and I can never escape. But I *can* deny my connections, break them, become a fragment" (p. 149). Kalnins does not examine critically Lawrence's concept of power. She eagerly embraces its positive qualities, and ignores its obvious negative aspects and ramifications as well as its practical and psychological problematics—the latter a theme Lawrence's fiction often focuses on. Kalnins caps this performance with a final platitude: "In our scientific and materialistic age there exists more than ever before the need to regain the imaginative and spiritual values which alone can restore that sense of living connection and wholeness" (p. 24).

This is uncriticism—yet quite significant because it reveals the intensity of the feelings, desires, and frustrations Lawrence's writings address, the continuing deep attractiveness of unexamined rejection of science and technology, the radical impulse toward connection and intimacy at all costs, the seductive notion that science, mathematics, and materialism are incompatible with full and authentic human life. But while the uncritical response is understandable, it also effectively obscures the text which the editor has been at great pains to establish. That text bears looking at.

Great distances separate Lawrence's *Apocalypse* from Kalnins's remarks and from the book of Revelation. Lawrence is not the transcriber of a divinely vouchsafed symbolic vision. He speaks for himself and of his feelings: "And I must confess, my first reaction is one of dislike, repulsion, and even resentment. My very instincts *resent* the Bible." His "own first feeling" about Revelation is that it is the fullest of mystification and least attractive book in the Bible (p. 59). The roots of this feeling reach deep into the repressive Nonconformist religion of Lawrence's youth:

Long before one could think or even vaguely understand, this Bible language, these "portions" of the Bible were *douched* over the mind and consciousness ... day in, day out, year in, year out expounded dogmatically, and always morally expounded.... The interpretation was always the same whether it was a Doctor of Divinity in the pulpit, or the big blacksmith who was my Sunday School teacher. Not only was the Bible verbally trodden into the consciousness, like innumerable foot-prints treading a surface hard, but the foot-prints were always mechanically alike, the interpretation was fixed, so that all real interest was lost. [p. 59]

Significantly, the texts of choice for these intoners and expounders, whose holier-than-thou piety and vulgarity so early repulsed Lawrence, are from Revelation: "With nonconformity, the chapel people took over to themselves the Jewish idea of the chosen people. They were 'it,' the elect, or the 'saved.' And they took over the Jewish idea of ultimate triumph and reign of the chosen people. From being bottom dogs they were going to be top dogs: in heaven. If not actually sitting on the throne, they were going to sit in the lap of the enthroned Lamb" (p. 63).

Lawrence Enters the Pantheon 163

From its early days into the present, Lawrence sees Christianity as split between the sublimated love and aristocratic humility of Jesus and the "popular religion, not thoughtful religion" (p. 63) symbolically articulated in Revelation: false humility, the attraction toward mean-spirited power, vengeful triumph over one's enemies (whether actual oppressors or simply those whose lives are fuller and freer), and such intense hatred of the world that its destruction is viewed as glorious fulfillment. Digging out radical contradictions of this sort is Lawrence's forte, a hallmark of his thought, and these first pages of *Apocalypse* embody typical qualities of the movement of his thought.

The movement is not "logical" or philosophical: it does not proceed through the enunciations of intellectual propositions, their explication, and the development of their relationships and consequences. It is closer to being phenomenological or psychological, closer to Lawrence's own insights into the nature of authentic thought. Strong spontaneous feelings and emotions, like those of the primitive or the child, are welcomed into consciousness, and become the matter of intellectual exploration while at the same time being allowed to guide the work of the intellect. Like Somers in *Kangaroo*, Lawrence lets buckets down into the unconscious; unlike Somers, Lawrence is able to tap his unconscious, think, and write. It is as if he were composing an Immortality Ode or a *Remembrance of Things Past*, a coming-to-terms with himself and life. That a good many other portions of *Apocalypse* do not match the fresh, subtly satiric, wide-ranging, vividly imagined, unpredictable, and genuinely interesting writing and thought of its opening sections indicates that Lawrence was unable to sustain his creative involvement with John of Patmos's bizarre, antipathetic book and his own project of explicating its subtexts and contradictions.

Lawrence's exposition emphasizes the tension between Christ's selfless spiritual love and John's urge toward vengeance and triumph against an idealized background or repressed "pagan" acceptance of life, power, connection, and corporeality. This treatment recalls the themes of *Studies in Classic American Literature*, as does the further contradiction Lawrence discerns between the literal meaning of John's visions and the lost text

Lawrence believes is at the basis of *Revelation:* an initiation ritual, similar to those in ancient, occult, and anthropological literature, from which John and his editors expurgated the unacceptable pagan message of positive, intimate connection with the cosmos while appropriating its symbolism for their own ends. Drawn from this ritual, the seven seals of Revelation, for example, are willful distortions of esoteric symbolism for seven "centers" of the initiate's body.

The symbolism of Revelation stirred Lawrence's emotions and attracted him from the first, unconsciously, despite his dislike of the book and its vulgarization in preacherly and popular religion. It spoke directly to his intuition of a joyful pagan world where men lived "breast to breast with the cosmos" (p. 130). Lawrence felt compelled to elaborate and substantiate that intuition, drawing time and again on the occult, which was as popular in his day as it is in ours. The occult furnished him with a store of remarkably congenial ideas that he freely blended with other congenial ideas and adapted to his needs. In *The Apocalypse Unsealed,* for example, James Pryse interprets Revelation as an initiation rite and the Seven Cities of Asia as symbols of the body centers or *chakras* of Kundalini Yoga, Kundalini being the power that lies coiled like a serpent at the base of the spine and rises along the spine and through the centers to the "third eye," or pineal gland, as the initiate attains enlightenment.[1] This material and snatches from Madame Blavatsky and other occultists are reimagined with striking creativity and verve in Lawrence's first versions of *Studies in Classic American Literature* (collected as *The Symbolic Meaning*), *Psychoanalysis and the Unconscious,* and *Fantasia of the Unconscious.* Material of this kind together with bits of the early Greek philosophers and other attractive poetic/intellectual fragments highlighting opposition, complementarity, symbolism, spontaneity, nonintellectual thought, and so on figure prominently in Lawrence's repeated attempts to put into satisfactory form his feelings on power, love, the sexes, and the union of the individual with the family, the state, and the living cosmos. Lawrence took seriously the amalgam of borrowings and personal notions he habitually drew upon when he reworked his ideas: he called the ensemble his philosophy.

Isolating and systematizing the content of his thought (a task Lawrence himself found difficult and uncongenial if endlessly seductive), emphasizing its truth value, situating it respectably in the ranks of world philosophy, finally transforming Lawrence into a kind of sage—we have been too eager, I think, to accord Lawrence's ideas the solemn, unreflective reverence due serious philosophy or uplifting dogma. The results are predictably dull and unconvincing. Like Ezra Pound, Lawrence was a village explainer, and it is the special personality, the spirit and style, *l'homme même,* of the village explainer that vitalizes his explanations and makes us read them, motley and uncanonical though they be. This is not intended to denigrate Lawrence's passionate convictions, merely to refocus our attention.

It would not be far off the mark to say that Lawrence never expressed ideas, he always expressed himself. His perceptive self-analysis in the foreword to *Fantasia of the Unconscious* points in this direction: "I am not a proper archaeologist nor an anthropologist nor an ethnologist. I am no 'scholar' of any sort. But I am very grateful to scholars for their sound work. I have found hints, suggestions for what I say here in all kinds of scholarly books, from the Yoga and Plato and St. John the Evangel and the early Greek philosophers like Herakleitos down to Frazier and his 'Golden Bough,' and even Freud and Frobenius. Even then I only remember hints—and I proceed by intuition."[2] The ancients looked up at the starry night sky, drew random points of light into patterns, projected their feelings upon the patterns, and elaborated luminous fictions upon them. Lawrence read extensively, guided by intuition toward hints that confirmed his intuitions and upon which his intuition could, in turn, build. His reading of scholarship, as of the occult, was unscholarly, creative; he was an intellectual *bricoleur,* collecting odds and ends of ideas and fashioning them into patterns that suited his psyche.[3] He is at his best when writing about ideas as if he were writing novels, weaving an often dazzling mythology of ideas.

From this perspective, *Apocalypse* and its associated texts present us with Lawrence in the act of rewriting a refractory text to suit himself, much as he asserts John and his editors refashioned the pagan initiation ritual. As we read, we follow his *bricolage*. It is almost like watching the film made of Matisse at work with its focus on his brushstrokes, at times in exquisite slow motion: we become involved in the idiosyncratic, sensuous manipulation and patterning of materials. Detailed study of these aspects of *Apocalypse* would run to many pages—and perhaps finally collapse of its own weight; more complex works like "A Study of Thomas Hardy," *Psychoanalysis and the Unconscious, Fantasia of the Unconscious,* and the various versions of *Studies in Classic American Literature* are more capable of sustaining such examination. And especially with a text by Lawrence, even when long passages are quoted, some features of the author's patterning and the reader's involvement in it will always elude analysis and criticism. Still, relevant points about Lawrence's ideas and the way he handles them can be made here.

Lawrence's ideas and works are permeated by a recurrent mythology of a pretechnological Golden Age where organic and physical yet mystical integration of human with nonhuman life ensured that power, passion, the emotions, physical sensations, and the spontaneous unconscious held their proper places in man's total psyche. Complementing this myth is one of the Fall. There have been many falls in Lawrence's view: into intellectualism, spirituality, technology, democracy, moralism, and all sorts of repressive one-sidedness. Yet the paradise which has been lost in the distant past is fitfully glimpsed in the lives of primitives, it tugs strangely at the unconscious in bits of art and ancient or occult symbolism, and the psyche still holds the creative potential to regain Paradisal integration in modern times through radical reorientation and revitalization of human relationships and thought: "Start with the sun, and the rest will slowly, slowly happen" (p. 149). In Lawrence, however, the myth of cyclic rebirth is presented in an ironic phase: the cycle is always painfully and yearningly stuck in a degenerate, problematic present, the darkest hour before a new dawn.

Lawrence Enters the Pantheon

In *Apocalypse*, Lawrence is less concerned with establishing a pagan substrate to Revelation and identifying its elements than with propounding the superiority of his vision or dream of pagan life:

Don't let us imagine we see the sun as the old civilisations saw it. All we see is a scientific little luminary, dwindled to a ball of blazing gas. In the centuries before Ezekiel and John, the sun was still a magnificent reality, men drew forth from him strength and splendour, and gave him back homage and lustre and thanks. But in us, the connection is broken, the responsive centres are dead. Our sun is a quite different thing from the cosmic sun of the ancients, so much more trivial. We may see what we call the sun, but we have lost Helios forever, and the great orb of the Chaldeans still more. We have lost the cosmos, by coming out of responsive connection with it, and this is our chief tragedy. What is our petty little love of nature—Nature!!—compared to the ancient magnificent living with the cosmos, and being honoured by the cosmos! [p. 76]

It is useless to argue for or against rather weak and contentless assertions of this kind even when distilled from their elaborate soapbox-style rhetoric. And it is dangerous to swallow Lawrence's antiscience, antitechnology, and other "anti-" notions whole. Both the assertions and the rhetoric are typical of Lawrence and indicate that he was commonly at least as interested in the potential of an idea as a stick with which to beat the degenerate present as for its own sake. He tends to use ideas for and develop them through attack, as a satirist, not a philosopher, does: his ideas and myths become vehicles for satire. Speaking of modern woman ensnared by the desire to be "significant," to "make something worthwhile" of her life, Lawrence writes:

So, tragic and tortured by all the grey little snakes of modern shame and pain, she struggles on, fighting for "the best," which is, alas, the evil best. All women today have a large streak of the police-woman in them. Andromeda was chained to a rock, and the dragon of the old form fumed at her. But poor modern Andromeda, she is forced to patrol the streets more or less in police-woman's uniform, with some sort of banner and some sort of bludgeon—or is it called a baton!—up her sleeve, and who is going to rescue her from this? Let her dress up fluffy as she likes, or white and virginal, still underneath it all you can see the stiff folds of the modern police-woman, doing her best, her level best.

Ah God, Andromeda at least had her nakedness, and it was beautiful, and Perseus wanted to fight for her. But our modern police-women have no nakedness, they have their uniforms. And who could want to fight the dragon of the old form, the poisonous old Logos, for the sake of a police-woman's uniform? [pp. 126–27][4]

Lawrence's powers as a satirist are considerable, his supple spoken and Biblical prose rhythms admirably suited to scolding sarcasm, innuendo, scorn, burlesque, invective, travesty, and even witty humor. This last quality is slighted in discussions of his work; the "dirty little secret" about Lawrence is that whether one agrees with his ideas or not, he is raffish and fun to read, even when dealing with the big issues closest to his heart. Perhaps most obvious in works like his essays on Ben Franklin or Walt Whitman or in *Fantasia,* refreshing currents of satiric laughter—including self-satire—and humor run through much of his work.

Now that Lawrence has been dead for more than fifty years and the content of his ideas has become both familiar and distant, his borrowings tracked down to their heterogeneous and heterodox sources, we would do well to "reposition" his "think pieces," to situate them more in the direction of Swift or Yeats or Wallace Stevens than that of, say, Bertrand Russell or T. S. Eliot. We might also examine them with more serious emphasis on their status as fictions, as subjective arrangements of ideas for aesthetic and psychological ends rather than for external validity and social value. We might pay more attention to how ideas, myths, and satire function within these arrangements to give shape to desire rather than on quarrying detachable propositions from them and building manifestos out of them. Jung's writings on archetypal symbols, mandalas, the integrated psyche, and symbolic designs and patterns are provocative background here, but his works are at once too close to Lawrence's thoughts and to many of his sources, too fully articulated a system of their own, and too ideologically loaded to be central to this effort; Frye and Lévi-Strauss may be more to the point. Lawrence shouldn't be reduced to a crypto-Jungian: too much is lost in the process.

Lawrence and his writings are more complex than his ideas. We need to pay less attention to his ideas and more to the actual ebb and flow of his thinking and writing, to the fluid alternations and combinations of exposition, satire, reminiscence, analysis, paean, scorn, and the other rich veins of feeling that give them life. Once this is accomplished, we may begin to notice the satire and deflation Lawrence brings to bear even on characters who spout his "philosophy" most articulately, but must come to terms with facts rather than fictions to deal with their situations. We may begin to see both his mythology of ideas and his fictional characters in more human, less dogmatic, terms.

Further volumes of the new Cambridge Edition of Lawrence's works will doubtless be as encumbered as this one by academic accretions and a desire to adore, yet they will give us the opportunity to come to terms with the facts of Lawrence's texts and an occasion for encountering the special qualities of the talent and personality that brought them forth. But scholarly editions are a peculiar genre, perhaps aimed as much at establishing a text as at a pedantic apotheosis of the author in question. The ironies of both ventures are many and as we read the Cambridge Lawrence they will doubtless often recall a very Lawrencian passage of Borges:

There is no exercise of the intellect which is not, in the final analysis, useless. A philosophical doctrine begins as a plausible description of the universe; with the passage of the years it becomes a mere chapter—if not a paragraph or a name—in the history of philosophy. In literature, this eventual caducity is even more notorious. The *Quixote*—Menard told me—was, above all, an entertaining book; now it is the occasion for patriotic toasts, grammatical insolence, and obscene deluxe editions. Fame is a form of incomprehension, perhaps the worst.[5]

Notes

1. James M. Pryse, *The Apocalypse Unsealed* (New York: John M. Pryse, 1910), pp. 14–16. This is the first book on yoga that Lawrence read.

2. D. H. Lawrence, *Psychoanalysis and the Unconscious and Fantasia of the Unconscious* (New York: The Viking Press, 1960), p. 54.

3. See Claude Lévi-Strauss, *The Savage Mind* (Chicago: Univ. of Chicago Press, 1966), pp. 16–36, for a discussion of *bricolage* as a mode of primitive and artistic thought.

4. See also p. 47 on stale buns, the New Jerusalem, and the Aunties of this world; pp. 50–51 on the supple, slippery Nymph Reason; pp. 87–88 on *Urdummheit.*

5. Borges, *Labyrinths: Selected Stories and Other Writings* (New York: New Directions, 1964), p. 43.

Medieval Literature in Historical Context

Derek Pearsall

> Janet Coleman. *English Literature in History 1350–1400: Medieval Readers and Writers*. English Literature in History series, ed. Raymond Williams. London: Hutchinson, 1981. 337 pp.

The question of the relationship in the Middle Ages between the study of literature and the study of history is one that has often been raised, perhaps more by literary scholars than by historians. The latter are, on the whole, content to "use" literature as one (generally inferior) source of evidence for the reconstruction of the past, and to assume, as indeed they are entitled to assume, that literature is "part" of history. Literary scholars are rather more uneasily conscious of the looming presence of the more comprehensive discipline and feel that they must pay at least lip service to the necessities of a historical consciousness in their reading of the literature of the past. It might be argued that the constraints under which both literary scholars and historians work are artificial and arise only from a rather arbitrary differentiation between the subject matters of their two disciplines. To some extent this is true, and there are certainly some forms of writing, in the Middle Ages as in any other, that fully engage the central interests of both parties. A poem with an overtly political and historical content, such as *Richard the Redeless* (otherwise known as the first part of *Mum and the Sothsegger*), would be a case in point. On the other hand, there are forms of writing, or verbal record, at the outer ends of the spectrum of "literature" and "history," which argue for a real if not readily definable difference of preoccupation between the interests of the two disciplines. Much of Chaucer's writing, for instance, defies any obvious kind of historical contextuality, while the roughage of the historian, the gravelly diet of accounts and documentary record, is for the most part indigestible to the literary scholar.

Whatever merit there may be in these distinctions and qualifications, it remains true that the inert hand of educational tradition, and the prejudice it encourages that the defined areas of study in the curriculum correspond to separate and definable areas of reality, lies heavy on all ventures into the no-man's-land between them. Historians continue to use imaginative literature as a quarry for information about the social and economic realities of the past, quite disregarding the complexities inherent in even the most transparent forms of literary realism in their relationship to the matter of actuality, and the many and more important impulses that may guide a writer other than the desire to give an accurate record of what he has observed. I note, for instance, that two respected social and economic historians of the Middle Ages, seeking information on that elusive reality, the home of the medieval peasant, go to the widow's cottage of Chaucer's *Nun's Priest's Tale*, and come to quite different conclusions about what is there represented—not surprisingly, given the heady brew of literary reminiscence and mock-heroic burlesque that Chaucer is concocting.[1]

But literary scholars are on the whole worse, and their attempts to use their version of quickly read and ill-digested history to provide background or occasions for literary works are often guilty of the most elementary error. It was long believed that Hulbert was right in associating the origins of the alliterative revival with some assertion of Englishness that grew out of baronial discontent with royal policies.[2] The explanation was neat and plausible and fit well with the cherished conviction among literary scholars that medieval barons were always discontented. More assiduous research revealed that at the critical time, for the poetry, the barons were not at all discontented—they were, indeed, unprecedentedly contented.[3] It was, in fact, the very explanation that would not do. Attempts to find historical parallels in the wars of Edward III for the events of the alliterative *Morte Arthure* have been similarly discomfited, and may be presumed to be based on a similar misconception of the role of contemporary (or supposedly contemporary) historical events in the activities of the imaginative writer.[4] As for Chaucer, who for the most part is skillful enough to elude the hunters of historical fact by not putting any into his poetry, it has been his fate, as the notes to Robinson's edition show, to have almost every one of his poems attached to some historical occasion. It is as if literary scholars believed, basically, that literature lacked some dimension of reality in lacking a date and occasion and attachment to history. This belief is a reflection of the generally inferior role accorded to literature and is laid bare in some of the fringe writing on the subject, of which the classic example for a medievalist must always be Hotson's attempt to attach the *Nun's Priest's Tale* to the quarrel between Mowbray and Bolingbroke.[5]

The reaction of some literary scholars to such assumptions about the nature of the relationship between literature and history has been to deny the relationship altogether and to concentrate on the structures of meaning that may be elicited from within the literary text. For those who begin with a distaste for history, the approach has much to commend it. But for those who do not wish to crawl for ever blindfold round the hermeneutic circle, there may seem to be still the possibility of a more positive approach, and of course there are ways in which even the newest New Critic or structuralist or phenomenologist, is going to be frustrated in his study of an old literature where the understanding of the very reference of the language depends on a total acknowledgment of the preeminence of the historical. The critic cannot expect the editor to do the work of the historical imagination for him.

The more positive approach, as I have hinted, is to position oneself in the middle of the spectrum of literary and historical writing, the area where they overlap and blur into each other, and to work out from this to some authentic understanding of "literature in history." This is the approach taken, and the title happily chosen, in the new series of which the present book by Janet Coleman seems to be the first offering. The author makes none of the elementary mistakes I have been drawing attention to, and she does not make the further mistake of attempting a comprehensive coverage of the period which she has chosen to deal with. Instead, she takes a number of themes or areas of concern where it seems to her that the study of different kinds of writing, theological and overtly didactic as well as literary and historical, is illuminating. There is little "history" of the conventional kind here—no battles or regnal dates—and indeed not much about the more "literary" kind of literature. Chaucer, for instance, puts in only a comparatively rare appearance. The concentration is rather upon literature and its relation to social and cultural change, and the idea of an age in transition, or even turmoil, inevitably figures large in Coleman's account of things. Chapter 2, after a brief introduction, deals with "Vernacular Literacy and Lay Education"; Chapter 3 (by far the longest) with "The Literature of Social Unrest"; Chapter 4 with "Memory, Preaching and the Literature of a Society in Transition," and Chapter 5 with "Theology, Nonscholastic Literature and Poetry." The contents of the different chapters are not entirely unpredictable: Chapter 2 covers some fairly familiar ground, though in a brisk and readable and well-informed manner; Chapter 3 deals with what might be called "historical" or "political" poetry, and gives extended accounts of such poems as the Anglo-Norman *Against the King's Taxes* and Gower's *Vox Clamantis* as well as *Mum and the Sothsegger* and the poems of MS Digby 102 (one of Coleman's advantages as a historian is that she does not have to make an effort to remind herself that English literature is not necessarily literature in English); Chapter 5 treats some of the ideas, such as those concerning free will and predestination, salvation by grace and by works, which came down from scholars like Holcot and Bradwardine to vernacular writers, principally Langland. Chapter 4 is a little less predictable, and rather less easy to understand. It brings together alliterative verse, the development of encyclopedic preachers' handbooks, and Lollardy, as well as a number of other things, in a discussion of the consequences of extended literacy in terms of the decline of memory and the increase in social mobility.

All the time one has the sense of being shown over a familiar building in the company of a bright, new, enthusiastic, rather breathless, and not very experienced guide. There is a mass of material here, a phenomenal amount of reading, including a perhaps disproportionate amount of the very recent, and high intelligence and ambition everywhere. But there are some problems with the digestion of such hastily assembled materials, and of course there has to be, with such ambition, a thesis. Coleman's thesis, briefly put, is that the expansion in literacy is associated with an increase in social mobility; that the literature of the age characteristically records and reinforces the role of the expanding "middle classes" (p. 14); that this literature itself expands to include a concern with theological questions and problems of social reform in which "the present reality" is confronted (p. 95); and that with this goes an increase in the interest shown in the individual and an increased sense of individual authorial responsibility.

Coleman sometimes presses this thesis rather hard. At the end of a discussion of fourteenth-century political verse, for instance, she generalizes thus: "What is significant however is that, while the early political verses were commissioned by kings and the nobility, by the mid-fourteenth century, if not earlier, the pressure to write about contemporary events in English was exerted from below" (p. 65). But, though some of the evidence points this way, some of it points the other, and some of it points in no way at all that is useful to Coleman. Another theme is that a voice of a new and "relevant public poetry" (p. 69) emerges during the latter half of the century, in which causes of social and religious complaint are merged. This contention is supported thus: it is difficult to make hard-and-fast distinctions between secular and religious poems; many romances have a homiletic element; some long poems, commonly called religious (such as *Piers Plowman*), have a strong interest in current issues. The conclusion is: "Poetry meant as didactic, social and religious commentary, rather than merely as entertainment, seems to have caught the prevailing mood of the times" (p. 71). I think there is some truth in this but feel more strongly drawn to conclude, by such modes of argument, that we need more and better distinctions between different kinds of literary work. Elsewhere, Coleman speaks of a tendency in the poetry of social complaint, at the end of the century, "to blame individuals rather than groups" (p. 117)—but there had always been this tendency in the genre of writing which favored it.

Chapter 4, which is glutted with ideas, is particularly troubled by a tendency to employ generalizations drawn out of context from secondary sources in the construction of further generalizations. "One of the effects," we are told, "of the growth in literacy on literature and the consequent development of fixed modes of discourse and a fixed logic to analyze discourse was the development of the use of allegory and figural interpretation as an attempt to 'read' and reinterpret aspects of the fixed, cultural tradition, not least the Bible" (p. 159). If this is saying, as it seems to be, that allegorization increases with the spread of literacy in the fourteenth century, how can it be true? The Bible had long been sufficiently allegorized, and the allegorical poetic tradition was long established; a decline in both was imminent; what possible connection can there be? Allegorization requires literacy of its practitioners, but not a spread of it; when more people can read, more will (probably) read allegorical writings, but this is no more than to say that more people can read. The effort here at a resounding generalization is not productive. Elsewhere, an attempt to associate Spearing's views on dream-poetry with an opinion derived from another source that dreams are somehow "oral" in origin (p. 165) is notably awkward. Likewise, Turville-Petre's account of the origins of the alliterative revival in written sources rather than oral tradition is duly alluded to (p. 162), but its value undermined by a reference to the passage in *Winner and Waster* condemning the new kind of entertainer, which is said to prove the demise of the oral tradition. If it was dead, it must have lived and been there to provide the continuity through oral tradition that Turville-Petre so fastidiously objects to. In any case, the lines in *Winner and Waster* are quite differently to be interpreted, and they accord with a genre of complaint to be found elsewhere, for instance, in *The Life of the Black Prince*.

Inevitably, in such an ambitious and wide-ranging and eclectic book, there are quite a lot of mistakes. Usk's *Testament of Love* is not in verse (p. 21); the "Christ of the Craftsmen" (p. 23) is no more; *William of Palerne* is not an ancestral romance

(p. 25); the Auchinleck manuscript does not comprise, in any significant sense, "French, Latin and English works" (p. 78); the determinism debate does not appear in the Nun's Priest's Prologue (p. 141); Holcot is not "Chaucer's source for the 'Nun's Priest's Tale' " (p. 178), only a partial source for part of it; Gower is not known to have been a civil servant (p. 275); and Furnivall would turn in his grave to find himself as "Furvinall" (p. 283).

But if Coleman gets a few things wrong, and finds herself barking up a few unpromising trees, or trying to shepherd too many unruly ideas through too small a hole in the fence, she can be forgiven much. The writing, occasionally clogged, generates a good deal of intellectual excitement, and she does succeed in her primary task, which is to take a refreshingly new look, unrestrained by the traditional prejudices of the historian or the literary scholar, at a large and important body of writing of the latter half of the fourteenth century. Everyone will learn something from her brave and ambitious adventure, and it will not be merely that it cannot be done.

Notes

1. G. G. Coulton, *The Medieval Village* (1925; rpt. as *Medieval Village, Manor, and Monastery*, New York: Harper Torchbooks, 1960), p. 99; R. H. Hilton, *A Medieval Society: The West Midlands at the End of the Thirteenth Century* (London: Weidenfeld and Nicolson, 1966), p. 98.

2. J. R. Hulbert, "A Hypothesis concerning the Alliterative Revival," *Modern Philology*, 28 (1931), 405–22.

3. Elizabeth Salter, "The Alliterative Revival," *Modern Philology*, 64 (1966–67), 146–50, 233–37. Coleman makes generous acknowledgment of her debt to the work of the late Professor Salter, whose work on particular poems provides, indeed, a model of the discriminating use of history by a literary scholar. See "The Timeliness of *Wynnere and Wastoure*," *Medium Aevum*, 47 (1978), 40–65, and "A Complaint against Blacksmiths," *Literature and History*, 5 (1979), 194–215.

4. See W. Matthew, *The Tragedy of Arthur* (Berkeley and Los Angeles: Univ. of California Press, 1960), and, for criticism of his interpretation, G. Keiser, "Edward III and the Alliterative *Morte Arthure*," *Speculum*, 48 (1973), 37–51.

5. J. Leslie Hotson, "Colfox vs. Chauntecleer," *PMLA*, 39 (1924), 762–81.

Responsible and Irresponsible Authorship: Recent Henry James Criticism

Ross Posnock

    Alwyn Berland. *Culture and Conduct in the Novels of Henry James.* Cambridge: Cambridge University Press, 1981. 227 pp.

    Nicola Bradbury. *Henry James: The Later Novels.* Oxford: Oxford University Press, 1979. 228 pp.

    Laurence Bedwell Holland. *The Expense of Vision: Essays on the Craft of Henry James.* Princeton, 1964; rpt. Baltimore: The Johns Hopkins University Press, 1982.

    Susanne Kappeler. *Writing and Reading in Henry James.* New York: Columbia University Press, 1980. xiv, 242 pp.

    Philip Sicker. *Love and the Quest for Identity in the Fiction of Henry James.* Princeton: Princeton University Press, 1980. xv, 196 pp.

    H. Peter Stowell. *Literary Impressionism: James and Chekhov.* Athens: The University of Georgia Press, 1980. xv, 277 pp.

The work of many of James's most penetrating critics proceeds not from a recognition that he is an interesting writer despite his difficulty, but rather that his difficulty is nearly inextricable from what makes him exciting. These critics have endeavored to understand how and why his work is difficult, while resisting as much as possible the impulse to reduce "the peculiarly fluid and unsettling reality" of his fiction, especially the later work, to "something far more stable and conventional," in the words of Ruth Yeazell, whose book on late James is admirable in its refusal to simplify.[1] Describing a quality of "genuine dialectical thought," Fredric Jameson writes in his *Marxism and Form* that "such thought is . . . essentially process: it never attains some ultimate place of systematic truth in which it can henceforth rest, because it is as it were dialectically linked to untruth, to that mystification of which it is the determinate negation."[2] This statement, which limits itself to a depiction of the "mental operation" of dialectical thinking, seems to me strikingly pertinent to Henry James's sensibility and art, for it suggests that a source of his notorious ambiguity, the open-ended plurality of his fictional world, can be located in a commitment to a profoundly relational conception of human experience. James enunciates his dialectical vision at the opening of his initial preface, where he notes that "really, universally, relations stop nowhere" and thereby states one of the defining conditions of his art, which strives for formal control while remaining aware that "experience is never limited and it is never complete," as he states in "The Art of Fiction." The artist's problem, then, says James, is to make relations "appear" to stop.

The novelist sustains the illusion of stasis as he creates an intensity of form commensurate with the dynamism of experience. Thus he solicits conflict and "convulsions" that exploit the genre's elasticity: in great works we take pleasure in feeling the "surface . . . bear without cracking the strongest pressure we throw upon it."[3] Among the pressures James exerts is his use of techniques from other arts—notably painting and drama—and the jealousies and suspicions generated between the competing genres are precisely the tensions he finds nourishing to his fiction. The great advocate of the economy and order of organic form also celebrates the novel's propensity to "appear more true to its character in proportion as it strains or tends to burst . . . its mould."[4]

James's acute sense of the dialectical was doubtless nurtured by his father's idiosyncratic education of his children at home, where, James recalls in a well-known passage from *A Small Boy and Others*, "the presence of paradox" reigned "so bright," and the "literal played in our education as small a part as it perhaps ever played in any, and we wholesomely breathed inconsistency and ate and drank contradictions." Under the tutelage of his father's iconoclasm James had the "amusement . . . of hearing morality, or moralism . . . made hay of in the very interest of character and conduct," and virtue was admissible only when it "was more or less ashamed of itself." In this "queer educative air," the senior James guided his sons "but by one word: convert, convert, convert!" The vagueness of his father's directive was deliberate, for the conversion of "every impression and every experience" had no concrete goal or purpose save the development of the imagination, which James was to link explicitly to the power of conversion in "The Art of Fiction": "When the mind is imaginative . . . it converts the very pulses of the air into revelations." Imagination conceived of not as an entity but as an activity of mind, a process that multiplies impressions rather than fixing them, is paramount for James, as it is for his brother, who defined consciousness as "standing for a function." And the sensitivity of both Jameses to plurality and process was developed by their father's "experiment," the effect of which "could only be to make life interesting," as the novelist recalled.[5]

James's suspicion of fixity and autonomy extends to a skepticism of the possibility of experience liberated from the "whole envelope of circumstances" that Madame Merle emphasizes in her famous debate with Isabel Archer. But while James would likely concur with Madame Merle's declaration that "there's no such thing as an isolated man or woman," he honors the ideal of the unrelated self by devoting a novel to a young woman's attempt to "affront her destiny" as a social being. Unconditioned experience is also a powerful myth for Merton Densher, who, late in *The Wings of the Dove,* believes his unmediated "vision" of Milly's death to be "not only possible but inevitable." Yet his conviction is compromised by the persistence of what he calls the "aesthetic instinct," which makes him unable to perceive Milly without a "vividness" of imagery that muffles the fact of her agony. Such an art, celebrating and mocking the deepest yearnings of its heroes, is "rooted in a kind of cosmic irony" characteristic of the dialectical mind's refusal to "say finally here is where Truth lies," to quote Martin Jay's description of Adorno's thought.[6]

Like the light in Strether's Paris, James's work reveals "what things resemble," illuminating by the refractions of analogy as it continually subverts conventional dichotomies: appearance and reality, theatricality and sincerity, reading and writing, form and content, and, inevitably, life and art. An insistence on the relational informs the distinctive structure of the Jamesian aesthetic experience, which is founded on the complicity among the novelist, his characters and readers. He described his characters as his "delegates," and he believed that when the writer "makes" the reader well, the latter does "quite the labor" of creation. Characters and readers are linked by their absorption in reading texts—be it in the social text (the code of conventions, customs, manners, roles that mediates personal communication) or the representation of that text in James's fiction. The pervasive textual metaphors in his novels and criticism suggest the analogies between social and literary sign systems, both of which must be interpreted rather than spontaneously perceived. And astute interpretation involves dissolving the polarities that organize and simplify social and literary experience, so as to discover and understand the ambiguous, fluid nature of Jamesian reality, where "nothing solid is its solid self," to borrow Wallace Stevens's phrase.

However familiar this sketch of the intricate texture of James's art, many critics simplify him by tacitly relying on the duality of form and content, which accounts for two of our most familiar images of the novelist: critics who emphasize content discuss Henry James the novelist of manners, moral analyst of the international theme in all its glamourous intrigue and romance. Critics for whom form has priority examine Henry James the rigorous and self-conscious formalist, high priest of the novel as symbolic art form, master technician of point of view narrative. Instead of maintaining these static, partial portraits of James, his most rewarding critics tend to focus on the interplay between these images by exploring the intimate, if indirectly expressed, relation between his prefaces and fiction, especially the late novels. To understand this complex relation is to discover that his formalism is not simply a narrow technical concern but a vision of experience that embraces the aesthetic and social realms, both of which rely on the exploitation of conventions, forms, styles of representation.

Richard Poirier, Leo Bersani, and Laurence Holland have vividly revealed the dialectical wholeness of James's "grasping imagination" by pursuing the exhilarating challenge of taking James "strenuously at his word," in Poirier's phrase.[7] Influenced by Blackmur's and Matthiessen's respective emphases on the prefaces and the late novels, these three critics have probed the implications of James's "compositional view of experience," which, as Poirier says, defines the "positive beauty" of "composition" (James's phrase) as a "mode of existence" and as a "form of art" (p. 107).[8] But to accept James's view of composition, Poirier points out, "raises quite disturbing problems about the nature of the human meanings we can legitimately extract from what might be, on James's part, a prior and more intense commitment to the shapeliness of human actions" (p. 108). Poirier has in mind such a scene as Strether's dismissal of Maria Gostrey in the final scene of *The Ambassadors,* an action that is an "artful expedient for mere consistency of form," as James confesses in his preface.

For Holland in *The Expense of Vision,* a moment such as the conclusion of *The Ambassadors* reveals less a "commitment to the shapeliness of human actions" than the intimate relation of this shape (as depicted in the novel's form) to James's vision. Since it is dictated in part by the demands of James's form, Strether's rejection of Maria's offer has the crucial effect, according to Holland, of implicating the novelist's art in the sort of manipulations Chad had profited from. And Strether, by his own profitable use of Maria previously, "enacts for James the exploitive sacrifice on which the novel is founded" (p. 281). James's entanglement, through the mediation of his form, in the action of *The Ambassadors,* is a prime instance of what Holland calls the "fully creative function of his form" (p. xii), which creates moral issues in its own right rather than simply confronting them. The novelist's "torment of participation" constitutes, in

Holland's view, his effort to bear the responsibility of authorship—to redeem, by his deliberate complicity, the inevitable sacrifices and betrayals incurred in the exercise of authority. For James the novel is the "most prodigious of literary forms," as he says in his preface to *The Ambassadors*, precisely because it is founded, as Holland observes, "on a process which is both treacherous and redemptive, betraying and redeeming its materials in the act of creation" (p. 173).

James's "distinctive fusion of moral and technical concerns" and the moral risks this fusion entails define the "crisis of creation" (p. xii) that Holland views as crucial to the prefaces and the drama of the novels, particularly those of the major phase, to which more than half of *The Expense of Vision* is devoted. According to Holland, the intimacy of "James's vicarious involvement in his medium," confessed in the actions of Strether, Kate, Densher and Milly, and Maggie Verver, turned the "representational novel" into the "intimate novel," which sought to help redeem the acquisitive world "which the late masterpieces confront and accept in the process of attempting to transform it" (p. 225). And James enacted this redemptive process "through the exercise of the imagination," an activity he shares with his fictional delegates. The novelist's exercise of power became "radically bold" in the late fiction because, says Holland, "the crises of transformation which he depicted in the lives and social destinies of his characters were joined to a crisis in his art, involving the formal conventions he used in the throes of transformation" (p. 224). These twin crises are most intensely rendered in *The Golden Bowl,* the subject of Holland's final and longest chapter, which reveals how the hazards of authority and the urgent need for redemption are faced explicitly in James's final preface, and confronted most profoundly in his fiction by the audacious Maggie Verver, James's "delegate" in the second half of his last complete novel.

Both author and character struggle to redeem forms in a state of crisis: the "funny form" of Maggie's adulterous marriage, and the conflict in James's novelistic form, where responsible and irresponsible authorship are disturbingly close. Their shared redemptive efforts, insists Holland, "cannot—and must not, to be effective—escape from their dependence on the very materials and instruments they seek to transform. To acknowledge that dependence is the crux of the redemptive act for Maggie as for James" (p. 387). Thus Maggie's decision to take responsibility for transforming her flawed marriage involves the sacrifice of her beloved father, who must be forced to depart, the infliction of pain upon Charlotte, and the surrender of the Prince.

"The muffled majesty of irresponsible authorship" that, James confesses, "ostensibly reigns" in the novel by virtue of the fact that it is narrated by an omniscient third person voice, must be redeemed by the novelist, who confronts this crisis in his preface. He topples the detachment of his narrative mode by getting down "into the arena" with his characters—the "bleeding participants" whose "struggle . . . provides for others . . . the entertainment of the great game," as he notes in his preface. James's intimacy with the characters he must exploit is revealed in his dependence on them to bear the burden of his form, which is founded on the exceedingly close register of two centers of consciousness—the Prince and Maggie. "It is precisely that willed dependence on, that deference to" his delegates, says Holland, that "redeems an otherwise irresponsible artistry" (p. 177).

Not only is James's narrative form undergoing crisis in the late fiction (recall the "palpable voids, the missing links, the mocking shadows" that James bemoans in his description of the form of *The Wings of the Dove*) but so are other aspects of his style: "friction among the pictorial, the dramatic, and the novelistic . . . the dialectic of combat within the imaginative process" generates the pressures and contortions that are the distinguishing qualities of James's late prose, which Holland calls a version of expressionism, "if that term is conceived as a generic mode of the imagination" (pp. 224, 76). The interaction between the "conspicuously wrought" expressionistic "contortions of insistent movement" (p. 78) and the more settled and ordered patterns of convention characteristic of mannerism, defines for Holland the tensions of Jamesian style.

In his remarkable chapter on the Prefaces, Holland calls them "a landmark in the history of expressionism," for they are a "celebration of a process, a mission and a form rather than a statement of theory" (p. 156). The Prefaces replace "the more contemplative and categorical aims of traditional aesthetics" with "modern features" that Holland summarizes as "the obsessive concern with the assets, hazards and limitations of the imaginative life, the attempt to validate the institution of the novel in a culture which ignores, debases, and assaults the arts, the double concern for *objectivity* and *intimacy* in the arts, the experiential, strenuously activist, orientation . . . the importance accorded to technique and an expressive medium, the tenor of crisis, the awareness of process and change, the concern for the writer's responsibility and the grounds of his authority" (p. 155). For Holland the Prefaces illuminate the fiction because they "draw on the same resources of experience and metaphor as do the creative works," primarily the myths and vocabularies of "religious sacrifice and exploitive capitalism" (pp. 156–57).

In outlining the preoccupations of the Prefaces, Holland, in effect, summarizes many of the concerns of *The Expense of Vision*, which shares with the Prefaces an insistence on the dialectical relation of the experience of life and the art of fiction. The interplay between them, as should be apparent, is central to Holland's study and is implied from the start, when he describes James's novels as avoiding simply recording and demonstrating "findings of earlier experiments of the imagination," but daring to "make the original experiments themselves" (p. xiii). Holland points to the crucial result of this activist conception: "The process of making his novels is what joined him to the world he knew and rendered in his art and kept him from sorting his characters into categories of good and evil with supremely Olympian assurance and detachment" (pp. xi–xii).

Holland's insistence throughout on the complexities and elusiveness of James's art was mistaken for obscurantism and an oversubtle formalism by some critics reviewing the book upon its initial publication in 1964. But Holland stresses James's ambiguities and complications not for their own sake but rather as the measure of the novelist's relational view of experience. And the expression and enactment of this vision in the complicities, analogies, and implications of form and substance are what he reveals in his readings of seven works. Early critics also complained that *The Expense of Vision* was insufficiently critical, far too celebratory. While Holland runs the risk of this charge, such a complaint ignores his work's principal intention and achievement, not judgment but the more difficult work of understanding. And this requires not only careful examination but imaginative engagement with his subject. Holland's nearly stunning grasp of nuance and his command of detail demonstrate the depth of his engagement with James's mind and art and repay the close rereading of this book. And if the density and intricacy of Holland's argument and prose deter some readers, they also manage to convey the texture of James's sensibility.

The Expense of Vision is not flawless: it never makes good on its prefatory emphasis on James's treatment of his reader, and there are a few passages that refuse to surrender their meaning. But the work's recent return to print, with an additional essay—on *The American Scene*—confirms its stature as the subtlest and most precise reading of James. The eighteen years since its first appearance have witnessed a steady recognition of Holland's seminal contribution, as Poirier, Bersani, Quentin Anderson, and Kenneth Graham, to name only a few, have acknowledged the importance of his work.

Recently, Holland's viewpoint has indirectly been given new currency with the assimilation of French poststructuralism by Americanists. John Carlos Rowe's deconstructionist reading of James in his *Henry Adams and Henry James* (1976) in effect puts many of the emphases of the dialectical approach in a philosophical context. Viewing the novelist through the lens of the Derridean critique of metaphysics, Rowe finds that James celebrates "neither an ultimate meaning nor a central symbol" but, instead, "the process of signifying." "To recognize the differences and ambiguity that compose man's world is a moral imperative in James's later fiction. This attitude refuses absolute truth, completed meaning and dogmatic tone."[9]

Not surprisingly, of the five recent works on James under review, the two most stimulating and valuable—those by Bradbury and Kappeler—are most fully alive to the dialectical quality of James's mind and art. But only Kappeler, with her poststructuralist orientation, fully explores the dialectical, which, in a sense, is the subject of her book. The three other works (by Stowell, Sicker, and Berland) prefer to approach James's fiction as a collection of themes to be isolated, singly, or in a cluster, for examination. Regardless of how astutely such themes are discussed, this approach tends to limit the success of one's critical enterprise from the outset because it ignores the interplay of form and content central to James's work—or to any important art, for that matter. And to isolate content commits the critic to the kind of substantialist thinking that runs directly counter to James's insistence everywhere on the relational. In addition, a thematic approach risks ignoring the novelist's unprecedented effort to create a poetics of fiction and to fully articulate his own aesthetic intentions, preoccupations that have more than tangential relation to his novels.

As the first full-length attempt at both defining impressionism as a literary genre and analyzing the "gradual achievement of quintessential impressionism" in James's career from *The Portrait of A Lady* to *The Golden Bowl*, Peter Stowell's *Literary Impressionism: James and Chekhov* seeks to fill an important gap. James and Chekhov share a "commitment to the rendering of perceived reality, capturing the actual act of perception," and thus create an art receptive to chance, the accidental, the unknowable, and "arbitrary and inconclusive ambiguity" (pp. 21, 24). Stowell also rightly emphasizes James's involvement with the impressionistic themes of change—"a character's responding to events through time"—and the fusion of "the inner ego with the outer world," the phenomenological relationship which "underlies the entire vision and aesthetic of impressionism" (p. 32). Impressionism, Stowell claims, is a label that has rarely been attached to James despite his frequent use of the word in his fiction and criticism.

But, strangely enough, Stowell devotes only seventy pages to analyzing James's impressionism in five novels. The rest of the book is devoted to a 40-page examination of impressionism in the context of intellectual history and a 105-page study of Chekhov, who, Stowell blithely admits, had not the slightest awareness of James and vice-versa. It appears that Stowell has merely yoked together two very different artists who are linked by some common aesthetic aims broad enough to be equally relevant to a number of other writers of the time. In short, this is less a book than a collection of three loosely connected essays.

Having allowed himself such limited space to discuss five complex works, it is hardly surprising that Stowell's readings of James are sketchy; but they are more seriously hampered by frequent rehashings of the familiar themes of point of view and the "epistemological effects of subjectivity" (p. 21). To be told that "both Isabel and Maisie are on a journey of perception, beginning in innocence and ending in perceptual acuity" (p. 187) is to learn nothing new. Equally unremarkable is Stowell's emphasis on the theme of change: that "change is ephemeral and ambiguous" (p. 198) is what James "discovers" in *The Sacred Fount;* that "change is continual," and that Strether comes to understand "what he cannot know and accept what he can" (p. 220) describes, for Stowell, Strether's ultimate apprehension of experience. And Maggie, the heroine of the novel which "brings to consummate resolution all the important elements" of impressionism, is blandly described as that rare character in impressionist fiction who does not simply "see and absorb change," but "effects changes in human relationships" (pp. 221, 226).

Stowell's reading of James might have been less pedestrian had his conception of impressionism been less thematic. Despite considerable talk of process, of "shifting relations," the "multi-dimensional world of surfaces and adult duplicities" (p. 174), these issues remain only matters of content with no relation to James's form. But a more important problem with his view of James and impressionism is Stowell's indifference to the fact that James's epistemology is at odds with impressionism's implicit belief in the spontaneous, innocent eye of perception. While James states that "any point of view is interesting that is a direct impression of life," in the same letter in which he makes this statement he goes on to remark: "You each have an impression colored by your individual conditions."[10] Thus the "direct impression," like the self, is created in interaction with "conditions"—social, historical constraints. By relying on a notion of the impression as the product of pure, immediate perception, Stowell makes the kind of error many of James's characters commit when they mistakenly believe that their vision is unconstrained and objective rather than an interpretation bound by context.

The belief in autonomous perception is, of course, part of the larger belief in the unconditioned self; both views ignore what James calls man's "exposed and entangled state," the fact that he is rooted in social reality. For a novelist who defines experience as our "apprehension and our measure of what happens to us as social creaures," the self finds meaning in relation to others, often by falling in love. The link between love and the attainment of selfhood is the subject of Philip Sicker's *Love and the Quest for Identity in the Fiction of Henry James*, which defines the "quest for love throughout the length and breadth of James's fiction" to be a "continual quest for identity in a universe that seems to deny both permanent, objective values and the integrity of the self" (p. 10). Love becomes the means by which man breaks out of the prison of his own mind and achieves an integrated identity. Sicker pursues his thesis across an impressive number of works, from 1868 to 1910, with special emphasis on the fiction written between 1895 and 1904. In this span of James's entire career, the novelist's view of love begins with "image love," an idealization of the beloved that depends upon distance rather than consummation. But later, love became a sexual and spiritual unity, and telepathic communication comes to be characteristic of Jamesian lovers, preeminently Densher and Kate.

Sicker makes a convincing argument in his opening chapter that James, more than any other English novelist except Lawrence, dedicated his fiction to an exploration of romantic love. This represents a significant departure from conventional opinion, which tends to label James and his work as "emotionally frigid," a characterization that began in his own lifetime and still prevails. Also successful is Sicker's fourth chapter with its analysis of the "disturbed midnight" (James's phrase) of the novelist's career—the sometimes baffling and eccentric works produced from 1895–1901, culminating in *The Sacred Fount*.

Sicker links their theme of solipsism to the near desperate sense of personal crisis that beset James in this period. Particularly illuminating are his discussions of "In the Cage" and *The Awkward Age*.

In his second chapter Sicker discusses James's affinities to and divergences from Pater, who shares James's belief that the self is "merely the sum of its experiences . . . a whirlpool of impressions"; and thus "there can be no stable source of identity within the conscious mind" (p. 23). But James rejects Pater's "cultivated solipsism," according to Sicker, who states that as James "developed his fiction he became increasingly aware of the individual's need to discover or create some coherent inner identity amid the ebb and flow of sensations" (p. 25). And man, in James's early fiction, creates an integrated self only through love, which begins with a belief in the fixed otherness of another person, a stable "love-image" that anchors the self.

Thus, in Sicker's view, the Jamesian self seeks wholeness and stability, for James has a "desire to find a principle of order in the self" (p. 25). But, regardless of how sensible this desire may seem, it is Sicker's rather than the novelist's, whose conception of identity is more problematic than Sicker suggests. Although Sicker is well aware that stability is an illusion and that society, which he perceptively defines as the quality of flux itself, obstructs the creation of an integrated identity, he simplifies the relation of social reality to the self by insisting that James asserts the self's need for unity. Sicker also contends that there is a "human need" to make one's social and psychological self "consistent—to appear in the world's eyes just as we appear in our own" (p. 51). But James is fascinated by characters who feel no such need for consistency but instead revel in the freedom of discontinuity, continually deferring a stable self. Sicker is aware of such characters and he accurately identifies and describes them: "Madame Merle, Kate Croy, Charlotte Stant—women who conceive of themselves primarily in terms of their manner, habits, tastes, and who strive to create a visible image of themselves for others to admire" (p. 44). Although these figures challenge Sicker's belief in a universal need for a stable identity, he defuses this challenge by relegating them to a category he labels "Jamesian dark women," thus implying that these characters are simply the immoral exceptions that prove the rule. And the rule, according to Sicker, is that "James's protagonists never simply adopt poses . . . but rather seek to discover their truest psychological and social self by discovering someone outside themselves. In short, they fall in love" (p. 52).

Here the demands of Sicker's thesis blind him to the actualities of the Jamesian world, where the behavior of the so-called "dark women" differs not in kind but only in degree from the self's everyday mode of behavior. Because, in James's view, we are social beings existing in potentially vulnerable relation to others (our "exposed" state, as James says), we represent rather than simply present ourselves to others. What James calls the "measured mask" is never dropped in social interaction; and this is not an impediment to self-expression but its defining condition. Thus to call the self theatrical is to insist on nothing more or less than man's status as a social creature. And the theatricality of James's "dark women" is not what makes them immoral, for all social interaction is governed by the manipulation of roles and conventions (including language itself).

One reason the social text in James is ambiguous is that the self seeks expression by adopting the improvisational fluidity of a manner, which is not static but engaged in a continual process of response and adjustment to others; thus the self possesses a certain mobility and has no intrinsic bias towards consistency or stability. "Manners, customs . . . forms," James insists in a letter to Howells, "represent an enormous quantity" of "human life" and are the "very stuff" of the novelist's work because in large measure they constitute the self. Sicker quotes this letter (p. 49) but fails to take James at his word, which would involve probing the statement's implications for a conception of self. Instead, Sicker compounds his misunderstanding of theatricality by his unfortunate reliance on Erikson's ego psychology, with its suspicion of " 'mere "roles" played interchangably . . . mere strenuous "postures" which cannot possibly be the real thing' " (p. 52). Although Erikson's devaluation of role playing and his positing of an a priori absolute (something called the "real thing") is blatantly un-Jamesian, Sicker somehow believes James would have "concurred."

Sicker's belief in a "truest" self uncontaminated by "poses," a belief shared by James's naive characters, is based on an implicit opposition between theatricality and sincerity, which is precisely a polarity that James seeks to collapse, most explicitly in *The Tragic Muse*. This dichotomy, and the misconceptions that it creates, can be surmounted, as the fate of Strether, for one, testifies. He begins his journey maintaining the Woollett view that the self is stable and consistent. But, of course, Strether's "double consciousness" eventually recognizes the egregious inadequacy of such a conception of the self, a realization that is born in his initial encounter with Chad's "sharp rupture of an identity." What Strether slowly discovers is that consistency is not a privileged standard and that discontinuity may also characterize the self. Strether's acceptance of the self's instability and the plurality of the social text, and his gradual understanding that in social experience deception and manipulation interact with sincerity and love, are some of the insights that make him one of the truly civilized figures in James's fiction.

The simplifications that hamper Sicker's book are misconceptions found too often in James criticism. Instead of taking James at his word, some critics ascribe to him conventional views that rob him of his power to disturb. To moralize about or ignore theatricality, to limit the self to a single need, be it stability or love, reduces the boldness of James's vision of social life to bland and familiar dimensions. As might be expected, Sicker's weakest chapter concerns the novel in which James makes one of his profoundest explorations of the theatrical self—*The Wings of the Dove*. Faced with that elusive and unabashed performer Kate Croy, whose character and motives are as complex as any in James, Sicker's thesis turns her into an ardent and earnest lover; her affair with Densher reveals that "only the mysterious warmth of shared love can melt the individual mold and bring two total consciousnesses into fusion with one another" (p. 125). Unfortunately, such inflated rhetoric is all too characteristic of this chapter, which depends too much on grand flights into the metaphysical and too little on the close examination of the nuances of the text. Thus we are told that the love of Kate and Densher allows them to "discover the fluid vastness of one's *total* being" (p. 128; Sicker's emphasis) and that ultimately they reach a "mystical merging of minds so complete that the lovers cease to be aware of themselves as autonomous beings" (p. 134). Not only is this diction grossly inappropriate to James but it ignores the awe and anxiety at the heart of Densher's response to Kate's unnerving theatrical panache. In this chapter and in his discussion of *The Golden Bowl* the limitations of Sicker's study are conspicuous; his indifference to James's form, his narrowly thematic approach and reliance on concepts of the self counter to James's view of identity impede his effort to illuminate two of James's most complex works. An examination of Sicker's bibliography reveals one explanation for his book's weakness: missing are many of the important works of James criticism written in the last fifteen years. Not only is there the obvious gap—John Bayley's *The Characters of Love*—but nowhere to be found are the works of Poirier, Holland, Bersani, Rowe, Yeazell, and Veeder. Surely Sicker's work would have profited by exposure to these critics, who deserve to be confronted either directly, or, at least, in footnotes.

Like Sicker's study, Alwyn Berland's *Culture and Conduct in the Novels of Henry James* is indifferent to most recent James criticism, and it offers a strictly thematic reading. Berland announces at the outset that the technical achievements of James's fiction will be set aside in favor of studying the novels in relation to his vision of civilization as culture. The implications of Berland's intentions are disconcerting: both his glib division of form and content and his ascription to James of a distinctly limited conception of civilization. Because these reductive premises are the foundation of his study, it is not surprising that Berland's readings of *The Portrait of A Lady, The Ambassadors,* and the three "public" novels are too often superficial and familiar.

The most interesting section of the book is its opening chapter, where Berland argues that James's "consecration of culture" was deeply influenced by Ruskin, Pater, and Arnold's conception of culture as "a structure of value and of belief to replace those religious certainties or sanctions which they felt to be no longer available" (p. 19). Most important for James was Arnold's emphasis on Stoicism and the conflicts of "Hebraism and Hellenism, the call to duty and the call to beauty." "Like Arnold, James rejected each of these two terms alone . . . the great dream of the Jamesian pilgrim is the Arnoldian ideal: the marriage of Hebraism and Hellenism" (pp. 30, 35). Berland rightly adds that James's heroes never achieve this "perfect marriage . . . but it is their striving toward such a synthesis" (p. 35) that is important. These observations are suggestive and are the most original aspect of the study, which is vitiated by Berland's admitted dislike of basic aspects of James: he repeatedly stresses the "limitations" in James's work, especially elitism, which involves an overemphasis on "acute personal awareness and intelligence" at the expense of the "full vitality" with which Hamlet (!) and Lear confront life (p. 3). Allegedly missing from James is the richness of lived experience present in the greatest writers. More than once Berland complains of the novelist's "disquieting individualistic emphasis" which ignores a sense of community. The culmination of these charges is Berland's judgment that James's fiction "yields extraordinarily little reflection or comment on the political, social, economic processes of history or of contemporary life" (p. 11). "The institutional life of men" is absent from James, for he conceives of civilization "primarily within the compass of the arts, as culture" (p. 105).

Are we to conclude, then, that Ruskin, Arnold, and Pater also hold this attenuated view and are to blame for James's limitations? Berland doesn't face this question, or the more important one: Why write about a writer one finds deficient in fundamental ways? Berland reads the novels on the basis of his image of James the sterile elitist, and his attack is clearly one more rehearsal of the "stereotype of James as Ivory tower exile" (a phrase of William Veeder's), an image that persists with critics who have little grasp of James's indirection and refusal of the literal (a legacy of his father's). Stephen Donadio, in his recent book on James and Nietzsche (Oxford Univ. Press, 1978), demolishes this stereotype; and not only Nietzsche, but Marx and Freud are profoundly relevant in discussing James's allegedly insular fiction. But rather than looking to these authors' writings on civilization and culture, Berland cites a single authority on the subject—Kenneth Clark, whose enumeration of civilized qualities—"gentleness, forgiveness, knowledge, courtesy"—is hardly worth the footnote Berland gives it. Even less excusable is Berland's neglect of the two most obvious and important texts in any consideration of James and culture—his monograph on Hawthorne and *The American Scene*. And to excuse oneself from discussing or even alluding to these works because only the fiction is to be studied is as willfully reductive as ignoring his technical achievements. But to have discussed these would have quickly exposed the shallowness of Berland's view of James. This study does a great disservice to a rich and fascinating topic, and although it contains enough material for a competent article, it is not up to the intellectual demands of the subject.

In vigorously pressing their narrow theses, the works of Stowell, Sicker, and Berland fail at one of criticism's essential tasks—to convey the distinctive texture of a writer's mind and art. Though each book offers readings of numerous texts, a remoteness from the particularities of James's sensibility and its expression in fiction persist as the inevitable result of thematizing and tendentiousness. It is a pronounced virtue of Nicola Bradbury's *Henry James: The Later Novels* that instead of confining itself to a snug thesis, it dares to return us to elementary and crucial questions: "Why do we read James? And how?" (p. 1). Because she knows that James's art "gradually diverts our curiosity from a search for answers towards an interest in the process by which questions arise" (p. 2), her primary purpose is to immerse the reader in that complex process as it is portrayed in the dense verbal surface of late James. She devotes a chapter to each of the late masterpieces, and what is most impressive about her readings is their assiduous attention to how meaning is created through the expressive use of diction, syntax, grammar, and other stylistic devices. Her study proceeds by careful, at times minute scrutiny of linguistic patterns, and is less concerned with a closely argued thesis than with patient and often illuminating verbal analysis.

Bradbury's introduction, "The Process and the Effect," amply demonstrates her grasp of nuance and the special demands late James places upon the reader. The reader, in fact, and his relation to character and author are prominent in Bradbury's approach, which stresses that "James himself links the how and why of author and reader through 'the process and the effect of representation' " (p. 2). In the first of the late novels, *The Ambassadors,* James increased the complexity of the novel process, according to Bradbury, which forced the reader to understand this complexity; analogously, Strether comes to appreciate process and to apprehend imaginatively the indirect, oblique character of social expression, qualities that Bradbury probes in her second chapter on "The Unspeakable and the Unsayable."

The expressive values of silence—conspiratorial, sublime, strategic, narrative—are fully exploited in James's fiction. "Silence is distinctive amongst units of expression in the flexibility of its form, or lack of form ... both a unit of specific expressive significance and an escape from the limitations of form" (p. 27). Silence is also significant, says Bradbury, for its moral resonances; for her, the Jamesian "ideal" involves "the poise between curiosity and restraint," a stance akin to Keatsian "negative capability" (p. 5). And this kind of silence, which she describes as "open" and "imaginative," is opposed to the silence of deliberate concealment. Silence, then, becomes a means of discriminating moral character: "James's 'heroes' (and heroines) are distinguished by their restraint from expression, while the villains manipulate both words and silence with equal ease" (p. 11).

While this is an intriguing view of silence, what is troubling is Bradbury's division of heroes and villains, whose "kinds of silence" allegedly express "opposite approaches to experience" (p. 11). Puzzlingly, her finely tuned awareness of process and complicity here lapses into melodramatic categorizations of characters' moral status. Indeed, categorization is a term that crops up at various points, most tellingly in the conclusion: "The damage caused by inadequate categorization of experience is clear in the miscarrying of the various plots of *The Wings of the Dove,* and of the good intentions of all the characters in the first volume of *The Golden Bowl*" (p. 218). But the fixity of categorization would seem to be precisely what James's (and Bradbury's) emphasis on process and the "open state" of the late novels is meant to avoid. Although Bradbury perceptively states that in the late novels "the hierarchy of 'meaning,' subject and expression becomes increasingly difficult to determine," and that the "categories of expression become fluid," these formal characteristics have little relation, in Bradbury's view, with the moral experience they depict (p. 12). She neglects to see that the antihierarchial, fluid qualities of James's form reflect, indeed enact, the equally subtle and elusive moral drama. In effect, Bradbury's acute insistence on the dialectical seems to pertain only to James's form.

Bradbury's refusal to grant James's moral "categories" the fluidity she finds in his "categories of expression" is apparent in her description of the "hero" Strether achieving "absolute imaginative morality," as he moves "amidst the greater truths of absolute right and wrong." And "in his final words, there is no uncertainty" (pp. 68, 70). Simultaneously, says Bradbury, Strether attains "negative capability" (p. 71), though how he can both dwell with absolutes and maintain Keats's "uncertainties, mysteries, doubts" is left for the reader to resolve. Fortunately, these simplifications and confusions are not in evidence when she discusses Maggie Verver, whose morally ambiguous character Bradbury accepts: "We suspend narrow condemnation," and resist dispelling "the radical ambiguity which remains in our assessment" of the novel and its characters (p. 219).

Henry James: The Later Novels never really lives up to its acute and highly suggestive introduction: although Bradbury stresses "the links between author, reader and protagonist," she tends to focus too much upon the latter two of this trio, and she seriously underestimates the extent and significance of James's complicity with his characters. Her astute claim that "in his fiction . . . James works out the 'poetics' he subsequently analyzed" in the Prefaces is not followed through. Nonetheless, on the whole this is a thoughtful and well-informed study, a worthy attempt to understand James's most complex works. Although Bradbury fully confronts James's difficulty only on a formal level, she recognizes that his difficulty creates some of the pleasure of reading.

The pleasures of reading the Jamesian text are central in Susanne Kappeler's *Writing and Reading in Henry James*, which has the laudable intention of recovering the sense of "fun" that James, if not most of his critics, insists is a central purpose of his art: "It all comes back to that, to my and your 'fun'—if we but allow the term its full extension," he remarks in his final preface. The full extension of fun is what Kappeler seeks to define and celebrate as the essential reason for reading James: "Above all it is 'fun,' and not, for instance, simply a matter of conveying (or extracting, respectively) a moral judgment on the society portrayed, for which so many critics of James's work are out" (p. 190). The fun James provides results from his conception of the "literary enterprise" as an "elaborate game" between reader and writer. And the difficulties of the game are the very source of fun, which would be "taken out . . . if all were told and the 'case' given away" (p. 190).

In her introduction Kappeler identifies Roland Barthes's aphorism that the "reader is properly the 'writer' or 'producer' of his text," as her "starting point" for an exploration of the " 'reader's share' in his experience of reading" (p. xiv). What makes James the ideal subject for such an analysis, in Kappeler's view, is the novelist's decisive rejection of the governing realist convention that the author is omniscient and the reader dependent on him for guidance. James radically alters this relationship: "The *bona fide* confidence between writer and reader of the realist novel is a contract which James refuses to sign. With the introduction of 'point of view' and the renouncement of omniscience the Realist guarantee of Truth is not granted, and the relation of reader and writer is built on a different basis. James has spoken out as the writer who wants to trick (not guide) his reader." Thus the reader is "invited to join the game" with James, and "take on the reader's share"; in short, "writer and reader are partners on equal terms" (pp. 52, 53). Kappeler's account of James's relation to realism is a version of what Fredric Jameson has called "the ideology of the text"—a "moralizing valorization" of the modern text (read Jamesian text) that reduces realism to a "straw man": "The concept of realism which thereby emerges is always that with which modernism has had to break, that norm from which modernism is the deviation." Like Barthes, who is the foremost exponent of this simplistic view, Kappeler has a conception of realism as "nothing but punctuation, a mere marker or a 'before' which permitted the phenomenon of modernism to come into focus properly," as Jameson describes the elusive term in Barthes's work.[11]

Kappeler's schematic and inadequate literary history should not obscure the acuteness of her description of the reader's relation to James. The dialectic of reading and writing is important in James's work and comprises the central thread of her study, which discusses a rather miscellaneous set of texts: "The Aspern Papers," the tales of artists and writers James wrote in the late eighties and nineties, the Prefaces, and, in her longest section, *The Sacred Fount*. This unorthodox selection of works reflects a certain eccentricity, apparent also in her chapter on metaphors of gardening in James. But if her disregard for major works and taste for the outré limits the scope of her book, her approach is often imaginative and produces numerous fresh insights.

Kappeler's insistence on collapsing the traditional dichotomy that opposes writer and reader finds support of course from James, who describes the writer as an "embroiderer of the canvas of life," and a reader of the "crabbed page of life." These metaphors suggest, in Kappeler's words, that "the novelist is as much an interpreter of the 'canvas of life' as the reader is an interpreter of the novelist's embroidery . . . in other words, the activities of writer and reader are singularly similar" (p. 159). And Kappeler well observes that James's sense of life as a "canvas" expresses his vision of reality as "already a completed artifact and not a 'natural' beginning" (p. 172). James's work "becomes a new canvas, appealing for interpretation," but a new set of rules governs the game now that writer and reader are partners. Kappeler describes "the predicament of the reader-interpreter" and the "peculiar nature of literary communication" once the "Realist guarantee of Truth is not granted": "In the literary dialogue . . . the author speaks but once and then leaves his critical interlocutor to spin out his answer as endlessly as he pleases . . . without offering any further assistance, correction or confirmation. The reader certainly is 'condemned never to know with any certainty whether his interpretations are exact'. . . . The quest for correctness is misplaced in a context where verification is impossible" (pp. 70–71). Thus, as she later notes, "no interpretation of an ambiguous text is ever going to be complete or 'correct'; but every consistent interpretation which is faithful to the text is spelling out a part of the work's ambiguity" (p. 192).

Having described the structure and rules of the literary game, she then turns to James's own fictional treatment of it in the numerous tales involving literary and artistic figures. These characters' behaviors reveal James's conception of the reader's share and what comprises fair play. One of her most interesting findings is that many of the tales articulate a taboo—"No literary intimacy must exist between the writer and his reader." The "delicate topic of checking back," of attempting to verify interpretations with the author, "is treated like a literary taboo" (p. 76). Her identification of this taboo as a concern of the tales is ingenious, and her discussion of the stories of artists and writers is one of the highlights of her study.

Kappeler's analysis of "The Aspern Papers" explores the consequences of the unverifiable nature of authorial intention: "Aware that he [the reader] is not in a position to verify the author's 'individual desire to express something,' he will refrain from limiting intention, or meaningfulness, to the deliberate, the rational and the conscious—to 'what happens in the mind' " (p. 71). Thus the Jamesian reader must become suspicious, alert to unintended revelations, as Kappeler demonstrates in discussing "The Aspern Papers," which, as a first person narrative, pits the reader against the nameless narrator, the "author" of the tale. As a skeptical, "non-docile" interpreter, Kappeler must "read 'through' the narrator's discourse . . . to form a view of the events which differs from the one intended and 'represented' by him" (p. 57). In judging events independently of the narrator's guidance, Kappeler attends to the "unconscious level" latent in his discourse. "The recognition that there is something else to be sought, some further puzzle to be solved" is crucial in the game of reading James, and Kappeler calls this other level "the second hermeneutic," in contrast to "plot hermeneutics," that form the "primary basis" of reading (pp. 53, 54). It is in pursuit of the "second hermeneutic" that the reader of James becomes the producer of the text rather than a passive consumer simply reading for the story. In his careful analysis of clues the reader assumes the role of detective and the narrator of "The Aspern Papers" is now his major suspect whose narrative aims at diverting the reader's suspicion. According to Kappeler, the narrator's principal ruse is to disguise his story as a simplistic folktale of heroes and villains, a tale that he hopes will lure the reader into sympathy and trust. What Kappeler's strenuous detective work uncovers, through a detailed close reading, is the narrator's sexual repression and displacement; his obsession with Aspern's papers conceals a quest for love.

While Kappeler makes vivid that James's reader must read beyond the story, her approach to "The Aspern Papers" suffers from her implicit adherence to the "ideology of the text" and its valorization of modernism. For her conviction that "in the modern first-person narrative we have a paradigm of the courtcase... discourse is under suspicion" (p. 55) describes, in fact, the condition of any first-person text, which is always signifying an unintended level, one that David Goldknopf, in his study of the English novel, has labeled "the confessional increment." "Everything an I-narrator tells us has a certain characterizing significance over and above its data value, by virtue of the fact that he is telling it to us... this increment is the most valid reason for using an I-narrator."[12] In short, it is in the nature of first-person narrative to operate on a "second hermeneutic" level, and it is not specific to the Jamesian (i.e., modern) text, although James perhaps consciously exploits this level more than his predecessors do. While Kappeler's implication that James alone demands a suspicious reader is misleading, her argument nevertheless remains interesting and illuminates the nature of the challenge the novelist presents to the reader.

Kappeler's reading of another first-person text—*The Sacred*

Fount—is less intent on tracking down the narrator than on letting him explain himself. She adopts this strategy to avoid the mistake of many other critics, who insist on reading the work "on a level above the text, on a place of parable or allegory, which adduces an entirely new stratum of meaning, to be superimposed upon the text" (p. 191). In effect, then, *The Sacred Fount* has been read by oversuspicious readers. Kappeler reserves her suspicion for other critics, particularly those who identify the narrator as an artist or as James himself. Because her reading "enters the text on its own level," she calls it "primary, that is, textual," as it "takes up the narrator's hypothesis about sacred founts and follows it through to the end" (p. 191). In so doing, Kappeler makes the important point that the narrator is most precisely described as an interpreter—his relentless analytical activity makes him at once a reader, critic, and creator, whose product is a theory not a tangible artwork. Her discussion of *The Sacred Fount* is scrupulous and inventive, continually alive to the interpenetration of reading and creating, appearance and reality, pretense and truth in the novel. In an appendix, "Critics and *The Sacred Fount*," Kappeler reveals that a "binary conception" has often simplified many critical readings and is the primary weakness of many players of the Jamesian game (p. 209).

Ironically, the dialectical subtlety of Kappeler's reading of *The Sacred Fount* does not inform her sense of literary history, which depends, as noted, on the imprecisions of binary opposition. But *Writing and Reading in Henry James* is a lively and challenging work, possessing the kind of "fun" she emphasizes in James. In his foreword to her book Tony Tanner asserts that Kappeler "shifts Jamesian criticism into a new key of sophistication." More precisely, her study, in combining theory and practical criticism, makes an admirable attempt at such a shift.[13]

Skeptical of "neat and complacent conclusions," James relished "impressions [that] could mutually conflict—which was exactly the interest of them." While James found "such rash multiplications of the candid consciousness" "splendid for experience," he confessed they were a "burden" for the artist. But without "multiplications" "no representation of life worth speaking of can go forward."[14] We have seen that the novelist's commitment to bearing the "burden" of representing the dialectical complexity of experience demands an analogous commitment by the critic if he hopes to achieve responsible authority in his own discourse. One reason Laurence Holland is James's most responsible critic is that in fully assuming the burden— the challenge of James's difficulty—he recognizes the "precarious footing" of authority, including his own as critic. "In a world where authority is problematical and is acknowledged to be so, where authority is challenged on all sides . . . responsible authority is that which acknowledges the challenge, recognizes the claims, and incorporates the challenge in its constituted forms and enactments" (p. 175). This definition of James's responsible authority also describes Holland's exemplary response to the master's challenge. Although sadly posthumous, the republication of *The Expense of Vision* is most welcome; the standard it has set for James criticism can properly measure the relation of any critic to his subject.

Notes

1. Ruth Bernard Yeazell, *Language and Knowledge in the Late Novels of Henry James* (Chicago: Univ. of Chicago Press, 1976), p. 2.

2. Fredric Jameson, *Marxism and Form* (Princeton: Princeton Univ. Press, 1974), p. 372.

3. Henry James, *The Art of the Novel*, ed. R. P. Blackmur (New York: Scribners, 1962), p. 304.

4. Ibid., p. 46.

5. Henry James, *Autobiography*, ed. F. W. Dupee (New York: Criterion, 1956), pp. 124, 126. "The Art of Fiction" can be found in Henry James, *Partial Portraits* (Ann Arbor: Univ. of Michigan Press, 1972), p. 388.

6. Martin Jay, *The Dialectical Imagination* (Boston: Little, Brown, 1973), p. 67.

7. Richard Poirier, *The Performing Self* (New York: Oxford Univ. Press,

1971), p. 108. See also Poirier's *The Comic Sense of Henry James* (New York: Oxford Univ. Press, 1967).

8. "Compositional view of experience" is Leo Bersani's phrase, found in his chapter "The Jamesian Lie," *A Future for Astyanax* (Boston: Little, Brown, 1976), p. 148. See also Bersani's "The Subject of Power," *Diacritics,* 7, No. 3 (1977), 2–21.

9. John Carlos Rowe, *Henry James and Henry Adams* (Ithaca: Cornell Univ. Press, 1976), p. 231. Richard Poirier also suggests that Holland's approach has affinities with poststructuralism. Poirier begins his foreword to the new edition of *The Expense of Vision* by stating: "Anyone who read *The Expense of Vision* when it first appeared in 1964 will have been prepared for much that has appeared since that time on the theory of the novel." He goes on to mention that Bersani, whose work on James is informed by "European critical thinking," "reveals a special gratitude" to Holland's book.

10. *Henry James Letters,* ed. Leon Edel, Vol. III (Cambridge: Harvard Univ. Press, 1980), p. 257.

11. Fredric Jameson, "The Ideology of the Text," *Salmagundi,* 31–32 (1975–76), 233. Another polarity crucial to the historical mythology of poststructuralism is also implicit in Kappeler's study: Derrida's "two interpretations of interpretation." Clearly James partakes of the joyous affirmation of the game of interpretation that characterizes Nietzsche in Derrida's view (see "Structure, Sign and Play," in *The Structuralist Controversy,* ed. Richard Macksey and Eugenio Donato [Baltimore: Johns Hopkins Univ. Press, 1972]).

12. David Goldknopf, *The Life of the Novel* (Chicago: Univ. of Chicago Press, 1972), p. 38.

13. To my mind a more successful fusion of theoretical and practical criticism applied to James is Shoshana Felman's Lacanian reading of "The Turn of the Screw," "Turning the Screw of Interpretation," *Yale French Studies,* 55–56 (1977), 94–207.

14. *The Art of the Novel,* p. 214.

Hoy's Bowers's Dekker

T. H. Howard-Hill

Cyrus Hoy. *Introductions, Notes, and Commentaries to Texts in The Dramatic Works of Thomas Dekker*, ed. Fredson Bowers, 4 vols., Cambridge: Cambridge University Press, 1980.

Although twentieth-century editorial theory and practice are substantially grounded in the study of early English plays, it is remarkable how few of the Renaissance dramatists listed among the "most frequently cited editions" of Professor Cyrus Hoy's commentaries on Dekker have modern editions. Brome (1873), Chapman (1910–14), Deloney (1912), Ford (1895), Greene (1905), Heywood (1874), Kyd (1901), Lyly (1902), Marston (1887), and Middleton (1885) are clear candidates for supersession, as possibly are more recent editions of Field (1950), Tourneur (1929), and Webster (1927). Deduction of Peele (1961–70), the unannotated Marlowe (1973), and Beaumont and Fletcher (1966–) presided over by Professor Fredson Bowers, leaves three editions of the first rank, editions that are greatly useful to editors of early English literature. They are R. B. McKerrow's pioneering Nashe (5 vols., 1904–10, revised by F. P. Wilson, 1958), the massive Herford and Simpson Jonson (11 vols., 1925–52), and the Massinger of Philip Edwards and Colin Gibson (5 vols., 1976). To this select group must now be added *The Dramatic Works of Thomas Dekker* by Fredson Bowers and Cyrus Hoy (8 vols., 1953–80). With the addition of F. P. Wilson's edition of Dekker's plague pamphlets (1925) and Professor M. T. Jones-Davies's *Un Peintre de la Vie londonienne: Thomas Dekker* (1958), Dekker is as well served in these times as any of his playwriting contemporaries.

Professor Hoy's title is "Introductions, Notes, and Commentaries"; his volumes consist of an introduction and a commentary (notes on words and passages) for each of the plays contained in Bowers's edition of *The Dramatic Works*, first published between

1953 and 1961. The line-numbering of Dekker's plays is based "on the 1970 reprint of vol. I of Bowers's edition, the 1964 reprint of vol. II, the 1966 reprint of vol. III, and the 1968 reprint of vol. IV" (I, vii), probably the most up-to-date combination of reprinted volumes at the time Hoy's work went to press but one not likely to be found in many libraries. (I have worked from the 1962 reprint of the first volume, the corrected 1964 reprint of the second, and the original third and fourth volumes.) The introductions "place the plays in their critical contexts" (p. vii); that is, they apparently treat of matters such as stage history, sources, and attributions, which should inform scholarly appreciation of the plays, rather than provide a critic's reading of the play itself as drama or literature. Hoy claims also to "provide a record of critical response to the plays" (p. viii), but there is almost nothing of the kind for Dekker's portion of *Sir Thomas More*, not surprisingly, or for *The Shoemakers' Holiday*, *Old Fortunatus*, *Patient Grissil*, *Satiromastix*, and *Sir Thomas Wyatt*, which are all the plays of volume I. Examination of volume IV, however, reveals passages which support the editor's contention. Considering his firm grasp of the issues which accompany the study of an author of so complicated an oeuvre as Dekker, Hoy should be commended for any attention he pays to critical issues at all. It is not in literary criticism that the accomplishment of these volumes lies or should be sought.

After an admirably compact recital of the details of dating and theatrical provenance, which places each play firmly within the chronology of the dramatist's career, the editor usually turns to sources. The examination of source materials is particularly prominent in the first volume. Dekker's use of Thomas Deloney's *The First Part of The Gentle Craft* occupies most of the introduction to *The Shoemakers' Holiday*. The discussion is somewhat inflated by a long quotation from Stowe's *Survey* about Simon Eyre and the building of Leadenhall. The significance for the play of this and subsequent discussion is not made clear; "Leadenhall" is not glossed in the commentary. Hoy is even more expansive in the introduction to *Old Fortunatus*. Dekker's 1599 play is his revision of one or more lost plays, possibly by him, written around 1596. Somewhere behind these plays lies a German *Volksbuch* of Fortunatus which Hoy identifies as Dekker's source, even though there was no sixteenth-century English translation of the 1509 and 1550 German editions or of Hans Sachs's dramatization of 1553. Whether Dekker read German is not mentioned. The *Volksbuch* is quoted from and summarized for nine and a half pages, but Hoy cannot decide how far "this rambling narrative" had been compressed in the old play of 1596. The main difference between the *Volksbuch* and *Old Fortunatus* is "the insistent morality of the play," an observation which might have been prepared for more economically, particularly as the *Volksbuch* has been already described at length elsewhere. Hoy is fascinated by the Fortunatus story: he devotes another three and a half pages to a German Fortunatus play acted at Graz in 1608 and partly modeled on Dekker's play. The information is drawn from a monograph by Paul Harms (1892) and tells the reader nothing more important about Dekker's play than that it, in turn, became a source for theatrical adaptations of the Fortunatus story.

Similar amplitude may be observed in the discussion of the sources of *Patient Grissil* in the same volume. The story, which entered literary history in Boccaccio's *Decameron,* eventually found dramatic expression in English in John Phillip's *The Commodye of pacient and meeke Grissill,* which is variously dated between 1558 and 1566. Hoy leads the reader through four and a half pages of discussion of Phillip's play, which he says "deserves more attention than it usually receives" (I, 134), but baffles him with the statement that "past scholars have been emphatic in their denial that Dekker['s] . . . play owes anything to Phillip's comedy" (I, 139). Hoy's comment that it is "a unique witness to what the preceding generation had found in the story, and to the conventions available to a dramatist of that generation for putting the story on the stage," seems to a point irrelevant. Nevertheless, the editor deftly uses the earlier play and the English tradition to demonstrate the contribution which Dekker and his collaborators made in their version of the increasingly familiar story. In later volumes the treatment of sources is less expansive and consequently less distracting to the reader. Indeed, with the small reservation mentioned above, Hoy's introductions must be commended for their comprehensive command of oftentimes complicated issues. The discussion of *Satiromastix* and the war of the theaters is particularly lucid and illuminating.

The commentaries draw extensively on earlier editions of Dekker's works and on standard sources for the study of English life, lore, and language, such as Cotgrave's *Dictionary* (1611), Florio's *World of Words* (1598), Halliwell's *Dictionary of Archaic and Provincial Words* (1847; rpt. 1924), Hazlitt's *Popular Antiquities* (1870), Nares's *Glossary* (1822), *Shakespeare's England* (1916), Skeat and Mayhew's *Glossary* (1914), Stow's *Survey* (ed. 1908), Sugden's *Topographical Dictionary* (1925), Tilley's *Proverbs* (1966), and Wright's *Dialect Dictionary* (1898–1905). Comparison of these volumes with single-text editions of individual plays is greatly to Hoy's benefit; his notes are precise and supply more information, without redundance. (Perhaps I might note that there is a typographical derangement affecting *Westward Ho* II.i.180 at III, 187.) Occasionally the editor was obliged to go beyond a concise gloss. A good example is the note to V.iii.88–90 of *The Welsh Embassador*. (Why does only this play have an old-spelling title?) The line is an allusion to the old St. Paul's Cathedral, which lacked a steeple from 1561. Hoy shows that the passage supports F. D. Hoeniger's defense of the authenticity of Dekker's poem "Paul his temple triumphant" against the charge that it was a Collier forgery: "Dekker's presumptive poem here [lines 215–20 of Hoeniger's text] echoes an image that is only to be found elsewhere in the Dekker canon in a work that Collier did not know" (IV, 165). Doubtless there are other nuggets of scholarship in the notes awaiting readers equipped to recognize them and assiduous enough to seek them out.

In volume IV occurs the "Index to the Commentary" which Hoy is at pains to explain "should not be regarded as a concordance" (IV, 169). Unfortunately, it is described as such in the publisher's brochure, which is more widely circulated than these volumes. The index contains references to the places in the separate commentaries, by act, scene, and line numbers, where the words and phrases are discussed; it is "an index to the vocabulary of Dekker's dramatic works." To this extent the index is both necessary and valuable. The casual user must remember that the entry words are in the old spelling and that references between variant spellings (e.g., *bombast* and *bumbast*) are not given. He must also be aware of what forms are used in Dekker; *quorum* is not listed nor is *corum,* but *in corum* and *Coram* are. There are cross-references between the two notes but not, in the index, between the often confused terms themselves. More greatly to the detriment of the best use of these volumes is the exclusion of index entries for "such matters as historical sources, or social and political allusions" mentioned in the commentaries—which is serious enough—and in the introductions. In this respect Hoy's volumes are less useful than McKerrow, Herford and Simpson, and Edwards and Gibson. It is hard to understand how an editor who must have consulted those indexes with advantage to his researches would not have seen the necessity of detailed indexes to his own work.

So much for the organization of Hoy's volumes. Despite his reluctance to deprive the editor of the respectful attention his labors so richly deserve, a reviewer cannot ignore the question of the relationship between Hoy's work and Bowers's, that is, between the commentaries and the critical edition to which they belong. One's admiration for Hoy's Bowers's Dekker is substantially unaffected by the fairly minor criticisms made so far. After all, when there is no fundamental weakness in the middle, one can only skirmish on the peripheries, and a few paltry ranging shots do no serious harm. On the other hand, when one turns attention to the whole work, the critical annotated edition of Dekker's plays, certain stresses and flaws may be detected. The most remarkable of these is the matter of the canon.

Fredson Bowers accepted E. K. Chambers's canon of Dekker's plays from *The Elizabethan and Jacobean Stage* (III, 289–

305) as guide to his endeavors, but he wrote after publication of his first volume, "It seemed to me appropriate for the major decision about the Dekker canon to come from the author of the supplementary volume since the defence of the selection would fall on him."[1] At that time he was inclined to favor inclusion of *The Welsh Embassador, The Noble Soldier, Lust's Dominion,* and *Blurt Master Constable* as "doubtful" plays in the fourth and last volume. In the event, all but the last were edited. *Blurt Master Constable* lacked external evidence of Dekker's authorship, and the textual editor was unwilling "to add [the play] on his own authority to the generally established Dekker canon." *Blurt,* together with *The Family of Love,* seemed "to belong most appropriately in the Middleton canon."[2] Arthur Brown, reviewing volume four in 1962, raised an important issue: "Will he be prevailed upon, one wonders, to edit further plays if his colleague responsible for the more critical material (and originally, one understands, responsible for questions of canon—he seems to have deserted Bowers on this matter!) decides that there are stylistic grounds for including them?"[3] The editors' responses appear to be negative. Hoy writes in a footnote that, to the pieces collected by Bowers, he "would add only the comedy of *Blurt, Master Constable* . . . [which] is certainly Dekker's in part, and probably is entirely his" (I,viii). This comment is amplified in the following volume, where he refers to "the impressive statistical analysis of the play's vocabulary in David J. Lake's *The Canon of Middleton's Plays"* published in 1975. Lake, who brought forward two pieces of external evidence of Dekker's authorship which were published too late to influence Bowers, concluded that "the evidence for Middleton is too weak to be relied on, and, unless and until more is discovered, we should assume that *Blurt* is an unaided play by Dekker."[4] So much for the obligation of the editors of Middleton to include the play in the edition currently going forward for the Clarendon Press. *Blurt* is not listed in the abbreviations of Dekker's dramatic works and is rarely mentioned in the commentaries. Occasionally—as with the reading *ptrooh* for instance—an unusual expression in Dekker's plays is noted as occurring also in *Blurt.*

The editor is careful to establish that the introductions, notes, and commentaries accompany the texts included in Bowers's edition, but in the preface which precedes all four volumes he equates those "twenty-five pieces" with "the canon of Dekker's *Dramatic Works*." In effect the responsibility which the textual editor assigned to his collaborator in matters of canon has not been discharged. Hoy's volumes contain no general discussion of Dekker's canon, and the variety of plays which have been associated with his name are mentioned, if at all (the lack of general index inhibits precision), only in passing in the introductions to the individual plays. Whether the textual editor was unwilling or unable to return to his editorial task or the editor of the commentary was neglectful of his is pointless to inquire. The fact is that the present eight volumes contain neither an investigation of the Dekker canon—which seems to remain where Chambers left it in 1923—nor of the canon of Dekker's dramatic works.

Blurt Master Constable is not the only important omission. Apparently unknown to Chambers or considered on account of its date beyond the scope of his investigation, a scribal transcript, *The Telltale,* is Dulwich College MS. xx; there is widespread agreement at least that the play was composed during the period of Dekker's connection with the theater. The manuscript was edited for the Malone Society by R. A. Foakes and J. C. Gibson in 1960. Shortly afterward, when the last volume of Bowers's Dekker was published, Arthur Freeman concluded that the play was "chiefly, if not entirely" the work of Dekker.[5] G. R. Price concurred: "This play is surely Dekker's."[6] So far as I can determine, *The Telltale* is not even mentioned in Hoy's work. There can be no two scholars better equipped than Freeman and Price to settle the claims of *The Telltale* for inclusion in Dekker's canon, yet, apparently because the publication of the established text is being allowed to freeze the canon where it was in 1923, this play, and *Blurt Master Constable,* are left in canonical limbo.

There are oddities surrounding another manuscript text, *The Welsh Embassador,* which was printed in Volume IV of Bowers's edition. The manuscript may be consulted in the Cardiff

Public Library by those with energy to seek it out: there is no evidence, for example, that Greg saw it when he wrote his magisterial *Dramatic Documents from the Elizabethan Playhouses* (1931). The editor of the Malone Society edition of 1920 seems, from his work there, to have been selected largely on account of his proximity to the library; and Bowers was obliged to print an appendix listing a substantial number of errors in the Malone edition which he had detected by comparing the reprint with photographs of the manuscript.[7] Since one cannot expect a definitive critical edition of a manuscript to be established from photographs, even with the aid of a manifestly defective diplomatic reprint, a reader will consult Hoy's commentary interested to learn whether he has supplemented the earlier work with independent examination of the manuscript. (The point is not spurious. A significant benefit from Hoy's volumes is his revision of readings admitted to the text in the first four volumes.) The evidence is ambiguous. At II.ii.131 Bowers's misprint of "scramblinge" for MS. "scamblinge" was probably detected when the editor attempted to gloss it; the correct reading was available in the Malone Society edition. At V.iii.41, where Hoy corrects Bowers's expansion of the Malone Society reading of "A‹s" from "Astynanax" to "Ascanius," he comments that the following *s* is no longer legible. My xerox copy seems to show the descender of the long *s* still, possibly the only part of the character which existed when the MSR was prepared, as the editor's caret suggests.[8]

Many reviewers of Bowers's volumes mentioned the difficulty of emending the text from consideration of the "physical evidence of the printed book together with the paleographical." Philip Edwards wrote: "Many of the textual notes, refusing to accept a previous emendation, are really part of an otherwise non-existent commentary, for they are essentially elucidations of difficult passages. On the other hand, the textual note emending *vāpres* to *vampies* (*Shoemakers' Holiday*, IV.i.12) dissolves in a cloud of mystery because no explanation of the word is given."[9] Naturally Hoy provides support for many of Bowers's emendations from passages in other Dekker works, and it should be cause of great satisfaction to Bowers that his text has survived the most rigorous scrutiny relatively unscathed. The editor of the commentary, who was trained in bibliographical studies by Bowers himself, justifiably argues against unnecessary emendation in nine places, sometimes proposing an emendation of his own.[10] One instance of unnecessary emendation occurs at *The Honest Whore, Part I,* II.i.355, where Bowers rejected Dyce's "Back-door'd," meaning sly or devious for Qq "Blacke-doord" in favor of his "Blacke-beard [Italian]." Hoy devotes nearly three pages to convincing the reader that Dyce's emendation was correct even if his interpretation of the expression was wrong; it seems that seventeenth-century Italians shared the reputation of the Greeks for "arsy varsy" (*Northward Ho,* IV.i.159) pleasures. On the three occasions when Hoy proposes a new emendation, his arguments have an authority and persuasiveness that only an editor totally immersed in his author's works can achieve.

Furthermore, Hoy supplies a variety of materials bearing on the textual history of Dekker's plays which are not found in Bowers's volumes. Edward Pudsey's commonplace book (Bodleian Library MS. Eng. poet. d.3) contains quotations from a number of plays acted around 1600, including *Satiromastix* and *I Honest Whore;* they are mentioned by Bowers. Hoy also gives, for instance, collations of the variants between the 1641 Q and British Library MS. Lansdowne 725 of John Day's *The Parliament of Bees* which contributes to *The Wonder of a Kingdom* (III:307–13) and *The Noble Spanish Soldier* (IV:132–36), an appendix of passages duplicated in *The Noble Spanish Soldier* and *The Welsh Embassador* (IV:167–68), and a collation of the text of the poem at *N.S.S.* I.ii.1–17 with Bodleian Library MS. Rawl. poet. 196. The upshot is (if it needs to be said) that even if one's first concern is with Dekker's text, attention cannot be confined to Bowers's volumes.

The simple conclusion is that *The Dramatic Works of Thomas Dekker* would be a better edition had the editors worked together on it instead of consecutively, as seems to have happened, or had either editor undertaken the whole task alone. Each was well qualified to assume the heavy burden. That has not occurred. Nevertheless, students have ample cause to rejoice in Cyrus Hoy's accomplishment; it not only completes at last the original design but displays judicious scholarship at its highest level.

Notes

1. Bowers, "The Cambridge Edition of Dekker," *The Library*, ser. 5, 10 (1955), 131.

2. Bowers, *The Dramatic Works of Thomas Dekker*, vol. IV (Cambridge: Cambridge Univ. Press, 1961), p. vii.

3. Brown, *The Library*, ser. 5, 17 (1962), 322. The unsatisfactory division of responsibility for the canon was also noted by Philip Edwards in *Modern Language Review*, 58 (1961), 96.

4. Lake, *The Canon of Thomas Middleton's Plays: Internal Evidence for the Major Problems of Authorship* (Cambridge: Cambridge Univ. Press, 1975), p. 89.

5. Freeman, "The Authorship of *The Telltale*," *JEGP*, 62 (1963), 288–92.

6. Price, *Thomas Dekker* (New York: Twayne, 1969), p. 175.

7. Bowers, "Errors in the Malone Society Reprint," *Dramatic Works*, Vol. IV, pp. 403–4.

8. I have checked Bowers's list against the manuscript; the following minor corrections should be made: II.i.67, for "c‹arringe" read "car‹ryinge"; II.i.142, for "(572)" read "(573)"; II.ii.SD, add "(774)"; III.ii.36, for "Wincheste" read "winchester" not "Winchestr," as in Bowers; IV.i.127, add "And] and (1439); ms. &"; IV.ii.33, the MSR reading is correct; IV.ii.54, the MSR reading is correct; V.ii.88, the MSR reading is correct.

9. C. T. Prouty, *MLN*, 71 (1956), 45; Edwards, *MLR*, 49 (1954), 498; see also J. R. Brown, *RES*, 14 (1961), 84. "Vampies," Hoy reveals, is "the forepart or upper leather of a boot or shoe" (I:54).

10. Hoy argues against emendation of the text at *O.F.* II.i.106; *P.G.* IV.i.124; *1H.W.* II.i.355; *W.H.* IV.ii.405; *N.H.* V.i.308–9; *V.M* II.i.24; *W. of E.* II.i.259, II.ii.126–7, and *W.E.* V.iii.41. He corrects Bowers's retention of original mis-

prints at *Sat.* II.i.233, IV.i.117, *1H.W.* I.i.27, and notes omissions, misprints and misnumeration in Bowers at *S.H.* III.ii.45, IV.iv.110–11, V.ii.167, V.v.173–7; *O.F.* Persons, II.ii.56; *2H.W.* II.ii.78; *W.H.* V.i.163–4, V.iv.246–7; *N.H.*. II.i.42, V.i.477.1–3; *R.G.* V.ii.26.1; *V.M.* I.i.130, II.ii.119; II.ii.42; *S.D.* II.i.82, II.i.90.1; *W.E.* II.ii.131.

Tennyson and the Histories of Criticism

Jerome J. McGann

The Letters of Alfred Lord Tennyson, Cecil Y. Lang and Edgar F. Shannon, Jr., eds., Cambridge: Harvard University Press, 1981. xxxviii, 366 pp.

The Letters of Edward FitzGerald, Alfred McKinley Terhune and Annabelle Burdick Terhune, eds., Princeton: Princeton University Press, 1980. Vol. I, 1x, 712 pp. Vol. II, xxxii, 629 pp. Vol. III, xxxiv, 753 pp. Vol. IV, xxviii, 653 pp.

The Letters of Arthur Henry Hallam, Jack Kolb, ed., Columbus: Ohio State University Press, 1981. xxx, 841 pp.

Robert Bernard Martin. *Tennyson: The Unquiet Heart.* Oxford: Clarendon Press, 1980. xii, 643 pp.

Peter Allen. *The Cambridge Apostles: The Early Years.* Cambridge: Cambridge University Press, 1978. x, 266 pp.

June Steffensen Hagen. *Tennyson and His Publishers.* University Park, Pa.: Pennsylvania State University Press, 1979. xxi, 233 pp.

Henry Kozicki. *Tennyson and Clio: History in the Major Poems.* Baltimore: Johns Hopkins University Press, 1979. xvii, 185 pp.

Robert Pattison. *Tennyson and Tradition.* Cambridge: Harvard University Press, 1979. 178 pp.

In his introduction to *The Letters of Arthur Henry Hallam* Jack Kolb says that *In Memoriam* "is not merely the most personal elegy in English, it is also the only major work in the genre in which specific details of its subject's life and character enter so largely into the process of the poem" (p. 34). This remark, which seems to me quite correct, points to the fundamental reason we wish to have a work such as the one that Kolb has produced. Hallam's letters help us to recover the significance of important details in Tennyson's poetry. They illuminate the aesthetic function of specific references and local fact. From our removed historical vantage, they supply the deficiencies which have developed through a lapse of time and shifts in cultural views.

Kolb's observation underscores the general critical significance that biographical and historical works have for poetry, including the documentary materials which these works depend upon and reproduce. We measure the value of such works, first, by the accuracy of what they set out to do. Kolb's edition, for example, is a good one: its texts are thorough and correct, and its annotations are useful and dependable. The editions of the Tennyson and FitzGerald correspondences can be relied upon as well, both for their texts and their editorial materials. Indeed, the edition of Tennyson's letters produced by Cecil Y. Lang and Edgar F. Shannon, Jr., is something like a model of accuracy and learning, and the edition of the FitzGerald letters is only slightly less praiseworthy. Considered just as letters, and for their historical significance, the FitzGerald correspondence is far the most important and interesting of these three collections. But considered as an edition, the Lang and Shannon work stands alone.[1]

Biographies and related works (like June Steffensen Hagen's *Tennyson and His Publishers*) are necessarily obliged to deliver their material through an interpreting narrative medium, but they too will and should be initially weighed in a balance that measures for accuracy. Robert Martin's biography is an excellent, in many ways a splendid, work—so much so, in fact, that one wishes to honor it with a few corrective annotations. Perhaps most important involves the matter of how much money FitzGerald loaned to Tennyson. Martin's biography deals with Tennyson's finances in important and illuminating ways, so that one wishes he had inquired more closely into the old story that

Tennyson and the Histories of Criticism 221

FitzGerald had loaned Tennyson £ 300 "for many years in Tennyson's poor days." A newly published letter from Fitz-Gerald to Tennyson (2 July 1835) suggests that the story is not true, and that the actual amount of the loan was "some ten to twelve pounds" on "occasion."[2] Another old story has it that the queen called on Tennyson in the summer of 1847. Martin accepts this account, but the fact is that Tennyson was on a water cure at the time of the alleged meeting and could not have seen her.

I shall instance one final, perhaps less important, matter here since it bears upon a subject I shall be taking up later in some detail: the circumstances surrounding "The Charge of the Light Brigade." Martin says that the poem was based upon an account of the charge which Tennyson read in the *Times* of 14 November 1854 in which the phrase "a hideous blunder" appeared; and, furthermore, that Tennyson wrote the poem on 2 December and sent it off to John Forster for printing in *The Examiner*. This account is once again based upon certain earlier accounts, on the one hand, and certain documentary evidence on the other—the most important of which are the notoriously problematic *Memoir* and the equally problematic *Journal* of Emily Tennyson. But there is no question that the account which Tennyson read was in the 13 November *Times* (the leader in the 14 November issue is very different, though equally interesting) and that the poem itself was written and sent to Forster on 6 December.[3] Hagen's book on Tennyson's publishing career produces an even more garbled account of these events; indeed, her book is excessively dependent for all its material, not on an examination of original documents, but on secondary and hand-me-down narratives. Consequently, her entire project—which seems to me of central importance for the study of Tennyson's poetry—suffers in her treatment from its willingness to depend upon unreliable guides.

An accurate transmission of facts is a sine qua non of criticism and scholarship, and a careful scholarly elucidation of obscure facts is only slightly less fundamental. All scholars accept these obligations, of course, though I am not entirely sure that they all understand equally well how such a concern for referential fact relates to the aesthetic operation of works of art, and hence to the pursuits and methodologies of literary criticism. I shall try to demonstrate these relationships at a later point in this essay through a detailed examination of "The Charge of the Light Brigade." Before we can turn to this example, however, we must first reflect on some other matters which bear upon the subject of poetry, specific poems, and the historical contexts that help to generate and support them.

I shall begin with a quotation from the introduction to Henry Kozicki's recent book *Tennyson and Clio,* a work that sets out to define Tennyson's "philosophy of history" and explore its poetic operations:

> The "meaning and purpose" of the past cannot obtain without both a conceptual system and intense convictions. And we cannot interpret properly a poem in which we deem Clio's influence operational unless we are able to identify both idea and emotion. For example, the presence of the notion of historical cycles does not bring meaning to a poem unless we can discover what the poet felt about that notion. The intellectual order that is a philosophy of history in Tennyson's major poems is, thus, an inextricable compound of concepts and convictions that must be determined in its totality, as a lifelong development, before it may be used as a sounding board to enhance any note elicited from a particular poem. Lest this be taken as an intentionalist intent (and a disregard of everything we have learned from the new criticism) I can only say, with Brooks, that "my basic concern has been to read the poem," but to note that, in order to do this, the critic must select "from scholarship those things which will help him understand the poem *qua* poem." [p. xii]

This is a promising set of remarks, for Kozicki seems to understand the relationships that function between specific poems and their ideological materials. Facts, whether referential or ideational, are always interpreted facts, and in a poetical context the ideological formatting assumes a paramount importance. This happens because the concrete utterances of poems incorporate not merely linguistic terms and their referential "objects," but a whole network of what has been called, at various times, "belief" (Coleridge), "ideology" (Marx), "social evaluation" (Bakhtin). According to a classic twentieth-century formulation: "The material of poetry is not language understood as the aggregate or system of linguistic possibilities (phonetic, grammatical, lexical). The poet does not select linguistic forms, but rather the evaluations posited in them. All the linguistic characteristics of the word that remain after the abstraction of these evaluations are not only unable to be the material of poetry, but cannot even be examples of grammar. For instance, a linguistic example is a conditional utterance: a pure linguistic form only lends itself to symbolic designation. A linguistic form is only real in the concrete speech performance, in the social utterance."[4]

Kozicki's work shows that he understands these matters only in a superficial way. For example, when he discusses the topic of the English Great House as it appears in Tennyson's work (pp. 56 ff.), he is unable to make critical distinctions between Gothic and neo-Gothic, or between the English Great House (which is one thing) and certain Victorian ideas about the English Great House (which are quite another matter). Kozicki sees these distinctions, it seems to me, but he does not understand them critically.

The weakness of his treatment—the sources of its failure as criticism—emerges clearly when we turn to Robert Martin's biography, where the topic of Tennyson's lifelong obsession with the English Great House is a recurrent one. Martin's treatment of this subject—like his treatment of Tennyson's relations with women—is good because he sees the fundamental contradictions that support Tennyson's attitudes. These contradictions are epitomized in Tennyson's early (and lifelong) contempt for his uncle Charles Tennyson d'Eyncourt, whose deep passion for the past appeared as an obsession with all the accoutrements of lineage and pedigree, as well as his single-minded commitment to the project of rebuilding Bayons Manor into the very image of his idea of the English Great House. Many of the things Tennyson most heartily despised in his uncle were essential features of his own central ideas and embedded attitudes.

Kozicki is not aware of these contradictions—many others could be instanced here—because he approaches Tennyson's "philosophy of history" in an uncritical fashion and spirit. The problem appears early in his work and operates throughout. Speaking of Tennyson's juvenilia, for example, Kozicki argues that their treatment of their subjects is not "tendentious" but "merely accurate" (p. 11). This remark might seem an odd one if we recall Kozicki's explicit comments on ideology in poetical works (some of which I have quoted above). But the remark explains itself in its immediate context, where Kozicki also says:

In these early poems, Tennyson may be indicating that for him pageantry, high passion, and monumentality possess the brightest colors on the literary canvas. But he also takes pride in an exact knowledge of his subject matter and, further, looks without squeamishness or illusions upon the ordained ways of the world (unless Christian orthodoxy is taken for illusion). He wants to understand history. And in the understanding, as it is revealed in these early poems, we may see the basic characteristics of Tennyson's philosophy of history. A divinity of some sort is working out its nature in history. History is occurring in apocalyptic cycles. The hero, either as individual or as collective spirit, somehow is a "free" agent of this divinity. [p. 11]

Kozicki's parenthetical observation is the giveaway: that is, we are dealing with a critic who shares Tennyson's views on these matters, whose own ideology (we must assume) merges with Tennyson's. Kozicki does not—apparently cannot—seriously entertain the idea that "Christian orthodoxy" might well embody a set of historic (and historical) illusions, or that Tennyson's so-called "philosophy of history" is actually a theology of history, and hence—to a non-Christian or humanist intelligence—necessarily illusive and illusory.

The ideology which Kozicki observes in Tennyson's poems is one of the subjects that appear throughout Peter Allen's *The Cambridge Apostles: The Early Years*. This excellent book describes the social and intellectual context in which Tennyson and his poetry were so deeply and reciprocally involved. The "philosophy of history" which Kozicki takes as his subject is traced

Tennyson and the Histories of Criticism 225

through its nineteenth-century development—which is to say, is traced from its (English) *fons* in the mind of Coleridge through its subsequent transformations and modifications in the work of various Apostles. Unlike Kozicki, however, Allen maintains his critical distance from his subject.

This comparison between Kozicki and Allen is not entirely fair, however, because Allen is not directly concerned with Tennyson's poems, whereas the poetry is the final point of reference for Kozicki's ideational discussions. A thorough criticism of poetry and poems must negotiate a difficult arrangement with its subject: on the one hand, it must remain sufficiently disinterested to see the work "as in itself it really is"; on the other, it must, like the poet, "bring the whole soul of man into activity." Poems are the foci of significant acts of social evaluation and human experience, and one of the central elements in a poem's focus is the reader of the poem (both original and subsequent). Kozicki reads Tennyson ideologically, which is as it should be. The weakness of his critical discussion is that his ideological position permits him no critical vantage on his subject matter. He cannot see the contradictions in Tennyson's poetry; by the same token, he cannot see that these contradictions are precisely the source of Tennyson's poetical strengths; and, finally, because Tennyson's work does not stand at a critical distance from his own ideas and ideologies, Kozicki's readings never have to bear the illuminating critique which Tennyson's (alien) views might have brought to light.

At this point one might reasonably object on the grounds that Tennyson's poetry does not involve contradictions in any ultimate way, that it is not a field in which tensions are promoted and maintained. In his *Tennyson and Tradition,* Robert Pattison says of *In Memoriam* that it "is a poem of syntheses [where] pagan and Christian myth [are] united in a single sense" (p. 110). In this view Pattison stands with Kozicki and almost all Tennyson commentators, who in fact do no more than reproduce the ideological stance which *In Memoriam* itself is bent upon promoting. (Thus Kozicki denigrates "Locksley Hall" as a poem full of "contradictions," whereas *In Memoriam*—a poem of resolutions and processive syntheses—is pronounced a success.)

That Tennyson's poetry aimed for and in large measure achieved a poetic of syntheses and resolutions cannot really be doubted. The history of his relations with the publishing institutions of his day, including his deep concern for and interest in the views of his readers and reviewers, bears eloquent testimony to the presence of this factor in his work. What appears in the verse as poetic theme and artistic form is matched, in the social arena of Tennyson's work, as a concern to reach as large an audience as possible—to forge a sympathetic contact with the widest possible range of Victorian society, with the greatest possible number of its class and interest groups. Tennyson's habits of composition, revision, and publication all testify to his interest in his audiences and their opinions. Indeed, many twentieth-century commentators have deplored this aspect of Tennyson's poetical work as a sign that he sacrificed his artistic integrity and authenticity in the pursuit of popularity.

I shall set aside for the moment any judgment on this matter and merely observe that Tennyson's verse style and form exhibit a genuine congruence and symmetry with his methods of production. Indeed, his *symboliste* poetical methods, which have so preoccupied the attention of recent criticism, involve a strategy whereby the poet is able to be, as it were, all things to all men. This is a strategy which traces its source to the philosophical, aesthetic, and theological ideas of S. T. Coleridge, whose impact in these areas, during the Victorian period, was profound— and not least profound on the Apostles. Tennyson's famous remarks, recorded in the *Memoir*, on the *symboliste*-allegorical method of his poetry, incorporate a rather clumsily expressed Coleridgean set of ideas:

"There is an allegorical or perhaps rather a parabolic drift in the poem." "Of course Camelot for instance, a city of shadowy palaces, is everywhere symbolic of the gradual growth of human beliefs and institutions, and of the spiritual development of man. Yet there is no single fact or incident in the 'Idylls,' however seemingly mystical, which cannot be explained as without any mystery or allegory whatever." The Bishop of Ripon (Boyd Carpenter) once asked him whether they were right who interpreted the three Queens, who accompanied King Arthur on his last voyage, as Faith, Hope and Charity. He answered: "They are right, and they are not right. They mean that and they do not. They are three of the noblest of women. They are also those three Graces, but they are much more. I hate to be tied down to say, '*This* means *that*,' because the thought within the image is much more than any one interpretation."

As for the many meanings of the poem my father would affirm, "Poetry is like shot-silk with many glancing colours. Every reader must find his own interpretation according to his ability, and according to his sympathy with the poet." The general drift of the "Idylls" is clear enough. "The whole," he said, "is the dream of man coming into practical life and ruined by one sin. Birth is a mystery and death is a mystery, and in the midst lies the tableland of life, and its struggles and performances. It is not the history of one man or of one generation but of a whole cycle of generations."[5]

Tennyson worked hard to fashion a poetic vehicle which was not merely designed to accommodate different views and alternate readings but which actively anticipated these differences—which (as it were) called out to them and offered Victorian readers a place where they would find their differences reconciled. The whole project of *The Princess* illustrates Tennyson's aesthetic of reconciliations. It is a "medley" of social, political, and sexual differentials that are held together in an equally heterogeneous poetical form. The accommodations which the poem makes—indeed, the ideology of accommodations which it promotes—are notably epitomized in the conclusion. Here Tennyson offers a series of tableaux marked by differences and differentials which are not characterized by serious strife or disruptions. More than anything else the conclusion manages an arrangement of variegated detail and accommodations of various people.

This ideology enters the style of Tennyson's poetry as a strategy of those unmistakable and Tennysonian ambiguities. *In Memoriam* offers a host of examples. The simplest type centers in Tennyson's use of the pun and associated forms of word play; for example, in Section 66:

> "The shade by which my life was crost,
> Which makes a desert in the mind,

Has made me kindly with my kind,
And like to him whose sight is lost.

The stanza opens with a pun on the word "shade" and closes with a word play in the final line whereby the referent of the pronoun "him" is rendered ambiguous. The latter effect requires the following stanzas to work itself out, but the point can be simply stated: Tennyson likens himself to "him whose sight is lost," but that phrase, in the context of the section as a whole, is so "worked" as to suggest a reference to Hallam. This small poetical event signals one of the poem's largest general ideas—that Hallam and Tennyson are "incorporate" (see Section 2, line 16). This is a poetical term of some importance in Tennyson's poem, and another example of a Tennysonian pun: that is to say, it is a word that suggests almost diametric opposites—both incorporeality, on the one hand, and physical embodiment on the other. Tennyson manages to suggest through this word that he and his dead friend become at once two in one flesh as well as two in one spirit.[6]

In such verse the reader finds himself encouraged to read in many different ways, for many different meanings. "Every reader must find his own interpretation according to his ability"; which is also to say that the poetry believes itself able to anticipate those multifarious readings and readers, believes itself ready to accommodate not so much all *levels* of reading as all the interests and ideologies of its readers. Many of Tennyson's critics, and not least of all his recent critics, have devoted their attention to the study of these symbolic effects, and to the thematized forms which Tennyson's symbolic style was developed to support. Pattison's book on Tennyson's employment of the idyl is a good case in point. The strengths of this book rest in its accurate presentation of the tradition of the idyl, on the one hand, and in its careful descriptions of Tennyson's special idyllic employments on the other. The book's weakness lies in its uncritical methods of examination. Pattison's reading of *In Memoriam* thematicizes the work as a poem of evolutionary syntheses, and his discussion of *The Idylls of the King* as a poem of "process" follows similar lines. Form and style in both poems combine into a vision of "a new, unified relation expressing the advance of civilization" (p. 151). This presentation is of course accurate enough, so far as it goes, but it does not go nearly far enough. Pattison's entire book offers these ideas not merely as Tennyson's ideology but as the triumph of Tennyson's poetic discourse—ideas we are expected to honor as if they offered us some elemental and unambiguous truth, some final solution (as it were) of the conflicts and contradictions which the poetry brings into focus.[7]

This is not the way to approach the statements and themes of a poetical work. Like matters of referential fact, ideas operate in a poetical discourse as historically specific elements of the artistic event. The "theme" of "universal process" in Tennyson's poetry (see Pattison, pp. 135–36) is not a transcendental category or idea, it is a specifically Victorianized form of thought that operates in Tennyson's work in a specifically Victorian way (it is quite different from a Romantic concept of "universal process," which is its most immediate source). More particularly, ideas enter a poetical medium as interpreted and polemicized ideas, as ideas that carry with them, into the poetry, various specific kinds of emotional attitudes and social valuations. This characteristic of the statement-level of all poetical works is crucial to bear in mind, for two reasons. In the first place, it is the source and ground of all the "ambiguities" and "contradictions" which poems are known to generate and promote. In the second place, it locates the gulf that eventually separates the author from the reader, that allows the reader to enter the poet's world *from a distance,* at a point of difference that encourages both sympathy and judgment.

Of course Tennyson's poetry explicitly sets out to short-circuit such differentials, to produce a poetry that builds a grammar of assent in order to solicit various agreements. His work is, in this respect, quite unlike (for example) the work of Blake or Byron. The latter was, by his own admission and will, "born for opposition," and his poetry was deliberately fashioned as a sign of contradiction. Blake's goals were somewhat different, but finally analogous. In *The Marriage of Heaven and Hell,* Blake allied himself with the Jesus who came not to bring peace, but a sword (Plate 17), and he explicitly wrote under the motto:

"Opposition is true Friendship" (Plate 20). Or, as he observed of those two "classes of men," the Prolific and the Devourer: "These two classes of men are always upon earth, & they should be enemies: whoever seeks to reconcile them seeks to destroy existence."

Needless to say, these are not Tennysonian ideas and attitudes. Where Blake and Byron seek to promote contradiction and conflict, Tennyson will always be aiming for reconciliations and syntheses. Nevertheless, because human experience in its historical passage is at all points marked by struggles, by blindness and self-deception, by contradictions—as well as by the continual effort to deal with these matters, to overcome whatever adversative forces one meets with; because this is so, and because poetry's subject is human experience in time, poetry inevitably reproduces the conflicts and contradictions which it is itself seeking to deal with, and even perhaps seeking to resolve. Tennyson's syntheses and resolutions are part of his subject matter, part of his Victorian materials; they are not the "answer" to the issues raised by his poetry, they are part of the problem—and, in a way, the most crucial part of the problem for this reason: that they bring into sharpest relief the conflicts and contradictions which the poetry has dared to call forth. At the heart of Tennyson's creative work lie a quest and polemic for a certain ideology whose subject is society and whose forms of thought are aristocratic, evolutionist, and synthetic. But precisely because this *is* an ideology, it remains subject to those (self-generated and unapparent) limitations which bring into focus the social and psychological conflicts which the poetry struggles with, and is itself a part of.

The ideological elements that operate in poems are not, however, an *aesthetic* problem for the works. Ideology functions in poetry not as generalized idea, abstract thought, reified concept, but as a specific and historically concrete manifestation of such things. Poetry, like all art products, can only exist in a medium of uniqueness. Its value lies in the sharp edge of its particularity, in its ability to evoke the sense of a complete human world by focussing upon some salient and specific matters of time, place, and circumstance. Like the particular referential elements in poems—the so-called historical facts which critics and editors will gloss for later readers—ideology in poems is a matrix of historical particularities: in this case, the particularities of belief and commitment, ideas written in a grammar of needs, feelings, and attitudes.

Ideology is not an *aesthetic* problem for poems, it is a *critical* problem. The fundamental uniqueness of a poetical work is threatened not by its own ideological commitments but by the ideological structures of literary criticism—and most particularly by the ahistorical structures of interpretation that have dominated criticism for the past fifty years. The threat arises because literary works are *parole* rather than *langue* structures. In contrast to art or music criticism, then, the critical medium which studies literary works employs (ideological) forms which are structurally congruent with the forms of literary works themselves. This structural congruence frequently betrays criticism into that characteristic pitfall of interpretive methods: the mirroring of the object of interest, the re-presentation of the work of art. As a consequence, the unique and particular work comes to us in a more generalized form of thought, and we are often seduced into taking the reflection of the work for the thing itself. This is the process by which contemporary culture subjects literary works to an ideological consumption. Poems are made to speak what the consciousness industries of the moment desire them to say. And one of the things such industries (principally, the academic industry) most want to find in the poetry of the past, in the Great Tradition of art which we inherit, is a Truth (or Truths) that may set one free (that has set one free, and that may be counted on to set one free again and again).

An authentic criticism must vigorously oppose these spurious forms which criticism itself sometimes assumes. The case of Tennyson is merely symptomatic—and an opportunity. The study of Tennyson's poetry must begin and conclude in a field of historical particulars. To do so requires, of course, that we be able to elucidate the specific sociohistorical contexts of the originary works themselves. However, because those works are at all points mediated in time by a series of readers and audiences, we cannot make contact with the originary works except through the social mediations and mediators which have handed them over to us. Consequently, before I turn to a specific Tennysonian text, I want to fill out the reception history which stands behind his work and which has so powerfully affected contemporary critical attitudes.

The first two reviews of Tennyson's poetry—W. J. Fox's in the *Westminster*, and Arthur Henry Hallam's in *The Englishman's Magazine*—are remarkable in several ways.[8] Both are brilliant assessments, and both introduced Tennyson to the reading public in highly laudatory terms. In addition, although Fox and Hallam had only Tennyson's early volume, *Poems, Chiefly Lyrical* (1830), to comment upon, their views can now be seen, from our privileged historical vantage, to have set the terms for the entire subsequent history of Tennyson criticism and interpretation.

Fox, a radical and a utilitarian, opened his review with a lengthy excursus on the moral and philosophical powers of poetry. "Why is Shakespeare the greatest of poets?" Fox rhetorically asked. His answer was not long in coming, nor any surprise: "Because he was the greatest of philosophers.... Extent of observation, accuracy of thought, and depth of reflection, were the qualities which won the prize of sovereignty for his imagination." And as for Tennyson's verse? "Here is a little book ... which shall beautifully illustrate our speculations, and convincingly prove their soundness." Fox speaks for a whole tradition of Tennyson readers that extends from his early admirers among the Cambridge Apostles to several later generations of (predominantly) Victorian readers, including that dear and honored lady Queen Victoria herself. In our own day this tradition has suffered an eclipse, though it preserves its authority in a variety of quarters which include such notable commentators as G. M. Young, Jerome Buckley, and A. J. Carr.

Hallam, a Cambridge Apostle himself, was a most reflective and philosophical young man with all the moral earnestness one could hope to find, even in a Victorian. His notice of Tennyson's early poems also opens with a long excursus on the general grounds of his criticism; but, unlike Fox, Hallam argues for a sensational and aesthetic view of art. "It is not true," Hallam says, "that the highest species of poetry is the reflective: it is a gross fallacy, that, because certain opinions are acute or profound, the expression of them by the imagination must be eminently beautiful. Whenever the mind of the artist suffers itself to be occupied, during its periods of creation, by any other predominant motive than the desire of beauty, the result is false in art." His position is largely an extreme statement of views developed by Coleridge and extrapolated by the chief ideologues among the Apostles. Coleridge never separated the two traditional functions of poetry—to please and to instruct—so radically as Hallam did. In fact, the sharpness with which Hallam drew this division reflects the accuracy and importance of his criticism of Tennyson's poetry, which displaces its truth content and referential connections—especially in the early work—to a marked degree.

Hallam's views would eventually gain an all but complete academic ascendency in the melancholy long withdrawing roar of the Victorian period. To the degree that Tennyson's poetry is taken seriously today, it is read almost exclusively against the grain of what we take to be Tennyson's Victorian frame of mind. Harold Nicholson initiated this movement when he distinguished between the "remarkable depth and originality of his poetical temperament and the shallowness and timidity of his practical intelligence." Nicholson established the line that there are two Tennysons, and that only one of them is worth reading. The bard of Farringford and Aldworth—Tennyson Laureate, the Victorian Sage—was quietly stored away in the archives of literary history so that the true poet could be permitted to emerge. No fact so dramatically illustrates this situation as the current status of a poem like "The Charge of the Light Brigade." Once a set-piece example of Tennyson's greatness—required reading and always anthologized—this great poem cannot be found in any of our currently standard collections of Victorian poetry.

An additional fact about the history of Tennyson's critical

reception needs to be emphasized. Along with the predominant distinction between Tennyson as Sage and Tennyson as *Symboliste* runs a related pattern of praise and critique. Today we generally value the symbolist Tennyson and denigrate the sage, and these two valuations tend to operate dialectically. In Tennyson's day, however, the approach was different. Fox and Hallam both praised Tennyson's early verse, though their critical grounds for doing so seem to us poles apart. Indeed, the history of Tennyson's Victorian reception shows very clearly that these same critical grounds were both employed to attack Tennyson's work. An extensive critical line, beginning with John Wilson's early assault upon Tennyson, denounced Tennyson's artificiality, aestheticism, and obscurity. This line included some of Tennyson's admirers as well, most notably R. C. Trench, who urged Tennyson to abandon the line which Hallam was promoting. "Tennyson," he said, "we cannot live in art."

Similarly, the grounds of Fox's praise were also the basis for the sharpest kinds of critique. Gladstone's and Goldwin Smith's famous remarks on *Maud* epitomize a line of Victorian criticism that attacked Tennyson's ideas and social attitudes. We know this line best through the sneers of people like Swinburne, whose grounds of complaint were aesthetic. People like Gladstone and Smith, however, launched their criticisms from moral positions. Tennyson's poems seemed uninteresting or worse because of their social attitudes and intellectual positions. Lest we think that such an approach has fallen into disuse, we have merely to recall the recent critical history of *The Princess* and *Maud*.

The purpose of this brief survey of the history of Tennyson's reception is to provide us today with the basis for a critical perspective on our own views. Critics spend a great deal of time—properly so—trying to arrive at critical assessments of the works they inherit, but they sometimes neglect to place their own views under the microscope. Until Harold Nicholson's epochal work, critics generally argued about the relative merits of Tennyson as sage and Tennyson as symbolist. Since that time, however, Tennyson's ideas and social attitudes have not seemed especially interesting to the critics, and least of all to those who admire his work and are seeking to reestablish Tennyson's high reputation. Lionel Madden is the spokesman of our moment when he says: "The modern reader who recognizes Tennyson's need to express social ideas may nevertheless feel considerable difficulty in accepting much of the official verse. Certainly many of the occasional poems are limited in significance by the specific nature of their themes."[9] This is merely Hallam's position in a new key. As such, it seems to me a limited view of Tennyson's artistic significance—and all the more limited because it is a position that dominates the approach to Tennyson in a way that Hallam's view, in his period, never dominated the critical discussion.

If it is true that the modern reader can accept Tennyson's "need to express social ideas," then I would argue that this modern reader is obliged to deal with those social ideas in the critical analysis of Tennyson's works. The fact that we today may have "considerable difficulty in accepting" many of Tennyson's works because we are uninterested in or hostile to the ideas they express seems to me as much a judgment upon our own ideas and their limitations as it is upon Tennyson's. More than this, I think such a view betrays a fundamental misconception of the function of ideas and ideology in poetical works.

I want to illustrate what I mean by looking closely at "The Charge of the Light Brigade," one of those occasional poems thought to be "limited in significance by the specific nature of their themes." Madden's view on this matter, we should recall, is a commonplace of our received notions about the "mode of existence of a literary work of art." That is to say, most readers today would take it for granted that a poem like "Tears, Idle Tears" is much less "limited in significance" than a poem like "The Charge of the Light Brigade." This assumption operates in criticism because the latter work seems to be "limited" by virtue of the explicit and specific character of its historical points of reference. "Tears, Idle Tears," on the other hand, appears an altogether more "universal" work because it takes up topics of so-called general human interest, because it does not display any explicitly "occasional" elements.

I would argue, on the contrary, that such views about the

nature of poetical works thoroughly mistake the relation which holds between a poetical work and its historical contexts (whether its original context or its subsequent ones). This is not the occasion to take up such general issues of literary theory. Nevertheless, what I wish to say here about Tennyson's poetry is based upon certain general ideas on the relation between poetry and history, so that a few remarks on this broader subject are in order.

I take it that poems, like all art products, can only operate in a medium of uniqueness. Their value is always a function of the sharp edge of their particularity. Because poems represent various sorts of human ideas, events, and attitudes, the character of their uniqueness is always socially and historically embedded. Consequently, if we are to appreciate or study, say, the religious verse of Christina Rosetti, we must find a way—either intuitively or with the self-consciousness of criticism—to grasp the unique religious character of Rosetti's poetry. Her Christian themes, and even her verse forms, are much in debt to the work of Herbert in particular, and they locate themselves within a recognizable and well-known tradition of religious verse. The business of literary criticism, however, is precisely to resist the impulse toward a general Christian (or even Anglican) thematics for her poetry, which is part of the context of her work, and to seek to formulate what *distinguishes* her work, what sets it apart from (say) Herbert's and within (say) the tradition of Anglican poetry. To perform these critical operations we must, I believe, find ways of defining the special historical and social terms within which her poetry emerged, and from which it drew its unique characteristics.

The same may be said of Tennyson's poetry (or of any poet's). In his famous essay on "Tears, Idle Tears," Cleanth Brooks located the poem's strength in the fact that its tears are "occasioned by no immediate grief [but] spring from a deeper, more universal cause."[10] This is an interesting critical remark, for several reasons. Most noticeable is Brooks's idea that universal causes for grief are somehow deeper and more telling than merely occasional ones: in literal fact, that a cause of grief which springs from the region of ideas is deeper and more important than one that springs from a simple matter of fact (say, the death of one we love). I shall pass without comment why Brooks may have believed such an idea and turn instead to Tennyson. For "Tears, Idle Tears" does in fact express a consciousness which suffers under an existential malaise, which experiences an ideological grief rather than a concrete or "occasional" one. This fact about the poem's subject is extremely important, for it gestures toward those qualities of the poem that specify and define its characteristics. "Tears, Idle Tears" is not the good poem that it is because its grief springs from deeper and more universal causes rather than from more immediate and occasional ones. This is what Brooks believes about the poem because this is what Brooks seems to believe about human life in general: that there are universal causes and factors and that these are deeper and more important than immediate and concrete ones.

One must point out, of course, that although Tennyson's poem itself expresses a sense of existential malaise, it does not assent to the truth of that malaise in the way that Brooks has done. When Tennyson says "Tears, *idle* tears," he begins to show us as well how and why he is disturbed and puzzled by the type of grief he is feeling. It is a "strange" type of feeling, especially when one compares it with any number of more concretely generated sorrows—griefs that spring from specific and clearly understandable occasions. In point of fact, such comparisons are precisely what the poem itself offers to the reader's consideration.

"Tears, Idle Tears" is not simply a poem about an existential malaise. It is a poem which dramatizes, as it were, a person's discovery that he suffers from such a feeling. Furthermore, it is a poem in which the feeling is consciously and resolutely explored—not in order to discover the *meaning* of the feeling, but in order to set forth its character and specific marks. This fact about the poem is what makes Leo Spitzer's critical analysis in "'Tears, Idle Tears' Again" so much more telling than Brooks's.[11] For whereas the latter is able to describe fairly well the "dramatic truth of the situation" which the poem evokes, Spitzer's account brings to the poem a degree of critical understanding which Brooks's does not. Spitzer examines the lyric in comparative relation to a number of similar works by Ovid, Quevedo, Hofmannsthal, and Hemingway, and his method has the virtue of being able to draw clear and concrete distinctions. Like Brooks, Spitzer confines his discussion to verbal stylistics; unlike Brooks, his analysis appeals to a methodology which is based in a historical approach to cultural products. The appeal remains implicit, but it governs every aspect of his paper.

The virtue of historical method in literary criticism lies in its ability to set poems in contexts, and thereby to provide them with an analytic structure that can reveal the unique features of the poems themselves. Spitzer's approach to "Tears, Idle Tears" is one of several that might be taken. The fact that he does not deal with the poem in terms of its immediate social context means that his analysis does not attempt a self-conscious explanation of the meaning of this poem in and for mid-Victorian England. The refusal to develop such an explanation—to set forth a comprehensive social and ideological analysis of the poem in terms of its original context—is significant because only that sort of analysis can provide a later reader—a reader in late twentieth-century America, for example—with a critical context for his (later) reading. To interpret "Tears, Idle Tears," to read it with sympathy and understanding, requires that we see it as in itself it really is. We cannot have it on any terms, least of all on our own terms, unless we understand the terms that are and are not possible. We may have it on our own terms—we may read the poem in terms of our own (implicit or explicit) ideologies—only when we are clear about the differences that separate us from the poem, and hence that permit us to sympathize with it.

In short, a historical method in criticism is always comparative and dialectical. To expose the mid-Victorian ideology that informs every part of Tennyson's poem is to define critically the specific shape and special quality of its humanness. The poem is moving and human *in its mid-Victorian* qualities. Recognizing this fact about the poem's aesthetic mode of operation is important for later readers because it provides us with a critical perspective upon our own ideologies. The peculiar shape and qualities of our own forms of humanness are exposed in the light of the past that appears before us through a poem like this.

Such an effect is especially salutary and dramatic when the critic chooses to take up a poem like "The Charge of the Light Brigade." We survey the reception history of this poem to find that it has not merely fallen out of favor, as Byron's and Swinburne's works once fell out, but that it has come to seem mildly ludicrous, slightly contemptible. Here is Tennyson at his most "official" and most "Victorian"—a period piece that even Tennyson's admirers are happy to have since it provides them with a contrast to those "deeper, more universal" poems like "Tears, Idle Tears." In my view, however, the force of this poem derives from its resolute and human particularity. Its importance for criticism—for criticism at the present time in particular—lies, first, in the critical light that it throws upon "deep" and "universal" readings of poems like "Tears, Idle Tears"; and, second, in the way it challenges the entire project of an ahistorical criticism and implicitly exposes the ideological limitations and biases of such a critical method.

These limitations appear with special clarity in the recent commentary, such of it as exists, on "The Charge of the Light Brigade." The only reader who has anything good to say about the poem is Christopher Ricks, and he confines his remarks to stylistic matters. Like everyone else, Ricks goes out of his way to avoid discussing the poem's subject matter—both the historical events and their ideological significance. The Crimean War, the famous charge at Balaclava, and Tennyson's own attitudes toward these matters are universally recognized by the critics, but only because they are universally regarded as embarrassments, both in themselves and to the poem.[12] My own view, however, is that such a critical stance has misunderstood the relation which exists between poems and their historical formats and that the significance of "The Charge of the Light Brigade," its achievement as a poem, can only appear through a critical elucidation of the work's historical aspects.

The topical character of the poem is established by its first printing, which was in *The Examiner* (9 December 1854) one week after Tennyson read of the events at Balaclava and wrote the poem. But the poem is not so much a commentary on the war and British foreign policy in the Crimea as it is a eulogy of the British character. As such, its specific location in time and place focuses the poem's choice of a certain ideological point of view, and that point of view in turn focuses the historical and human drama which the poem embodies and represents. Let us begin to elucidate that drama, to clear away the vaguenesses which have gathered about the poem and permit it to recover its aesthetic resources.

As we have seen, the poem was from the outset a "popular" work—it took its origin in a newspaper report, and it first appeared in the popular press. Indeed, the poem in many respects is a distilled interpretation of the popular reaction to the charge as that reaction was expressed in the newspapers. The *Times* leader of 13 November 1854 carried the first reasonably complete report of the event, and it began as follows: "We now know the details of the attack on Balaclava.... We have ... in the despatches before us nearly the whole of the loss, which it would be vain to conceal is most lamentable, and all the more so because it seems to have arisen from some misunderstanding.... The disaster ... is not more, but it is not much less, than the annihilation of the Light Cavalry Brigade.... Even accident would have made it more tolerable. But it was a mere mistake—evidently a mistake, and perceived to be such." The note of puzzlement in this passage will be picked up and repeated throughout the many press rehearsals of the events at Balaclava. The question put in the *Times* leader on the next day, 14 November, brings into clear focus the central concern expressed in the public reaction: "What is the meaning of a spectacle so strange, so terrific, so disastrous, and yet so grand?" The press reports themselves were to work out their explanations, and these had a profound influence on Tennyson's poem, as we shall see. But the press influence reached Tennyson, first, in the request for an explanation, the demand for a meaning. "The Charge of the Light Brigade" is in great measure a response to the question set out in the *Times*.

We may begin to elucidate Tennyson's answer by looking at

Tennyson and the Histories of Criticism

the newspaper text of the poem, which was its first printing. *The Examiner* prints a version of lines 5–6 which contains an interesting variation on the received reading.[13] The latter has: " 'Forward, the Light Brigade! / Charge for the guns!' he said." In the first printing, however, these lines read: " 'Forward, the Light Brigade! / Take the guns,' Nolan said." *The Examiner*'s reference to Capt. Lewis Nolan is a concrete detail which would have focused contemporary audience response to the poem in a particular way. Nolan was not just another cavalry officer, but a highly respected and even celebrated figure, a recognized authority on the management and tactics of cavalry units. In 1853 he published two books "which created a sensation in military circles—*Cavalry, Its History and Tactics* and *Nolan's System for Training Cavalry Horses.*"[14] That he took part in the charge of the Light Brigade, indeed, that he was killed in that charge, was of course common knowledge by the time of Tennyson's poem. Indeed, the detail is only there in the text because Nolan's career and his death *were* common knowledge.

In the reports which reached England immediately after the charge, Capt. Nolan's name was linked with the infamous "blunder" that sent the brigade to its fate. Controversy boiled around the degree of his responsibility for the disaster, and he characteristically was made the focus of all the explanations. This happened because Nolan epitomized in the public mind "a cavalry enthusiast, who had but lately published his opinion that cavalry could do everything in war," as the *Times* leader put it. Part of the explanation for the charge at Balaclava, then, lay in the rash enthusiasm of what the *Times* called "a proud Dragoon officer."

When Thoreau commented on the events at Balaclava from his alien American vantage, he took them to demonstrate "what a perfect machine the soldier is," and in particular what a thoughtless and rather brutish character was the typical British recruit.[15] But Thoreau's view of the poem and its recorded events is based upon a gross misreading not only of the objective facts of the situation but of the British response to those events. Once again we have to exercise our historical imaginations a bit if we are to see the human drama of this poem as in itself it really is. As we do this, we must at all times remember that the narrative I am reconstituting here is one that was common knowledge at the time.

Tennyson, like everyone else in England, first read a full account of the charge in the *Times* leader of 13 November, and his poem in fact follows this narrative in a number of details, and even uses some of its exact phrasing. The famous lines "What though the soldier knew / Some one had blundered" rework a passage in the newspaper report which says that the cavalry officers "knew well what they were about" when they made their charge, were fully aware that "some hideous blunder" had occurred. Indeed, this is the passage which also supplied Tennyson with the phrase "the valley of Death." "With nothing to lose but themselves, and no inducements out of their profession," the Light Brigade "risked on that day all the enjoyments that rank, wealth, good social position, and many fortunate circumstances can offer.... Splendid as the event was on the Alma, yet that rugged ascent ... was scarcely so glorious as the progress of the cavalry through and through that valley of death, with a murderous fire, not only in front, but on both sides, above, and even in the rear." The last part of this passage clearly anticipates some of the most well-known lines in Tennyson's poem. Furthermore, the newspaper account draws attention to a crucial aspect of the poem which will not be found in it *literatim* but which is nonetheless present and important: the social standing of the cavalry officers, and the image which the public at the time had of the light cavalry, and especially of the particular units which had been sent to the Crimea. The newspaper's reference to the battle of the Alma, only recently fought, highlights these matters in a way that would have been unmistakable to any contemporary of Tennyson's, but which is necessarily obscure to us now. We must clarify that obscurity.

The charge of the Light Brigade was carried out in three lines. The first was made up of the 13th Light Dragoons and the 17th Lancers; the second of the 11th Hussars; and the third of the 4th Light Dragoons and the principal body of 8th Hussars. This body of light cavalry was in all respects like the rest of the regiments sent to the Crimea; that is to say, they were all the most socially elite units in the British army, spit and polish, dashing, and notoriously affected groups which had never seen a battlefield. The units had not seen action since Waterloo, and when they were chosen for the Crimean campaign over the experienced field-tested troops from the Indian frontier, the decision caught the public notice and generated some controversy. Questions were raised whether these "wasp-waisted, dandified army officers, whom the comic magazines loved to caricature, [would] prove to have any of the mettle of the Peninsular or Waterloo" combatants.[16] This question is implicit in the conclusion of *Maud* when the hero of Tennyson's poem declares: "Let it flame or fade, and the war roll down like a wind, / We have proved we have hearts in a cause, we are noble still" (III. 54–55). "The Charge of the Light Brigade" is Tennyson's attempt to show not merely that the English aristocracy has not lost its leadership qualities, but in what respect this historically threatened class still exercises its leadership.

This aspect of Tennyson's meaning emerges when we recall that the battle of the Alma was regarded by the English as a noble victory of the English infantry forces; and furthermore, that in the English mind the infantry and the cavalry were distinguished along class lines; and finally, that the cavalry sent to the Crimea was a special object of public concern, and even at times contempt. The charge of the Light Brigade took place in the context of these facts and attitudes, and the popular explanation of the charge which finally emerged (in its first complete form in the *Times* leader for 14 November) took account of them—as Thoreau's remarks did (and perhaps could) not do:

The cavalry in our service is supposed to have always claimed a species of rank over the infantry. Its frequent attendance on the person of Royalty, its splendid uniforms, and the exemption from colonial service, have made it the favourite resort of the aristocracy, and infected it with the weakness of caste. This has long been so notorious as to be the subject of caricature, which would not have been understood had it not appealed to popular estimate. With these feelings on the two sides, it is no wonder if the cavalry have acted during this campaign with a dignity that rather interfered with their use, and if, on the other hand, the infantry thought the cavalry were saving themselves somewhat too carefully. We believe that this feeling arose much more from the want of a good understanding and a sort of jealousy between the services than from any particular facts; yet, so it is, that from one reason or another the cavalry did little at the Alma, where it was much wanted, and had no other opportunity of distinction during the campaign. We may presume that feelings of this sort would be rather aggravated by the hardships and dangers of the siege, in which, of course, the cavalry could do but little, and by the general want of occasion for its service. Such suspicions and insinuations, unfounded as we believe them to have been, would not be long in finding their way; nor is it likely that such sensitive, high-spirited men, as Lords CARDIGAN and LUCAN would be wholly proof against them. Nothing is more natural than that every feat of daring done by any other branch of the service would be felt as a new summons to do something worthy of the rank assumed by the cavalry. Let us suppose the Light Brigade in view of the enemy on the 25th with such feelings, and spectators of the victorious charge of the Heavy Brigade. Let us further imagine them receiving a written order, in terms that seemed to leave no discretion, to advance and recapture the guns in the hands of the enemy. Let the order be borne, interpreted, and enforced by a cavalry enthusiast, who had but lately published his opinion that cavalry could do everything in war, storm any battery, break any square, whether supported or not. Let the order be passed from officer to officer, each one more jealous of the other, and adding, possibly, personal feelings to a wounded *esprit de corps*. There you have in the proud Dragoon officer, in the stimulating example, in the grand occasion, the crowd of spectators, the absolute order, the enthusiastic messenger, and peremptory interpreter, too ample explanation of a noble but disastrous deed—a fatal display of courage which all must admire while they lament.

Tennyson's poem grounds itself in the ideological focus which this passage has taken. The six-hundred dead cavaliers are "noble" still, not merely by virtue of their actual class position, but by reason of their deeds, and the spiritual "nobility" which their deaths have shown. They have not merely equaled, at Balaclava, the victory achieved at Alma by "the lower orders," they have surpassed them altogether and regained their rightful place in society: not its political leaders, but its spiritual models.

Tennyson and the Histories of Criticism 245

Tennyson's poem sets out to make the same kind of statement. This is partly why it does not always attract a later middle-class audience, which may find it difficult to generate a sympathetic attitude toward a patently aristocratic poem. Originally the work was able to cross class lines because the event itself exerted a national impact, because in the context of a foreign war class differences and conflicts tended to dissolve in national sympathies. In such a context it would be well for all the social orders if the "superior orders" were *not* in fact effete and socially ineffectual.

One of the principal technical means which secured this meaning for Tennyson—which in fact enabled his poem to cross class lines and speak to the nation at large—is hidden in the iconography of the poem. The images in "The Charge of the Light Brigade" are drawn from the newspaper accounts of the day, but the form of those images is based upon an iconography of heroism that Tennyson appropriated. His sources are French, bourgeois, and painterly, and his use of them in his English, aristocratic, and verbal work represents another struggle with foreigners which the entire English nation could sympathize with. In this struggle Tennyson means to settle an old score with the French, and to complete, as it were, Wellington's victory at Waterloo: to complete it at the level of ideology.

The key fact about the charge, for Tennyson, is that it took place despite the fact that the cavalry officers understood a blunder had been made somewhere, that the charge was, from the point of view of military tactics, a terrible mistake. The inexorable rhythm of Tennyson's poem—"Half a league, half a league, / Half a league onward"—perfectly mirrors the cavalry's implacable movement, and both of these correspondent motions reveal the human elements in the situation that Tennyson wishes to emphasize: the men's steadiness of purpose, as well as their entire understanding of what is involved in their action. "They went with their eyes open," the *Times* reported, "as if under a spell."

> Cannon to right of them,
> Cannon to left of them,

> Cannon in front of them
> Volleyed and thundered;
> Stormed at with shot and shell,
> Boldly they rode and well.

The reports which came back to England from the battlefield repeatedly emphasized the orderliness of the charge, its steadiness and fearfully determined resolution: "in perfect order," said the *Times*, "to certain destruction." The English cavalry was generally acknowledged to be manned by the best horsemen in Europe, though it was also widely recognized as a cavalry that had not achieved the successes commensurate with its equestrian talent. Balaclava came to seem what the *Times* called the "glorious doom" of the Light Brigade, their mission and their fate. "They went as fanatics seek the death that is to save them, and as heroes have sought death in the thick of the fight, when they could no longer hope to conquer. . . . There was organization and discipline; there was even experience and military skill, at least enough to enable the chiefs to know the terrible nature of the deed. . . . This was not war, as the French General said; it was a spectacle, and one worthy of the 'cloud of witnesses' that encompassed the performers" (*Times*, 14 November). All these attitudes were to be gathered up into Tennyson's poem, where the Light Brigade's suicide mission becomes, paradoxically, its crowning glory:

> When can their glory fade?
> O the wild charge they made!
> All the world wondered.

These lines refer specifically to the newspapers' widespread reports of the astonishment which the charge produced in those who observed it—in particular, in the allied French soldiers. The words of *The Morning Chronicle* typify the accounts in all the newspapers: "French officers, who saw with dismay the madness of the act and the certainty of destruction, express themselves amazed by the invincible spirit of our men." The remark of the French general Bosquet was reported everywhere and perfectly captures Tennyson's own understanding of the event: "C'est très magnifique mais c'est ne pas la guerre."

But Tennyson's poem gives an altogether new meaning to Bosquet's famous remark. Tennyson insisted that he was not a person who favored or delighted in war, and of course later ages have had little difficulty seeing through his ideological confusions on this matter. If we shift the overtones of Bosquet's observation just a bit I think we may see past the evident confusions in Tennyson's mind to its (perhaps) not so evident clarities. For "The Charge of the Light Brigade" describes a cruel and stupid military event as if it were a spiritual, even an aesthetic, triumph. *But of course* this isn't war, it is magnificence, it is glory. The poem's images present the cavaliers as if they were cast in a tableau, or in a heroic painting—and in one case at least, as if they were statues. The Light Brigade comes before us in Tennyson's poem as an aesthetic object, as we see very clearly in the fourth stanza, where the riders are made to assume the classic pose of the equestrian hero in action. Such a figure lived in the nineteenth century's eye in a whole array of paintings and statues, some great (e.g., in the work of David, Gros, Géricault, and Delacroix), some merely ordinary (e.g., in the statuary familiar throughout the cities of Europe): "Flashed all their sabres bare / Flashed as they turned in air."

The fact that the military gestures in "The Charge of the Light Brigade" are modeled upon a certain tradition of heroic military art is extremely important to see. For that artistic tradition is almost entirely French, and it emerges out of the Romantic styles that were connected with Napoleon, the First Empire, and the exploits of the *Grande Armée*. One has merely to compare, say, David's famous portrait of Napoleon with any of the portraits of Wellington, or even of Nelson, in order to perceive the gulf which separates their ideological points of view. Like Gros's portrait of Murat at the Battle of Aboukir, or Géricault's famous picture of the chasseur of the Imperial Guard, David's picture is charged throughout with various signs of Romantic motion, force, and energy. English painting of the same period never triumphed in this style. Consequently, in the immediately subsequent history the French chasseurs of the

Napoleonic wars become heroic models throughout European art and culture, whereas the English cavaliers are either models of equestrian decorum, or objects of broad ridicule—in the last instance, mere aristocratic dandies. Besides, the fact that the heroic French chasseur did not come from the well-born and elite classes of society was an important element in his ideological significance. In this respect he came to stand for the human meaning of the historical events that tore Europe apart at the end of the eighteenth century. Napoleon's world-historical import was epitomized in the figure of the French chasseur, whose exploits in battle overshadowed and surpassed in glory the military acts of Europe's congregated elite forces.

Wellington had won the battle of Waterloo, but England had lost to France the ideological struggle that followed. Indeed, the ancestors of Tennyson's Light Brigade had been present at Waterloo, but their presence was hardly noted and not decisive. Out of the defeat of Napoleon's grand army, artists like Gros and Géricault snatched a brilliant aesthetic triumph. Tennyson's poem deliberately, if perhaps only half-consciously, enters into this complex historical network in order, as it were, to gain for the English cavalry the emblems of the heroism they deserve but have never had. Thus it is opportune that it should have been the French who stood by at Balaclava to comment upon the English cavalry's charge. "All the world wondered" at this charge, but that worldwide wonder was appropriately registered in a French accent. More than anyone else they would have understood the meaning of the charge, for it was carried out in a famous French manner: the measured, deliberate pace of the Light Brigade's advance had been the wonder of Europe since the grand army invented and defined it.

Tennyson's poem, then, represents an effort to appropriate for an English consciousness those images of heroism which had been defined in another, antithetical culture. The poem conceals an act of revisionist historical criticism, an "Englishing," as it were, of certain French possessions. This revisionist act emphasizes the predominant motive of the entire poem, however, which is to institute through the art of poetry a change of meaning analogous to the one which Gros and Géricault instituted earlier through their painting. All the world's wonder at Waterloo had been focused on Napoleon and his armies, despite the fact that England and Wellington had won the military encounter. But the Light Brigade's act at Balaclava offered to Tennyson the chance to change the outcome of England's spiritual and ideological defeat.

Tennyson's method, therefore, is founded in a set of paradoxes, the most fundamental of which is that his model should have been French and Romantic rather than English and Victorian. Out of this basic paradox Tennyson constructs a series of new and changed views on certain matters of real cultural importance. Most clearly he wants to show that the charge was not a military disaster but a spiritual triumph, and that the men of the English cavalry are not dandified and enervated aristocrats—that they are not merely "noble still," they are the deathless spiritual leaders of their country. These changes of meaning are epitomized in the poem's most notable linguistic transformation, whereby Tennyson manages to suggest that the name of the "Light Brigade" carries a meaning which transcends its technical military significance. The pun on the word *light* points to the quasi-religious identity and mission of this small brigade of cavalry. Indeed, in that pun we observe Tennyson moving his poem out of its secular and nonverbal French models into a Victorian set of attitudes peculiarly his own.

This historical reading of Tennyson's poem is an attempt to restore it to our consciousness on its own original terms. The purpose of such a reading, however, is not to make us sympathize with the poem on its own terms—to submit to the poem's peculiar mid-Victorian ideological attitudes. On the contrary, the aim of the analysis is to make us aware of the ideological gulf which separates us from the human world evoked through Tennyson's poem. "The Charge of the Light Brigade" embodies certain specific ideological formations, and it attaches these attitudes and feelings to certain specific events. Everything about this poem—everything about every poem that has ever been written—is time and place specific. This we sometimes forget. But we also tend to forget, when considering the employment of a historical criticism, that every reader of every poem is equally time and place specific. The function of a historical criticism, properly executed and understood, is to clarify the historical particularities of the entire aesthetic event, whether observed from the vantage of the original work, on the one hand, or of the later reader(s) of that work on the other. A collision of ideologies and consciousness will necessarily take place when such a criticism is set in motion.

Out of that conflict—which *is* the aesthetic experience—emerges the sort of light and understanding poetry was meant to bring: what I would have to call critical sympathy. In "The Charge of the Light Brigade," we reexperience the original Victorian response to that most pitiful of all events: a blundered tragic action. Some of Tennyson's contemporaries, and a large part of Tennyson himself, saw the charge at Balaclava as a kind of heroic tragedy—in the words of one correspondent, "a *grand national sacrifice.*" But another part of the population, and another part of Tennyson, understood that it was only a *kind* of heroic tragedy, and that its blundered and failed aspects gave it a different quality altogether. For in the end the poem rests in an evident, a simple, yet a profound contradiction which is the basis of all its related sets of contradictions. The Light Brigade achieved, in its famous assault, an immortality, a final spiritual triumph. In the event it suffered as well, in the words of the *Times,* a human "catastrophe," an "annihilation." This triumph is also "The disaster . . . of which the mere shadow has darkened so many a household among us." Tennyson's poetry is in the pity even as it is also in the glory.

The poem, in other words, embodies an original set of contradictions that can be of use to us as its inheritors, as its subsequent readers. For we too, like Tennyson and his contemporaries, intersect with our own age and experience—including our experience with this poem—in certain specific and ideologically determined ways. "The Charge of the Light Brigade" is important for us precisely because of the differential which it necessarily represents. Indeed, I should even venture to say that its importance as a cultural resource, for us today, will be a function of our immediate disinterest in it or hostility toward it. Time and human experience—which are the measures of all future experience—have sanctioned the achievement of this work. Whatever immediate or practical usefulness it may have rests with us, and particularly with those of us (or that part of ourselves) who feel most alienated from the (piteous, not tragic) human experience enacted in this poem.

Thirty-five years ago a book was published which has since been seen to have defined the subsequent period of academic criticism in its attitude toward art objects (as verbal constructions, or "texts"), as well as in its attitude toward the criticism of art objects (antihistorical). The position taken by Cleanth Brooks in *The Well Wrought Urn* is epitomized in the following passage: "I insist that to treat ... poems ... primarily as poems is a proper emphasis, and very much worth doing. For we have gone to school to the anthropologists and the cultural historians assiduously, and we have learned their lesson almost too well. We have learned it so well that the danger now, it seems to me, is not that we will forget the differences between poems of different historical periods, but that we will forget those qualities which they have in common."[17] This is a farewell salute to the nineteenth-century tradition of philological studies and a manifesto of a new antihistorical criticism. Its limitations as a critical method are now, two generations later, quite clear to everyone who reflects upon these matters. Brooks's words, once the veritable epigraph of a new tradition of academic readers, now appear as its inevitable epitaph. For the danger which Brooks then saw is now unapparent, whereas the one he dismissed—"that we will forget the differences between poems of different historical periods," as well as the aesthetic significance of those differences—is only too clear.

Being a part of history we must follow Brooks in time, and so we also mean to follow him in thought. We too may want "to treat ... poems ... primarily as poems," but when we do so it will be in the light of another tradition of thought that we also must follow. For it is philology which shows us that to treat poems *as* poems means that we must encounter them in the full range of their concrete particularity. This means that we must grasp them in their historical uniqueness. Like Ahab, every poem has its special humanities. It is the business of literary criticism to reveal the human histories of its subjects, a task which will—which must—include the acknowledgment of criticism's own historical limits. Both of these subjects together constitute the field in which literary criticism undertakes to read and study the works of the poets.

Notes

1. The qualitative difference between the editions of the FitzGerald and the Tennyson letters is graphically illustrated in the letter from FitzGerald to Tennyson of 2 July 1835 (previously unpublished; each of these new editions has a text of the letter). This is an important letter—see my discussion in the superior text—which presented a difficult editorial problem: the four-page manuscript letter is badly stained and multilated. The text produced by Lang and Shannon is almost twice as long as the text produced by the Terhunes, and the difference measures certain important scholarly characteristics: of judgment, care, editorial persistence and scrupulousness, and (finally) results.

2. See Lang and Shannon, *Tennyson Letters*, p. 134.

3. See *The Letters of Emily Lady Tennyson*, ed. James O. Hoge (University Park, Pa.: Pennsylvania State Univ. Press, 1974), pp. 70–71; for discussion of what Tennyson took from the *Times*, see the later parts of the present essay; see also *Lady Tennyson's Journal*, ed. James O. Hoge (Charlottesville: Univ. Press of Virginia, 1981) pp. 40–41.

4. P. N. Medvedev and M. M. Bakhtin, *The Formal Method in Literary Scholarship* (Baltimore: Johns Hopkins Univ. Press, 1978), p. 122.

5. *Alfred Lord Tennyson: A Memoir by His Son* (London: Macmillan, 1897), II, 127. Tennyson told his son that he "considered [the allegorical readings of his poems] the best" (p. 126).

6. See Pattison, p. 169 n. 29, where this characteristic of Tennyson's verse style is nicely touched on.

7. The lack of a particularized historical sense weakens Pattison's book even at some of its best moments—e.g., in his excellent discussions of the tradition of idyl (see especially pp. 18–22, 29). Pattison discusses the idyl form in its various actual manifestations as if the form contained, in itself, certain poetic qualities and powers; and furthermore, as if the characteristics of these qualities and powers were uniform in all their historic incarnations.

Tennyson and the Histories of Criticism

8. For convenience of reference, in my discussion of the reception history of Tennyson's poetry I will cite only texts that can be found in J. D. Jump's excellent *Tennyson: The Critical Heritage* (London: Routledge and Kegan Paul, 1967).

9. Lionel Madden, "Tennyson: A Reader's Guide," in *Writers and Their Background: Tennyson,* ed. D. J. Palmer (Athens, Ohio: Ohio Univ. Press, 1973), p. 18.

10. Cleanth Brooks, *The Well Wrought Urn* (New York: Reynal and Hitchcock, 1947), pp. 153–54.

11. Leo Spitzer, " 'Tears, Idle Tears' Again," reprinted in *Critical Essays on the Poetry of Tennyson,* ed. John Killham (New York: Barnes and Noble, 1967), pp. 192–203.

12. See Christopher Ricks, *Tennyson* (New York: Collier Books, 1972), pp. 244–45. The best contextual discussion of the poem to date is in Michael C. C. Adams, "Tennyson's Crimean War Poetry: A Cross-Cultural Approach," *Journal of the History of Ideas,* 40, No. 3 (July–September, 1979), pp. 405–22.

13. My texts of the poems here will be cited from *The Poems of Tennyson,* ed. Christopher Ricks (London: Longmans, 1969).

14. Cecil Woodham-Smith, *The Reason Why* (New York: McGraw-Hill, 1953), p. 167.

15. *H. D. Thoreau: Reform Papers,* ed. Wendell Glick (Princeton: Princeton Univ. Press, 1973), p. 119.

16. Adams, "Tennyson's Crimean War Poetry," p. 419; and see as well Woodham-Smith's discussion of these and related matters, *The Reason Why,* pp. 134–35.

17. Brooks, *The Well Wrought Urn,* p. 197.

The Reader as Hero and Bully: Stanley Fish and F. R. Leavis

Alan C. Purves

Stanley Fish. *Is There a Text in This Class? The Authority of Interpretive Communities.* Cambridge: Harvard University Press, 1980. ix, 394 pp.

William Walsh. *F. R. Leavis.* Bloomington: Indiana University Press, 1980. 189 pp.

Stanley Fish writes clearly. By this I mean that Fish uses words and syntax in a fashion common to many users of the language—literary critics, teachers, philosophers, editors, people in general. At least I perceive his uses of language to be common in their absence of too many metaphors or puns or too much use of involved syntax or allusion. Having described my perception, I must acknowledge that twenty years ago I received a doctorate in English and comparative literature, studying the English Romantic poets, the English eighteenth century, Milton, and the English and Continental renaissance, as well as critical theory, and metrics, which at that time was embroiled in structural linguistics. I was educated into a community of shared terms, assumptions, and allusions. So was Stanley Fish, and our communities were quite similar. I believe that this is the principal reason his writing strikes me as clear.

Such is not the case when I read Jacques Derrida, Cary Nelson, or Wolfgang Iser. I have to struggle with them. The first and third were educated in different traditions; the second was educated in my tradition a decade later. Derrida, Nelson, Iser, and Fish say similar things about literature and readers, but I understand Fish. And Stanley Fish would like that, for he establishes a community of readers as a construct upon which to expound a theory of criticism and a theory of literature. Fish and I belong to the same community. Iser and Derrida are members of two neighboring European communities; Nelson is a member of the younger generation of our community. Any community establishes what a text is, what aspects of that text should receive attention, what interpretive norms should hold, what criteria of literary excellence should obtain. The last is not included in Fish's definition, but I shall return to the point later in a discussion of William Walsh's biography of F. R. Leavis.

The thrust of *Is There a Text in This Class?* follows a relatively old tradition, although not a particularly popular one in critical circles.[1] It is a tradition that asserts the primacy of the reader as a maker of meaning. To varying degrees it has been followed by such literary critics as Coleridge, Northrop Frye, Louise Rosenblatt and supported by linguists such as Edward Sapir and Benjamin Lee Whorf and by psychologists such as Sigmund Freud, Charles Osgood, and Richard Anderson. The substance of the tradition holds that individuals are held together in communities, communities which are to a great extent bound by language, and particularly by a common semantic space. Groups of people hold similar meanings for words and sentences when those words and sentences are placed in a common context. Take the familiar lines from Shakespeare's *Cymbeline:* "Golden lads and girls, all must, / As chimney-sweepers, come to dust" (IV.ii.262–63). One group of people would assume that Shakespeare belongs to a Renaissance community that held certain beliefs about morality and so would interpret the lines as *meaning* that death comes to young and old, rich and poor, noble and commoner. And that assumption seems reasonable, since we know when Shakespeare lived and we know that "dust" could hold in the seventeenth century, as it can today, the connotation of death ("dust thou art and to dust thou shall return"). At the same time other people know that in seventeenth-century English, a spent dandelion was called a "chimney sweeper" and the young blossom a "golden lad." These people assume that they inhabit with Shakespeare a floral community and that the lines are much less serious in their portrayal of the inevitability of change and perhaps death.

Which community did Shakespeare inhabit? Which of the interpretations does the text really support? Or does it mean

The Reader as Hero and Bully: Fish and Leavis

something completely different? Fish asserts that we cannot know—the text cannot be used to answer these questions, for the text is a human production viewed by humans who may or may not be members of the same community as the writer. Similarly, one cannot go to the writer except in the most general sense—Shakespeare was *not* referring to dust from atomic bombs although a modern reader might make that inference.

To set forth the argument of the position briefly and in terms somewhat different from Fish: a text is a linguistic utterance of a writer. Any linguistic utterance has two properties, a semantic core that is shared by the writer and many contemporary readers and an overlay of associations held by the writer and not necessarily shared. Recent research in schema theory indicates that the core and overlay exist at the level of the word, of course, but also at the level of larger units of discourse, such as paragraphs and stories. Earlier genre theory had espoused a similar position, that a reader was given a signal that a text was a particular genre and so had certain expectations, which the text either fulfilled or denied.

But, as Fish observes, the issue is even more complex, for readers have long read texts with other sets of presuppositions about how the text should be read. A philologist may look at a text differently than a moralist. In her recent *The Reader, The Text and the Poem*, Louise Rosenblatt (whom Fish unfortunately barely acknowledges) observes that readers may read a text "efferently" or "aesthetically"—to take away a message or to take pleasure. Within the class of aesthetic reading exist several subclasses, which Fish calls "interpretive communities." Communities share certain assumptions, or certain *stock responses*, to use I. A. Richards's term. These communities may be large or small; they may persist over long periods of time, perpetuating themselves primarily through educational systems, formal or informal.

In sum, Fish holds that a reader cannot "know" the text as "in itself it really is"; all the reader can know for certain is his perception and understanding of the text and can verify it by reference to his community, those who share his schemata and semantic space:

Here, I suspect, a defender of determinate meaning would cry "solipsist" and argue that a confidence that had its source in the individual's categories of thought would have no public value. That is, unconnected to any shared and stable system of meaning, it would not enable one to transact the verbal business of everyday life; a shared intelligibility would be impossible in a world where everyone was trapped in the circle of his own assumptions and opinions. The reply to this is that an individual's assumptions and opinions are not "his own" in any sense that would give body to the fear of solipsism. That is *he* is not their origin (in fact it might be more accurate to say that they are his); rather, it is their prior availability which delimits in advance the paths that his consciousness can possibly take. [p. 320]

What I have called schemata, Fish calls beliefs; his term connects to theology and philosophy, mine to psychology, but the terms are complementary.[2] A critic acquires a set of schemata, or belief systems, and operates within their governance. Critics are bound by these systems much as speakers of a given language are bound by that language and members of a culture bound by the semantic space of that culture. When a critic reads a text and interprets it, he does so within the confines of his system and so creates, as Louise Rosenblatt says, a poem. Each critic creates a somewhat different poem, but critics are able to communicate both because of a certain fixity of the text and because of the nature of the community.

Stanley Fish's volume sets out to address this general position in two ways: first, as a retrospective collection of essays, the book shows how Fish progressed to his present position and how he responded to various attackers, notably Meyer Abrams and John Reichert; second, it presents a series of attacks on the pomposity of various critics, particularly the stylisticians who keep hoping to prove that if you can count it, it must be true. Fish would go so far as to assert that meter is a set of conventions readers and writers apply to texts. Long ago I reached the same conclusion as Stanley Fish: people inhabit communities that make meaning, and the potential variety of communities is vast given the number of possible aspects of a "text" that could be discussed and the number of approaches—analytic, classificatory, interpretive, and evaluative—that could be taken. The community means to influence its members' very initial approach to a text and guide their mental operations as they work through to an interpretation.[3] Some of those communities are determined by a general culture: many European students reading William Carlos Williams's "The Use of Force" believe that the doctor acts professionally throughout and criticize the girl. They appear to do so because the cultural norm holds that doctors are always right—even when brutal.

Other communities are determined by schooling, as Fish observes in his title essay, which shows how he has channeled his students to be members of his community (he is much more honest about himself than are Norman Holland and David Bleich, who appear almost surprised by the Freudian interpretations of their students):

The question sometimes put to me—"If what you are saying is true, what is the point of teaching or arguing for anything?"—misses *my* point, which is not that there is no perspective within which one may proceed confidently but that one is always and already proceeding within just such a perspective because one is always and already proceeding with a structure of beliefs. The fact that a standard of truth is never available independently of a set of beliefs does not mean that we can never know for certain what is true but that we *always* know for certain what is true (because we are always in the grip of some belief or other), even though what we certainly know may change if and when our beliefs change. Until they do, however, we will argue *from* their perspective and *for* their perspective, telling our students and readers what it is that we certainly see and trying to alter their perceptions so that, in time, they will come to see it too. [pp. 364–65]

In fact, one might go further than Fish and assert that all interpretations result from schooling of one sort or another. In countries where literature forms part of the curriculum, students learn which questions are "appropriate" to ask of a text—questions of "hidden meaning" in the United States, questions of historical background in Italy. Reading literature and reading in general are acquired skills limited by cultural norms. Communities—some national, some class-bound, some regional, all schooled—acquire norms for reading texts, for writing essays, for judging literary quality.

One might justly argue that Fish substitutes group solipsism for individual solipsism. But, as cultural anthropologists and psycholinguists have argued for a generation at least, group solipsism appears best to describe people's perceptions of many phenomena, not the least of which is a literary text. One might also say that Fish is recapitulating and defending the medieval hermeneutic tradition, which allowed for finding Christian allegory in any text examined. Today's scholastics, however, Fish would asseverate, can find whatever allegory is current in their community—be it Freudian, Marxist, moralistic, jingoistic, new critical, post-structuralist, or whatever the current community is "into." His dictum to the current literary student, were Fish to be using the jargon of the sixties, might be "Do thy thing; but know thy bag."

It *might be,* and it would be the dictum of a pure deconstructionist, but in affirming the importance of "communities," "institutions," "canons," and "contexts," Fish separates himself from purely solipsistic readers like Derrida and Nelson. He also avoids making the critic as important or more important than the writer, although he asserts, as have Frye, Rosenblatt, and others, that a text comes alive only when read. The point about communities asserts the social bond between writer and reader, a bond of language. Some of the bonds are very broad so that communication of information over space and time is possible (if writer and reader share the same context); some of the bonds are much more narrow as contexts narrow. Fish and I may have been graduate students at the same time, taking similar courses, but we were at different universities and we have since pursued different careers. Yet he and I appear to share many contexts in our readings of seventeenth-century poetry, and neither of us appears to be particularly comfortable in Freudian circles. The point is, nonetheless, that contexts can be circumscribed, but, more importantly, described so that readers can reach consensus, or at least, can communicate. Perhaps the broadest level of consensus is the most valid interpretation, although frequently not the most interesting; a reader can be apprised of

The Reader as Hero and Bully: Fish and Leavis 261

a different interpretation from those previously known and can assent to it as another possibility.

Fish talks only in interpretation, and some critics say that the function of the critic is not to interpret but to evaluate, to assert or deny the worth of literary works and writers. Does Fish's notion of a community hold here as well? I think it does, and I think William Walsh's *F. R. Leavis* supports the contention. Walsh has written a hagiographic "critical" biography—a brief biography with notes on the master's criticism. As a biography, it is illuminating to the American reader aware of Leavis's power and influence but somewhat unsure of his position in British academe and letters of the first half of the century. As criticism, it strikes one as an exercise in pedestal-building, for Walsh places Leavis with Dryden, Johnson, Coleridge, and Arnold. I cannot understand why one would do so, based on Leavis's own writing. Stanley Fish helps me understand.

F. R. Leavis was an outsider in Cambridge all his life—a bright town boy in a university where locals were not supposed to be luminaries. So Leavis established a community that created its identity by attacking the establishment. And he got so in the habit of doing so that he seemed never quite to recognize that he had become the establishment—or a new establishment. What Leavis's writing accomplished was a new canon. In *New Bearings in English Poetry, Revaluation, The Great Tradition,* and particularly in *Scrutiny,* Leavis established T. S. Eliot, Johnson, Donne, Pope, Wordsworth, Shelley, Keats, Jane Austen, George Eliot, Henry James, and Joseph Conrad as the major figures in English literature. As a result of his community building, these figures—and a few single works by others, particularly Dickens and D. H. Lawrence—became the "glass[es] of fashion" for at least two generations of graduate students, if not in England, certainly in the United States. Leavis accomplished this feat less by argument than by intimidation and proselytization. Leavis's work is full of *obiter dicta;* he ends a paragraph on *Little Dorrit,* "It is all significant" (quoted by Walsh, p. 151). Like Arnold, Leavis asserted what was good, what constituted the "best that has been known and said in the world." Arnold sought to build a community in the face of prospective anarchy, Leavis in the face of a donnish hegemony. Both succeeded.

Walsh spends some time documenting the campaign; Leavis and his wife, together with several adjutants, such as Denys Thompson, D. W. Harding, and Frank Whitehead, established a critical-pedagogical movement which operated at two levels, the first of which Walsh discusses at great length, the level of critical writing. Leavis was not an interpreter in Fish's sense; his style was not that of an explicator. He wrote of the importance rather than the import of authors and texts—importance both personal and to other authors. He sought to make an English literary heritage, to extend it through various contemporary writers, and to have the works included in the university canon.

The other aspect of Leavis's movement, less fully discussed by Walsh, is probably more important in the long run. Through Thompson and others involved with the journal *The Uses of English,* addressed to secondary-school teachers, there emerged in the period 1940–1960 an approach to the school study of literature that was personal and moral, quite different from the prevailing historical approach. The new approach coincided with the shifts in British education that brought about the comprehensive school, and its adherents formed the core of teacher trainers and textbook writers of the present generation. As a result of Leavis, the contemporary English community of readers differs greatly from that in the United States.[4] They are not necessarily better or worse, but they are different. The broad American community of readers appears to have come about as a result of a curious melding of New Criticism and various interpretive critics, particularly the psychological, and, to a lesser extent, the heirs of Irving Babbitt. The general British community today results in great part from Leavis.

Critics build interpretive communities and they also build canons. As Stanley Fish might observe, but doesn't, both situations are normal literary counterparts to religious communities and other intellectual and social groups. In fact, Fish's analysis of hermeneutics parallels much of social psychology. One wonders why such a view should be the object of attack, but then one remembers that no sect likes to be told that it does not own the truth. Recently I shared with my son the results of a study of student ratings of another student essay. "But Dad," he said, "that's what the essay is." The essay isn't, but the perceptions of that essay are shared by American students like my son, and to them the perceptions are truth. So, too, with interpretive communities: they cannot admit the relativist's view of themselves but must assert that such *is* the nature of the text. Stanley Fish is somewhat like the boy in "The Emperor's New Clothes" (as *I* perceive both of them), but the emperors will always want to strike back.

Notes

1. This lack of popularity is evidenced in a recent article in *Newsweek*, 22 June 1981, pp. 80–83. The reports indicate fear of the deconstructionists among the older critics. *Newsweek* intimates that Derrida, Hartmann, et al. are in league with those devils Nietzsche and the linguists (whom *Newsweek* has castigated for years over issues related to the teaching of English).

2. One might trace twentieth-century criticism psychologically rather than (as Fish does) philosophically. There was a long period from early Richards through the 1960s, when criticism followed behaviorism with the text the stimulus to the reader's response. The newer approach follows the psychology of the cognitivists and the perceptual psychologists. Such a shift, of course, parallels the shift in linguistics marked by the work of Chomsky.

3. See Alan C. Purves, with Victoria Rippere, *Elements of Writing about a Literary Work: A Study of Response to Literature* (Urbana: National Council of Teachers of English, 1968). In that volume we identified over 120 separate kinds of statements on the basis of an examination of essays by students, teachers, and professional critics in five countries. See also Purves, with Sharon Silkey, "What Happens When We Read a Poem," *Journal of Aesthetic Education*, 7 (July 1973), 63–72.

4. For a fuller statement of the Leavisite position, see John Dixon, *Growth through English* (London: National Association of Teachers of English, 1968).

Annihilating the Poet in Donne

John T. Shawcross

John Carey. *John Donne: Life, Mind, and Art.* New York: Oxford University Press, 1981. 303 pp.

Both the literary-critical thinking of the greater part of the twentieth century and its current practitioners are so totally ignored in John Carey's recent book on John Donne that one might suppose Edmund Gosse were the last significant writer on Donne, David Masson's the last perceptive investigation of Milton's poetry, and names like Cleanth Brooks, Kenneth Burke, Ernst Cassirer, or Jacques Derrida not even names, let alone people with important critical ideas. *John Donne: Life, Mind, and Art* offers an interpretation of Donne's poems (and of Donne) seen through the biography of the poet. However, the book is neither a biography nor a critical study. It is a reading of poems (with excursions into some prose, largely for biography or interpretative "evidence") in terms of biography with sallies into a half-disguised and wholly unestablished psychological analysis. At fault is methodology; even more significant for readers are the frequently indefensible results of that methodology. Lamentably, then, the positive elements in the discussions are tainted, and, for some of the poems, such matters as biographical and psychological contexts are obliterated altogether.

Halfway through the first chapter, "Apostasy," one clearly understands what the book will be doing, and most informed readers will tune out, realizing its speciousness. After discussing the *fact* that Donne was born into a Roman Catholic family and grew up in an anti–Roman Catholic political world, Carey declares Donne's rejection of Roman Catholicism, which thus becomes apostasy, and its centrality to Donne's personality and his concerns: "The poetic evidence of this crisis is Satire III—the great, crucial poem of Donne's early manhood" (p. 26). Carey does not quite state that the poem is not a satire, but his discussion in no way accords with what a literary satire is and thus suggests that the author either ignores such generic labels or does not know what such generic labels imply for literary understanding: "For most of its length it is not a satire at all, but a self-lacerating record of that moment which comes in the lives of almost all thinking people, when the beliefs of youth, unquestionably assimilated and bound up with our closest personal attachments, come into conflict with the scepticism of the mature intellect" (p. 26). The contents of the poem are read as close biographical counters: the section on the Catholic Graccus, for instance, reflects Donne's personal bitterness toward the one "right" church, which concept he "gave up" but "still clung to." Thus the sonnet "Show me deare Christ" "reveals the lasting disorientation his apostasy entailed," and that apostasy "leads to almost comic contradictions in his sermons." "When Donne renounced Catholicism isn't known," but "Satire III shows . . . that he has been able to prise his intellect away from the old Faith, otherwise there'd be no need to set out on a search for truth" (p. 30). Ultimately, the reader's problems with this book concern not only the interpretation of a poem or the acceptance or non-acceptance of matters in Donne biography, but also the question of the preconceptions of the book's author. Carey clearly accepts all Church doctrine as dogma and conceives of church dogma as encompassing all truth that might exist in any sphere. From such a preconception arises then the premise that Donne could not speculate on varied aspects of religious truth, allowing all sides their voice, could not, that is, write a work of the imagination. Indeed, there is no "voice" in any of the poems; there is only the poet.

Carey's readings of different kinds of poems manifest his inability to perceive literary voice. Of the love elegy "The Bracelet," for example, he writes, "In this poem *Donne* has lost a gold chain belonging to *his* girl" (p. 39, my italics); in "Womans Constancy," he again finds the speaker to be Donne; he reads the poem to Rowland Woodward beginning "Like one who'in her third widdowhood" as though it presents some of Donne's thoughts unaltered by rhetoric or poetic form ("His doubts about selfhood make it imperative that he should imprint a firm self on the poems" [p. 270]); and in several holy sonnets he sees the "speaker" as always the same and always a self-dramatizing Donne who "is, or says he is, poised on the brink of eternity" (p. 203). While surely there are biographical elements in the Woodward poem and these holy sonnets, those elements are fashioned into a literary statement, the first in rhyming tercets, the second as sonnets with definite octaves and sestets. Carey fails to heed the literary voice in the poems. The "firm self" being stamped on the poems is equated with contrived portraits and puns on Donne's name, and, "like the scratching of a signature in a window, they are all subterfuges to clarify the identity" (p. 170).

Where this approach to the poems leads—the directly biographical context, the lack of literary context, the ignoring of voice—can be seen in Carey's reading of "The Relique," which he calls a death-wish poem. "At first Donne's intellectual contempt for Catholicism dominates," he writes. "When his skeleton and its hairy bracelet are hauled from the grave they will, he prophesies, be added to the Church's grisly bric-a-brac and adored by silly women. Donne confounds these misguided worshippers by launching into a defiant humanist manifesto, which segregates himself and the girl he loves from their pious follies" (p. 44). Not only is Donne the man directly the "I" of the poem, but the situation is purported to reflect a real association between Donne and some amour. The lines "Difference of sex no more wee knew, / Than our Guardian Angells doe" launch Carey into a speculation that this is residue from Donne's "childish article of faith" that there are guardian angels "commissioned to watch over him, which had been instilled into him as a child" and which persists in his mature beliefs. A further technique of this methodology is to propose something that is said not to be proposed, which, of course, thus plants the idea in the reader's mind: "If we were to try and [sic] explain the poem in terms of Donne's psychology we might say that his rejection of Catholic superstitution (relics, miracles) had left his hunger for holiness without a focus, so he invents a version of human love elevated enough to satisfy it. Love fills the crater left by apostasy. 'The Relique' cannot be reduced to such formulas, but they are a part of its life" (p. 45).

Carey has missed the wit and ironies of "The Relique" by his relentless application of thesis. I do not say that biographical residue does not exist and, indeed, what I will suggest is a more telling instance of the "rejection of Catholic superstition" in its pornographic jibe. The point is that Carey does not read the poem as a piece of literature, written by a poet with imagination, pulling in image, symbol, and wit for his reading audience (originally, probably, a coterie of friends who also tried their poetic hands at various topics, situations, techniques, desired effects, and often enough, obscenity). The poem begins, "When my grave is broke up againe" and continues: "And he that digs it, spies / A bracelet of bright haire about the bone" (lines 1, 5–6). A frequent love-token in Donne's time was a bracelet of a loved one's hair worn around the wrist (cf. Egeus' reference in *A Midsummer Night's Dream* I.i.28–29, 32–33: "Thou, thou, Lysander, thou hast given her rhymes / And interchang'd love tokens with my child;" "And stol'n the impression of her fantasy / With bracelets of thy hair, rings, gauds, conceits"). But Donne makes the lines in his poem function not only as an indicator of love-token but as a witty comment that even though in life she was a miracle who apparently did not allow the seal that nature sets free to be touched (or broken), in death, in the grave, there is "more than one a Bed," and the woman's seal has now been metaphorically "injur'd" by older, natural action. The bracelet of bright hair will lead the digger to "thinke that there a *loving* couple lies" (my italics); along with other double entendres (like "Comming and going" with its to-and-fro or up-and-down connotation), the image is phallic, the bone (not simply *wrist* or *arm*) encircled by bright hair (not simply that acquired when she was young, but pubic). The *loving couple* becomes graphic; the second guest has indeed been *entertained;* the difference of sex which they did not know first, they know second, for then they did not know "what [they] lov'd, nor why"; now they do.

I hope I am not being morally naive by suggesting that Donne would not have been so indecorous as to provide such obscene readings had he been the "I" of the poem, sincerely presenting a real love experience, conditioned by a deeply personal contempt for Catholic practice. There is certainly blasphemy in the poem (and the lines "Thou shalt be'a Mary Magdalen, and I / A something else thereby" come to mind), but it is device (no matter how contemptuous Donne may have been) to produce a witty paradox between the religion of love and the religion of faith. If we must speculate about poems, let us speculate about the audience for which the poem was written and its reaction, and we can hear Donne's friends chuckling and guffawing over his expertise in being able to present something which could hoodwink readers not attentive to the puns and parallelisms. A similar point can be made about "The Good-morrow," often read as an avowal of great love for someone, sometimes for Ann More, when we consider the third and fourth lines again: "But suck'd on country pleasures, childishly? / Or snorted we in the'seaven sleepers den?" Carey's comment on the poem is: "The cloister image [as womb in *La Corona*] derives from a matins hymn used in the Roman Church for feasts of the Blessed Virgin. Donne's rendering of it inevitably reminds us of the love in 'The Good-morrow' which 'makes one little roome, an every where,' and the link-up suggests how closely Donne's early religious training influenced his love poetry, though a different 'deare wombe' was involved" (p. 51). But "The Good-morrow" is no more straight autobiography than is "The Relique"; rather it presents another love situation for the poetic hand to delineate. The male, who has had various sexual experiences in the past and who assumes his present love partner has had too—surely he would have been able to decide that during the last evening—asserts that this night of lovemaking has been so gratifying that it reduces all his past sexual experiences to child's play or mere relief with prostitutes. And he wonders whether indeed this is going to be a true love and continued liaison or just the one-night stand it apparently started out to be.

Carey does not offer a view of Donne the poet because he does not treat the poetry as poetry but ultimately only as versified biography. Thus he ignores a main avenue into the poems as literature, the voice in the poems and the author's manipulation of his reader by what he does in the poems. Even in agreed biographical poems the limitation creates an unbalanced reading; for example, in his reading of "A Burnt Ship," where Donne's sense of *play* (the ludic content) is nowhere to be found. In comparison with Ralegh's account of the historical event behind the poem, Carey finds Donne less humane, pitiless, hard, jubilant in tone, rhapsodizing: "Donne treats the slaughter as a joke: the pretext for a smart paradox" (p. 95). Of course! The problem is that Carey underneath it all demands "serious" treatment for "serious" subjects, for he is frequently literal-minded and always unconcerned with the act and art of poeticizing. Had Donne wished to present this event in a "serious" way, he would not have chosen the epigram to do it (not that epigrams cannot be serious, as some of Ben Jonson's attest), but rather a different subgenre, perhaps a lyric form like those verse letters written to various male friends, or, indeed, something like "The Storme" or "The Calme." I would start the other way around from Carey and emphasize that Donne has written a witty epigram built on puns and the admixture of incompatible opposites—fire and water—and that he used as subject an event which he had read about (to suggest that he may have been an eyewitness, as Carey does, is against biographical knowledge). In other words, Carey emphasizes tenor in his treatment of "A Burnt Ship"; I would emphasize vehicle *for this poem*.

Elsewhere I find Carey wrenching the significance of the word *Pilgrimage* in "Goe and catche a falling starre" (p. 38); still relating "The Autumnall" to Magdalene Herbert (p. 81), although he gives ample reason for rejecting Walton's connection of the two (actually one has only to read the poem and note its images to realize how preposterous Walton's statement is); calling "A Letter to the Lady Carey, and Mrs. Essex Riche, from Amyens" (the only poem we have in Donne's holograph except for two Latin epigrams inscribed in books) "a totally worthless set of verses" (p. 84); viewing *Biathanatos* as a fully serious "giant suicide note" (p. 209); revealing his own antifeminism ("We are careful to talk, nowadays, as if we believed that the male ought to respect the female's individuality. Donne is above such hypocrisies, and states, with measured resonance, his lethal hunger" [p. 100]); overreading, as in the "massive erection" he sees in "To His Mistris Going to Bed"; and sweeping away interpretations of the *Anniversaries,* which apparently do not have or require "any semblance of sense" and which "are about as touching as a brass band" by epitomizing them as essays in exorbitance (pp. 101–3). Another dangerous methodology is the relating of words and images in disparate works written at different times and perhaps in differing contexts. It is the main procedure for the discussions in the last half of the book, but it should be evident that the underlying assumption is a consistency in Donne's thinking, attitudes, language and uses of language. Snidely Carey tries to demolish all antibiographical critics as "for the most part . . . persons with literary gifts infinitely smaller than Gosse's" (p. 72). And on pages 90–91 he further betrays his inadequacy for the job of dealing with Donne's poetry when he asks, "Would he not have been an even greater and more prolific poet if he had not squandered his time turning out verse letters, epithalamions and funerary tributes? Might we not have had more *Songs and Sonnets?*"

Unfortunately, I must mention yet another problem with the book: its writing. Carey strives to achieve informality by using contractions, omitting commas, using colloquial phrasing and word order (e.g., "the essential quality which makes Donne Donne" [p. 4]), repeatedly using "so" as a conjunction, and indulging in occasional bad grammar and questionable vocabulary ("Donne did not get as much money out of her [the Countess of Bedford] as he had hoped" [p. 80]). This sort of informality is so pervasive at the beginning of the book—when presumably Carey is trying to build reader interest—that the reader is alternately bored and insulted. And too often Carey manipulates language instead of coming out and saying what he means.

But as I have remarked there are positive elements in the discussions and, for some of the poems, significant matters like biographical and psychological contexts. The reader familiar with Donne's works will rethink those works, even when Carey has not pursued those particular items. For example, the problem of nothingness and suicide is seen to pervade *Essays in*

Divinity, poems like "A Nocturnall upon S. Lucies Day," *Devotions, Biathanatos,* the sermons: "Though seeking nothingness, Donne prizes himself as a special kind of nothing. . . . This illogicality strikes us as psychologically true, not just because it sounds so like Donne, but also because it reproduces the mixture of feelings contained in bereavement" (p. 172). To Carey, Donne the poet and Donne the theologian is each of two minds in the fascination with nonentity, and he is, we remember, "a little world made cunningly." The Holy Sonnet is as much concerned with self-hate and death-wish (annihilation) as these other works, while maintaining a sense that the poet is important enough for God to direct His "fiery zeale" toward consuming that world which the poet is.

Further there is in the second half of the book a greater attention to imagery in chapters entitled "Bodies," "Change," "Death," "The Crisis of Reason," and "Imagined Corners." For example, after looking at poems in which the human body is a basic subject or image, Carey turns to "The Flea," reviewing briefly but meaningfully flea poems and Donne's variant. "The delicate intentness of that last line ['An cloysterd in these living walls of Jet'] treats a flea as no flea had been treated in English before." "The transformation of the flea to a temple and a cloister . . . reminds us . . . of Donne in his sermon clambering through the body's vaulted edifice" (pp. 146–47). Also he carefully examines evaporation as a motif, citing "A Feaver," "The Expiration," the sermons, "The Perfume," "The Bracelet," "The Progresse of the Soule" ("Metempsychosis"), pp. 183–84. "Of the fifty-four *Songs and Sonnets,* thirty-two—well over half— find some means of fitting death in" (p. 201), Carey tells us, and proceeds to review the preponderance of the subject, image, or motif in those and other poems as if backed off and taking survey of all the poems. The procedure interrelates the works and places many of the poems into the larger contexts they deserve. An example: "Metempsychosis" is related to *Essays in Divinity* and both to "Reason is our Soules left hand, Faith her right," "Elegie on Prince Henry," and the sermons through the struggle of faith against the violent conflict of reason. These

Annihilating the Poet in Donne 273

works have not been so treated previously, except that some have entered investigations of reason versus faith in Donne.

Throughout these later chapters Carey provides much information drawn from the history of ideas and philosophy and ranging through other authors like Aldous Huxley and Walter Pater. On pp. 244–48 follows the reason or faith issue seen in Ockham, Bacon, Comenius, Ralegh, and others; according to Carey, "He belongs ... to a dying tradition, not of the brave new Baconian world" (p. 248). The earlier chapters too supply important information, like that about Margaret Clitherow (pp. 40–41), which builds the religious atmosphere surrounding the younger Donne, or like that about the British expeditions (pp. 66–69), which supplies historical contexts, or like that about various noblemen sought out for preferment (pp. 83 ff.), which helps develop a picture of Donne the person and opportunist. In all these instances, however, the reader will recognize, the emphasis is upon the information, not upon the poems.

Carey's discussions of "The Progresse of the Soule" (pp. 148–58, 175, 269–70, 274) should be specifically pointed out since he is one of the few critics who have taken the poem seriously and have anything intelligent to say about it, and conclusions like that advancing the possible authorship of "Sapho to Philaenis" (pp. 270–71), denied by some critics, have cogency through his demonstration of a poem's congruency with Donne's concerns. The strong points of this examination of Donne's psychic biography and its impingement on the works are Carey's focus on the importance of context—biographical, historical, ideational—and the useful information he supplies in each of those areas. It is unfortunate, however, that Carey has been so little concerned with literary matters that he has allowed his thesis of a kind of schizoid Donne to occasion a serious misreading of the poems and that he has offered up a structure of Donne's imagination which, while framing its individuality, ignores that which is at base not individual, only adapted.

The (De)Construction of Sister George: Eliot's Second Hundred Years

Victoria S. Middleton

Jeannette King. *Tragedy in the Victorian Novel: Theory and Practice in the Novels of George Eliot, Thomas Hardy, and Henry James.* Cambridge: Cambridge University Press, 1978. viii, 182 pp.

Hugh Witemeyer. *George Eliot and the Visual Arts.* New Haven: Yale University Press, 1979. xiii, 238 pp. 36 illus.

U. C. Knoepflmacher and George Levine, eds. *Nineteenth-Century Fiction, Special Issue: George Eliot, 1880–1980.* Berkeley: University of California Press, 1980. Vol. 35, No. 3. 202 pp.

Judith Wilt. *Ghosts of the Gothic: Austen, Eliot, and Lawrence.* Princeton: Princeton University Press, 1980. xii, 307 pp.

If the ensuing discussion of four critical studies dealing with George Eliot has a grammar or plot, it may resemble a polysyndeton. The choice of a cumulative structure might seem a function of the variety of subjects treated by the books—tragic drama, literary pictorialism, Positivism, conservative politics, Gothicism, and others. But diverse subjects can be drawn together by a synthesizing mind like George Eliot's own. Rather than attempt such a feat, I more modestly prefer to set up a comparison that is inclusive ("both/and"), not exclusive ("either/or"), in nature. Implicitly, there are two models of criticism reflected in these four studies. The first and more established is a positivistic, evolutionary model that views Eliot's books (as she told us to) as organic products of distinct phases in the evolution of her own consciousness. That is, we can regard Eliot's novels as organisms (fabrics, webs, tissues, organs) with complex internal structures and complex relations to each other and to their intellectual environment. All four studies to some extent accept the organic model of a literary tradition, whether they discuss Eliot's personal development or that of the English novel. In *Tragedy in the Victorian Novel,* Jeannette King classifies Eliot as a lesser member of a triad of Victorian tragic novelists. Her mastery of tragic themes and techniques, King implies, is superseded by that of Thomas Hardy and Henry James in the refinement of the novel as a tragic form. Hugh Witemeyer's *George Eliot and the Visual Arts* is another study of growth, though the connective tissues he analyzes are links between literature and painting. Where King feels that Eliot suffers by comparison with other artists, Witemeyer finds much to celebrate. The *Nineteenth-Century Fiction* special issue is more judiciously appreciative in considering Eliot's relation to other women novelists, to essayists, to her fellow Victorian conservatives, Positivists, and scientists. At the same time that this collection of essays affirms the organicist model—whether perceived in Eliot's work or applied to it—it challenges that model. Articles by Catherine Gallagher and, especially, J. Hillis Miller not only undercut a positivistic reading of *Felix Holt* and *Middlemarch,* they also argue that Eliot deconstructs such readings within those novels. This second critical perspective calls into question realistic fictions and disconfirms facile correspondences between reality and the ways we perceive and structure our responses to it. Eliot's skepticism and irony have received too little attention, with the unfortunate consequence that skepticism and irony are sometimes leveled at what is positivistic and syncretic in her vision. Without preferring one model of criticism over the other, the editors of *Nineteenth-Century Fiction* stress the pluralism of the views they present, rather than their latent contradictoriness. They emphasize that Eliot resists a single interpretation. The articles themselves remind us that our very idea of George Eliot is a construct, or rather that there are many ideas and that some are antithetical.

Judith Wilt's study of *Ghosts of the Gothic* again places Eliot in a context or tradition, but it recreates our notion of that tradition—what we mean by Gothicism and realism. Her paradigm is more compelling and attractive than those of King and Witemeyer because it yields a reading of Eliot that is neither disparaging nor honorific. Further, it avoids the static or explicative quality of those books. Wilt's argument runs some of the risks of inductive hypotheses (of which no one was more wary than George Eliot), especially a tendency to claim as Gothic certain fictional situations that are better accounted for in other critical terms, and a countertendency to lose sight of the thesis about Gothicism in analysis of individual novels. Still, she uses her hypothesis creatively, challenging and opening up our readings of realistic novels, in part by examining her own thesis analytically. Her book departs from received notions about realism and Eliot's commitment to it, while *Nineteenth-Century Fiction* holds the contrary stances in suspension, implying that George Eliot is at once syncretic and deconstructive. Clearly, while my discussion of these four texts has an "and then" structure, it is inevitable that equal value cannot be ascribed to each book. What seems important, as Eliot criticism enters its second century, is that, whether as feminists or deconstructionists, we claim George Eliot's work as contemporary by reading her in ways that reflect our world view, and by not unquestioningly, unanalytically accepting what we take to be her own.

Both Jeannette King and George Eliot would find my judgment of *Tragedy in the Victorian Novel* somewhat unfair, for it sacrifices the whole to the part. In focusing almost exclusively on her treatment of George Eliot's work, I risk committing the same injustice that King herself verges on in her comparison of Eliot to Hardy and James. To distinguish Eliot from the other two novelists, King stresses Eliot's belief in communal progress through individual suffering and her emphasis on the mutual cooperation and connectedness of parts of the social organism. King seems to me to exaggerate Eliot's optimism, for Eliot's novels dramatize, as she says Hardy's and James's novels do, the tragedy of "wasted potential" (p. 127). The gap that King senses between Eliot and the two more "modern" male writers seems smaller than King allows. The contrast she sets up does imperfect justice to Eliot and vitiates King's own theory; in correcting what I believe to be distorting, I hope to show what is valuable in King's work. Her view of tragic themes and forms represents a version of literary history that is old-fashioned but not therefore uninteresting or uninformative. Her view of tragedy has the same kind of strengths and flaws she attributes to Eliot's fiction: faith in an evolution of literary forms: a tendency to subsume the individual fact or organism (or novel) under a general law or principle; a commitment to certitude, expressed in generalizations, paradigms, and aesthetic closure.

King argues that the locus of the tragic spirit in nineteenth-century English literature was the novel, not the drama. (She mentions Ibsen only in passing: one would like to hear more of his impact on novelists and even, hypothetically, what Eliot would have made of his treatment of women.) King examines the philosophy of tragedy, the clash between determinism and free will, and shows how it found expression in the contemporary form of the realistic novel. "Classical tragic drama not only does without, but requires the absence of, realism" (p. 50); that is, close description of ordinary life would seem antithetical to the sublime passions and universality experienced in tragic plays. In the hands of Eliot, Hardy, and James, however, the novel was transformed into the appropriate vehicle for the distinctively Victorian conception of tragedy. In their works, Fate or Necessity takes the deterministic guise of biology, heredity, and environment (p. 60). The heroic individual becomes, often, the middle- or lower-class individual struggling against these determining conditions (pp. 65–67). The three novelists dramatize the outcome of tragic suffering differently: George Eliot stresses the absorption of the individual's suffering by the ongoing, evolving communal life and the absorption of tragic elements by novelistic closure that affirms the continuity of ordinary life. Hardy rages against a meaningless, indifferent cosmos whose laws conspire against the individual; his novels question classic tragic forms themselves and the order they affirm. James's work is preoccupied with the individual's struggle between freedom and forms that are internal, social, or aesthetic. Each novelist defines the essential tragic plot differently: for Eliot, it lies in "the irreparable collision between the individual and the general" (p. 84); for Hardy, it consists of "the worthy encompassed by the inevitable" (p. 100); for James, it is "unfulfilled intention"

(p. 127). King says that the tragic novels of Hardy and James are preoccupied with "loss and waste" (p. 157)—with the terrible realization that suffering might have had a different result.

But King does not focus on tragic waste in Eliot's work. She grants Eliot's masterful depiction of "her vision of modern tragedy—the woman's situation, with its enforced passivity and pathos, and the stifling of the individual by artificial social roles" (p. 78). At times, however, King accuses Eliot of making her heroines' suffering pathetic rather than tragic, helpless and unconscious rather than heroic, to affirm society's progress. I would suggest instead that Eliot exploits the conflict between women's heroic potential and their opportunities for displaying heroism; her tragic vision indicts the circumstances that rob women's lives of grandeur. In showing reality, she does not inevitably affirm it—especially its "wasting" the potency of Maggie Tulliver, Dorothea Brooke, and Gwendolen Harleth. King assesses George Eliot's achievement in terms of the merit of her tragic vision. Two problems arise from her approach. First, King seems to criticize Eliot's theory of tragic fiction rather than her practice. Perhaps Eliot did not intend her novels to be read as tragedies; or, perhaps, as King allows, she meant us to see that "tragedy is absorbed into the novel" (p. 93). While King acknowledges that Eliot intends to assimilate tragedy and realism, at times she criticizes Eliot for denying or turning away from tragedy: "the tragic tension is weakened" (p. 93); there is "more tragic tone" in the work of Hardy and James (p. 35); Eliot's "redefinition of tragedy resulted finally in an avoidance of tragedy" (p. 158). Eliot's endings don't fulfill her own ideal of "faithfulness to life" (p. 75)—they seem static, arbitrary, and overly simplistic compared with James's " 'unfinished' endings" (p. 95). This comparison distorts Eliot's purpose.

The second problem with King's judgment of Eliot is her own faith in progress. She regards Eliot's work as an early phase in the evolution of tragedy through the realistic novel (its ultimate incarnation being *Jude the Obscure*) to the theater of the absurd. In the company of Artaud, Eliot's tragic vision must seem quaint, with its emphasis on morality, duty, submission, resignation. (Of course, as Judith Wilt shows, when Eliot's Gothic vision is appreciated, it prefigures Kafka's in no quaint and trivial way.) While I would hardly argue for Eliot's modernity, I don't think she is as unambiguously positivistic as King seems to, or that her novels always end with moral certitude and compromise. Perhaps King ignores the possibility that adaptation to tragic necessity—as in a woman's fateful choice of a husband—itself is tragic, and that Eliot's tragic form and vision are one.

I would further challenge King's reading of certain novels. The predicaments of Mrs. Transome and Gwendolen Harleth seem unmitigatedly bleak and impossible to put out of mind regardless of the barely credible happiness of the heroic males (Felix Holt and Daniel Deronda). These exceptional women are left in dreadful isolation (an apt punishment for their naively superior separateness earlier in the novels); though they may not comprehend and rage against the fate they have met, the narrator's voice (as King effectively points out) intervenes and reconciles us to the inevitable. To put it another way, King should have seen how the inarticulate suffering of Mrs. Transome and Gwendolen Harleth, or the sublime passion of Maggie Tulliver and Alcharisi, have much in common with the elevated suffering and consciousness of Tess, Sue, and Jude, or Isabel Archer, Kate Croy, and Milly Theale, and that Hardy and James also elucidate the unconsciousness of their characters to reconcile us to their fate (p. 89). For Eliot, as for Hardy and James, suffering brings consciousness, which inevitably involves language. In the work of all three, the articulation of lived suffering is shared between characters and novelist, an achievement made possible by the fusion of novel and drama.

While Jeannette King analyzes features shared by drama and novel, Hugh Witemeyer stresses George Eliot's view of the relation of literature to the plastic arts. According to Witemeyer's *George Eliot and the Visual Arts,* Eliot uses the pictorial analogy or description as a proscenium arch: she draws the reader from graphic to dramatic scene (p. 42). Witemeyer's study focuses on the technical means by which Eliot sets the scene or introduces a character to the inner or outer drama. His historical approach attempts to avoid two critical excesses he identifies in

The (De)Construction of Sister George

George Eliot criticism: the overemphasis on psychological action in her fiction (p. 4) and the formalists' injunction against going outside the literary text for meaning (p. 5). Two countertendencies make his own study timely, he feels: recent art criticism shows increased favor toward Victorian painting and literary criticism is currently receptive to exploring correspondences and analogies between the arts (p. 5).

Witemeyer scrupulously defines his own sense of what constitutes the pictorial in literature: the novel must "overtly recall (1) an identifiable work of art, (2) a tradition of graphic or plastic representation, or (3) an established convention of pictorialist rhetoric such as the formal character-portrait" (p. 7). Witemeyer documents the influences on Eliot's pictorial writing: her own knowledge of artists and paintings; G. E. Lessing on literature's aesthetic properties and G. H. Lewes on empirical psychology (p. 35); and, most significant, the influence of Ruskin's moral aesthetics (p. 16). Having justified his own historical situating of Eliot, Witemeyer discusses four kinds of painting or pictorial description in Eliot's novels. In descending order of their importance, these are: portraiture; sacred and heroic history painting; genre painting; and landscape (p. 8). Eliot's use of portraiture evolves from her belief that appearances mirror reality (Dinah and Seth in *Adam Bede*), through moral condemnation of real evil underlying apparent innocence (Hetty Sorrel and Mrs. Transome), to recognition of the gap between the static picture and the changing persona as a normative one (Dorothea and Gwendolen) (p. 45). Witemeyer offers an interesting interpretation of Hetty Sorrel's portrait as the implicit undercutting of traditional rhetorical patterns about *belle donne*: "George Eliot implies that the convention itself involves a projection of male desire which has little to do with the real nature of women" (pp. 53–54). He credits her with a sophisticated feminist stance, in a sense, and rightly.

Eliot used history painting to render concrete her belief in a secularized typological symbolism (p. 75), which let her associate noble human faces such as Mordecai's with Biblical exemplars, idealizing the living human being (p. 77). Eliot's own "taste for massive, Amazonian figures" in sculpture (and in life) is expressed in "imposing creatures" like Maggie Tulliver and Gwendolen Harleth (p. 80). It is interesting that Eliot liked Raphael's "classical, spiritualized, and serene" beauties but at the same time responded (guiltily) to Rubens's "baroque, fleshly, and dynamic" representations of women (p. 23). Witemeyer expands our awareness of how George Eliot portrayed the English and Jewish characters of *Daniel Deronda* as separate—the English are treated with "ironic portraiture," the Jews with "ennobling" (p. 92), the latter following Ruskin's idea that the Venetian, coloristic style of painting is more Oriental and more spiritual (p. 100).

Genre painting is less central than portraits and history painting to Eliot's representation of the reality beyond appearances. Witemeyer feels critical attention has exaggerated Eliot's reference to Dutch genre painting in *Adam Bede* (p. 21). He shows how Eliot used "conversation" paintings to convey both family intimacy such as that of the Garths (p. 111) and its inverse, through the telling absence of lawful members such as the fathers of Mrs. Transome's and Lydia Glasher's children (pp. 122–24).

Finally, Eliot's landscapes are not picturesque in a sentimental way but are sublimely Ruskinian in spirit (pp. 142–43), rendered with Pre-Raphaelite detail and Wordsworthian involvement (pp. 136–37). Witemeyer confirms the observation of Edward Dowden, whose contemporary criticisms of Eliot were so often discerning, that Mordecai in *Daniel Deronda* is usually placed in a "Turnerian and visionary" landscape (p. 141). The human drama would always be foregrounded in Eliot's work; but Witemeyer shows how carefully and aptly drawn the background landscape is.

In a final chapter Witemeyer analyzes Frederic Leighton's illustrations of *Romola*, which may have fed the "boundless public appetite for visualized narrative" (p. 157) but which remained, perhaps necessarily, more faithful and sensitive to "stylistic and iconographic traditions" of painting than to the text of *Romola* (p. 161). George Eliot quickly discerned that "Leighton's Romola is . . . very different from the Romola of the text. . . . Tonally, the illustration is to the text very nearly what a negative is to a photograph" (p. 167). Given Witemeyer's critique of the drawings (eight of which are reproduced), the reader appreciates why Eliot supplied her own verbal portraits, conversation pieces, and landscapes.

Rather like Eliot's fictional word-paintings or analogies to real or invented pictures, Witemeyer's study has a static quality. For Eliot, art follows from and serves to show empirical and moral reality; for Witemeyer, showing or displaying the paintings in George Eliot's gallery (a richer collection than we might have suspected) suffices. For the most part he accepts received critical interpretation of her thought and art and passes few judgments on Eliot's success. In the course of cataloging, explicating, and classifying Eliot's paintings, however, Witemeyer shares discoveries that win new respect for her ability to transmute aesthetic knowledge into art.

To borrow from Witemeyer's use of the analogy between fiction and painting, one could say that the *Nineteenth-Century Fiction* special issue deals with George Eliot primarily as a history and genre painter. (One contributor, J. Hillis Miller, would even have us see flashes of modernistic technique in *Middlemarch*.) The collection of essays sets off Eliot's artistry by showing analogies to and influences by, not the other plastic arts, but other literary texts—for example, those of eighteenth-century women writers who come before and twentieth-century women writers who had to rewrite Eliot, to go beyond her monumental example in order to write themselves. Other articles highlight Eliot's transmutation of material ranging from politics to Positivism, using fictional techniques (the organic metaphor, the journalistic essay) that she borrowed and refined or devised herself.

Rather like Witemeyer, the editors and contributors assume that we know much about Eliot's achievement following the three-decade-long renaissance of Eliot scholarship. This volume does not for the most part offer readings of major novels (*Adam Bede*, *The Mill on the Floss*, *Silas Marner*, *Middlemarch*, or *Daniel Deronda*). Rather, it fills in gaps in our knowledge of Eliot's place in literary history—lacunae these articles make us aware of for the first time. Yet they are in no sense mere footnotes to existing scholarship. The essays linking Eliot to a tradition of women's writing redefine our sense of her literary inheritance and legacies. Others focus on Eliot's integration of Victorian forms (the journalistic essay) and ideas of form (the organic metaphor). Several articles connect nineteenth-century political theory and action to lesser-known novels (*Romola* and *Felix Holt*), while others reassess Eliot's use of and commitment to social evolutionary theories and to Positivism. Finally, three leading Eliot scholars (Barbara Hardy, J. Hillis Miller, and Richard Poirier) demonstrate that there is always something new under Eliot's sun, offering three diverging readings of Chapter 85 of *Middlemarch*, to "suggest something of George Eliot's continued resistance to any single critical 'key' " (p. 256). Despite the editors' emphasis on Eliot's fictive and protean persona (p. 254) and her "life-giving resistance to any single—and hence entombing—interpretation" (p. 255), this volume is not a kaleidoscope of readings. It does not offer quick changes in critical perspective, startling new apercus, or (with a few exceptions) glimpses of a radically new George Eliot. But if the effect is not dazzling, neither is it dizzying; there is little sense of thematic discontinuity, considering how varied the subjects of the essays are. The impression left is of sound, interesting, valuable scholarship that sees George Eliot steadily, so that we may see her achievement more whole.

Margaret Doody traces George Eliot's predecessors among eighteenth-century women writers who sought to combine Fielding's sure authorial commentary with Richardson's sensibility, expressed by his imperfect, impassioned, suffering heroines (pp. 263, 265.) Doody shows how eighteenth-century novels by women used the paradigmatic plot of a heroine hampered by faulty education and experience, abandoned by parents and befriended by other women—the plot of great nineteenth-century novels like *Jane Eyre* and *The Mill on the Floss* (p. 268). Besides depicting women characters as the incarnation of a sympathetic principle (p. 271), eighteenth-century women writers turned to social history (pp. 276–77). To dispense social analysis and judgment confidently, they sought "a wise humorous persona" (p. 282). Doody offers Fanny Burney as the

The (De)Construction of Sister George

first to unite the author's superior judgment of and identification with her characters, using *style indirect libre* (p. 287), an achievement culminating in Eliot's ironic yet sympathetic narrative voice.

Doody's article continues the work of identifying and interpreting a women's tradition in the history of the English novel, to which Elaine Showalter made an important contribution. In this volume Showalter herself analyzes Eliot's stature among women writers and readers of the twentieth century. Showalter suggests that while nineteenth-century women resented Eliot as a formidable superior, modern women like Virginia Woolf and Katherine Mansfield identified with her and sought to reclaim her reputation from the hands of male critics (p. 310). The "demystification" of Eliot's madonna image and her reincarnation as an "imperfect, impulsive, and attractive sister" (p. 299) have been made possible by a second wave of recent feminist criticism that no longer insists on only heroic female role models in literature but honors Eliot's sympathy for and fellowship with ordinary women. Feminist readers of *Middlemarch* are at present more disposed to tolerate Celia than to resent Dorothea's failure, Showalter feels. Ironically, while male critics share in the pervasive contemporary appreciation of Eliot, male novelists "still use Eliot as an example of dreary moralism" (p. 310). In contrast, women writers like Simone de Beauvoir, Margaret Drabble, and Gail Godwin do homage to Eliot's plots and themes even when they seem to correct them. John Cheever writes Eliot off; his novelist daughter Susan rewrites her (p. 310). George Eliot's persona indeed seems to be growing younger, Showalter implies in "The Greening of Sister George," as she becomes (like all great artists) our contemporary.

Dealing with Eliot's place in another tradition, Robert Stange discusses Eliot's essays and reviews as a "prolegomenon to novel writing": "It was inevitable that a novelist should emerge from this kind of writing" (pp. 321–22). Stange sees Eliot adopting traits of both Lamb's Elia and Lewes's Vivien (p. 326) but using the male persona for her own "almost private irony," as for example when she gives mocking advice about the treatment of "our wives" (p. 317). The mask slips a bit at times, such as when Eliot rhapsodizes about Liszt during a trip to Weimar (p. 318). *Theophrastus Such* marks a return to the personal vein after the detachment of *Daniel Deronda* (pp. 328–29); it represents an incipient attempt to address monumental and enormously varied moral questions in brief, intimate essays (pp. 320, 323). Though Stange's discussion of the relations between Eliot's fictional and nonfictional voices is informative, his admiration for *Theophrastus Such* and his belief that it is a "first step" toward a new persona reflect a rather uncritical faith in the idea of artistic development.

David Carroll treats progress differently—as an idea and a technique in Eliot's storytelling. Carroll examines how Eliot "fictionalize[s] an organic process" in "Janet's Repentance" (p. 331)— how the tale reflects Eliot's "Coleridgean dialectical vision" which regards tension and reconciliation between opposites as necessary to growth, to revival of dead forms of life (pp. 334, 333). In the first part of "Janet's Repentance," it is Milby that is moribund and revived by Evangelicalism (p. 339). In the second half of the story, the organic myth is reenacted in the psychological drama between the Dempsters and the Reverend Tryan (p. 340). Eliot adopts the conventional love triangle to show Janet's soul as the prize to be won (p. 348). In her awakening to spiritual growth and consciousness, Janet is the prototype of Maggie Tulliver, Esther Lyons, and Gwendolen Harleth in the later novels. Carroll shows that the idea of the organic led Eliot to revive stereotypical and "dead" literary forms in her own fiction.

In the same critical vein as David Carroll, redefining and expanding current interpretations of Eliot's ideas, are the articles by K. K. Collins and Martha S. Vogeler. Collins publishes for the first time some late essays which argue against an easy assumption that Vogeler reviews nineteenth-century Positivists' reactions to Eliot in order to clarify how Positivistic her fiction is. Both writers dissociate her from major intellectual positions of the nineteenth century and affirm her intellectual independence. Collins quotes Eliot on her dislike of "that irrational exclusiveness of theory" she found in Spencer and other Victorian social scientists and scientists (p. 389). (We might say that

The (De)Construction of Sister George 287

this skepticism extended to Positivism, though Vogeler sees other factors behind Eliot's and the Positivists' mutual reserve; among these were her dislike of didactic fiction and her preference for personal freedom over rigid views on marriage.) Collins's essay reaffirms Eliot's distrust of inductive theories—she believed laws were fictions guiding research, not producing facts (p. 400). Eliot saw myth, language, and other cultural achievements as strategies for weathering the world, responses to conditions, and limitations that surround us. Good acts precede moral laws, for Eliot; and Collins reminds us in a nice phrase that Eliot believed "it is up to us to design—to save—ourselves" (p. 403).

Eliot was more comfortable reviving and reforming existing structures than contemplating new and revolutionary ones. Eliot's conservative politics in *Felix Holt* are treated by Joseph Butwin and Catherine Gallagher from different perspectives. Butwin focuses on Eliot's characteristically Victorian fear of the mob. She idealized crowds that were communal expressions of shared values, as in *Adam Bede* (p. 353); she anathematized crowds that acted on abstract principles or theories, as in *Romola* (p. 354). Eliot distrusted a public governed by ideas transmitted by journalism rather than by lived and inherited values. Similarly, she feared and felt distant from crowds of alienated urban dwellers (p. 371).

Examining the values of individual speakers in *Felix Holt*, Catherine Gallagher offers a more radically new reading of Eliot's growing conservatism in the 1860s. Eliot's awareness of a disjunction between "facts and values," of a gap between appearances and essences, led to her dissatisfaction with "metonymic realism" (p. 375). This aesthetic and epistemological crisis paralleled a crisis in Eliot's liberalism—her gradual loss of faith in democratic principles of aggregation and inclusion, expressed in a transition from metaphors drawn from the communal family and the free marketplace to conservative ones based on the church and the hierarchical family. Gallagher interprets *Felix Holt* as a problematic fiction in which the titular hero resists being read as a representation of reality; the omniscient narrator "seems undermined by Felix's own 'cultured' mode of beholding reality" (p. 379). He insists that culture consists of values that are absolute and detached from facts. Felix's abstractness is at odds with the narrator's inductive realism. He is an abbreviated and rather crude encoding of Eliot's fears for culture in the 1860s, fears expressed less didactically in later works. *Middlemarch* handles the conflict more artfully, while *Daniel Deronda* rejects inductive realism altogether (p. 384).

Gallagher sees Eliot as a precursor of modernism in her ultimate rejection of realism; J. Hillis Miller seems to treat Eliot as a postmodernist. In deconstructing Chapter 85 of *Middlemarch,* he shows how Eliot uses an epigraph from *Pilgrim's Progress* to set up her own realism as integral to narration (p. 444), only to emphasize the allegorical quality of both texts (pp. 446–47). Miller argues that "the ethical and the epistemological dimensions of George Eliot's humanist allegory contradict one another. The ability to do good in George Eliot's novels always in one way or another depends on ignorance, while the novels themselves show over and over the terrible dangers of ignorance" (p. 447). I must confess that I find unsettling Miller's claim for "the unreadability of ch. 85 of *Middlemarch,* as of the novel as a whole" (p. 448). I am not persuaded that the question with which he ends is the paramount one that Eliot's novel asks of us: "We cannot know whether it is better to read *The Pilgrim's Progress* or to read *Middlemarch*" (p. 448). Yet it is imperative to do more than trace allusions and note organic filaments connecting works, to cite sources and analogues as if there exists certitude and consensus about Eliot's meaning. Miller's undercutting of the tendency to see progressive, evolutionary paradigms in Eliot's texts (and her life) opens up our responses to *Middlemarch,* making possible a new reading. But if Eliot deconstructs texts within her own novel, she does so to affirm value and meaning, not to deny them. Knowledge of values may be problematic, but Eliot does not rest with demonstrating this. Miller's commentary does not follow Eliot's text in its passage from skepticism to commitment. Still, it is a brilliant exegesis.

The three glosses on Chapter 85 reflect both the traditionalist and the iconoclastic views of Eliot. Barbara Hardy, like Miller, raises the issue of analogy or interdependence between Chapter

The (De)Construction of Sister George 289

85 and *Middlemarch* as a whole. Miller sees the chapter as "synecdoche" (p. 441) that questions similitude, while Hardy perceives organic, anatomical connection. Hardy sees Chapter 85 of *Middlemarch* as an organ related to the body of the text. The chapter "dilates and contracts" even as the language and narrative stance do, making us feel the pain and growing consciousness of the Bulstrodes, whose marriage is revived from its mere formality through their shared grief (p. 435).

In contrast, Richard Poirier connects Chapter 85 to a whole new tradition of texts; he feels it implies a "radical critique of American epic fiction of the nineteenth century" (p. 452). In this chapter he hears "the accents of feminist revenge," not merely in the murder of "significant males" (Casaubon, Lydgate, Bulstrode), but also in Eliot's relentless "domestication of life": "All the failures of male ambition are transformed by women . . . into modest forms of social reality, social accommodation" (pp. 452–53). While Poirier indeed offers another, new persona—Eliot as a British lioness commenting on the manly American novel—his reading strikes a jarring note. To give the last word, as he does, to Fred and Mary Garth's "family life" is to forget that Mary writes books. It is to underemphasize the intellectual superiority, the self-confidence modulating into compassion, the authoritativeness, the implied ambition that are integral to Eliot's persona and to the fabric of her vision. Other essays in this volume—from Margaret Doody's to J. Hillis Miller's—capture the masterful complexity of this vision effectively.

The editors of *Nineteenth-Century Fiction* rightly maintain that Eliot invites pluralistic, even contradictory readings. She uses analogies, she deconstructs them; she embraces a male persona, she destroys men to celebrate female domestication of the household. Whether deconstructing texts or constructing personae, the various articles confirm Eliot's belief in what K. K. Collins calls our need "to design . . . ourselves." I found myself wondering whether this centennial issue would have been improved by a summarizing essay accounting for these contradictions, for Eliot's predilection for pluralism. Still, the fact that a reader looks for such a summing up in a periodical issue compliments the editors' choices. The volume stimulates new ways of reading and takes existing interpretations further. Eliot's work may be the sole possible synthesis or capstone to the myriad topics raised by these critics.

There is no lack of a strong, unifying thesis in Judith Wilt's *Ghosts of the Gothic,* and the fact that Eliot is one of several authors dealt with does not result in distortion of her work to fit this paradigm. In these two respects, Wilt's book is more satisfying as a scholarly whole than either King's study or the *Nineteenth-Century Fiction* special issue. *Ghosts of the Gothic* shows how the ghosts of power, desire, and isolation haunt novels of the great tradition. Her study focuses on Austen, Eliot, and Hardy to show that Gothicism and realism are not mutually exclusive, though they are at odds; each novelist reconciles or integrates impulses toward self and toward society, power and submission, isolation and community, *within* "realistic" novels. In a sense, realism is the punishment of Gothic rebellion, excessiveness, and desire; the reality principle may take the form of the father's law (p. 25) or the narrative's relentlessly sane realism (p. 303). Its power may be felt as dread, even before the crime or sin is committed.

When Wilt claims that elements of the Gothic are present in all novels in the form of suspense, violence, obsession (p. 99), however, her definition of the Gothic becomes excessively elastic and inclusive. Further, I would quibble with minor points of interpretation of individual novels. *Frankenstein* seems not simply to punish male usurpation of female generative power— the birth role (p. 63). Mary Shelley punishes the scientists, I think, to exorcise dread at her own usurpation of male logic and law. But on the whole Wilt does get at the subterranean dread, horror, out-of-control romanticism, and suspense in what we usually regard as classics of realism. She shows how the Gothic interpenetrates the vision of reality in Austen, Eliot, and, more predictably, Lawrence. While she acknowledges that the Gothic heritage encompasses Scott, Charlotte Brontë, and Dickens, her purpose is to show that the great tradition, dominated by female and foreign writers, actually contains heresy rejected by orthodox writers like T. S. Eliot or antiorthodox writers like Joyce. By focusing on the central place of Gothicism in the great

The (De)Construction of Sister George 291

tradition, Wilt shows the sublime and heroic manifestation of what she feels is rendered less darkly in Scott, Brontë, and Dickens. There "childish" fantasies that portray reality as overwhelming seem truer than "adult" strategies that deny death (pp. 117–18). In Austen, Eliot, and Lawrence, ghosts haunt people more terrifyingly because they do so in the daylight of adult situations.

Wilt's placement of Gothicism in the cellar of the house of realistic fiction attests to its covert but essential function in the realistic novel. Her approach yields ingenious readings that enliven orthodox interpretations of Austen, Eliot, and Lawrence without itself becoming heretical. In Wilt's view, for example, Austen celebrates, she doesn't entirely debunk, Gothicism. She practices a kind of "aesthetic Ludditism," breaking up Gothic machinery (castle settings, tyrannical heroes, churches, overimaginative heroines), but reassembling them for her own psychological purpose to make anxiety seem "high" or serious (p. 126). In Lawrence, the Gothic machinery seems less radically disrupted than in Austen's novels. For Lawrence, the Father's law is the old order that is dead; the suffering Son must be transcended; and the Holy Ghost's advent is awaited. Corresponding to these phases are the Gothic trappings of the ghostly (the work ethic and industrial machine) (p. 250); the vampiric murder of the self, especially in marriage (p. 265); and the power of place (pp. 276–77). (America, until it failed Lawrence, seemed a new repository of promise and power.) Lawrence's "often admirable feminism" (p. 275) identifies with the potent and uprooted female, yet, as Wilt points out, eventually lapses. For example, Lawrence cannot envisage adult relationships among women, and he sees women's bodies as "temporary possessions," as vehicles for childbearing (p. 279).

George Eliot's work may seem less Gothic than Austen's or Lawrence's, but Wilt uncovers new implications in Eliot's partially suppressed excursions into romance. Eliot brings to the foreground what Austen keeps "offstage"—the sublime forces of death and marriage (p. 173). Dread and pain must be embraced and used if a world larger than the ego is to be admitted (p. 177). Eliot's novels use several Gothic "machines"—the dangerous mob, marriage-as-murder, and the Dead Hand (pp. 178, 181–82). In fact, as Wilt perceives, it is Eliot's "drifters" or aliens who survive, while the orthodox theorists like Casaubon and Bulstrode are "decreated" (p. 203).

Wilt resolves the somewhat hackneyed critical problem of integrating the apparently disjunctive plots of *Daniel Deronda* by seeing the novel's action as "the stealthy divergence of human lots" (p. 216). When Daniel Deronda seems about to rescue Gwendolen Harleth, the narrative itself restores the separateness of the two characters (p. 209). Horror comes in two gender-linked varieties: women have no possibility of heroism, and men have too much "heroic responsibility" (p. 219). The novel deals with separate destiny in yet another sense. Zionism, or history-as-surprise, preserves Deronda's apartness: he is both Jewish and feminine or, as Wilt says, his mother's daughter (p. 223).

The principal women in *Daniel Deronda* have a kinship that seems to me even more important than Deronda's kinship network. The actress Alcharisi rejects all but "self-created roles," and Gwendolen, while lacking her genius, also tries to avoid enslavement (p. 228). I believe Deronda to be a spokesman for the patriarchy (the dead father's law, in this case, grandfather Daniel Charisi's) rather than his mother's spiritual heir(ess). Still, Wilt's interpretation of the Gothic mysteries' eruption into Eliot's realism is compelling. It gives us a simultaneously psychological and formal vehicle (the Gothic machine) to accompany Eliot's flights into romance. In the novels of Austen, Eliot, and Lawrence (as well as Doris Lessing, Wilt adds), Gothicism is a subcurrent insisting on the mysteries of life against "the sanities of narrative" (p. 303). "Normality" may win and reason may punish, but the self's sublime drive toward power and its attendant dread, guilt, and self-punishment are integral to realism's profundity.

Approaches to George Eliot—like those of *Nineteenth-Century Fiction* and *Ghosts of the Gothic*—that enliven our readings are of greater value than those that simply confirm existing ways of seeing Eliot. King's and Witemeyer's books increase the units of our knowledge without examining the categories under which these are subsumed. That is, they integrate ideas of tragedy and pictorialism into a configuration of ideas about community, progress, and realism, performing a mathematical addition rather than a chemical combination. More productive are the operations performed in the other two books, whether deconstructive or revisionary.

Judith Wilt and, for the most part, the contributors to the George Eliot issue of *Nineteenth-Century Fiction* do not sacrifice Eliot or a single novel to any inductive hypothesis. They use existing paradigms of interpretation but swerve from them in creative ways. As Wilt implies, a little heresy is more stimulating than orthodoxy, and it evokes the sublime more dramatically. George Eliot is more attractive as a sinful sister than as a madonna. It is salutary to be reminded of mysteries, ambiguities, and insurrectionary tendencies in her work. Though her novels may seem as definite as a declarative sentence, we should recall Eliot's injunction that closure is illusory, that every ending is, like every beginning, "a make-believe" (*Daniel Deronda*). Both *Ghosts of the Gothic* and a number of the articles in *Nineteenth-Century Fiction* remind us that Eliot's commitment to sanity, morality, and compromise comes in spite of and because of the pressure of their antitheses. Eliot criticism should portray her realism not as the static, inevitable product of an evolution, but rather as the dynamic image of a constantly reenacted struggle.

Merton's Affirmation and Affirmation of Merton: Writing about Silence

Victor A. Kramer

Thomas Merton. *The Collected Poems of Thomas Merton.* New York: New Directions, 1980. 1048 pp.

Thomas Merton. *Merton on St. Bernard.* Kalamazoo: Cistercian Publications, 1980. 242 pp.

Thomas Merton. *Love and Living.* Naomi Burton Stone and Brother Patrick Hart, eds. New York: Farrar Straus Giroux, 1979. 232 pp.

Thomas Merton and Robert Lax. *A Catch of Anti-Letters.* Kansas City: Sheed, Andrews, and McMeel, 1978. xiii, 128 pp.

Deba Patnaik, ed. *Geography of Holiness: The Photography of Thomas Merton.* New York: The Pilgrim Press, 1980. xii, 128 unnumbered pp.

William H. Shannon. *Thomas Merton's Dark Path: The Inner Experience of a Contemplative.* New York: Farrar Straus Giroux, 1981. 221 pp.

Monica Furlong. *Merton: A Biography.* San Francisco: Harper & Row, 1980. xx, 342 pp.

James Forest. *Thomas Merton: A Pictorial Biography.* New York: Paulist Press, 1980. 102 pp.

George Woodcock. *Thomas Merton, Monk and Poet: A Critical Study.* New York: Farrar Straus Giroux, 1978. 200 pp.

Ross Labrie. *The Art of Thomas Merton.* Fort Worth: Texas Christian University Press, 1979. xiii, 188 pp.

Sister Thérèse Lentfoehr. *Words and Silence: On the Poetry of Thomas Merton.* New York: New Directions, 1979. ix, 166 pp.

James Finley. *Merton's Palace of Nowhere: A Search for God through Awareness of the True Self.* Notre Dame: Ave Maria Press, 1978. 158 pp.

Daniel J. Adams. *Thomas Merton's Shared Contemplation: A Protestant Perspective.* Kalamazoo: Cistercian Publications, 1979. 361 pp.

Elena Malits. *The Solitary Explorer: Thomas Merton's Transforming Journey.* San Francisco: Harper & Row, 1980, xiii, 175 pp.

Gerald Twomey, ed. *Thomas Merton: Prophet in the Belly of a Paradox.* New York: Paulist Press, 1978. xiii, 237 pp.

Brother Patrick Hart, ed. *The Message of Thomas Merton.* Kalamazoo: Cistercian Publications, 1981. xvi, 213 pp.

Thomas Merton chose to be a cloistered contemplative within one of the most austere religious orders in the United States. Paradoxically, while his affirmation of that enclosed way of life was an affirmation of silence, his career as contemplative led to his being one of the most prolific writers in the modern world. When he decided in 1941 to be a Cistercian monk, he knew that he might forego being a published writer. Of course that did not happen, and as he grew in his love of the contemplative life he also matured as a writer who voiced aspects of that quiet. Recent books about him demonstrate that solitude allowed him to treasure community, and silence allowed him to honor words. His silent way of life led him to experience the necessity of writing in a world that seemed out of touch with the contemplative aspects of existence. Merton wrote scores of books and hundreds of articles during his twenty-seven years at the Abbey of Gethsemani in Kentucky, and we are now beginning to see the complexity of what this man of silence affirmed through his writing. He died in 1968 while in the prime of life, yet new writings keep appearing, and no doubt this will continue for years. During the past decade several new collections of Merton essays have appeared as well as the meticulously edited *Asian Journal*.[1] A proper assessment of only the books by Merton which have been published since his death would require a substantial essay. The present review will focus only on some of the recent books by Merton and about his life and work.

The day will come when there may be more books by Merton published after his death than the fifty he saw through the press before he died. In view of the rudimentary known facts about Merton's vast outpouring of words, that will hardly be surprising, for it was largely through the printed word that he affirmed his vocation. Merton wrote volumes of poetry, autobiography, scores of essays, and numerous reviews. He also wrote enormous numbers of letters, and there are detailed journals for each phase of his life. Two book-length bibliographies have been published about his work.[2] Since his accidental death in 1968, books by him have flowed from presses at a steady rate. Several of these were in process at the end of his life. In the years since 1968 Merton books on prayer, collections of poetry, a novel, collections of essays, and photographs as well as the composite *Asian Journal* have appeared.[3] We know that there will be several additional volumes of essays and journals and that eventually the correspondence will begin to be edited. Also, Merton's orientation notes, accumulated during the years he was Master of Scholastics and Novice Master, will be published. Those lecture notes will run to a dozen volumes (a project already under contract). As an example of the prolific industry of this contemplative, one should note that the extant correspondence alone at the Thomas Merton Studies Center of Bellarmine College includes approximately 1,826 separate files, and that in some cases there are scores of letters spanning decades. Letters to Jacques Maritain, Jean Leclerq, Daniel Berrigan, and Ernesto Cardenal would make a minimum of four books. Correspondence with literary friends and editors, such as Robert Giroux, Naomi Burton Stone, James Laughlin, Sister Thérèse Lentfoehr, and Robert Lax, would constitute several more. Letters to fellow monks would make yet more additional volumes. Such material promises to add to the Merton corpus in the decades to come.[4]

Then there is the secondary material. Much of it can be called "second generation" Merton scholarship, for a considerable amount of valuable critical writing was accomplished while he was still alive, or appeared shortly after his death. Much of the "first generation" material is especially valuable because it was written by persons close to him—as friend, fellow monk, literary associate. Now a new body of scholarship is developing, generated not so much out of close acquaintanceship with Merton but from close attention to his published works. The large number of graduate theses on Merton, completed and in progress, is still another indication of his continuing importance in American culture. His books remain in print, and his writings are being discussed. The new books examined in this essay demonstrate his continuing value as poet and writer; they are a further sign of his promise for the future. To appreciate the variety of work which current scholars are producing, some awareness of the books which appeared immediately after his death (but which do not constitute the subject of this review-essay) is necessary. The first collection of essays about Merton was appropriately called *Thomas Merton, Monk*. These close-up portraits, edited by Brother Patrick Hart, O.C.S.O., are mostly essays by persons who were close to Merton.[5] Frequently cast as remembrances, the essays provide valuable glimpses of Merton's multifaceted personality. The next step involved evaluating some of his relationships with society. That book of essays, entitled *Thomas Merton, Prophet in the Belly of a Paradox* (1978), is much more analytical and shows that a definite distancing has taken place. Still a third significant step has been taken by another recent collection, *The Message of Thomas Merton* (1981), a gathering by many hands which traces the complexity of Merton's thought and suggests how his message will be studied in

Thomas Merton: Writing about Silence

the future. The two most recent collections, reviewed in this essay, reveal the present directions of Merton study.

Throughout these three collections of essays about Merton we see scholars gradually distancing themselves from a man who was foremost a monk but who was always aware of the world. He realized his obligations in (and to) the world; thus he must be seen both as a contemplative and as a social critic. Like Emerson and Thoreau, he knew that the contemplative and active aspects of existence reinforce each other. Man needs both. Yet Merton realized that considerable discipline is essential if humanity is to find its proper relationship with God and with other men.

This approach was made clear in the first several books about Merton. Now, with still more primary material available and several additional studies completed, we can see even more clearly that language was always at the center of Merton's personal discipline. When Dennis McInerny, John J. Higgins, James Baker, Frederic Kelly, and Raymond Bailey published their books, *The Collected Poems of Thomas Merton* had not yet appeared. Consequently none of these five writers spent much time with the poetry. They did valuable groundwork, but in retrospect their books already seem in need of revision, in part because their themes are so closely tied to theological or social frameworks. We now know that there never were two separate Mertons. As monk and writer, and as man of God seeking God's mercy, he lived his life as a whole—and while he did so he formed reflections of it, for himself and others, through his concern with language.

Higgins's 1971 study *Merton's Theology of Prayer* (republished by Doubleday as *Thomas Merton on Prayer*) offers "a synthesis of Merton's understanding of prayer, showing its centrality within the thought of his spirituality."[6] Higgins tells us that Merton's concern with prayer involved no radical changes but was a gradual unfolding, as he became more aware of the mystery of God. If what Higgins stresses is true (and I think it is), then the emphasis on social criticism in Baker's book of the same year needs more qualification. Yet Higgins's book does not always distinguish carefully between the early and later Merton. It remains rather abstract.

Thomas Merton—Social Critic (1971) by James Thomas Baker is a kind of companion volume to Higgins's work. Baker provides an overview of Merton's social outlook and tells how in the course of his life he seemed to become increasingly aware of his obligations to the world.[7] Baker minimizes the fact that Merton's social criticism developed slowly over a period of decades and flowered under the monastic influence.

This relationship becomes clearer in a book which was published three years later and, in some fundamental ways, is a synthesis of the types of work done by Higgins and Baker. Frederic Joseph Kelly, Jr.'s, *Man before God: Thomas Merton on Social Responsibility*, appeared in 1974 from Doubleday.[8] Kelly examines Merton's writing on social topics, yet in his treatment we see that the social dimensions of religious man grow out of Merton's love of God. Responsible social action, Kelly points out, must grow from a proper relationship to God. And clearly that was what Merton's life and writings were all about. Thomas Merton, who became Father Louis, became a mystic precisely because he would not forget the world.

Thomas Merton on Mysticism by Raymond Bailey (Doubleday, 1975) traces the main steps in Merton's journey inward.[9] In this study we see how Merton's attitudes about the mystical life changed; they became more simple as he became more aware of the radical simplicity of life itself. Bailey's book is an excellent guide to the interrelationship of Merton's life and writings as he developed stronger ties with various mystical traditions. William Shannon's *Thomas Merton's Dark Path* (discussed in more detail below) provides information on these subjects and shows that Merton refined his appreciation of mysticism through formal writing at the same time that he was also refining his life.

Throughout his dual career Merton remained fascinated by the relationship between silence and the word, between the contemplative state and the need to articulate awareness. The first books to appear after his death dealt with questions which grew out of Merton's concern with prayer, theology, mysticism, social concern, and responsibility. These books were important

Thomas Merton: Writing about Silence

initial steps toward understanding Merton's complexity. We are now witnessing a further step in Merton scholarship, a greater awareness of the relationship between his aesthetics and his love of art as his approach to both God and man.

The poetry reveals the unity of Merton's vision more consistently than anything else, for it is here that he comes closest to verbalizing what will never be verbalized. This fact alone makes the *Collected Poems* valuable. In the poetry, the intensity of contemplative need and an awareness of articulation manifest themselves strongly. This is true of Merton's early formal modernist poetry as well as his later poetry, which was anything but traditional. Merton himself called it "anti-poetry." The *Collected Poems of Thomas Merton*, now available as a paperback, is a prodigious opus, hardly what he would have planned himself had he lived to see such a volume through the press.[10] In more than one thousand pages, it presents the bulk of the poems as they first appeared, together with a very large number of uncollected, manuscript, and fragmentary verse. It will prove of great value for understanding this ambitious, enigmatic poet.

When his poems are finally studied systematically, they will be seen to have value on many levels. Often successful as technical exercises, they also reveal his spiritual development. His poems chart American culture in the nineteen-forties, fifties, and sixties, that thirty-year period when he was active as a writer and during which time he became ever surer of his identity as Father Louis, the monk. To absorb the hundreds of pages of Merton's poetry will take a long time, and scholars should first remember that he himself raised many questions about how best to write poetry. The early lyrics of *Thirty Poems* (and *Early Poems*) are technically tight and intellectually challenging, yet almost too predictable in their patterns. The later poems are open, experimental, alive, questioning. Some readers have not yet accustomed themselves to this apparently radical change in poetic manner. There was in fact little radical change; he simply became more willing to admit that he did not have all the answers, and that the wisdom of others (other traditions, styles, philosophies) could help him approach more closely the infinite wisdom of God. The collected poetry is uneven, but this would be true for anyone who wrote so much while living such a full life.

It is fortunate that New Directions has made the *Collected Poems* available in paperback. (The cloth edition, priced at $37.50, appeared in 1977 and is already out of print.) The paperback gathers all the poems published in separate volumes between 1944 and 1969 including a reprinting of the Anvil Press *Early Poems 1940–42* which first appeared in 1971, essentially a selection of poems omitted from the first book (*Thirty Poems*, 1944). In addition it provides invaluable appendixes that include poems which Merton gathered for another volume, "Sensation Time at the Home"; uncollected poems; humorous verse; a French poem; translations of French poems; translations from many other languages; drafts and fragments; and even a selection of concrete poems—almost four hundred pages in all. These appendixes alone would constitute the subject of an extended study.

The Collected Poems of Thomas Merton documents both Merton's personal development and the changes in American culture as it moved through World War II, racial discord, and Vietnam. Merton's earliest volumes reflect his mastery of modernist technique and his revulsion from the contemporary mentality which easily accepted war. Many earlier poems catch a younger poet's delight in having been led to the monastery. As his poems develop, Merton affirms more and more his knowledge that quiet, peace, solitude, contemplation, and inner peace are first essential within each person if individuals are to play significant roles in a rapidly changing world. Each poem reflects Merton's journey, always a combination of contemplation and action.

The need for such a balance clearly attracted Merton to the poetry of Chuang Tzu. *Collected Poems* includes selections from his readings from Chuang Tzu, but not as they originally appeared in Merton's carefully designed text with illustrations, and without the author's note and essay, "The Way of Chuang Tzu." Sixty-two readings were included in the original edition; only fifty appear in the collected poetry volume. The appendix ideally should have provided a separate section for these "readings," since Merton was not the translator. As he explains in his earlier note, he relied upon four translations—two French, one German, and one English. The misleading label of these "readings" as "translations" suggests one of the editorial problems of *Collected Poems*. Another results from a uniform typeface used for all titles, thus obscuring some visual subtleties of the original printings. Similarly when poems are reset, as is the case for the earlier volumes, line length occasionally changes. Other editorial changes have also been introduced. The poem "In April When Our Land Last Died," for example, is retitled "A Mysterious Song in the Spring of the Year." Merton likely made an emendation in a personal copy of which the editors were aware, but an editorial note would have clarified such matters.

There are other basic editorial problems with this gigantic volume. No editor is listed, and while care was apparently taken to see that the poems correspond to the printed texts of the various separate editions, some minimal apparatus in the later sections would have been helpful. Especially is this the case in the appendices. Poems published during Merton's life are reproduced next to notebook poems (for instance, materials published in *The Asian Journal*). Dates are provided for uncollected poems, yet not places of publication. Within a given section some poems are not dated, while others are. The poems in the section of "drafts and fragments" especially should have been dated. Still another problem is that while some of these translations first appeared in *Emblems of a Season of Fury* along with introductory notes, and thus should have been reprinted as part of that book within *The Collected Poems*, they are silently moved to an appendix, and the notes are omitted. Such problems are, however, relatively insignificant, and we should be pleased that this volume is available. In time it will become necessary to collate, verify, date, and document variants for these poems. In the meantime this volume will provide an enormous fund of information, pleasure, and entertainment for its readers. Better than any other single book available it reflects the energy of Thomas Merton. It also suggests the work remaining for scholars.

Merton was able to cultivate diverse fields of interest simultaneously: autobiography and poetry, essays on theology and on the contemporary culture, on the liturgy, on art. And he did so because his his search for God expressed itself in varied modes, depending upon the situation in which he found himself. Merton would put all of his energy into whatever project was at hand—in prayer, in conference with a novice, in revision of galleys, in writing a letter. As he grew in the contemplative vocation, he accepted the use of words as a valuable means of placing himself within the particular moment. Imagine the sheer fun he had writing a letter to Robert Lax, a close friend since their shared days at Columbia. The correspondence in *A Catch of Anti-Letters* clearly reflects this friendship, and these *Anti-Letters* are unlike anything we might easily imagine.[11] While in one sense personal letters, they are also prayers, statements of acceptance of where both writers "are" as a result of some twenty-five years of friendship. They are finally an excellent example of Merton's characteristic exuberance. These are private documents, but they also reveal much about the human spirit and Merton's realization that one finds the greatest satisfaction in the simplest things of life. He was lucky to have Bob Lax as correspondent, and the bond of their friendship is everywhere evident in these "anti-letters," these celebrations of the immediate. They are about the joy of being oneself, about the joy of pain and sorrow, and about the fact that even in the most isolated circumstances one can remain aware that one is united with others through language.

One brief excerpt can suggest the seriousness of Merton's and Lax's play. They were both artists; so while the subject matter of the poem-letters is wide, the question of art is central. One Merton letter begins: "How long you think you can hide from the long arm of the postoffice? Where have you been? Have you grown the beard and put on the moppit and entered the sketes and lavras? Where is the long black vestment? Do you know that the sketes and lavras have missed the boat of aggirnamento or perhaps aggornamountain. Let the motto cry out from the captain's bridge as we sail round and round the Agios Horos: 'Aggiorna-Mount-Athos.' This pun will tickle the feet of the Protos" (p. 47).

These dense letters reveal a good bit about Merton's enthu-

Thomas Merton: Writing about Silence 305

siasms, interests, techniques, and affirmation of life—which of course, also includes death. There are, for example, beautiful letters toward the end of the volume about the death of their mutual artist-friend Ad Reinhardt. Fascinated by Reinhardt's black canvases, Merton sings of his death:

> Tomorrow the solemns. The requiems alone in the hermit hatch. Before the ikons the offering. The oblations. The clean oblations all round thunder quiet silence black picture oblations. Make Mass beautiful silence like big black picture speaking requiem. Tears in the shadows of hermit hatch requiems blue black tone. Sorrows for Ad in the oblation quiet peace request rest. Tomorrow is solemns in the hermit hatch for old lutheran reinhardt commie paintblack. Tomorrow is the eternal solemns fending off the purge-fire place non catch old skipper reinhardt safely by into the heavens. Tomorrow is the solemns and the barefoots and the ashes and the masses, oldstyle liturgy masses without the colonels and without the sergeants yelling sit down. Just old black quiet requiems in hermit hatch with decent sorrows good bye college chum.
>
> It is all solemns and sads all over beginning to fade out people in process before comes the march of orges and djinns. Well out of the way is safe Reinhardt in his simple black painting the final statement includes all. [p. 120]

To sing of death in this way is also to affirm life.

Merton's real subject was affirmation, both in the life and in the writing. The early Merton, perhaps too smug in the joy of enclosure at Gethsemani, tended to emphasize that enclosure. Later, more generous and open themes developed. Barriers between self and others were broken down as new ways of seeing developed and new metaphors of transformation were sought. Elena Malits's book *The Solitary Explorer,* examined in detail later in this essay, charts the significant stages in Merton's writing as he witnessed himself changing and thus realized the need of new metaphors to suggest that change. The record of his personal journey was at first a "secular" diary and then a purgatorio. Later it became an examination of the mystery of being in a whale; then of the paradox of voicing the silent life; and ultimately of the irony of the conjectures of an innocent (and finally guilty) bystander. These metaphors helped affirm Merton's situations at a particular time. Yet often it took a good many words to work his way through to affirmation. Bearing such facts in mind, we read the diverse essays of the recently published *Love and Living* as one of the final steps in Merton's journey—a step that so often involved looking again carefully at what we as a people have ceased to notice.

The essays in *Love and Living* deal with different subjects and are important because they show how Merton was capable of reaching out in many different ways. These essays keep turning back on related ideas: live well; love now; celebrate what you are and have; and in that immediate fact of loving, you will begin to come to an awareness of God. Merton's concerns are with essences. Editors have divided the book into three sections: "Love and Living"; "Seven Words"; and "Christian Humanism." Some minimal scholarly apparatus to date these essays would have been helpful. The first group treats questions about man's loss of contact with truth, living, communication. Included here is an essay transcribed from a conference given for Novices at Gethsemani on "Cargo Cults of the South Pacific" which gives valuable insight into the long poem *The Geography of Lograire*.[12] The second section meditates on words such as *death, ethics, war*, with which modern man has lost contact. The final section is a hopeful look to the future.

At the core of Merton's concern, as in earlier books such as *New Seeds of Contemplation* and *The New Man,* is his fascination with the virtues of silence:

> There is a silent self within us whose presence is disturbing precisely because it is so silent: it *can't* be spoken. It has to remain silent. To articulate it, to verbalize it, is to tamper with it, and in some ways to destroy it.
>
> Now let us frankly face the fact that our culture is one which is geared in many ways to help us evade any need to face this inner, silent self. We live in a state of constant semi-attention to the sound of voices, music, traffic, or the generalized noise of what goes on around us all the time. This keeps us immersed in a flood of racket and words, a diffuse medium in which our consciousness is half di-

luted: we are not quite "thinking," not entirely responding, but we are more or less there. We are not fully *present* and not entirely absent; not fully withdrawn, yet not completely available. [p. 40]

The most important single fact revealed in these newly collected essays is Merton's affirmation of man's proper place in the universe. Yet he reminds us that that peace is found, paradoxically, by finding one's true self and by not allowing other things to infringe. The essays here reflect the mature Merton, reaching out to his world.

The most recent addition to Merton primary material, *Merton on St. Bernard,* gives a glimpse of a much earlier writer, one who twenty years before had quietly been building the base for later work as teacher, Novice master, and mature thinker. These essays on St. Bernard appeared in disparate places in the early nineteen-fifties; together they show that already early in the career Merton was concerned with combining the contemplative with the active. His systematic inquiries, while sometimes loaded with Latin quotations and occasionally pedantic in tone, reveal a Merton who is sure of his vocation. Though early, they are also vintage Merton, full of hints at how he made connections fundamental to his life. The book includes essays on "Action and Contemplation in St. Bernard" and "St. Bernard on Interior Simplicity." The concluding section concerns "Transforming Union in St. Bernard of Clairvaux and St. John of the Cross." Jean Leclercq's introduction illuminates Merton's approach to Bernard and the timeliness of the subject. Merton saw the need to emphasize a balance between the active and the contemplative, yet, as Leclercq notes, he has assimilated Bernard's theology; thus the essay on Bernard's *The Spirit of Simplicity* is expressed "with precise vocabulary, but also with such breath that what he says is valid not only for the Cistercian Order but for all Christians" (p. 17). Merton's study of St. Bernard demonstrates that he had given serious thought, early on, to the relationship between the active and contemplative lives. He emphasizes that they are not separate; one feeds the other. Merton is frankly amazed at his discovery:

It is abundantly clear from all these texts that the contemplative life, as St. Bernard conceives it, is by no means a life of study, still less of research scholarship. However, since mystical understanding is a penetration of the mysteries of our faith and since contemplative wisdom is nourished by the Word himself, it is clear that we prepare ourselves for it by our *lectio divina*. Contemplation is simply the procession, by experience, of what we have read in Scripture. Hence the soul spontaneously seeks God in Scripture, *sciens se ibi absque dubio inventuram quem sitit*. This thirst is not to be satisfied by anything less than the "kiss of his mouth"—by God himself, giving himself secretly to the soul in mystical experience, casting aside the sensible images and figures in which he came disguised. St. Bernard knew that these hidden meanings of Scripture were revealed more perfectly to the soul meditating in the woods than to the student in the scriptorium. [p. 56]

To look carefully, to enjoy being in the woods, is to be contemplative. Merton's looking involved many hours in the forests of Gethsemani. (He even once courted the possibility of being the resident forest ranger, thereby acquiring a ready-made hermitage as well as running the risk of an ivory-tower existence.)

As he came to love particular trees and places, his appreciation of those particulars deepened. This love is recorded in poems and journals, but also through the lens of a camera; for during the final several years of his life Merton proved himself to be an accomplished photographer. And what better reminder is there of what Merton studied, taught, assimilated, than a series of one hundred of his best photographs? Merton the contemplative—but always artist by instinct—had a gift with the camera which was strengthened by his association with John Howard Griffin. Some of that story is made clear in Griffin's *A Hidden Wholeness*,[13] a volume which might well be read as preface to a new collection of photographs fittingly called *Geography of Holiness*. Deba Patnaik's loving selection and arrangement of some of Merton's best photographs provides yet another important avenue of entry into his world. John Howard Griffin encouraged Merton to use the camera, and he made striking progress in a relatively short time. The photographs of this new collection, which is beautifully printed and bound, demonstrate that Merton learned to look everywhere for a hidden wholeness. Here is the visual expression of what Merton said when he examined St. Bernard. In addition, Patnaik's introductory text provides access to the aesthetics of Merton and shows the reader how those aesthetics were closely allied to spiritual insights.

All this newly available primary material sets the stage for the scholars (dozens of them) who have published work about Merton in the last few years. William Shannon has produced a new book which also includes primary material. Shannon's *Thomas Merton's Dark Path: The Inner Experience of a Contemplative* is valuable for several reasons. First, it provides extensive sections from Merton's unpublished manuscript "The Inner Experience." That manuscript is a reworking of and addition to earlier projects, and it provides insight into Merton's appreciation of the nature of contemplation. Shannon also shows his readers what is significant in each of Merton's books about contemplation. And through textual study he demonstrates how these texts grew. Thus the chapters on *Seeds of Contemplation* and *New Seeds of Contemplation,* on "The Inner Experience," and on *Contemplative Prayer* are deliberate and thoughtful textual investigations of how manuscripts were revised, ordered, and rearranged to bring about the books.

Shannon's book is much more, however, than an occasion for reprinting Merton's unpublished manuscript, and tracing textual variants in others. Shannon provides an introduction to Merton's books on the subject of contemplation. Taking them in systematic and chronological order, he provides a summary of the important aspects of Merton's development from his earliest stance, in books such as *What Is Contemplation?* and *Seeds of Contemplation,* to the final consideration of these subjects in *The Climate of Monastic Prayer.* Because Shannon is concerned with the evolution of Merton's thought, he summarizes the development of that thought. His successive chapters trace the evolution of Merton's ideas and experience into the complex works which they are. Shannon insists: "It was because Merton was attuned to experience that he was preeminently a theologian—a contemplative rather than a dogmatic theologian. His theology was not an expounding of the truths of revelation in order to offer an intellectual appreciation of them; rather, it was the theology of one who could talk about God because he had first walked with God. For him, God was the burning mystery of Reality. God was the Great Experience beyond all experiences. No one in the twentieth century has articulated that Experience with such clarity of vision as Thomas Merton" (p. 223). Contemplation is ultimately inexplicable, but through his own systematic study Merton makes us aware of its value, and Shannon demonstrates how Merton's study and affirmation of the contemplative experience progressed.

Merton's career was extremely full, and it will be a long time before we have a complete biography. A valuable intermediary step is Monica Furlong's *Merton: A Biography*. Her book focuses on high points in Merton's life, however, and the resulting picture is too full of crises. It is as if Furlong sought a book with a hero—tortured, frustrated, disappointed, but strong— and found him in Merton. All these qualities are there no doubt, but we should remember that Merton also wrote about the other side of these facts. Monastic life, with all of its problems, brought pleasure, satisfaction, and above all, union with God and man in a way not readily available outside the monastery. Ed Rice's informal biography *The Man in the Sycamore Tree* (actually a title for one of the novels which Merton wrote in the nineteen-thirties, but destroyed) was similarly skewed. Rice sometimes tended to make a martyr out of Merton while minimizing the strength of his interior life (the very thing of which Merton wrote so convincingly). Rice's account of Merton's determination to have a hermitage, and how "he was forced to trickery and pressure and evasion to obtain it," give only one version of the story which Furlong qualifies significantly.[14] Her account of the move to that hermitage comes closer to the truth:

> As the 1960s wore on, Merton was moving steadily toward the restructuring of his monastic life. It was as if the fantasy he had woven around his cinder-block building in the woods had come true in the minds of other people as well as himself, and it was becoming less and less a kind of outpost of the monastery, where it was proper to

converse with the "separated brethren" (although the Baptists and Episcopalians and Jews continued to come) and more and more the hermitage of Merton's dreams. Merton's sheer persistence in asserting that he needed time alone, coupled with the enormously heavy workload he had carried for years at the monastery and the kind of insouciance in the face of authority with which he had survived the "terrible" years of the 1950s, somehow made it inevitable. [p. 270]

As an overview, Furlong's biography of Merton is useful, and stimulating. Her narrative allows us to see sides of Merton which were hidden before. Her research on the early years in England is especially good. Yet almost chapter by chapter we are compelled to see still another crisis develop, and the book moves along slowly toward its inevitable conclusion, the mysterious death in Bangkok. Her method allows her to build on the crises of Merton's life, but the truth of his life was that it must have been at once more simple and more complex than the life presented in this nicely written book.

There are several problems with Furlong's method. Because the author needs to make the book exciting, she relies for the early parts rather too heavily upon the narratives which Merton himself wrote. The famous *The Seven Storey Mountain* and the earlier books, *The Secular Journal* and *My Argument with the Gestapo*, do provide much information about Merton, but real problems emerge when these books are used as major sources. Especially is this true of the novel, an imaginary journey to the England and France which Merton had known from earlier years. Furlong makes it seem as though Merton were writing of actual people he had known in England, yet with scant novelistic distancing. Another problem basic to Furlong's book is her constant search for problems; thus, for example, she overdoes the terrors of Merton's relationship with his Abbot Dom James Fox whom she casts as the villain in this biography. Merton was sometimes exasperated with the difficulties of being under the wing of Dom James, but at the same time Merton's appreciation of the care and concern of Dom James should also be traced and stressed.

A similar deficiency occurs when Merton's correspondence

with Rosemary Reuther is presented as if he were corresponding with no one else during those months. The letters do help tremendously in understanding Merton, and we can be grateful that the Merton Legacy Trust has allowed generous quotation from them. But while Reuther's exchange with Merton was clearly valuable, Furlong makes too much of it:

> And now here was a woman and a Catholic, a better theologian than himself, flatly arguing with him and contradicting him, questioning the validity of his vocation and refusing all attempts to charm her out of her cool dismissal of his motives. Merton might, I suppose, have been very angry indeed. In fact, he was fascinated and delighted.
>
> Yes, he said honestly in reply, he was in a crisis, and he was much too defensive, and he became frightened of her being so cerebral "probably because I resented my mother's intellectuality." Yes, he did need to get out of the place and move around a bit, only his Abbot wouldn't let him and refused even to discuss it. [p. 305]

Furlong has taken certain episodes in Merton's life and built them into a compelling narrative, but this is hardly the whole picture. Other biographies must fill in other parts of the mosaic.

In progress now is an authorized biography by Michael Mott, who is continuing a project begun by John Howard Griffin. One hopes too that some of Merton's literary friends, perhaps Daniel Berrigan or Bob Lax, might write memoirs. And contributions by his many editors and by fellow monks would also be welcome. James Forest's writing about Merton is an example of the value of personal, even biased, views. As did Ed Rice's biography, Forest's gives insights into a side of the man not immediately available through the published works. For instance, Forest's essay, written for the Twomey collection *Thomas Merton: Prophet in the Belly of a Paradox,* provides many valuable insights into the Merton he knew who was involved in writing for the peace movement. Eventually all such facts can be combined; at present our information is fragmentary.

James Forest's *Thomas Merton: A Pictorial Biography* is not a personal remembrance or a memoir but is rather an introduction to Merton's life. The text is brief and undocumented; Forest tells us that he could have provided footnotes, but he decided to let the photographs speak for themselves, and they do. In seventeen brief sections of prose which support the photographs, Forest provides the outlines of Merton's life. This book is a tribute to Merton: and, importantly, it will stimulate additional interest in his work among a wide audience.

Furlong sees Merton as a man increasingly sure of his vocation, yet she does not show that the monastic vocation itself was clarified by the act of writing. This omission is understandable: many of the monks who lived with Father Louis during his twenty-seven years at Gethsemani were only vaguely aware that the Father Louis of their monastery was a world-famous author. This says much about the monastic life, of course: it is also almost as if Merton himself conspired to keep his literary reputation hidden. As the books appeared year by year he must have found it difficult, however, to keep the roles of writer and contemplative separate. The published work led to still more writing, done while secluded from other monks and from the world. For decades Merton was separated from others (especially from other artists) and from most contemporary literature. This isolation made him a special kind of writer. During years of seclusion he first had to raise questions about the nature of his writing and then about his responsibility as a monk and writer. For a period in the late forties and early fifties, he even wondered (in print) if he should cease writing altogether. Of course he did not, and through this intense questioning he worked out an accommodation. For him writing became an activity essential in relation to his contemplative way of life and this vital relationship is the real key to his career. In writing about silence he affirmed his way of life, but also, and more significantly, in writing about silence he developed a firmer grasp of what others in the world needed. Like Emily Dickinson or Henry Adams in their self-imposed exiles, he embraced the mystery of a contemplative life and came to a surer understanding of what other men could not so easily articulate. He also learned to write, and then to let go of that writing; thus, paradoxically, his personality as a writer assumed less importance over the years.

Merton's poems were at first what allowed the young writer

to move from being an intellectual and an aspiring novelist to being a contemplative monk; yet the poems also constitute a link with that earlier experience of the world and were the avenue which would lead the mature writer back into contact with the world. A similar pattern informs Merton's journals; detailed records of the moment serve as meditations which ultimately reveal the impossibility of any radical separation from the world.

Several recent studies about Merton show how important writing was for him. In different ways each of the three books by Woodcock, Labrie, and Lentfoehr go beyond the life, as outlined by Furlong, to shed significant light on the development of Merton's aesthetic. All stress that he was an artist because he was first a man of God, but it is equally clear that he was a contemplative because of his constant concern with writing. He was nurtured under rather strange circumstances (at least by contemporary standards) yet isolation had advantages. Through discipline and solitude Merton saw that his world needed writing which would strike correct chords for readers beyond the monastery.

Although isolated from contemporary art, Merton never lost contact with the vital sources of imagination which feed a good poet. He went his own way and little by little developed his own approach to writing, finally even his own variety of poetry. He was, however, carefully reading poets such as William Carlos Williams and Louis Zukofsky during the years after he ceased modeling his work on that of Eliot and Dylan Thomas.[15] He also continued to write to friends, as we have seen with Robert Lax. (There is, for example, another volume of letters waiting to be edited, those between Merton and his Columbia teacher Mark Van Doren, part of a network of contacts which helped him to progress as artist, while simultaneously gaining strength in separation.)

The first of the new books which approaches Merton as artist is George Woodcock's *Thomas Merton, Monk and Poet*. It is valuable as the reasoned study of an outsider, not even, Woodcock says, a practicing Christian. The result is an approach to Merton which is clear-headed, balanced, and objective. Woodcock reminds us that while Merton was separated from the world, the subject matter became more and more the world beyond. Merton's role reflected his vocation as priest. Woodcock writes, and qualifies with Merton's own words:

> And if Merton believed that eremitic reclusion was really a necessary extension of monasticism, a pushing of outposts into the farther desert, he also believed that it was quite consistent with his priestly vocation. For to Merton what made the priest different from other men was not his pastoral role, his activities of teaching and advising other men or consoling and praying for them. It was not even that the priest is a man of God, for "The monk is a man of God and he does not have to be a priest." What distinguishes the priest is his sacramental role, his role as a "Visible human instrument of the Christ who reigns in Heaven," and this role is carried out when he re-enacts Christ's death and sacrifice in the mystery of the Mass.
>
> This explains at once the beauty and the terror of the priestly vocation. A man, weak as other men, imperfect as they are, perhaps less well endowed than many of those to whom he is sent, perhaps even less inclined to be virtuous than some of them, finds himself caught, without possibility of escape, between the infinite mercy of Christ and the almost infinite dreadfulness of man's sin. [pp. 80–87]

Woodcock's study demonstrates that the art and the life reinforced each other. Merton truly believed in the "mystical body," but he maintained much of his "existential communion" through the writing. Why else all those poems, letters, essays, cables, diaries, translations, prayers, and finally antipoems, but simultaneously to praise God and to keep reminding man of what he had forgotten?

Woodcock makes helpful suggestions for future study of Merton's poetry. He does not explicate the poetry in detail; he only isolates its predominant features. In a few pages he identifies the best of Merton's earliest work, but often he merely labels this or that poem as "effective." Woodcock is best when he picks up resonances between the life of the choir and the poems which grew out of that cloistered life. For example, his study of *Bread in the Wilderness,* a book in which Merton discusses the psalms as poetry, is quite well focused. Woodcock demonstrates that Merton wrote "poems of the choir" in which one hears the religious poetry which Merton had theoretically adumbrated in *Bread in the Wilderness*. Woodcock avoids any kind of synthesis, however, and merely gives several good examples. A similar approach is taken to important poems from other moments in Merton's life. Woodcock isolates what is of value but only occasionally stops for analysis.

Woodcock's wise but often cursory introduction suggests that Merton's monasticism led him more surely to compassion. Concern for others (expressed through essays about race, the liturgy, or the need for paramonastic communities) became the dominating force. If we go the next step and examine Labrie's recent study of Merton's work as art, we are reminded in some detail that it was precisely the developing aesthetic sense which allowed Merton to go back toward the world, not to criticize its errors so much as to celebrate its unity.

Woodcock's book provides valuable glimpses, and it covers a large body of material. Ross Labrie's *The Art of Thomas Merton* is, by contrast, more carefully focused on questions about art and is much less concerned with Merton as a particular type of person. Woodcock provides a valuable appreciation; Labrie works more as a scholar bringing together many pieces of evidence. Labrie attempts to show Merton's "versatility in mastering various literary forms" (p. xi), and within this framework he has succeeded admirably. Labrie demonstrates how the pressures Merton experienced in producing literary works alternated with a desire for solitude. He also considers some of the problems which Merton experienced within a strict religious order which, for example, required censorship. (Merton's relationship with his censors would also constitute a book length study.)

Labrie notes that "Merton's problems with writing were the result of his own anxieties about his dual vocation as both contemplative and artist" (p. 7). Merton's artistic drives provide the primary focus for Labrie; skillful use of unpublished notes, letters, and essays is evident throughout this study, especially in the opening chapter where Labrie outlines Merton's aesthetic. Labrie's examination of the dilemma of how a modern artist might find ways "to restore the face of nature and the rhythm of natural time as against the abrasive and synthetic pattern of modern life" (p. 17) is valuable. Yet because Merton produced so much, Labrie's task is immense. He too can only begin to provide the main outlines of what, inevitably, other critics must later pursue.

The Art of Thomas Merton is a beautifully printed book, and it is also available in an attractive paperback format. The care in its production reflects Labrie's precision. It is fitting that a book which has as its subject Merton's art should be so attractively produced. A handsome drawing from the Thomas Merton Studies Center collection of Bellarmine College is used on the cover of both the hardback and paperback editions. The book, which is handsomely printed, was designed by Judith M. Oelfke and set in ten-point palatino. There are six chapters: the first provides an introduction to the "contemplative and artist"; the next four survey his work as narrative writer, diarist, essayist, and poet; and a short chapter, "A Final Approach," concludes the volume.

The opening essay provides an overview of Merton as artist. The author shows how Merton's approach to art developed, and how he came to realize that he would never get certain types of experience into his words. There is mystery in life, and especially so in the life of a contemplative. As Labrie makes clear, this very mystery makes it possible for Merton's writing to continue to "open up." Labrie reveals Merton's concern with symbolism as an approach to mystery:

Merton saw the modern artist as frustrated in his search for the vital symbols that he believed had been buried alive amid the contemporary hunger for information and explanation. He pictured the most gifted artists of the age as driven by desperation, "running wild among the tombs in the moonlit cemeteries of surrealism." The flight from conventional symbolism became perverse and self-defeating, however, since the artist and his audience both had a basic human need for myth and symbol. In becoming instinctively suspicious of that "for which we are starved," the artist may simply aggravate his problem in communicating. Lamenting that ancient symbols had lost their meaning, the artist may become "hostile and uncommunicative, frustrating the desire for meaning by declaring that there are no meanings left and that one has to get along without them." [pp. 19–20]

This especially helps in understanding the later poetry, which was quite ambitious, but which sought to return to what was fundamentally important by making man aware of his losses.

Merton may have tried to do too much in too many ways, and this tendency causes problems for an investigator such as Labrie. Forced to categorize the writing into various types—narrative, diary, essay, and poem—he must ignore much of Merton's oeuvre in order that the framework of the study remain intact. Further, the impression is created that Merton somehow kept his writings in discrete categories. In reality one "genre" fed another, just as the monastic existence contributed to the flow of the writing. Like some of the earlier studies of Merton's thought, Labrie's book does provide another valuable category for our evaluation of Merton.

One of the deficiencies of a relatively brief study like Labrie's is that when he assumes responsibility for large categories of writing, he can only provide a limited amount of explication. He himself confesses that the essays gave most trouble. This had to be the case because of the sheer bulk (over 150 essays). There are similar problems with the poetry. Labrie cannot do justice to entire books, collections which took years to develop, in a few pages. Still there are many good things in this book. Labrie studied the existing critical commentary on Merton, and he is well attuned to the changes within the later poetry. That poetry was finally received with enthusiasm by critics aware of changes in contemporary American poetry, and Labrie explains how this poetry represents a considered accommodation with post-1930 contemporary verse. For this reason alone Labrie is worth studying.

Labrie knows that Merton used language consciously to make art. Thus his discussion of the diaries and journals centers around Merton's (or perhaps his superiors') awareness that he might one day turn them into finished works. Labrie discusses the charm of the published journals: here Merton could "converse" with other writers and reveal what he had been reading and thinking. At the same time the journals are in large part a conversation with himself. They therefore work on several levels. Labrie suggests that it is in *Conjectures of a Guilty Bystander* that this is most obvious. *Conjectures* is the most artfully contrived of Merton's journals; it covers the longest period; and it would require an extended study of manuscripts, reading notes, private journals, and letters to appreciate fully the craft of this seemingly simple document.

Woodcock and Labrie present selective overviews and so they are limited; this is also the case with Sister Thérèse Lentfoehr in *Words and Silence*. But with Lentfoehr a process of selection had already taken place because of her background as poet, and because of the valuable relationship she developed with Merton through correspondence over the entire period of his monastic life. Hers is a careful and systematic critique of the poetry, informed both by a close relationship with the poet and by continued study of the poetry.

Lentfoehr's appreciation of Merton's poetry is more than that of an admiring poet or correspondent. She has absorbed this poetry and can discuss it with wit and sparkle. She knows that it is good, and the organization of her book reveals a knowledge of many layers in Merton's poetry. Her writing retraces a familiar journey, one she apparently has made many times before. After reading Lentfoehr we realize that we can repeat the journey ourselves.

The three-part structure of Sister Thérèse's book corresponds to stages in Merton's career. The first three chapters introduce us to Merton as poet and to the early poetry, which is hardly ever static. Thus, in her succinct study of the fifth book of poems, published in 1957, she writes: "It has been apparent that in certain poems of *The Tears of the Blind Lions* Merton was already tentatively initiating a new manner—poems all but shorn of religious imagery, with a lean verbal structure frequently nonreferential, and with more than a hint of an ironic vision. Here we have it as a more or less general working technique" (Lentfoehr, p. 27). Her middle chapters are called "Zen Mystical Transparencies," "Surrealistic Patternings," and

"Recurrent Themes." The chapter on themes shows how Merton kept returning to basic ideas. Her pages about children (pp. 85–89), about elegiac poetry (pp. 89–94), and about the city (pp. 94–96) show how certain threads make up the fabric. Again, extended studies of all these thematic patterns could be made by others.

The final part of Lentfoehr's book is built around studies of *Cables to the Ace,* and *The Geography of Lograire,* and Merton's "central vision." She writes: "Merton's uniqueness as a religious poet lies in his focusing on the 'inner experience,' as he called it, the God-encounter in the depths of one's being and his striving to articulate it in his poetry. That this essential theme has its relevance for contemporary man in his seeking for transcendent experience is beyond dispute. And all of this Merton could validly contain within the scope of his monastic commitment" (p. 143). What I have suggested about Lentfoehr's book does not really indicate its full value. The work would profit from having its endnotes printed as footnotes, for there is much implied in references made to manuscripts, letters, and other materials in Sister Thérèse's private collection. We have here a poet-critic who knows another poet well, who has had access to manuscript material unavailable for others, who has been carefully reading this poetry for years—yet she is someone who refuses to idolize Merton. She keeps her distance, a distance of love and respect.

I stressed earlier that Merton's isolation from contemporary art was both asset and liability. In Sister Thérèse's study we can see this complexity illustrated. Probably if Merton had experienced more contact with other artists and with contemporary poetry, his movement away from a somewhat predictable "modernist" variety of poetry could have come more quickly. Yet Lentfoehr's exposition of the development of his poetry, and of the way certain patterns developed, demonstrates that many of the strains which were later considered innovative were indeed already present early in the career. In some basic ways Merton remained predictable.

Lentfoehr strengthens an argument for his genius. In *Words and Silence* she traces the important patterns in his poetic creations and shows how each stage grew out of the preceding one. Unfortunately (or fortunately, depending upon how much time is available), this means that for others to understand Merton's affirmation of silence, they have to spend as much time with his writing as his best critics have.

Merton's accomplishment as artist was fundamental to his life. But even more significant is the fact that his life, as reflected in the writing, became a model for others. The writing as a paradigm for others unifies the three additional studies of Merton's work reviewed here. Each of these books might be called theological in approach, although such categorization does not do justice to these studies of Merton's investigations into man's participation in the continuing paradox of the contemplative journey. One thing is clear; as Merton learned to affirm the mystery of his own journey, he articulated something of significance for a large audience too. As Elena Malits makes clear in *The Solitary Explorer,* it was as if through the writings Merton discovered his own life: "There is a ... sense in which we can say that autobiographical writing was Merton's work. The effort to articulate what was happening in his life was for him essential to the process of self-discovery. That enterprise actually served to shape Merton's identity, because writing about himself consciously engaged the man in the task he described as trying 'to be what I am' " (p. 140). Beyond this is the equally important fact that Merton's significant writing (Sister Elena would perhaps attempt to limit this to the autobiographical writing) does have a "power that renders it fascinating to others. The stories of his initial and continuing conversion, apparently, have brought some sort of religious conversion in numerous persons" (*The Solitary Explorer,* p. 153). Awareness of this fact unifies the books by Malits, Finley, and Adams. Future scholars will often be concerned with the effect of his writing upon other lives and other writers. Merton was primarily preoccupied with finding his own way, yet in that single-mindedness of quest he provides directions for other travelers. As he became surer of his abilities as artist, he ceased being very much concerned with the work of art as finished object. Writing then was recognized as a reflection of a personal process. It became more a matter of keeping a record of where the writer happened to be. Yet that state, of its nature, was not to be finished in the temporal world. As Merton himself noted in *Conjectures of a Guilty Bystander,* "He who arrives is ruined." But to keep arriving and knowing that one is but on one's way spiritually was finally one of the most important facts he came to live, love, and write about. That fact helps to account both for the nature of his quest and the open-endedness of his writing, especially in the final years.

In the three books by Finley, Adams, and Malits, the effect of Merton's systematic quest is seen more clearly than in examinations which focus upon his work primarily as art. Clearly both types of studies are needed, and ultimately what will become necessary will be still more examinations which will combine these approaches (study of art and record of quest). These two aspects of writing and living did not remain separated in Merton's existence. Through art Merton leads readers into silence, not just the silence of his own journey, but into the silence which all must embrace if they are to find wholeness. Merton lived his life moment by moment, and he put all his energy into particular moments. Depending upon how readers come to know him, they may appreciate one aspect over another, for Merton played many roles. We might express this another way; both Lentfoehr and Finley knew Merton, the first through reading and correspondence, the other through spiritual friendship and then by careful reading and study. This fundamental difference helps to account for the types of books they produced as well as to suggest the complexity of Merton who could be both a Novice Master and a poet. If you read only these two books, you might wonder if they are about the same man. Sometimes Merton seems so extremely concerned about words, yet often at those very times he is extremely specific about mystery. What we need to remember is that he lived a mystery which he could hardly articulate, right down to those months and weeks documented in the *Asian Journal,* the record of his journey to the "palace of nowhere." His mystery is always one crafted through words, although ultimately even the best metaphors only hint at what is beyond.

Jim Finley's title, *Merton's Palace of Nowhere,* is fittingly taken from the *Asian Journal,* and it suggests the mystery of a quest which Merton had come to embrace. Finley's volume is valuable but not easy to read. It is the fruit of a long period of gestation, the result of Merton's influence as Novice Master and as friend. (Another category of books awaiting careful study is the works written *because of* Merton's influence. Here we would have to include books by Ernesto Cardenal and Henri Nouwen.) Finley's procedure is scholarly. His primary concern is with man's need to be aware of the "true self" while he is pulled into all kinds of activities which are reflections of a "false self." Finley draws upon many Merton texts, and his reading of Merton's *The New Man* (1961), a book which has not been properly assimilated into the Merton canon, provides a major thrust for his discussion. Finley's explanation of Merton's struggle to articulate how we realize the true self is a way of understanding both Merton's affirmation and everyman's:

> Our struggle does not remove us from our simple, every day self but confirms its ultimate dimensions. Our prayer does not carry us off into realms unknown for it reveals the unknown depths of each passing hour. Nevertheless the struggle is a real one. The realization of the true self does not fall into our lap like ripe fruit. It is true that in God we live without effort, but it is also true that it calls for a divestiture of self to live without effort. The following text not only refers to the present reality of God's presence but also to the only way for us to realize it.
>
> > The desert becomes a paradise when it is accepted as desert. The desert can never be anything but a desert if we are trying to escape it. But once we fully accept it in union with the passion of Christ, it becomes a paradise. . . . This breakthrough into what you already have is only accomplished through the complete acceptance of the cross. [pp. 114–15]

While Finley's study is not literary, it provides insight into the literary production which reflects Merton's concern with the "true self." Finley's assimilation of his subject suggests that Merton has entered the mainstream of contemporary thought. Reading Merton has made a difference for Finley, and reading Finley will have an effect upon others. While it may seem to be a detour from the essential concern of this essay, it should be noted that what Merton accomplished in theologizing, in journals, and in the "Zen Mystical" poetry has parallels with contemporary poetry. And while I know of, for example, no direct connections between the poetry of Robert Creeley or Gary Snyder and Merton's work, parallels do exist. Merton insists that we must vastly simplify if we are going to make a breakthrough into the essential truth, and these poets come to similar realizations. The parallel studies of Zen by Snyder and Merton would provide material for a lengthy monograph.

Still other possible studies are suggested by the careful work of Daniel Adams who, in *Thomas Merton's Shared Contemplation,* approaches Merton's vocation as a monastic writer with the objectivity of an historian. Writing as a Protestant, Adams examines how Merton's themes emerge and how they relate to other themes in Western Christianity. The stress, again, is on the balance and combination of contemplation and action. Adams has chapters which are at times almost esoteric, while others are quite down to earth. The result is an overview of Merton's developing uses of contemplation as a subject which ties back in with living. Shannon provides the base for an examination of Merton's books which deal explicitly with this subject; Adams demonstrates how the consistent interest in the contemplative grows out of wider traditions. In the end, Adams comments not just on what Merton writes but also on how the writing connects with life both for Christians and for those in other traditions. Adams's book provides a very valuable approach for anyone who wants to understand Merton's place in the mainstream of Western culture, yet who also is skeptical about an apologia from a "Catholic" perspective. As a Protestant, Adams comes to his subject with skepticism, but he demonstrates that there is a solid foundation to what Merton achieved. His systematic chapter concerning the foundations of Merton's thought—an appraisal of the modern Thomists, St. Augustine, St. Thomas Aquinas, St. Bernard of Clairvaux, Platonic mysticism, the Desert Fathers, St. Gregory of Nyssa, St. Theresa of Avila, and St. John of the Cross—suggests both the value of Merton's work and the extent of further investigation still to be done. For without a doubt if these nine categories have provided the outline for one chapter by Adams, his thoroughness makes it clear that these major building blocks in Merton's spiritual formation could be studied in more detail. For example, Adams makes use of the articles which Merton wrote about Bernard and which first appeared in *Collectanea Ordinis Cisterciensium Reformatorium* in 1953 and 1954 and have subsequently been edited by Brother Patrick Hart in *Merton on St. Bernard* (discussed above). But clearly much more will be done in tracing the synthesis which Merton made. The same point could be made when Adams shows the applicability of Merton's thought to today's world.

Thomas Merton's Shared Contemplation provides a systematic investigation of the theoretical base upon which Merton investigates his world. All of its chapters are valuable, but the later ones are especially so. Here Adams shows us that the eremitic life, such as Merton lived it, may be the model we all will have to follow in the future, for we hardly have the communities we earlier dreamt were possible. He points out that *eremus* means " 'a certain physical separation from the affairs of the world, but it is intended to indicate our attitude' " (p. 262). Precisely because Merton had learned to accept solitude (and thus come to terms with himself) he was able to affirm mankind, since in solitude one begins to find the image of God in oneself and in others. Merton insists that "we must be able to discern the image of God in others." We can easily overlook that image if we are not first of all aware of God's image in ourselves. Merton believed that "all things carry within them an image of God" (p. 283). Looking toward the future, several important points are clear. Adams builds one of his chapters, "Contemplation in a World of Action," around the idea of the impossibility of an "either/or" choice and explains that Merton came to learn that monks, too, had their illusions. The monastery was hardly a place to get away from the world. Yet Adams also states that true monasticism serves well as a model for dispersed Christians living in a diaspora.

Because it combines approaches, Elena Malits's book may be the most successful of these final three. Malits is primarily concerned with Merton's continuing conversion, and therefore the patterns she traces in his writing are reflections of his continuing progress in being a Christian. She pays close attention to the text. Her only problem seems to be her insistence that it is in the prose autobiographical writing where the metaphors best manifest themselves, so she ignores most of the poems and pays little attention to essays which Finley and Adams examine. Nevertheless, Elena Malits does an excellent job tracing the significant metaphors of Merton's writing. She stresses his growth in solitude and wisdom. This enabled him to see that ideas attracting him bore implications far beyond his life. In one section, she examines phrases that recur throughout his career: "to leave the world," "to live in the desert," and "to seek God." These are classic formulations about the monastic experience, yet Merton's use of them allowed him to clarify his own existence and to transform them into metaphors in such a way that Christians who were not monks could apply his meaning to their lives. In each instance, she demonstrates his movement from somewhat simplified views of what it means to become a solitary toward a more complex view involving pain, suffering, and difficulty. Early during the monastic experience it seemed as if Merton had fled from the destructive tendencies in the world: soon he came to realize that one of his fundamental jobs was to accept such destructive tendencies, especially those existing within himself. When that was done, it was possible for Merton to take another affirmative step and to seek God while also remaining aware that there is really no way to leave the world.

Malits stresses that Merton wrote so that readers would identify "with him and his capacity to articulate the deep desires of the human heart" (p. 2). Her opening chapter provides an overview of the changing nature of Merton's "journey" and "his commitment to continuing conversion" (p. 20), while the second traces the actual movements of his life; these two overviews of works and life thus prepare her reader for the ensuing analysis. In the third chapter she bears down on the implications which this configuration of movement (expressed in the writing, but lived in a physical sense) had within the work. What follows is a careful analysis of someone who "was quite essentially a *monachos*" (p. 53) and therefore paradoxically someone who had to articulate his concerns, first for himself and then for others. Malits points out that for Merton there could finally be "no authentic seeking God unless a person knows how to let go, move on, and plunge ahead. Such are the 'skills' that the solitary painfully learns to acquire. The discipline of monastic life—and in particular of solitude—prepares one to go beyond the frontier. 'The real function of discipline,' Merton wrote in 1968, 'is not to provide us with maps, but to sharpen our own sense of direction so that when we really get going, we can travel without maps.' Traveling without maps, like moving beyond the frontier, was a metaphor for the capacities of mind and heart that represented for Merton genuine spiritual development" (p. 73). Malits's treatment of Merton's decade-long investigation into the nature of Zen and its relationship to Christianity, and even more importantly its meaning for him, is a fine example of the success of her method. Always paying close attention to texts, she demonstrates the gradual refinement of Merton's understanding. The same success attends her judgments about his refinement of the understanding of the self. Her chapter "A Mind Awake in the Dark" traces his systematic enunciation of how, if we are to become "new men," we have to reverse Adam's journey.

As one surveys these various approaches to Merton, it is as if each writer uses a magnifying glass to look carefully at an intricately crafted object, yet of course we know the object is a symbol. Woodcock, conscious of his distance from the object, concentrates rays of light on moments of conjunction which provide the broad outlines of Merton's dual journey as monk and poet. Labrie, working more as scholar and therefore with a concern for categorization, moves closer. This allows him to look carefully at individual items, details which suggest how the art functions. Sister Thérèse (who in a sense has had more access to Merton's private world as writer than anyone else) focuses only on the poetry, and she begins to investigate the intricacies of that poetic world, yet she never forgets it is part of a larger world. Elena Malits, looking at Merton from the point of view of a religious studies scholar intrigued by Merton's uses of metaphor and storytelling, chooses another aspect for examination so that we can see how the personal journey was a continuing one, yet one expressed through a language of clarification. Each scholar holds up a magnifying glass. Whether general outline, specific kinds of art, theological background, or the journey itself, the words crafted by Merton are guideposts for a journey. It is as if all these scholars are on the same journey and with their magnifying glasses they pause to see what Merton has left behind. In the meantime he seems to have taken still more steps forward.

Merton's complexity is made clear in the two recent collections of essays about him and his work. Gerald Twomey's collection is mostly about the social implications of the writing. Just as Merton's photograph was literally posted on the wall of Daniel Berrigan's prison cell, Merton's thought has remained with many during the past several decades. A few lines by Berrigan suggest Merton's impact in relation to social issues: as a contemplative Merton stood back from his society, not just to criticize it, but to say he had found something else much better.

> In prison remember
> Dame Poverty, her strait issues of man;
> Merton's photo, friend, confident brother under the skin
> . . . . .
> Merton: that cool brusque cavalier's glance at the
> world: No sale[.][16]

Gerald Twomey's collection of essays examines Merton's life and writing in its positive implications for modern society. Articles by James H. Forest and Gordon Zahn provide important information about Merton's role as peacemaker and pacifist. Other pieces of John Howard Griffin, Twomey himself, and Sister Thérèse Lentfoehr examine the social implications of the writing in relation to questions about race, war, civil rights, and the third world. Still other pieces in the book show Merton's concerns with the East, Church, renewal, and history. Twomey himself shows how Merton's monastic vocation supported his social vision:

> Ironically, Merton's eremitical years (1965–1968) spawned many of his most incisive social commentaries in the crucial areas of race and peace—another sign, "in the belly of a paradox." This expression of concern dovetailed with Merton's basic vision that the task of monasticism is intimately bound to "the whole question of the reconciliation of all men with one another in Christ." In reflecting on the moral climate of the United States at mid-century, he reiterated the concern of Pope John in *Pacem in Terris* that human fear must give way to love, "a love that tends to express itself in collaboration." [p. 97]

Twomey's collection indicates that scholars and friends (sometimes they are both) bring remembrance and systematic investigation to bear both on Merton *and* for the future. Twomey's book was planned to appear on the occasion of the 1978 tenth year celebrations of Merton's death. It seemed appropriate when that book was planned to focus upon the social themes in Merton's work. Twomey's collection is then a conscious step beyond Brother Patrick's earlier collection, *Thomas Merton, Monk.* Viewing Merton as prophet, it helps us to see that the contemplative life might easily lead to involvement.

In a sense involvement is the critical message in the last book to be reviewed here. Called *The Message of Thomas Merton,* and edited with a valuable introduction by Brother Patrick Hart, these essays by scholars from many disciplines examine aspects of Merton's thought and art. This volume is important for several reasons. The introduction by Brother Patrick is a masterful summing up of the basic ideas and themes in Merton's work. The twelve essays, each different, seem to have been chosen to provide directions for future study. Some of the essays in *The Message,* such as those by Elena Malits and William H. Shannon, extend work which these authors have published in their books. Other essays are speculative and seem to be designed to provide experimental modes of analysis. Victor A. Kramer's "Merton's Published Journals: The Paradox of Writing as a Step toward

Contemplation," John F. Teahan's "Merton's Life and Thought," and George Kilcourse's " 'Pieces of the Mosaic Earth': Thomas Merton and the Christ" are valuable as new ways of looking carefully at the writing. Teahan's provocative suggestions about parallels between Merton's awareness of silence and similar patterns in other twentieth century writers and philosophers promises to be an important area in future study. Other approaches in this collection radiate outward and suggest connections which other scholars will be pursuing. Especially valuable are insights about ecumenism by E. Glenn Hinson, about "Asian Religious Thought" by Deba Patnaik, and about solitude as suggested by Chalmers MacCormick. MacCormick investigates some of the implications in Merton's thought about solitude and man's need for it beyond the monastery:

> One of the respects in which Merton matured was that in his later writings he showed a greater sensitivity than he had shown earlier to the needs of the married for solitude. Previously he had, to be sure, commended marriage as a particular mode of contemplation and a high vocation, but he had not yet envisaged some kind of union of this vocation with the monastic. In his very important essay on "Ecumenism and Renewal," however, he reveals a concern, awareness, and germinal wisdom on this theme that might, had he lived longer, have developed into a major statement about solitude and marriage. (This may seem improbable, but it is not unimaginable.) He wrote: "Why could there not be monasteries, with a nucleus of permanently dedicated monks, to which others come temporarily for two or three years, for periods of training or for retreat (as for instance in Zen Buddhist monasticism)? Why could not married people participate temporarily, in some way, in monastic life?" [pp. 125–26]

Connections in other essays are made with tradition and with the present. Both the essays by Lawrence S. Cunningham, "The Life of Thomas Merton as Paradigm: The View of Academe," and Dennis Q. McInerny, "Thomas Merton and the Tradition of American Critical Romanticism," show that Merton's work cannot be read in a vacuum. His concerns must be related to all other aspects of life. As these diverse essays indicate, many areas about Merton will occupy scholars in the future. There will also be close textual studies of individual works and studies of influence. Such study will help us to see the unity of Merton's career. There will be still more considerations of the implications of Merton's thought for others—and especially for those outside monastic life.[17]

As noted earlier, unpublished Merton manuscripts and additional studies of him will continue to appear for decades. Selecting from unfinished materials for publication will take years. Along with lecture notes, notebooks, and correspondence, there are even some finished manuscripts awaiting publication. Our knowledge of him will continue to develop for many years as this man of silence continues to speak. More and more we see that writing made his life as it was. Still another book, not available at the time of the composition of this review, is the forthcoming *Literary Essays of Thomas Merton*. This book promises to substantiate the importance of writing for Merton. The preliminary table of contents indicates that it will be of value. The book includes reviews, essays on many writers, several on major figures such as Faulkner and Camus as well as studies about the nature of art and poetry.[18] Most of this material has been published, but in scattered places. The fact that there is now so much interest in Merton, as evidenced by the books reviewed here, will make this forthcoming collection useful.

Merton never claimed to be an original scholar, but perhaps that was part of his originality. As a contemplative who experienced flashes into eternity, he remained truly concerned about the world. He therefore affirmed the need to approach that world. Through his insights, both about eternity and the present, we approach the Merton most hidden from us. Continuing to write about liturgy, literature, art, history, race, war, politics, society, solitude, poetry, myth, he was led to other topics which could never be fully explored. Nevertheless his explorations are of immense value. There are some who unabashedly compare Merton to the Fathers of the Church. This comparison is not farfetched. It simply expresses the significance of what this compulsive writer, both a monk and a poet, had to say, and prophesies his role for the future.

Notes

1. *The Asian Journal of Thomas Merton,* edited from original notebooks by Naomi Burton, Brother Patrick Hart, and James Laughlin; consulting ed., Amiya Chakravarly (New York: New Directions, 1973). The journal includes selections from travel journals, personal diaries, and reading notes. Appendixes, including letters, and an extensive glossary of terms are provided.

2. Marquita Breit, *Thomas Merton: A Bibliography* (Metuchen, N.J.: Scarecrow Press, 1974), and Frank Dell 'Isola, *Thomas Merton: A Bibliography* (Kent State: Kent State Univ. Press, 1975). Breit's bibliography includes a listing of secondary sources about Merton. Dell 'Isola's is a systematic bibliographic description of Merton's books as well as a listing of periodical contributions, miscellanea, poetry, translations, and juvenilia.

3. These books include *Contemplative Prayer* (New York: Herder and Herder, 1969); *The Collected Poems of Thomas Merton* (New York: New Directions, 1977), clothbound edition; *My Argument with the Gestapo* (Garden City, N.Y.: Doubleday, 1969); *Contemplation in a World of Action* (Garden City, N.Y.: Doubleday, 1971); *The Monastic Journey* (Kansas City: Sheed, Andrews, and McMeel, 1977); *A Hidden Wholeness: The Visual World of Thomas Merton,* photographs by Thomas Merton and John Howard Griffin; text by Griffin (Boston: Houghton Mifflin, 1970). Other books of interest are the two collections edited by Gordon Zahn called *Thomas Merton on Peace* (New York: McCall Publishing, 1971), republished under the title *The Non-Violent Alternative* (New York: Farrar Straus Giroux, 1981); and *Ishi Means Man: Essays on Native Americans,* with a foreword by Dorothy Day (Greensboro: Unicorn, 1976). Also of value are the appointment calendars for 1979 and 1980 (Sheed, Andrews, and McMeel) which include texts and original drawings by Merton. The 1981 calendar, issued by the same publisher, includes photographs by Merton. Much of the material in these calendars had been unpublished.

4. The major repository for Merton manuscripts, tapes, books, photographs, and other materials is The Thomas Merton Studies Center at Bellarmine College in Louisville. It publishes *The Merton Seasonal of Bellarmine College,* which includes a listing of publications by and about Merton. An example of the continuing work being done at the center is the recent publication of selected foreign prefaces to editions of Merton books. Edited by Robert A. Daggy, this collection is called *Introductions East and West: The Foreign Prefaces of Thomas Merton* (Greensboro: Unicorn Press, 1981).

5. *Thomas Merton, Monk: A Monastic Tribute* (New York: Sheed and Ward, 1974).

6. *Merton's Theology of Prayer* (Spencer: Cistercian Publications, 1971), p. ix.

7. *Thomas Merton—Social Critic* (Lexington: Univ. Press of Kentucky, 1971).

8. *Man before God: Thomas Merton on Social Responsibility* (Garden City, N.Y.: Doubleday, 1974).

9. Bailey, *Thomas Merton on Mysticism* (Garden City, N.Y.: Doubleday, 1975).

10. Reviews of *The Collected Poems* have ranged from disapprobation to enthusiasm. See, for example, Daniel Berrigan's comments in "The Seventy Times Seven Storey Mountain," *Cross Currents*, 27 (Winter 1977–78), 385–93.

11. See pp. 79 ff., 240 ff., 287 ff., 408–9 of *The Seven Storey Mountain* (New York: Harcourt, Brace, 1948) for evidence of their friendship.

12. *The Geography of Lograire* (New York: New Directions, 1969) contains an author's note and notes compiled by editors (included in *The Collected Poems of Thomas Merton*) which this new material qualifies.

13. See note 3.

14. *The Man in the Sycamore Tree: An Entertainment.* (Garden City, N.Y.: Doubleday, 1970), p. 80.

15. See, for example, Merton's review of *All the Collected Short Poems, 1956–1964* by Louis Zukofsky, in *The Critic*, February–March 1968, pp. 69–71, and "Zukofsky: The Paradise Ear," *Peace News* (London), 28 July 1967, pp. 8 ff., reprinted in the forthcoming *Literary Essays of Thomas Merton*.

16. From "We Were Poor Poor Poor" and "Strip Mining," in *Prison Poems* (New York: Viking, 1973), pp. 87, 109.

17. A recent example of how a specialized study of one aspect of Merton's thought has implications for mankind in general is Richard Anthony Cashen, *Solitude in the Thought of Thomas Merton* (Kalamazoo: Cistercian Publications, 1981). Ultimately, says Cashen, Merton's concern about solitude is about "the very nature and destiny of man" (p. 178).

18. To be published by New Directions. The tentative table of contents includes fourteen literary essays (1959–1968); seven essays on Albert Camus; nine essays introducing poets in translation; and six additional essays on related literary questions. The three appendixes include the 1939 M.A. thesis written at Columbia, "Nature and Art in William Blake"; fourteen early reviews; and two transcriptions of conferences on William Faulkner.

An Eleventh-Century *Beowulf*?

Ashley Crandell Amos

Kevin S. Kiernan, Beowulf *and the* Beowulf *Manuscript*. New Brunswick, New Jersey: Rutgers University Press, 1981. xvi, 303 pp.

When, how, and why did *Beowulf* come to be written, and who was the poet (or the last poet) who shaped its literary form? These questions are of great interest to students of Old English literary history, but they are questions most scholars believed could not be answered on the surviving evidence. Kevin Kiernan believes they can, and he sets forth his answers in a controversial book about the *Beowulf* manuscript.[1] Beowulf *and the* Beowulf *Manuscript* consists of three sections: a sixty-page argument that the poem was composed during Cnut's reign ("The Poem's Eleventh-Century Provenance"), a hundred-page discussion of the codex, attacking previous work and arguing that *Beowulf* constitutes a codex within Cotton Vitellius A.xv independent of the three prose pieces and *Judith* ("The History and Construction of the Composite Codex"), and a hundred-page discussion of the manuscript form of the poem, with particular attention to lineation, corrections, erasures, etc. ("The *Beowulf* Codex and the Making of the Poem"). A four-page preface surveys material published after the completion of Kiernan's book but before its publication.

Kiernan's theory is, as he himself admits, "revolutionary" (p. xii), and he writes always as an advocate.[2] He uses and cites sources selectively, sometimes misrepresenting the material to which he alludes. As a result the reader quickly grows skeptical and wary; that "polemics" rather than dispassionate investigation will be the natural response to this book, as Kiernan astutely predicts (p. xiii), is a function of his own style of argumentation. His brief preface serves as an apt illustration. The preface suggests that there is wide-ranging scholarly support for Kiernan's line of argument, but the two books he cites which are now in print are not fairly represented in his summary. He claims that my monograph, *Linguistic Means of Determining the Dates of Old English Literary Texts* (Cambridge: Medieval Academy of America, 1980), demonstrates "that the old linguistic tests alone cannot rule out a contemporary MS of *Beowulf*" (p. xi). But, as I explicitly state on page 17 of my monograph, I make no attempt to date individual poems, and I make no judgment at all about the evidence of the language of *Beowulf* as to the date of its composition. It would be fairer to quote my conclusion that most of the old linguistic tests are not reliable indicators of date, and to present further deductions as his own. Papers presented at the Toronto symposium on the date of *Beowulf* (now published as *The Dating of* Beowulf, ed. Colin Chase [Toronto: Univ. of Toronto Press, 1981]) are also cited selectively. Kiernan notes that Thomas Cable finds that *Beowulf* and the eleventh-century *Death of Edward* draw on the same metrical paradigm (p. xi), but he fails to mention that Cable argues that the same "strict metre was composed for four centuries between *Caedmon's Hymn* in the second half of the seventh century and *The Death of Edward* in 1066," and within that period that Cable distinguishes *Beowulf* on metrical grounds from those poems composed after the mid-tenth century.[3] Kiernan also mentions the articles by Roberta Frank, Alexander Callander Murray, and R. I. Page discussing *Beowulf* and Scandinavian matters, and notes that neither they nor other conference participants specifically discuss Cnut's reign as a possible time of composition (pp. xi-xii).[4] That that omission was due to misinterpretation of Ker's dating of the *Beowulf* manuscript, as Kiernan suggests, is ridiculous. Only the scholars involved can explain why they did not favor a date after 1016, but an explanation more plausible than their ignorance of conventions of palaeographic dating is that they found no particular evidence pointing to a date after 1016. Kiernan cites Frank's parallels between *Beowulf* and late tenth early eleventh century skalds—but does not mention her early and mid-tenth century parallels or the skaldic material on Sigurþr that seems to rule out a date after 950.[5]

It may seem niggling to complain at length about Kiernan's

brief summary of two recent studies, but his treatment of these works is typical of his use of evidence throughout the volume: the arguments and conclusions of other scholars are misrepresented in summary in order to make a point. There is an ad hoc quality to Kiernan's argumentation. On page xi he recognizes that "the negative assumption that *Beowulf* could not have been composed during the Viking Age of the 9th and 10th centuries has lost its former hold"; he does not question the arguments to that effect presented by Page, Murray, and Frank, and he cites Nicholas Jacobs's article, which forcefully argues the point, in his bibliography (p. 282).[6] Yet on pages 20–23 he approvingly repeats Whitelock's arguments that the poem could not have been written during the ninth and tenth centuries, unless in the Danelaw, without considering the various rebuttals of her argument. Such inconsistency is at least partly due to the fact that *The Dating of* Beowulf (though not Jacobs's article) appeared after Kiernan had written his book; it is unfortunate that the two studies appeared so nearly simultaneously that neither could respond to the arguments of the other. *The Dating of* Beowulf should be required reading with Kiernan's book; its fourteen articles provide a useful perspective and corrective on many of Kiernan's points.

Kiernan's discussion of the evidence the language of *Beowulf* presents for its date of composition (pp. 23–63) is seriously flawed. His treatment of the linguistic tests is unclear and superficial, drawing almost solely on Frederick Klaeber's summary rather than the original works.[7] Kiernan does not attempt to describe or analyze the language of the poem, but only to refute any statements previously made about it that would contradict his hypothesis. He does not convey to us the fact that the language of *Beowulf* is different from datably late (and from datably early) poems, that, for example, the poem is remarkable in the richness of its vocabulary or in its frequent use of weak adjectives without articles.[8] His discussion of contraction, pages 25–27, misses the point. It is not a question of whether a reader could recognize the occasional verse which had to be read in a de-contracted form to scan, or whether a poet could retain the use of a few formulae, but of whether, once contraction of vowels juxtaposed after loss of *h*, *j*, or *w* was complete, and the diphthongs produced by such contraction indistinguishable from the original long diphthongs of Old English, a poet could recognize which words had undergone contraction and which contained original diphthongs. Could any poet divine that *ēam* ("uncle") had originally had an intervocalic -*h*- and could thus be treated as dissyllabic (as it is, for example, in *Beowulf* line 881), while *tēam* and *bēam* develop from original diphthongs and must always be monosyllabic? The *Beowulf* poet and other Old English poets do not make such mistakes; they do not treat words as de-contracted which could never have undergone contraction. It is this question which Kiernan should answer: not whether and how the verses could be scanned, but how they could be composed long after contraction was complete.[9] Kiernan's proposal that *wundini golde*, line 1382a, should be read as a compound, *wundungolde* (pp. 30–37), is striking and perhaps right, but his insistence on the importance of the manuscript reading *wundmi* is unconvincing in light of his own admission of scribal inconsistency in joining minims and the fact that *dini* is on the damaged, heat-marked edge of the folio. Readers should compare two discussions of the word in *The Dating of Beowulf*—John C. Pope's in "On the Date of Composition of *Beowulf*," pages 189–91, and E. G. Stanley's in "The Date of *Beowulf*: Some Doubts and No Conclusions," page 208.

The remainder of the language section suffers from several methodological flaws. Kiernan refers throughout to "standard Late Old English," which he introduces as another term for the late West Saxon referred to by Quirk and Wrenn as a standard form of Old English, the language of Ælfric (pp. 37–38). But later he refers to certain spellings as late Old English and others as late West Saxon and appears to distinguish the two (pp. 56, 57). Certainly some of the features he ascribes to late Old English, like "the ubiquitous *æ/e* variation" (p. 58), are not characteristic of late West Saxon at all, and since he never identifies manuscripts whose spellings serve as examples of the late Old English dialect (as the grammarians do for all the major dialects), what he means remains unclear. Kiernan appears to consider the "poetic dialect" Sisam has defined as a dialect in the same sense as Campbell's Kentish or Mercian, which are used merely to describe the language of particular texts, and his use of the phrase "literary dialect" is confusing, for all the Old English dialects are written, and Aldred's Northumbrian and the Vespasian Psalter's Mercian are surely as much literary dialects as Ælfric's West Saxon.[10]

Kiernan's interpretation of *phonological* and *orthographic* is unfortunate: he repeatedly dismisses the "purely orthographic" as though spellings were not the only evidence for written dialects like the Old English dialects.[11] His discussion of "the mixture of forms in *Beowulf*" (pp. 50–61) is rendered useless by its many omissions. He organizes his discussion according to the lists of forms in P. G. Thomas's "Notes on the Language of *Beowulf*" (*Modern Language Review*, 1 [1906], 202–7) and overlooks additional examples relevant to his categories of forms subject or resistant to breaking, *i*-umlaut, back umlaut, palatization, etc., which are listed in Klaeber's language sections (pp. lxxi-xciv, 274–78) and in Cameron et al. (pp. 38–75).[12] Symptomatic of the confusion of Kiernan's language section is his analysis of *wæs*, line 407, for the imperative *wes* (p. 52 and n. 61). Thomas calls the form Northumbrian, as Kiernan notes, and Campbell would concur (§743) or consider it typical of the dialect of the Mercian gloss to the Rushworth Gospels (Ru¹, §328). Kiernan tries to show that the form is West Saxon, but none of the authorities he cites is to the point. He cites Klaeber that ǣ for WS ĕ is "sporadically found" in non-Anglican texts, but Klaeber means Kentish and "Saxon patois" (i.e., Mercian) texts, not West Saxon ones as Kiernan would have it (see Klaeber, p. lxxiv). Kiernan then adverts to the "frequent confusion between the graphs *æ* and *e*" in late West Saxon and Ælfric (p. 52)—but no such confusion exists, although in texts of Ælfric, as elsewhere in Anglo-Saxon scripts for Latin and for Old English, *ę* (*e*-caudata, or tailed *e*) is occasionally used as an alternate graph for *æ*. He cites in support two sections of Klaeber's analysis, the first (p. lxxvii, presumably §9.1) irrelevant since it refers to *æ* as the monophthongization of $\overline{ea}$, the second

(p. lxxv, presumably §7.5, n. 1) without any suggestion that the variation between *æ* and *e* is "purely orthographic" (which Kiernan cited it to demonstrate). Kiernan's final citation of DeCamp on the West Saxon shibboleth of *æ* for *e* is also misplaced, since DeCamp is referring to WS *ǣ* for nWS *e* from PrimGmc *ǣ*, known as *ǣ*,[1] not to *ĕ* for *ĕ*.

That the *Beowulf* manuscript could have been copied after 1016 may be just possible on palaeographic grounds, though that would be to place the manuscript at the late extreme of its likely period. That the fact that it was copied then is "beyond reasonable doubt" (p. 61), however, Kiernan has signally failed to prove, much less that the poem was composed in the eleventh century. His historical arguments are considerably less convincing than those for other periods, and his linguistic arguments are faulty. He adduces no evidence in Part I that the poem was either composed or even copied in the reign of Cnut.

Parts II and III form the heart of Kiernan's book and attest to his fascination with and close scrutiny of the *Beowulf* manuscript. He argues that *Beowulf* formed a separate codex by itself within the Nowell codex, itself a discrete medieval manuscript later joined to the Southwick codex to form British Museum MS. Cotton Vitellius A.xv. Kiernan further argues that the varying numbers of lines per folio, the damaged and inconsistent numbering of the fitts, the later corrections in the text, and the worn and retouched surface of folio 179 (182) are best explained by assuming that the poem as it survives is a composite of two earlier poems joined (and perhaps even written) by the second scribe. I am not a palaeographer, and Kiernan specifically excludes those who have not had prolonged access to the manuscript itself from evaluating his arguments, but certain comments seem obvious.

Kiernan's description of the codex and its history (pp. 66–85 and ff.) is interesting and useful, recapitulating much of Max Förster's major description, but also extending it and correcting it in minor points.[13] He repeatedly alludes to "the curious neglect" of the *Beowulf* manuscript, asserting that "the *Beowulf* MS has scarcely been studied at all" and hinting at a scholarly conspiracy to ignore the evidence of a manuscript thought to be centuries later than the composition of the poem (pp. 3, 65, 168, 245). In fact the *Beowulf* manuscript has been studied about as thoroughly as the other great poetic codices, and facsimiles of the poem, of the Howell Codex, and of both Thorkelin transcripts have long been available; the Greenfield-Robinson *Bibliography of Publications on Old English Literature* catalogues nineteen studies of the manuscript, approximately the same number of studies as have been made of the other poetic codices.[14] Kiernan's ardent concern (pp. 81–110) that the so-called "MS foliation," one of the several schemes of foliation of the manuscript, be adopted as standard is idiosyncratic; any arbitrary system of reference, if unambiguous, will do to identify a particular folio. Kiernan's repeated assertion (pp. 71, 132, 169) that for *Beowulf* to have been copied as a separate codex would indicate more contemporary interest than if it were to be copied as the fourth item in a codex is puzzling and unconvincing. Indeed, Kiernan's conclusion that *Beowulf* constituted a separate codex and the analysis of quire size and structure on which he bases it (p. 126) are unconvincing; the analysis of the quires of the Nowell Codex in Leonard E. Boyle's "The Nowell Codex and the Poem of *Beowulf*" (*The Dating of Beowulf*, pp. 23–32) is far more persuasive, especially in its analysis of the varying numbers of lines per folio over the codex as a whole.[15]

Kiernan argues that the number and type of corrections in *Beowulf* suggest unusual care and contemporary, even authorial, revision of the poem. By his count there are eighty-eight written corrections and over ninety erasures in the seventy folios of the poem (pp. 194–95); these numbers are high for an Old English manuscript, but far from unique, and it would be surprising if every correction could be shown to be without doubt contemporary, despite Kiernan's confident assertion (p. 216, n. 43).[16] Kiernan accepts the theory advanced by Tilman Westphalen that folio 179r (182r) is a palimpsest, and carries what struck a reviewer of Westphalen as an "astonishing theory" a step further by arguing that the palimpsesting was intentional, performed by the B scribe for the purposes of revision (p. 245).[17] Fred C. Robinson suggests that "such a theory is not really provable from the evidence at hand, and . . . will probably remain but an interesting conjecture."[18] Few if any scholars other than Kiernan have accepted Westphalen's palimpsest theory, and ordinary wear seems more plausible as an explanation for the current state of the folio, since folio 179r (182r) begins a quire. Moreover, if the touching up represents authorial revision, it is unimpressive, and the dragon episode does not begin on this folio with line 2207, as Kiernan claims (p. 249), but on line 14 of the preceding folio with line 2200.

Kiernan's conclusion (pp. 270-78) is terse, dramatic, and largely unconvincing. It is not true that previous editors "assiduously ignored" palaeographical evidence, or that "taken all together, the evidence sustains the view of a contemporary MS" (p. 270). The poem was probably copied as the fourth item in the Nowell Codex, not as a separate codex, as Kiernan argues, and Boyle's article explains the inserted lines in the eleventh gathering, the anomalously ruled tenth gathering, and the confused fitt numbers without recourse to a revising author (*The Dating of* Beowulf, pp. 25–31). Kiernan's distinction between "correction" and "emendation" is not clear (p. 274); certainly corrections like the ones he terms emendations are found in many Old English manuscripts. By and large it is not true that the two scribes followed discrepant orthographic traditions (p. 274), and to the extent that they did, there are parallels in contemporary manuscripts (see Cameron et al., p. 37). There is no need to assume two different exemplars (p. 275).

From the preceding discussion it will be clear that I disagree with much of Kiernan's interpretation (e.g., of the language of the poem and of previous scholarship) and remain unconvinced by his arguments; I deplore his tendency to denigrate previous work (e.g., Förster's, Malone's, and Sisam's). Nevertheless, I read his book with close interest: it is always absorbing to examine work from a fresh perspective. Kiernan's writing is lucid, and he treats major issues; even those who accept no part of his argument can benefit from an occasional observation (*Beowulf* "becomes a poem that was itself largely the product of antiquarian interests," p. 61) and from Kiernan's emphasis on reading the poem in its manuscript context.

Notes

1. Kiernan argues that the poem was composed "during the reign of Cnut" (p. 61) from "two originally distinct MSS, and two originally distinct poems" (p. 258), and that the reviser of the composite poems was probably the second scribe "as the paleographical and codicological evidence encourages one to believe" (p. 278).

2. "This study of the *Beowulf* MS is not totally objective, for it is founded on the premise of a contemporary MS" (p. 270).

3. Thomas Cable, "Metrical Style as Evidence for the Date of *Beowulf*," *The Dating of* Beowulf, p. 79.

4. See Murray, "*Beowulf*, the Danish Invasions, and Royal Genealogy," pp. 101–11; Page, "The Audience of *Beowulf* and the Vikings," pp. 113–22; Frank, "Skaldic Verse and the Date of *Beowulf*," pp. 123–39, all in *The Dating of* Beowulf.

5. Frank, p. 136. "I cannot prove that *Beowulf* was composed then: nevertheless, accepting that the poem came into existence between 890 and 950 solves far more problems than it poses" (p. 137).

6. Nicholas Jacobs, "Anglo-Danish Relations, Poetic Archaism, and the Date of *Beowulf*: A Reconsideration of the Evidence," *Poetica*, 1978, pp. 23–43.

7. Frederick Klaeber, ed., *Beowulf and the Fight at Finnsburg*, 3d ed. (Boston: D.C. Heath, 1950), pp. cviii-cx, 274–78.

8. The preponderance of weak adjectives without articles may not necessarily be a sign of early date. Kiernan suggests that it "may be simply due to the poet's wish to be more archaic" (p. 24), but Mabel Falberg Dobyns points out that Wulfstan uses over twice as many constructions of the form preposition + weak adjective + noun as of the form preposition + article + weak adjective + noun in eighty-some examples (*Wulfstan's Vocabulary: A Glossary of the Homilies*, Diss., Univ. of Illinois, 1973, pp. 7–8).

9. I believe, in fact, that such verses could be composed long after the diphthongs produced by contraction had merged with the other long diphthongs. An examination of the metrically attested de-contracted forms in *Beowulf* (see Klaeber, *Beowulf and the Fight at Finnsburg*, pp. 274–75 and Angus Cameron et al., "A Reconsideration of the Language of *Beowulf*," in *The Dating of* Beowulf, pp. 33–75, esp. pp. 45–46) shows that some might represent analogical addition of endings (*gān, gǣð, dōn, dēð*), while most of the others have uninflected or inflected forms attested which preserve the intervocalic

h lost in the contracted form (*nēan/neah, hēan/heah, sēon/seah, flēon/flugon*) and others closely resemble a single pattern (*rēon, tēon, slēan, þēon*, etc.).

10. Kenneth Sisam refers to "a general Old English poetic dialect, artificial, archaic, and perhaps mixed in its vocabulary, conservative in inflexions that affect the verse-structure, and indifferent to non-structural irregularities, which were perhaps tolerated as part of the colouring of the language of verse" ("Dialect Origins of the Earlier Old English Verse," in his *Studies in the History of English Literature* [Oxford: Clarendon Press, 1953], p. 138. Cf. Alistair Campbell, *Old English Grammar* (Oxford: Clarendon Press, 1959), § 18.

11. E.g., pp. 50, 53. It is not true that "purely orthographic variations are ignored in the standard grammars" (p. 47, n. 54)—although they ignore variation in letter shapes, for the most part orthographic features like ‹th› for ‹þ› and ‹ð›, ‹u› for ‹þ›, ‹ccg› for ‹cgc› or ‹cg› are catalogued with care.

12. Additional relevant examples are listed in Cameron et al. in §§ A2.1, 2.3, 2.7, A3, A4.2.3.1, A5.4, A6, A7, etc.

13. Förster, *Die Beowulf-Handscrift,* Berichte über die Verhandlungen der Sächsischen Akademie der Wissenschaften zu Leipzig, philologisch-historische Klasse, 71, 4 (1919).

14. Julius Zupitza, ed., Beowulf *Reproduced in Facsimile from the Unique Manuscript, British Museum MS. Cotton Vitellius A.XV,* 2d ed., rev. Norman Davis, EETS 245 (London: Oxford University Press, 1959); Kemp Malone, ed., *The Nowell Codex: British Museum Cotton Vitellius A.XV Second MS,* EEMF 12 (Copenhagen: Rosenkilde and Bagger, 1963); Kemp Malone, ed., *The Thorkelin Transcripts of* Beowulf *in Facsimile,* EEMF 1 (Copenhagen: Rosenkilde and Bagger, 1951); Stanley B. Greenfield and Fred C. Robinson, *A Bibliography of Publications on Old English Literature to the End of 1972* (Toronto: Univ. of Toronto Press, 1980). Items 191–205 in the bibliography include nineteen articles and books dealing with the *Beowulf* manuscript; for comparison, the bibliography lists seventeen entries for the Exeter Book (207–20), twenty-four for Junius 11 (222–35), and twenty-six for the Vercelli Book (237–58).

15. Boyle argues that the three prose pieces, *Beowulf,* and *Judith* form a single codex, and that the B scribe started copying the last quires of *Beowulf* before the A scribe had finished the earlier quires, so that extra lines had to be squeezed in the middle quires in order that the work of A and B might mesh neatly.

16. Angus Cameron shows that Old English manuscripts were read, corrected, and annotated well into the Middle English period ("Middle English in Old English Manuscripts," *Chaucer and Middle English Studies in Honour of Rossell Hope Robbins,* ed. Beryl Rowland (London: Allen and Unwin, 1974), pp. 218–29.

17. Tilman Westphalen, *Beowulf 3150–55, Textkritik and Editionsgeschichte* (Munich: Wilhelm Fink, 1967). The book is reviewed by Kemp Malone in *Speculum,* 44 (1969), 182–86.

18. See Robinson's review of Westphalen's book in *Anglia,* 88 (1970), 363–68.

The *Review* Association

Major funding for *Review* is provided by a grant from the Research Division and the College of Arts and Sciences at Virginia Polytechnic Institute and State University. Additional support is provided by The *Review* Association, a group of major universities which support the aims and purposes of the series. Member universities are as follows:

Columbia University
Duke University
University of Minnesota
Pennsylvania State University
Princeton University
University of Virginia

Contributors

ASHLEY CRANDELL AMOS is Junior Fellow at the Pontifical Institute of Mediaeval Studies, University of Toronto.

T. A. J. BURNETT is Assistant Keeper of Manuscripts at the British Library.

J. A. BURROW is Professor of English at the University of Bristol.

WILLIAM E. CAIN is Associate Professor of English at Wellesley College.

STUART CURRAN is Professor of English at the University of Pennsylvania.

RICHARD J. DUNN is Professor of English at the University of Washington.

T. H. HOWARD-HILL is Professor of English at the University of South Carolina.

IAN JACK is Professor of English at Pembroke College, Cambridge University.

ROBERT S. KINSMAN is Professor of English at the University of California, Los Angeles.

VICTOR A. KRAMER is Associate Professor of English at Georgia State University.

M. E. KRONEGGER is Professor of English at Michigan State University.

RICHARD KUCZKOWSKI is Book Review Editor of the *New York Arts Journal*.

HAROLD LOVE is Reader in English at Monash University, Melbourne, Australia.

JEROME J. McGANN is Dreyfuss Professor of Humanities at the California Institute of Technology.

VICTORIA S. MIDDLETON is Assistant Professor of English at Franklin and Marshall College.

DEREK PEARSALL is Professor of English at the Centre for Medieval Studies, University of York.

SAMUEL PICKERING, JR. is Associate Professor of English at the University of Connecticut.

ROSS POSNOCK is Assistant Professor of English at the College of William and Mary.

ALAN C. PURVES is Director of the Curriculum Laboratory at the University of Illinois, Urbana-Champaign.

JOHN T. SHAWCROSS is Professor of English at the University of Kentucky.